Sport and Society

A Student Introduction

Sport and Society

A Student Introduction

edited by

Barrie Houlihan

SAGE Publications
London • Thousand Oaks • New Delhi

Introduction © Barrie Houlihan 2003
Chapter 1 © Peter Donnelly 2003
Chapter 2 © Barrie Houlihan 2003
Chapter 3 © Martin Polley 2003
Chapter 4 © Michael F. Collins 2003
Chapter 5 © Tess Kay 2003
Chapter 6 © Nigel Thomas 2003
Chapter 7 © Ben Carrington and
    Ian McDonald 2003
Chapter 8 © David Kirk 2003
Chapter 9 © Leigh Robinson 2003
Chapter 10 © David Stead 2003
Chapter 11 © John Amis and
    Trevor Slack 2003
Chapter 12 © Barrie Houlihan 2003
Chapter 13 © Guy Jackson and
    Mike Weed 2003
Chapter 14 © Holger Preuss 2003
Chapter 15 © Michael F. Collins 2003
Chapter 16 © Trevor Slack 2003
Chapter 17 © Murray Phillips and
    Tara Magdalinski 2003
Chapter 18 © Ian P. Henry 2003
Chapter 19 © Barrie Houlihan 2003

First published 2003

SAGE Publications Ltd
6 Bonhill Street
London EC2A 4PU

SAGE Publications Inc
2455 Teller Road
Thousand Oaks, California 91320

SAGE Publications India Pvt Ltd
B-42, Panchsheel Enclave
Post Box 4109
New Delhi 110 017

British Library Cataloguing in Publication data

A catalogue record for this book is available
from the British Library

ISBN 0-7619-7033-9
ISBN 0-7619-7034-7

Library of Congress control number available

Typeset by C&M Digitals (P) Ltd, Chennai, India
Printed in Great Britain by The Cromwell Press Ltd,
Trowbridge, Wiltshire

Contents

Figures

Tables

Boxes

Contributors

John Amis is Associate Professor of Sport & Leisure Management at the University of Memphis. His research is focused predominantly on the strategic management of organisations. This has included various analyses into how sports organisations engage in large-scale transformations and how firms use sports sponsorship as a strategic resource. While he is continuing to work in these areas, he is also currently engaged in a stream of research that explores the ways in which organisations use intangible resources. He has given invited lectures in several countries and is currently editor of the *International Journal of Sports Marketing & Sponsorship* and on the Editorial Boards of *European Sport Management Quarterly* and *Journal of Sports Management*.

Ben Carrington teaches Sociology and Cultural Studies at the Chelsea School, University of Brighton. He is co-editor, with Ian McDonald, of *'Race', Sport and British Society* (Routledge, 2001).

Michael F. Collins is Senior Lecturer in Sport and Leisure Management at Loughborough, and was Head of Research, Strategy and Planning at the Sports Council for many years. He is author of *Sport and Social Exclusion* (Routledge, 2003). Besides that topic, his research interests include sport and its social, environmental and economic impacts, the labour market for sport, and the structure and role of voluntary sport and its relationships with the other sectors.

Peter Donnelly is currently Director of the Centre for Sport Policy Studies, and a Professor in the Faculty of Physical Education and Health, at the University of Toronto. His research interests include sport politics and policy issues (including the area of children's rights in sport), sport subcultures and mountaineering (history). Recent books include: *Taking Sport Seriously: Social Issues in Canadian Sport* (Thompson Educational Publishers, 1997; 2nd edition, 2000), and *Inside Sports* (with Jay Coakley, Routledge, 1999).

Ian P. Henry is Professor of Leisure Policy and Management and Director of the Institute of Sport and Leisure Policy at Loughborough University. His research interests lie in the field of sport and leisure policy and politics and his recent publications include *The Politics of Leisure Policy* (2nd edition, Palgrave, 2002) and, co-edited with Chris Gratton, *Sport in the City* (Routledge, 2002).

Barrie Houlihan is Professor of Sports Policy in the Institute of Sport and Leisure Policy at Loughborough University. He has written widely in the area of sports policy and recent publications include, *The Politics of Sports*

Development: Development of Sport or Development through Sport? (with Anita White, Routledge, 2002), *Dying to Win* (2nd edition, Council of Europe Publishing, 2002) and *Sport, Policy and Politics* (Routledge, 1997).

Guy Jackson is currently Sports Marketing Manager for Loughborough University. He was, until recently, a lecturer in the Institute of Sport and Leisure Policy. His main research interests and publications are in the inter-relationship between sport and tourism and its economic and environmental impacts. He has also published in the area of sports development and sustainable tourism management. Recent publications include *Sustainable Tourism Management: Principles and Practice* (edited with B. Bramwell, I.P. Henry, A. Goytia Prat, G. Richards, and J. van de Straaten, 1996, Tilburg University Press).

Tess Kay is Senior Lecturer in the Institute of Sport and Leisure Policy at Loughborough University. Her main research interests cover the relationship between sport, leisure and social structure. She has a particular interest in the interaction between gender, sport and leisure and has undertaken a number of studies in this area. Her work includes analyses of gender differences in men and women's leisure behaviour, the sports experiences of women and girls, and analysis of gender equity policies. She has participated in a number of Europeran Union research projects in family-related policy and is a member of the Editorial Board of *Leisure Studies* journal.

David Kirk is Professor of Physical Education and Youth Sport at Loughborough University. He also holds Adjunct Chairs at the Universities of Queensland, Australia, and Limerick, Ireland. He has published widely on school physical education and youth sport, and was awarded the IOC President's Prize in 2001 for his contribution to research and development. His most recent book is a Foucauldian genealogy of physical education in Australia and Britain (*Schooling Bodies: School Practice and Public Discourse, 1880–1950*, Continuum, 1998).

Tara Magdalinski is a Senior Lecturer in the Faculty of Arts and Social Sciences at the University of the Sunshine Coast. She has published widely in Sports Studies and focuses on the cultural construction of performance enhancement, the role of nature in the bodies and site of the Sydney 2000 Olympics, and the corporate motives of Olympic education. Her first book, co-edited with Timothy Chandler, *With God on their Side: Sport in the Service of Religion*, was published by Routledge in July 2002.

Ian McDonald teaches Sociology and Politics at the Chelsea School, University of Brighton. He is co-editor, with Ben Carrington, of *'Race', Sport and British Society* (Routledge, 2001).

Murray Phillips teaches history and sociology in the School of Human Movement Studies at the University of Queensland. His research interests are in the epistemological status of sport history, sport and gender, the football codes, swimming and coaching history. He has recently published *From Sidelines to Centre Field: A History of Sports Coaching in Australia* (UNSW Press, 2000), and is currently editing *Deconstructing Sport History* (2003).

Martin Polley is Senior Lecturer in Sport Studies at the University of Southampton. He is a past Chairman of the British Society of Sports History. He is the author of *Moving the Goalposts: a History of Sport and Society since 1945* (Routledge, 1998), *A–Z of Modern Europe since 1789* (Routledge, 2000) and a number of articles on different aspects of sports history, including diplomacy and amateurism in such journals as *Contemporary British History*, *The Sports Historian* and *The International Journal of the History of Sport*.

Holger Preuss is Assistant Professor at the Institute of Sports Economics and Sports Management at the German Sport University, Cologne. From 1995 to 2002 he was scientific assistant at the Faculty of Sports at the Johannes Gutenberg-Universität Mainz. There he taught Sports Sociology and Sports Economics and was a member of the Research Team Olympia. From 1990 to 1995 he studied Economics and Physical Education at the University of Göttingen. In 1992 he was in Seattle for half a year and 1995 he attended the postgraduate seminar on Olympic Studies in Olympia, Greece. His research focuses on economic impacts of mega-sport events, especially the economic implications of hosting the Olympic Games from Munich 1972 to Salt Lake City 2002.

Leigh Robinson is a Lecturer in Sport and Leisure Management in the Institute of Sport and Leisure Policy at Loughborough University. Her main research area is the management of sport and leisure organisations and recent publications include: 'Is quality management appropriate for public leisure services?' (*Managing Leisure: An International Journal*, 2002), *Quality Management* (with Matthew Crowhurst, 2001, ISRM), *Performance Measurement for Local Authority Sports Halls and Swimming Pools* (with P. Taylor, A. Bovaird, C. Gratton and S. Kung, 2000, Sport England).

Trevor Slack is Professor and Canada Research Chair in Sports Management at the University of Alberta. His current research is on changes in sports organisations in emerging economies. He is the former editor of *Journal of Sports Management* and the current editor of the *European Sports Management Quarterly*. His work has appeared in such journals as *Organization Studies*, *Journal of Sports Management*, *Journal of Management Studies*, *International Review for the Sociology of Sport*, *Human Relations* and *European Journal of Marketing*.

David Stead is a Lecturer in Sociology of Sport in the School of Sport and Exercise Sciences at Loughborough University. Formerly concerned with youth sports policy, his current research interests are in globalisation and sport, the personal and professional experiences of elite athletes and the inter-relationship between sport and the media. Recent publications include '"Rite de passage" or passage to riches? The motivation and objectives of Nordic/ Scandinavian players in English league soccer' (with Prof. Joseph Maguire, *Journal of Sport and Social Issues*, 2000).

Nigel Thomas is Principal Lecturer in Sport, Health and Exercise at Staffordshire University. He began his career in higher education following ten years in local authority and governing body sports development roles, specifically focusing on the development of opportunities for young disabled people. His research interests include the media coverage of disability sport and the integration of children with special educational needs into main-stream physical education. He is currently completing his PhD at Loughborough University on 'Policy process in disability sport'.

Mike Weed is a Lecturer at Loughborough University, based in the Institute of Sport and Leisure Policy within the School of Sport and Exercise Sciences. He was previously Director of the Research in Sports Culture (RiSC) group at the University of North London. Much of his research interests focus on 'meso-level' approaches, and previous publications have been in the areas of sports tourism, sport and leisure policy and the social dynamics of sports groups. He is co-author (with Chris Bull) of *Sports Tourism: Participants, Policy and Providers* (Butterworth-Heinemann, 2003).

Introduction

BARRIE HOULIHAN

THE GROWTH OF INSTITUTIONAL AND POLICY COMPLEXITY

In the fairly recent past, the late 1950s and early 1960s, the number of roles that an individual might fulfil in relation to sport was limited to those such as participant, spectator, consumer of sports news and reports mainly through the newspapers and radio, or voluntary club administrator or official. There were few professional athletes and even fewer professional administrators; the symbiotic relationship between the television companies and sport was only just emerging; and the rampant commercialisation of sport, especially football, was still some years away. The organisational infrastructure of sport was similarly simple. National governing bodies of sport and their clubs were the organisational core of the sports system in the UK; the government considered sport as an area of social activity that did not warrant treatment as a matter of public policy; and the schools were left to provide a combination of physical training and some sports. The involvement of the state in sport was sporadic, substantially limited to the occasional committee of enquiry into a sports-related problem (such as the Moelwyn–Hughes Report in 1946 which followed the collapse of safety barriers at Bolton FC's ground), a police presence at major sports events and the Queen handing over the trophy to the winners of the FA Cup Final.

Today, however, the picture is radically different: the roles have multiplied, the infrastructure is much more complex and the state is now at the heart of sport. Individuals consume sport in a broad variety of ways through spectating, both at home and as travelling fans, and through a plethora of specialist sports radio stations, television channels (both free-to-air and pay-to-view), and newspapers and magazines. Far more people participate in sport and physical activity utilising publicly provided facilities (mostly built since the early 1970s), commercial facilities, especially fitness clubs (most of which date from the last 15 years), or voluntary clubs. Furthermore, as the public and commercial sectors have expanded, so too have the career opportunities in the sports industry. The limited range of administrative and officiating roles available in the 1960s has been augmented by new careers in sports development, sports science and fitness instruction, vastly expanded ranks of coaches, managers and agents, as well as the incorporation of traditional business professions, of accountancy, marketing and strategic planning into previously amateur and voluntarily run clubs and sports governing bodies.

Not surprisingly, the organisational and policy infrastructure for sport is far more elaborate, encompassing, for example, specialist sports colleges, a national curriculum for physical education, specialist elite sport regional institutes, dedicated funding programmes for sport through the National Lottery as well as other sources, an increasingly rationalised structure of governing bodies and clubs, sports media, and an elaborate governmental infrastructure comprising specialist agencies, sports councils, in each of the home countries plus one for the UK as a whole, and a Cabinet-level department.

The attitude of governments has also changed dramatically over the last 40 years or so. In the 1950s and early 1960s most governments in Europe and North America considered sport to be a matter outside the remit of the state – a matter for private decision in keeping with the idea of sport as something that took place in one's free time. State involvement was rare, inconsistent and certainly did not constitute a 'sports policy'. Yet today few countries do not have a recognisable sports policy supported by allocations of public funds and an administrative infrastructure to oversee implementation. Most governments support strategies designed to achieve elite success and many also support the promotion of mass participation, but sport is increasingly

found at the heart of other social, economic and foreign policies. Sport is often perceived by governments as a useful instrument in achieving non-sports objectives, whether these be the social control of male adolescents, the rebuilding of social capital in fractured communities, improvement to health and the reduction in obesity, improving diplomatic relations, job creation and the economic regeneration of urban and rural areas, and the stimulation of tourism.

THE STRUCTURE OF THE BOOK

Whereas in the 1960s sport was primarily an important social phenomenon, today it is, in addition, an important economic and political phenomenon. The focus of this volume is to locate the individual within the complex pattern of policy and institutions that form the fabric of sport in the early twenty-first century and to explore the patterns of engagement between the individual and sport as mediated by an increasingly complex policy and organisational infrastructure. The book is arranged around four broad themes: perspectives, inclusion, commercialisation and international comparative context.

The three chapters that deal with different perspectives on sport (Part I) are designed to introduce the reader to ways of understanding and investigating sport in society. Peter Donnelly's chapter on sport and social theory reflects the debts that social science students of sport owe to sociology. The sociological analysis of sport is well established and has generated many important insights into the relationship between the individual and society. Peter Donnelly's focus on the tension between structure and agency, and how the differing emphases on structure and agency affect our analysis of issues such as sport and health or drug abuse by athletes, illustrates not only the richness of insight that sociology can provide, but also the care that is required when evaluating competing interpretations of behaviour. Barrie Houlihan's review of the contribution that political science can make to our understanding of contemporary sport highlights the importance of understanding power and its distribution and use in shaping modern sport and, particularly, in creating or denying individual life chances in relation to sport. Organisational power and particularly the power wielded by the state is shown to be a dominant element of the context of modern sport. But, as with sociology, the reader is made aware of the competing interpretations that political science can generate and the need to temper theoretical commitment with empirical research. Martin Polley's chapter on history and sport provides an important reminder of the extent to which the contemporary pattern of opportunity for sport is constrained by long-established patterns of social relations, power distribution and institution building. It is simply not possible to understand issues such as gender equity in sport without a knowledge of the male domination of early sports organisations, nor to understand contemporary globalisation without an awareness of colonial history, nor the pattern of sports opportunities in schools without an understanding of the debates between advocates of competing conceptualisations of physical activity evident in the second half of the last century.

The discussion of the different perspectives on sport provides an important context for the next set of chapters comprising Part II, which examine aspects of the opportunity structure for sport. Michael Collins focuses mainly on wealth and class as factors affecting participation, but he also provides an overview of the multiple and layered nature of social exclusion. What is made abundantly clear is that the tackling and removal of one barrier to participation in sport all too often merely exposes the next barrier. Furthermore Michael Collins and other contributors in this part of the book, especially Tess Kay, Nigel Thomas, and Ben Carrington and Ian McDonald, show clearly the slow pace of change in challenging and lowering socially constructed barriers to participation. Tess Kay traces the recent history of women's exclusion from sport and draws attention to the variety and subtlety of the debates that seek to explain female under-representation as participants, officials, coaches and administrators. The depth and persistence of patriarchy within contemporary sport are amply exposed. Of especial significance is that Tess Kay points to the paradox, according to which many women perceive participation in sport as 'contradictory to femininity', while those who do participate experience little role conflict and report a sense of empowerment reflected in increased self-esteem, personal development, physical power and well-being.

The importance of ideology in providing a deep structure of beliefs and values which shapes sports opportunities is not just apparent in discussions of gender equity, but is also of profound importance in the discussions of disability sport and race and ethnicity. Nigel Thomas reviews the persisting tension between medical and social models of disability and the power of those models, almost exclusively designed by the able-bodied, to determine the parameters of sports participation. But what comes across most strongly from Nigel Thomas's chapter is the complexity of the politics of disability sport. Not only is there a multiplicity of disability sports organisations, but there is also a marked lack of consensus regarding the strategy for widening opportunities for disability sport, in particular whether disability sport should be organised separately or work more closely with mainstream sports governing bodies. These debates take place against a backdrop of consistent and continuing success of UK elite athletes in the Paralympic Games.

The significance of acknowledging the ideological context within which issues in sport are discussed is emphasised in the contribution from Ben Carrington and Ian McDonald. In their critique of the evolution of public policy toward race and ethnicity in sport, the authors trace the slow shift away from an assumption that the route to more equitable participation lay in uncovering and addressing the constraints to be found within ethnic communities to an acknowledgement of the barriers to participation evident within sports institutions. The anti-racism efforts of major sports, such as cricket, and the impact of the New Labour government are evaluated and lead the authors to conclude that while there is evidence of progress in tackling racism and inequity in opportunities, 'discrimination continues to structure the reality of sport for black and ethnic minorities in Britain in complex and often contradictory ways'.

The final contribution to Part II by David Kirk provides ample illustration of the extent to which contemporary practice in physical education has been shaped by the sharply contested history of the subject. Not only was there disagreement over the form of physical 'education' best suited to different social classes (sports for the children at fee-paying schools and military drill for those in the state system), but there was, and to an extent still is, a fierce debate about the purpose and value of physical education within the curriculum. Within this sharply contested context

David Kirk reviews key research findings in relation to the training of physical education teachers, the impact of curriculum design on the construction of gender, and the continuing tension between physical education and sport. As with the earlier chapters, the author explores the interplay between ideology, institutionalised power and contemporary politics in shaping the engagement between children and sport.

If the recurring themes that run through Chapters 4 to 8 are policy, the state and ideology, then the next seven chapters in Part III 'The impact of commercialisation' give greater weight to the significance of business for contemporary sport. Business has always been involved in sport, but the intensity and ubiquity of the business presence in sport is a phenomenon of the late twentieth century. Yet far from usurping the position of the state, business involvement with sport has prompted closer public sector involvement often seeking to regulate corporate activity in sport. Leigh Robinson provides an overview of the increasingly close relationship between sport and commerce and explores not just the variety of involvement, from online betting to sponsorship, but also the impact on professional sport and the structure of the sports industry. The author explores the unique characteristics that make sport so attractive to the commercial sector and discusses whether the relationship is best described as dependent, symbiosis, manipulation, mutual benefit or exploitation. Whatever description is preferred, the reader is left in no doubt as to the significance of the sport and leisure industry to the national economy.

Some of the themes introduced by Leigh Robinson are developed in more detail in David Stead's examination of the relationship between sport and the media. This relationship is the axis around which commercial interest in sport revolves. In addition to raising issues of audience manipulation through the media presentation of sports events, David Stead also explores the key question of access to sports products that are increasingly delivered in a pay-to-view format. The issues the author raises have a clear resonance with the earlier discussions of social exclusion. Given the pace of commercialisation and the investment by governments in national governing bodies of sport, it is important to understand the significance of organisational change for the way in which sport is managed. John Amis and Trevor Slack not only supply a conceptual language for the analysis of sports organisations, but also provide a wealth of examples drawn from both the commercial and voluntary sectors. Of especial importance is the analysis of the change in the structure of sports organisations from voluntarily run, simply structured and poorly resourced 'kitchen table' bodies to professionally managed, structurally differentiated and well-resourced boardroom organisations in which volunteers play an increasingly marginal role.

The professionalisation of both the participation in, and the administration of, sport is nowhere more clearly exemplified than in relation to the issue of doping. The rewards of sporting success, the proliferation of specialists (dieticians, masseurs, coaches, doctors, physiologists, etc.) within an athlete's entourage and the global character of the sports competition circuit have all made the successful development of an effective anti-doping policy more challenging. Barrie Houlihan discusses the attempts to develop a global policy response to doping and illustrates the extent to which anti-doping efforts by sports organisations have been supported, and occasionally submerged, by the regulatory activity of states.

Guy Jackson and Mike Weed then examine the rapidly growing phenomenon of sports tourism. Following a review of the nature of tourism supply and demand, the authors explore the impact of sports tourism. As is made clear, the hosting of major sports events can have substantial impacts on the local economies and environments: a point which Holger Preuss emphasises in relation to the hosting of the Olympic Games. However, as the authors also make clear, the sport tourism market is still in its infancy and is certainly not limited to the hosting of major events. While the clear impetus for market expansion has come from the commercial sector and from governments keen to attract lucrative mega-events, there is also the potential to use sports tourism to achieve other objectives more closely associated with sport for all and fitness and health. In his analysis of the Olympic Games, Holger Preuss explores in detail the argument that the hosting of the Olympic Games is an unalloyed benefit for the local community. The author shows clearly that while one might reach a conclusion that, on balance, the net benefits of hosting the Games outweigh the costs, the beneficiaries and those who bear the costs are often different groups in a community. Not surprisingly, business interests and the local or regional state are often able to use the Games to achieve organisational objectives associated with profit or urban regeneration, but the costs are often borne by poorer local residents who are displaced to make way for stadiums and can rarely afford the ticket price for the Games themselves. Holger Preuss's chapter provides a powerful illustration of the close association between commercial interests and state power.

The final contribution to this part of the book considers the relationship between sport and the environment. Michael Collins uses a series of case studies to highlight both the positive and negative impacts of sport on the environment. Linking with a number of conclusions from Holger Preuss's chapter, the author examines the potential for sport, and especially the hosting of major events, to facilitate the rapid regeneration of inner-city industrial areas. In addition, Michael Collins illustrates how competing uses of the countryside for sport can be reconciled, but also how relations between sporting and non-sporting users of the countryside can break down. Acknowledging that sport can generate significant negative environmental impacts, the author makes it clear that sport can also bring substantial environmental benefits if managed sensitively. The reclamation of brownfield sites for stadiums and mineral quarries for sailing, climbing and shooting, the development of community forests and the deliberate protection of biodiversity in the design of golf courses, all attest to the potential for commerce and sport to prosper without inflicting environmental damage.

The fourth part of the book encourages the reader to consider the pattern of sport in their own country in comparison to that in other industrialised countries and also in relation to the emergence of supranational and global institutions affecting sport. Trevor Slack's discussion of aspects of sport in the United States and Canada paints a vivid picture of the extent to which commercialisation in the United States dominates intercollegiate sport and also the degree to which the role of the public sector has been marginalised. Although the public sector is still more prominent in Canada, the trend is towards greater commercialisation and a greater reliance on voluntary community provision. Of especial interest are the problems created for professional sport in Canada as a result of the economic power of the USA. The

chapter also provides an interesting insight into the privileged position ascribed to the (usually male) high school athlete and the corrosive effect on broader school values.

Murray Phillips and Tara Magdalinski provide another point of comparison in their discussion of the sports system and culture in Australia. After stripping away the rhetoric that pervades many discussions of sport in Australia, they reveal a sports system and culture which disadvantages women and discriminates against Aboriginal athletes. The authors also describe a society where the mythology of Australian sport has such a strong hold that few questioned the substantial sums of public money that were used to underwrite the Sydney Olympic Games. Not only does Australia exemplify the strengthening role of government in managing the sports system, but it also illustrates the impact of increasing commercialisation. Perhaps of especial interest is their discussion of the interweaving of immigrant identities with a sense of Australian identity.

Identity is also an important aspect of Ian Henry's discussion of the increasingly prominent role of the European Union in sport. Given that so many of the world's major sports events are located in member states of the European Union, the impact of EU involvement in sport extends well beyond its boundaries and comprises an increasingly important element of the context of sport for many countries. The EU has shown itself to be an effective regulator of both commercial sports interests and also of aspects of public provision. Moreover, the Union has a strong interventionist tradition and, as the author makes clear, has ambitions to define a European model of sport which will stand in opposition to the highly commercialised North American model outlined by Trevor Slack and also referred to by Leigh Robinson and David Stead.

The last contribution to this section and the final chapter in the book is Barrie Houlihan's examination of globalisation and sport. In the opening section of this introduction emphasis was placed on the extent to which the context for modern sport had altered at the national level, with the steady rise in governmental interest in sport running in parallel with global commercialisation. The final chapter explores the process and outcome of globalisation and suggests that while the significance of globalising pressures is undeniable, the direction of change and the consequences for sport and for communities are far less clear. Nevertheless, while the trajectory of globalisation might be obscured, the role of the state as both an engine and a mediator of globalisation is clear.

CONCLUSION

At one time it was often argued that sport was an oasis in an increasingly complex and compromised society. Sporting values were clear (and laudable) and sporting practice made the concept of 'free time' a reality. As this volume shows, if this perception were ever valid, it certainly is no longer today. Sport, sports organisations and sports practice are at the heart of a number of major social issues either in their own right as sites of tension over social values such as gender equity, racial equality and social inclusion, or as policy instruments of government, such as those designed to achieve economic regeneration or gain diplomatic prestige. While each of the chapters in the book can be read independently, they provide strong collective evidence of the need to see sport located at the core of our consideration of many contemporary social issues, as an integral part of the industrial economy, and an increasingly valuable political resource. In the preface to his landmark study of the relationship between cricket and West Indian society, C.L.R. James famously adapted lines written by Kipling to ask 'What do they know of cricket who only cricket know?' It is the foundation of this volume that not only can our understanding of sport be enriched by using perspectives developed across a range of disciplines, but that the study of sport can also cast substantial light on major contemporary social and economic issues.

Part One   *Perspectives on Sport*

1

Sport and Social Theory

PETER DONNELLY

'[T]he discovery of sociology can change your life. It can help you to understand the social forces you confront, the forces that constrain and free you as you go about living your life. This understanding offers a liberating potential: To gain insight into how these social forces influence your life allows you to stand somewhat apart from at least some of them, and thereby exert more creative control over your own life.' (Henslin, 1999: 1–2)

Overview

→ Structure and agency in sociology
→ Synthesis
→ The history of sociology of sport
→ Methods of sociological analysis
→ The future of sociology of sport

In the opening quotation, James Henslin is paraphrasing Peter Berger's (1963) *Invitation to Sociology*. Discovering the sociology of sport can also change your life – if you are an athlete, and/or a student in sport studies or the sport sciences. It can help you to understand the social forces that affect your involvement in sport and physical activity, and that knowledge may help you to exert more control over your participation. This chapter is concerned with the fundamentals of understanding in sociology – social theory. It begins with an extended example, a demonstration of the way in which an analysis of the relationship

between sport and social class reveals the two main schools of thought in sociology. The example outlines the strengths and weaknesses of these two approaches, and shows how they are connected to political decisions that are made about health, sport and physical activity. This is followed by a synthesis of the two schools of thought showing how, in combination, they provide a much clearer understanding of the ways in which social forces influence participation. The latter part of the chapter presents a brief history of the development of sociological thought in the sociology of sport, and an even briefer analysis of the methods used in research in the sociology of sport. The chapter concludes with some ideas about the future of this field of study.

One of the most frequent research findings in the sociology of sport concerns the relationship between social class and participation in sport and physical activity. Statistics consistently show a linear relationship – the higher a person's income and/or level of education, the more likely he, and increasingly she, is to participate in sport and physical activity. But, as every scientist knows, statistical relationships are tricky things. They show that *a* is related to *b*; they do not show that *a* caused *b*. If we find a relationship between, for example, wearing brown shoes and achieving high marks on examinations, we have no problem seeing it as a meaningless relationship. Unless we are very superstitious, we are likely to attribute it to coincidence. Other relationships may cause us to think more. If, for example, we found a relationship between bodybuilding and feelings of sexual inadequacy, we might think that there are reasons to suspect such a relationship. It is certainly a theme that has recurred in some fitness industry advertising, where bodybuilding is supposed to relieve such feelings.

The explanation of a relationship is referred to in science (including the social sciences) as a theory. It is the best, currently accepted, explanation of the available evidence of a relationship or a natural phenomenon – why the apple fell from the tree; why the bath water rises when you get in; why everyone is soon aware that there is a flatulent person in the seminar room. New evidence may confirm the theory, or lead to newer explanations – the theory of creation becomes the theory of evolution; Newtonian physics is supplemented by the theory of relativity. In the natural sciences, the process of explanation is continual, and

in many cases relatively straightforward. The process of explanation in the social sciences – social theory – is not nearly so straightforward. As Giddens notes:

1 We cannot approach society, or 'social facts', as we do objects or events in the natural world, because societies only exist in so far as they are created and re-created in our own actions as human beings ...
2 ... Atoms cannot get to know what scientists say about them, or change their behaviour in light of that knowledge. Human beings can do so. Thus, the relation between sociology and its 'subject-matter' is necessarily different from that involved in the natural sciences. (1982: 13–15)

Thus, our theory about bodybuilders is easily overturned by 'sexually inadequate' individuals who decide to stop participating because of what it might reveal about them, or by 'sexually adequate' individuals who don't give much credence to the theory and decide to become involved for other reasons.

THE TWO SOCIOLOGIES

To return to the relationship between social class and participation, explanations tend to fall into one of the two main historical approaches to social theory – what we will refer to here as *agency theories* and *structure theories* (formerly, these were often referred to as social action theories and social system theories). Our explanation is easier if we place participation in sport and physical activity in the larger context of health, and if we start with the notion of agency. A major justification for participation – for the existence of public and private fitness centres and government expenditure on sport – is that we are supposed to be responsible for our own health. A number of neo-liberal governments now claim that they can no longer afford publicly to fund health care for a population that does not take some responsibility for its own health. Thus we find a whole catalogue of advice, demands and moral suasion designed to encourage the population to become more active and take better care of itself. The following is a recent example from British Medical Officer, Liam Donaldson:

TEN TIPS FOR BETTER HEALTH

1   Don't smoke. If you can, stop. If you can't, cut down.
2   Follow a balanced diet with plenty of fruit and vegetables.
3   Keep physically active.
4   Manage stress: e.g. talk things through, make time to relax.
5   If you drink alcohol, do so in moderation.
6   Cover up in the sun, and protect children from sunburn.
7   Practise safer sex.
8   Take up cancer screening opportunities.
9   Be safe on the roads: follow the Highway Code.
10 Learn the First Aid ABC – airways, breathing, circulation. (Cited in Raphael, 2001a: A8)

None of these 'tips' is unfamiliar to us. We have heard similar messages often, in the media, in government statements, in health and physical education classes. They take many of the well-known causes of illness, injury and premature death and suggest how to avoid them. And what they all have in common is the assumption of individual responsibility and choice with regard to lifestyle decisions.

Agency, or action, refers to the freedom that individuals enjoy to act in a manner of their own choosing. It refers to behaviour that is not determined by outside forces; and it tends to be associated with individualism, voluntarism and free will. At its most extreme, it leads to statements such as Margaret Thatcher's view of 'society': 'There is no such thing as society, only individuals ...' Students of sport often concur with this view of society. They produce, observe and are impressed by individual efforts; some even tend to see team sports as a collection of individuals temporarily working together. They are often impressed by psychological explanations of individual effort, and success or failure. Furthermore they are likely to be convinced that individuals ought to be active and live healthy lifestyles because people are, or ought to be, responsible for their own health. In sociological terms, the emphasis of agency theories tends to be more on the ways in which individuals create and give meaning to their world. Sociological theories emphasising this approach include: ethnomethodology, methodological individualism, phenomenology and some of the other interpretive sociologies (cf. Donnelly, 2000).

Agency theories represent one of what Dawe (1970) termed 'the two sociologies'. Standing in contrast are structure theories, which are based on the premise that our actions are determined by social forces and social structures. Sociological theories emphasising this approach include: some forms of Marxism, structuralism, and some forms of structural functionalism. At its extreme this approach argues that, so powerful are the institutions, social processes and social forces that govern people's lives, that individual actions (agency) are ineffectual. However, the emphasis given to structure in sociology tends to be on relationships between social structures, or on social relations, rather than individuals.[1]

If we return to our social class, health and physical activity example, a search of the literature indicates that a great deal of solid evidence is ignored when the causes of disease are related only to lifestyle choices. Articles in leading medical journals, and a great deal of evidence summarised in books such as Evans et al. (1994) *Why Are Some People Healthy and Others Not?* and reports such as Raphael's (2001b) *Inequality Is Bad for Our Hearts*, suggest that poverty and lack of education are far better predictors of disease than inappropriate lifestyle choices. In other words, these data indicate that social structure (e.g. the class system, social inequality and social relations between the social classes) is a better predictor of disease than agency. The evidence is summarised by Giddens:

Working class people have on average lower birth weight and higher rates of infant mortality, are smaller at maturity, less healthy, and die at a younger age than those in higher class categories. Major types of mental disorder and physical illness including heart disease, cancer, diabetes, pneumonia and bronchitis are all more common at lower levels of the class structure than towards the top. (1989: 215)

The magnitude of the effect is quite striking. Raphael (2001b) cites a recent study in Toronto, Canada, which showed that your chance of dying from a heart attack increased 10 per cent for each drop of $10,000 in income.

Raphael (2001a: A8) notes that, '23% of all premature years of life lost prior to age 75 in Canada can be attributed to income differences'. Of these lost years, 22 per cent result from heart attack and stroke, 17 per cent from injuries, and 14 per cent from cancers. Thus, 'the material conditions under which we live – especially during childhood – are far greater determinants of whether we die from illness than our adult "lifestyle choices"' (Raphael, 2001: A8). Evans et al. (1994) show that 'top people live longer', and they do so despite all types of statistical

controls for 'lifestyle choices' such as smoking and physical activity. Current views of this difference point, not to greater knowledge of health care due to higher levels of education, or the ability to purchase 'better' health care, but to the sense of being in control of one's life:

Higher incomes are related to better health not only because wealthier people can buy adequate food, clothing, shelter and other necessities, but also because wealthier people have more choices and control over decisions in their lives. The sense of being in control is intrinsic to good health. (National Forum on Health, 1997)

This sense of the effects of structure (the social and material conditions of our lives) rather than agency (our lifestyle choices) led David Gordon at Bristol University to devise:

AN ALTERNATIVE TEN TIPS FOR BETTER HEALTH

1 Don't be poor. If you can, stop. If you can't, try not to be poor for long.
2 Don't have poor parents.
3 Own a car.
4 Don't work in a stressful, low-paid manual job.
5 Don't live in damp, low-quality housing.
6 Be able to afford to go on a foreign holiday and sunbathe.
7 Practise not losing your job and don't become unemployed.
8 Take up all benefits you are entitled to, if you are unemployed, retired or sick or disabled.
9 Don't live next to a busy major road or near a polluting factory.
10 Learn how to fill in the complex housing benefit/asylum forms before you become homeless and destitute. (Cited in Raphael, 2001a: A8)

You will notice that Gordon does not even mention physical activity. There are good reasons for this because population activity studies – which define some people as 'inactive' or 'sedentary' – raise serious concerns about research that is based on middle-class assumptions about white-collar jobs and exercise as a lifestyle choice – they usually only measure recreational physical activity:

Housework, child care, manual labour, work that involves being on your feet, and the activities that some define as leisure and others as a chore (e.g. gardening) ... [which] account for the majority of energy expenditure of Canadians – remain unrecorded in most surveys. (Donnelly and Harvey, 1996)

Since lower-income people are far more likely to be involved in manual work, to use public transport, and to have less access to child care and house cleaning services, assumptions about, and measures of 'inactive' populations are likely to be misleading.[2]

THE TWO SOCIOLOGIES: A SYNTHESIS

The extended example above provides an ideal account of 'the two sociologies' – what Gouldner (1975) referred to as 'man on his back' (structure) and 'man fighting back' (agency). Each provides a highly plausible explanation of the relationship between social class and sport and physical activity, and each is well supported by evidence. As individuals (agents) we ought to make healthy lifestyle choices; but can we be blamed for the circumstances of our lives – for having poor parents or for having to live and work in unhealthy environments? Lower levels of participation among lower-class individuals are attributed to a lack of motivation, and a lack of concern by those adopting an agency interpretation. Structural interpretations are likely to point to

involvement in manual labour, low incomes, low education levels, and other structural and environmental circumstances in the lives of low-income people. In addition to the dilemma this creates, each interpretation is quite political, which is another element of sociological theory that must be considered. Agency explanations of the relationship, when attempting to account for the failure of some people to participate in sport and physical activity, or engage in other healthy lifestyle practices, can have the following consequences:

- they lead to victim-blaming – moral sanctions, or threats to withdraw health care from individuals who appear to have made unhealthy lifestyle choices;
- they lead to patronising attitudes about individuals who are considered not to know better, or to be too weak-willed to make healthy lifestyle choices; and
- they lead to poor policy decisions with regard to creating education programmes, public service advertising campaigns, and the provision of sport and fitness programmes and facilities that do not take into account the circumstances of people's lives.

Structural explanations of the relationship, when attempting to account for the failure of some people to participate in sport and physical activity, or to engage in other healthy lifestyle practices, can have the following consequences:

- they lead to criticisms about cuts to public spending on programmes and facilities, when such programmes and facilities were not necessarily ones that were supported by all individuals;
- they lead to compassion, and occasionally patronising attitudes, about the structural circumstances of people's lives without any real sense of how to involve

people in changing those structural circumstances; and

- they lead to poor policy decisions with regard to creating sport and fitness programmes and facilities which address some of the structural barriers to participation, but often fail to take into account individual needs, interests and choices.

In political terms, agency interpretations tend to be favoured by the neo-conservative end of the political spectrum while structure interpretations tend to be favoured by the social democratic end of the spectrum. Unfortunately, the political centre often combines the worst of both.

In sociology, however, the struggle to develop a synthesis, or a compromise, between 'the two sociologies' has been under way for some time. In fact, 150 years ago Marx recognised that: 'Men make their own history [agency], but they do not make it just as they please; they do not make it under circumstances chosen by themselves, but under circumstances directly encountered, given and transmitted from the past [structure]' (1852/1991: 15). Thompson and Tunstall asked: 'Do the two approaches of social systems and social action theory simply correspond to our own ambivalent experience of society as something that constrains us and yet also something that we ourselves construct?' (1975: 476). Berger and Luckmann's (1967) ideas about 'the social construction of reality', Giddens' theory of structuration, the theoretical work of Pierre Bourdieu, and the critical cultural studies developed at the Centre for Contemporary Cultural Studies at Birmingham University, have all consciously attempted to effect this compromise.[3] For Berger and Luckmann, 'society forms the individuals who create society [social construction of reality] in a

continuous dialectic' (Jary and Jary, 1995: 664). Giddens, as noted previously, argues that 'societies only exist in so far as they are created and re-created in our own actions [agency] as human beings' (1982: 13), and he resolves the dilemma by proposing the 'duality of structure' – ' "structure" is both the medium and the outcome of the actions which are recursively organized by structures' (Abercrombie et al., 2000: 8). Bourdieu's approach is evident in the work of one of his former students, Loïc Wacquant's (1992) study of boxing in an African American neighbourhood of Chicago. Wacquant locates the actions (agency) of the boxers within the class and racial structures of the United States, and the subculture of the boxing gym. Although each of these theoretical approaches has influenced the sociology of sport, it is critical cultural studies which has had the greatest impact on the field in the last 20 years.

The relationship between social class and participation in sport and physical activity is much more complex than it is possible to explain by either agency or structure interpretations alone. Individuals do choose whether to participate or not, if the circumstances of their lives permit such a choice. And even if the choice is available to an individual, a whole host of circumstances from that person's past (e.g. whether his/her family had been involved in sport, or had encouraged participation; the person's experiences in school physical education classes, etc.) and present (e.g. whether transportation and child care are available; whether it is safe; and whether people are made to feel welcome and comfortable participating) may affect his/her decision. Donnelly and Harvey (1996: 23–4) outline a whole series of structural barriers to participation in sport and physical activity, which they classify as:

- *infrastructural barriers* – associated with the material means of access (e.g. cost, available transportation, time etc.);
- *superstructural barriers* – associated with ideas about access (e.g. policies, knowledge, prejudice etc.); and
- *procedural barriers* – associated with the course of action available to individuals to attain access (e.g. social support, citizens' rights, organisational structure and management style).

In addition, two types of access are identified:

- *participational access* – when individuals have information; when they are able to cope with procedures associated with access (e.g. registration); and when they meet competent staff who are sensitive to diversity; and
- *representational access* – when participants (i.e. those with participational access) are also present in the structure and decision-making process.

Donnelly characterised the latter as 'a fully democratised sport and leisure environment [which] include(s) both the right to participate, regardless of one's particular set of social characteristics, and the right to be involved in determination of the forms, circumstances and meanings of participation' (1993: 417). In other words, the *agency* of participants is involved in creating and re-creating the *structural* circumstances of their participation.

Another example

An additional example, involving athletes' use of performance-enhancing drugs, shows first how agency and structure interpretations have become a part of our everyday

lives and, second, how social theory helps to resolve these overly simplified interpretations of human behaviour. On the one hand, an athlete has to decide to ingest or inject a banned substance; it is a conscious act, and the athlete is almost always aware that it is an illegal act in the world of sport.[4] Thus, given the assumption of agency, it is appropriate to blame the athlete, who is attempting to win by illegal means, and to impose what sanctions there are available.

This would be fine if athletes lived alone in a vacuum, but they are also a part of society and are influenced by its structures. Those defending rather than blaming athletes for taking banned substances may point to the cultural context in which athletes now live:

- the 'culture of excellence' which only values winning;
- the medicalisation of society, in which drugs are developed and sold for a whole range of conditions that were not previously defined as 'medical';
- the rationalisation of the body, in which the body is treated and trained as an 'object' somehow removed from the personhood of the athlete;
- the professionalisation of sport has added income to the ego boost of winning (in a culture of excellence) – a dangerous combination encouraging individuals to take risks in order to be the best; and
- public demand for records, and more spectacular athletic performances.

In addition, they might consider the subculture of sport, and look at drug use from the athlete's perspective. In 1991, after the Ben Johnson scandal and the exposures of the Dubin Inquiry, Canadian sprinter Angella Issajenko made the following statement: 'Athletes will do whatever they have to to win. They know that random testing is in [introduced in Canada as a result of the Dubin Inquiry], and they are still prepared to take the risk.'

The elements that help to explain such risk taking from an athlete's perspective include:

- *positive deviance* – athletes overconforming to the norms of sport (Hughes and Coakley, 1991), which includes taking risks;
- *the social relations of sport*, which often involve a controlling relationship between coach and athletes, and which may extend to the implicit or explicit condoning of drug use;
- *an athlete's commitment to sport*, which involves so much time, cost and sacrifice on the part of the athlete, and his/her family, and which may lead to an athlete seeking an 'edge' in order to justify their sacrifices;
- *the structure of sport*, in which government and sponsor funding, and a place on national teams, is only available to athletes who achieve and maintain a certain level of performance;
- *the abusive nature of sport*, which always includes punishing one's body, and which may include abusive dietary practices, a variety of therapies (some ethically questionable) for the rapid rehabilitation of injured athletes, and 'psychodoping' (Coakley, 1992), creates a context in which the use of 'natural' chemicals (e.g. testosterone, HGH) seems normal; and
- *the athlete information network*, in which information is informally and easily shared among athletes competing internationally – information concerning who is using drugs, what they are using and in what dosages, and how they are getting away with it.

So, is it the athlete's fault? Is it society's fault? Or is the fault in the system of sport that we have created? Of course, the 'fault' (a word which implies that we have already judged the situation, so 'cause' might be a better term) lies in all three. The society in which the athlete lives, and the social formations and networks in which the athlete trains and competes, exist in a dialectical relationship with the athlete. Decisions made by the athlete cannot be independent of those contexts; the athlete will make a decision about the use of banned substances, but that decision can only be understood in light of the circumstances in which it is made.

A research project on the use of banned substances in sport using, for example, a critical cultural studies perspective, would take into account:

- the perspectives of the athletes (using participant observation and in-depth interviews);
- the perspectives of those individuals who 'support' high-performance athletes (coaches, medical staff, psychologists and other sport scientists, agents, sponsors, sport organisation officials, the media, family and friends, etc.);
- the structure of the sport system; and
- the values of the society that support the sport system and the athletes.

And such a study might ask searching questions about power relations and vested interests in that sport system; or why only the athlete is punished for taking banned substances and not the suppliers of drugs, the suppliers of information about their use, and those who turn a blind eye to undetected use because their position and income depend on the performances of the athlete.

The simple assignment of blame, to the athlete or the system, makes a good pub argument, and is carried out in the media.[5] But, as we have seen here, it is quite asociological. To paraphrase Douglas, 'human actions [cannot only] be explained in terms of concrete individual factors (such as individual will, choice, or the concrete situations individuals face) or in terms of something outside of the individual (such as culture or social structure) that determines or causes what they will do' (1980: 183). Our understanding of human actions can only be developed when we tease out the complex interaction between the individual and the social structures in which he/she lives.

THE DEVELOPMENT OF THE SOCIOLOGY OF SPORT

In many ways, the development of theory in the sociology of sport parallels the process outlined above. Separate, and often unreflexive concerns with structure and agency in the early stages of development eventually lead to a more sophisticated synthesis of the two in more recent research.[6] A separate subdiscipline of sociology recognised as the sociology of sport began to emerge in the mid-1960s in the United States (Kenyon and Loy, 1965; Loy and Kenyon, 1969). Its origins were in both sociology and physical education, its practitioners were often advocates for, and fans of, sport and, as a consequence, little of the early work was critical in nature. This is problematic since sociology is often considered to be a 'critical' science – everyday assumptions about social relations, and aspects of social life that are considered to be 'common sense', are exposed to analysis to determine whether such assumptions and aspects of common sense are supported by evidence.[7] The development of the sociology of sport can be traced through three relatively distinct phases: namely, reflection, reproduction and resistance.

Reflection

The early, uncritical work in the sociology of sport was rooted in the assumption that 'sport reflects society' or, to put it another way, 'sport is a mirror [or microcosm] of society' (the reflection thesis). This view is not incorrect; in fact, it is quite obvious. How could a major cultural institution such as sport not reflect the societies in which it is practised? If the economy is capitalist, and women have less social power than men in a particular society, is it likely that the major cultural institutions such as sport will be characterised by socialist economic principles and gender equity? This approach was connected to structural functionalism, the predominant theory at the time in US sociology, and the most significant initial influence on sociology of sport almost everywhere that it began to emerge. And within structural functionalism:

If there was a theme that seemed to best articulate the mission of the sociology of sport in the early period, it was socialization. It was inclusive: Within it one could look at 'sex' differences, race differences, child development, who entered into organized sport and how, categoric differences in enculturation, moral development, and so forth. (Ingham and Donnelly, 1997: 367)

Thus, sport was considered to be beneficial and functional. Through sport individuals learned how to become members of their social system – to set goals, maintain discipline, manage aggression and adapt to change.[8]

Since structural functionalism, especially as expressed in the work of Talcott Parsons, is often considered to flip-flop between agency and structure (as opposed to subsequent attempts to discover a synthesis between the two), this was evident in the sociology of sport. Agency was evident in the assumed voluntary nature of social action – individuals participated in sport, and behaved in the ways they did, because that was their choice. The emphasis on individuals was also evident in the close relationship between the sociology and psychology of sport during their early manifestations; and in the early studies of sport from a symbolic interactionist perspective, which examined the individual actors' definitions of the situation and creation of meaning in sport subcultures. In contrast, the individual disappeared when analyses turned to structure, deriving from Parsons's later emphasis on social systems. The sociology of sport focused on social processes (e.g. socialisation, social change), and social institutions such as sport and the related institutions (e.g. education, politics). This also represented a more valid adaptation of Parsons's system needs (see note 8).

While the reflection thesis is accurate, it is also obvious, and passive, but not necessarily uncritical (if one takes a dim view of gender inequity, that criticism is unlikely to stop short of criticising sport). The consensus view outlined above came to be challenged by a conflict view of sport which focused on social problems, and began to emphasise the sexist, racist and exploitative nature of sport (cf. Hoch, 1972; Scott, 1971) – issues that reflected those concerns in the larger society. Sport was seen as the new 'opiate of the masses', socialising individuals into an uncritical acceptance of status quo inequities.

Reproduction

It soon became evident that the reflection thesis did not explain the relationship between sport and society. However, while it only served to describe a status quo, it was an important initial stage for the sociology of sport. It helped to overcome a view that sport was a distinct sphere, somehow separate from, and perhaps even transcending, social life (e.g. Novak, 1976). The rather primitive Marxism of the conflict perspective was an important transitional stage, leading those concerned with a critical sociology of sport, and those critical of the status quo in sport, to search for more sophisticated theoretical tools. They found them in European sociological theory, and in a sociology of sport that was emerging in France and Germany. Work by Brohm (1978), Rigauer (1969) and Vinnai (1973), in English translations, began to have a powerful impact on North American and British sociology of sport, and became part of what Ingham and Donnelly (1997) referred to as the 'critical shift' in the subdiscipline.

The European neo-Marxist critique of sport argued that sport socialised individuals into work discipline, hyper-competitiveness and assertive individualism. In other words, sport not only reflected capitalist society, but also helped to reproduce it, to reproduce dominant social and cultural relations in society as a whole (Hargreaves, 1986). The idea of social reproduction was drawn from Pierre Bourdieu's (1970) work on education, in which he demonstrated how the French educational system helped to reproduce the social class structure of French society. Thus, in the sociology of sport, rather than passively mirroring society, sport could now be seen as actively helping to maintain a particular set of power relations in an inequitable society.[9]

A shift in the sociology of sport in the 1980s led to far greater attention being paid to gender and race than to social class, and here the reproduction thesis proved to be valuable. Sport came to be seen as a 'school for masculinity' – at a time of rapidly changing gender relations and increasing social power for women, sport was considered to be one of the last bastions of masculine power. In addition to helping to reproduce gender relations, sport also came to be viewed as one of the barriers to changing race relations – helping to maintain the notion that certain racial characteristics (mental and physical) existed, and promoting stereotypical views of them. However, the reproduction thesis is rooted in structural thinking. There is no agency evident in analyses that focus on social processes and social relations. The reproduction thesis came to be considered as an accurate and dynamic, but partial attempt to characterise the relationship between sport and society.

Resistance

The reproduction thesis characterises a dynamic, but one-way relationship between sport and society. If the status quo is effectively reproduced from generation to generation, then no changes in the relative power of social groups, and their social and cultural relations, will occur. Individuals are rendered as passive agents: either as falsely conscious consumers of the new 'opiate of the masses' (viz. sport), unaware of the forces involved in producing and reproducing inequality and maintaining their subordinate status; or 'as passive learners "molded" and "shaped" by "society"' (Coakley, 1993: 170). If individuals are to play some part in understanding, giving meaning to and shaping their destiny, then it is necessary to reintroduce agency. Despite the overwhelming differences in social power that exist between a wealthy ruling elite and everyone else, we are not powerless. The resistance thesis attempts to capture the two-way process in which reproductive forces are resisted – in which agency confronts structure.

The first, and still one of the more valuable attempts to characterise this process, to synthesise agency and structure in the sociology of sport, is Gruneau's (1983) *Class, Sport, and Social Development*. His solution is developed from the ideas of Gramsci, Williams and Bourdieu. The resistance thesis, sometimes referred to as hegemony theory, is rooted in Antonio Gramsci's ideas about social power. Before Gramsci, hegemony referred to the straightforward domination of, for example, one nation or social class over another. Gramsci recognised that hegemony worked in more subtle ways, often aided by the compliance of those in the subordinate position.[10] As Williams noted:

A lived hegemony is always a process ... Moreover ... it does not just passively exist as a form of dominance. It has continually to be renewed, recreated, defended, and modified. It is also continually resisted, limited, altered, challenged by pressures not all its own ... That is to say, alternative political and cultural emphases, and the many forms of opposition and struggle, are important not only in themselves but as indicative features of what the hegemonic process has in practice had to control. (Williams, 1977: 112–13)

These ideas permitted sport to be seen as not only dominated by elites such as the International Olympic Committee, FIFA, sporting goods manufacturers and media conglomerates, but also as 'contested terrain', as the 'site of struggles' over 'the forms, circumstances and meanings of participation' (Donnelly, 1993: 417; see also Donnelly, 1988).

In the resistance thesis, individuals are seen as active, self-reflexive agents (a) who 'might quite consciously value sports as meaningful and beneficial aspects of their lives, while at the same time being aware that ruling groups attempt to use sport as an instrument of control' (Hargreaves, 1982: 43; see also Gruneau, 1983: 151–2); (b) who have the capacity to change the conditions under which they practise sport and recognise and change the conditions that maintain their subordinate status; and (c) whose attempts at resistance sometimes have an opposite effect, serving to reinforce the conditions of their subordination (cf. Donnelly, 1988). Thus, the resistance thesis focuses on sport as an aspect of culture, produced (socially constructed) by the participants but not always in the manner of their own choosing. Critical cultural studies of sport have examined, among other things, sport subcultures, sport media, gender and racial relations in sport, and more recently globalisation processes. As such, these studies become part of the 'struggles', because they expose the hegemonic process. For example, some recent studies of gender and the media (Cluer et al., 2001; Duncan and Messner, 2000) appear to show that a sustained, evidence-based critique of media sources regarding their marginalisation and trivialisation of women's sports is having an impact in terms of increasing and more equitable sports coverage for women.

A NOTE ON FIGURATIONAL SOCIOLOGY

This discussion of agency and structure in sociological theory – as evidenced in the sociology of sport – would not be complete without taking note of the important contribution of the work of Norbert Elias and Eric Dunning to this field of study (Dunning, 1999; Elias and Dunning, 1986). Their work, and that of others following Elias's figurational (or process) approach to sociology (e.g. Maguire, 1999), have been prominent in sport studies in the UK and The Netherlands, and increasingly in Japan. Rather than attempting a synthesis/dialectical relationship between agency and structure, or the individual and society, Eliasian sociologists argue that this is an artificial distinction. Their focus is on constantly changing social configurations produced by the interactions among interdependent individuals, and on the social processes that are simultaneously produced by, and produce, these social configurations. Work in this area of theory tends to take a much longer-term, historical view of social processes than other sociologies, and important work has been achieved in analyses of such processes as globalisation, democratisation, sportisation (the process by which sports developed and spread), parliamentarisation, and the civilising process. In addition to studying the development of sport (and specific sports such as rugby and boxing), Elias, Dunning and others are best known in the sociology of sport for their work on soccer hooliganism, the globalisation of sport, and health and injury issues in sport.

A NOTE ON METHODOLOGY

The growing sophistication of sociological theory (for the interpretation of data) occurred in parallel with the use of increasingly sophisticated sociological methods (for the collection of data).[11] Some of these methods were developed in sociology, but others have been borrowed from history, anthropology and literary studies. Perhaps the best known of these is survey research, employing written or oral questionnaires. Methods range through various forms of textual analysis (from content analysis to discourse analysis), to observation, participant observation and in-depth interviewing.

The last group of methods is now often referred to as ethnography – an in-depth analysis of a social setting or social phenomenon in an attempt to understand it from the participants' perspectives. Growing sophistication is most evident in the use of multiple methods, not just for the purposes of 'triangulation' (Denzin, 1970) – where various methods are used in order to determine the validity of results from one of the methods – but also in recognition of the complexity of social phenomena, and the need to obtain as many sources of data as possible in order to generate a more complete understanding.

For example, a study of Olympic television coverage might include analyses of:

• *the audience* – a broad-based audience survey to determine who they are and what they watched (this might include secondary analysis of the media's own audience surveys); in-depth interviews with selected audience members to discover the meanings they attached to the coverage; and participant observation with individuals or groups watching the Olympics in order to understand how they watch, what they see, and how they interpret what they see;

• *the content* – quantitative content analyses to determine exactly what was shown, when and for how long; and more qualitative textual or discourse analyses to discover how sports were shown, and what meanings were given to the coverage by the broadcasting crews, the sponsors, etc. This could include analysis of the commentary, the content, and the way in which that content was selected and presented; and

• *the production* – in order to discover how Olympic broadcasts are made, a researcher (or research team) might interview key production staff; examine (content and textual analysis) broadcast policy documents produced by the International Olympic Committee, the local organising committee, the host broadcaster, sponsors and advertising agencies, and the actual broadcaster (CBC, BBC, etc.); and observe planning and production meetings, editing and production suites, and on-site commentary and electronic news-gathering crews.

Even if the research team decides to limit its research to one Olympic sport, it is evident that a complete study – which takes into account the three primary elements of media analysis (production, content and audience) is a complex and expensive undertaking.

FUTURE TRENDS IN THE SOCIOLOGY OF SPORT

Predicting future trends is always risky, especially at the time of writing when it is not yet clear if the events of 11 September 2001 will have a long-term impact on, for example, processes of globalisation or systems of social control. The sociology of sport is also an extremely wide-ranging and active field of research, so any predictions must also be partial. However, the following issues seem to be attracting attention:

• the globalisation of sport, including its relationship to local and regional sport practices, and to issues of identity;

• continuing critical analysis of the commercialisation of sport, including the parts played by sponsors, media conglomerates and national and international sports organisations;

• growing interest in the contradiction between sport as a healthy practice and the high degree of risk and injury evident in many sporting practices, and the institutionalisation of sports medicine;

- the production of sporting mega-events (Olympics, World Cups, etc.), including the involvement of various levels of government, citizen involvement (or lack of), the development and construction industries, the spaces that are dedicated to such events, and environmental concerns;

- a revival of interest in social class, and its intersections with gender and ethno-cultural heritage, in relation to sport and physical activity practices and barriers.

Social theory provides the interpretive tools for analysis of these and many other issues of interest to those involved in the sociology of sport.

Chapter summary

- There are two main schools of thought in the sociology of sport, one which empha-sises agency, the freedom of individuals to act in a manner of their own choosing, and the other which emphasises structure, the extent to which individual actions are con-strained by social forces and social structures.
- A synthesis of these two schools of thought is possible whereby variation in participa-tion in sport, for example, may be explained in terms of the involvement of participants as agents in creating and re-creating the structural circumstances of their participation.
- Sociology of sport has moved through a number of phases of analysis – reflection, reproduction and, most recently, resistance.
- Future concerns within the sociology of sport include globalisation, critical analysis of commercialisation, the tension between health and injury in sport, mega-events and social exclusion.

Further reading

Henslin (1999) provides a sound introduction to the major concepts and schools of thought in sociology and Donnelly (2000) illustrates their application in the sociology of sport. Wacquant's (1992) analysis of boxing in the black community of Chicago illustrates the insights to be gained from a synthesis of structure and agency approaches in sociology. Ingham and Donnelly (1997) provide an overview of the development of the sociology of sport.

NOTES

1 While the focus of this chapter is on sociology and sociological theory, it should be pointed out that social thought regarding the structure and agency dilemma is evident in all of the social sciences – anthropology, political economy, history and even economics.

2 Of course, physical activity does not automatically lead to good health, as many coal miners, injured athletes and anorexic figure skaters could attest. We do have con-cerns about the health of those involved in heavy physical work, and physical activity, in unhealthy environments. Ingham put this in perspective with regard to recreational physical

activity when he wrote: 'The fusion of new right ideology and right-thinking common sense ... promotes a lifestyle which exhorts us to save our hearts by jogging in the arsenic filled air of Tacoma' (1985: 50). His comment has proven to be prophetic since a recent California study shows a direct link between lung disease and air pollution among children involved in outdoor sports: 'the most active children in high-smog communities developed asthma at a rate three times that of children in the low-smog areas' (Mittelstaedt, 2002: A8).

3 However, as Jary and Jary have noted, despite many disagreements regarding the relationships between the two concepts, and problems of definition 'most forms of sociological theory can be located ... as recognizing the importance of both structural determinacy and individual agency' (1995: 663–4).

4 Athletes in East Germany in the 1970s were often not aware that they were being given banned substances; and, until athletes were warned about contamination of health food supplements, a number of those who tested positive for nandrolone were probably unaware that they had ingested a performance-enhancing drug. This example of the structural circumstances in which athletes use drugs is drawn from Donnelly (1991).

5 Readers might wish to try a similar case study, exposing explanations of athletic success, for example, to detailed analysis. Is it only a result of individual effort involving both mental determination and physical prowess? Or is it a result of a sophisticated talent recognition and sport development system using all of the most up-to-date knowledge from sport science and coaching science?

6 Parts of this section are drawn from Donnelly (1996), who develops reflection, reproduction and resistance theses from Alan Ingham and John Loy, and from Ingham and Donnelly (1997), who provide the most recent analysis of the development of sociology of sport. This section provides a simplified description of the development of this field of study.

7 Students often view criticism as destructive. However, in science criticism is considered to be a constructive process involved in the development of knowledge. In the social sciences, criticism often exposes the assumptions and power relations that exist in everyday views of what is considered to be 'common sense'. Lazarsfeld (1949) exposed the dangers of 'common sense' when he revisited the findings of a well-known study of The American Soldier in World War II. He presented a series of findings of the study (e.g. 'As long as the fighting continued, men were more eager to be returned to the States than they were after the German surrender') that appeared to be 'common sense' (of course, they didn't want to be killed); and then revealed that he had reversed all of the findings (the eagerness to return to the US increased after the surrender – during the war, there was an important job to be done; after the war, they wanted to get on with their lives). Since both the false and the actual findings can be explained by 'common sense', the actual data, and the way in which they are interpreted, are shown to be of far more importance than 'common sense'.

8 The system needs identified by Parsons – adaptation, goal attainment, integration and pattern maintenance – were intended to apply to aspects of social systems (e.g. pattern maintenance was related to socialising institutions such as families and schools), but were often presented in the sociology of sport in terms of the socialisation of individuals.

9 It is interesting to note, however, that focus on the reproduction of social class had a far more significant impact on the sociology of education than the sociology of sport.

10 Subordinate compliance may be determined by feelings of powerlessness, or by the belief that the social order is appropriate (such beliefs often being encouraged by institutions such as education, politics, religion and the media). In British terms, it has been noted that the Conservative Party, often considered to represent the interests of wealth, would never be elected without a working-class 'deference vote'. And the widespread support for the Royal Family often surprises outside observers who see royalty as enshrining ideas of inherited privilege, rather than merit.

11 Following work by Ingham and Gruneau, Donnelly (1996) presented three levels of analysis – categorical, distributive and relational – that tend to parallel the reflection, reproduction and resistance theses.

REFERENCES

Abercrombie, N., Hill, S. and Turner, B. (2000) *The Penguin Dictionary of Sociology*. 4th edn. London: Penguin.

Berger, P. (1963) *Invitation to Sociology*. New York: Bantam.

Berger, P. and Luckmann, T. (1967) *The Social Construction of Reality*. London: Allen Lane.

Bourdieu, P. and Passeron, J.-C. (1970) *Reproduction in Education, Society and Culture*. London: Sage.

Brohm, J.-M. (1978) *Sport: a Prison of Measured Time*. London: Ink Links.

Cluer, S., Donnelly, P. and MacNeill, M. (2001) 'Lessons learned: a case study of CBC television coverage of men's and women's diving at the Sydney Olympics'. Paper presented at the North American Society for the Sociology of Sport Annual Conference, San Antonio, TX, 31 October–3 November.

Coakley, J. (1992) 'Burnout among adolescent athletes: a personal failure or a social problem?', *Sociology of Sport Journal*, 9: 271–85.

Coakley, J. (1993) 'Sport and socialization', *Exercise and Sport Sciences Reviews*, 21: 169–200.

Dawe, A. (1970) 'The two sociologies', *British Journal of Sociology*, 21: 207–18.

Denzin, N. (ed.) (1970) *Sociological Methods: a Source Book*. Chicago: Aldine.

Donnelly, P. (1988) 'Sport as a site for "popular" resistance', in R. Gruneau (ed.), *Popular Cultures and Political Practices*. Toronto: Garamond Press, pp. 69–82.

Donnelly, P. (1991) 'The culture of excellence: drug use by high performance athletes'. Paper presented at the Annual Conference of the International Committee for the Sociology of Sport, Tallin, Estonia, 26–29 June.

Donnelly, P. (1993) 'Democratization revisited: seven theses on the democratization of sport and active leisure', *Loisir et société/Society and Leisure*, 16: 413–34.

Donnelly, P. (1996) 'Approaches to social inequality in the sociology of sport', *Quest*, 48: 221–42.

Donnelly, P. (2000) 'Interpretive approaches to the sociology of sport', in J. Coakley and E. Dunning (eds), *Handbook of Sports Studies*. London: Sage, pp. 77–91.

Donnelly, P. and Harvey, J. (1996) *Overcoming Systemic Barriers to Access in Active Living*. Report prepared for Fitness Branch, Health Canada, and Active Living Canada.

Douglas, J., Adler, P., Fontana, A., Freeman, C. and Kotarba, J. (1980) *Introduction to the Sociologies of Everyday Life*. Boston: Allyn & Bacon.

Duncan, M. and Messner, M. (2000) *Gender in Televised Sports: 1989, 1993 and 1999*. Los Angeles: Amateur Athletic Foundation of Los Angeles.

Dunning, E. (1999) *Sport Matters: Sociological Studies of Sport, Violence and Civilization*. London: Routledge.

Elias, N. and Dunning, E. (1986) *Quest for Excitement: Sport and Leisure in the Civilizing Process*. Oxford: Basil Blackwell.

Evans, R., Barer, M. and Marmor, T. (1994) *Why Are Some People Healthy and Others Not? The Determinants of Population Health*. New York: Aldine de Gruyter.

Giddens, A. (1982) *Sociology: a Brief but Critical Introduction*. London: Macmillan.

Giddens, A. (1989) *Sociology*. Cambridge: Polity Press.

Gouldner, A. (1975) *For Sociology: Renewal and Critique in Sociology Today*. Harmondsworth: Penguin.

Gruneau, R. (1983) *Class, Sport, and Social Development*. Amherst, MA: University of Massachusetts Press.

Hargreaves, J. (1982) 'Sport, culture and ideology', in J. Hargreaves (ed.), *Sport, Culture and Ideology*. London: Routledge & Kegan Paul, pp. 30–61.

Hargreaves, J. (1986) *Sport, Power, and Culture*. New York: St Martin's Press.

Henslin, J. (ed.) (1999) *Down to Earth Sociology: Introductory Readings*. 10th edn. New York: The Free Press.

Hoch, P. (1972) *Rip Off the Big Game: the Exploitation of Sports by the Power Elite*. Garden City, NY: Doubleday.

Hughes, R. and Coakley, J. (1991) 'Positive deviance among athletes: the implications of overconformity to the sport ethic', *Sociology of Sport Journal*, 8 (4): 307–25.

Ingham, A. (1985) 'From public issue to private trouble: well-being and the fiscal crisis of the state', *Sociology of Sport Journal*, 2: 43–55.

Ingham, A. and Donnelly, P. (1997) 'A sociology of North American sociology of sport: disunity in unity, 1965–1996', *Sociology of Sport Journal*, 14: 362–418.

Jary, D. and Jary, J. (1995) *Collins Dictionary of Sociology*. 2nd edn. Glasgow: Harper Collins.

Kenyon, G. and Loy, J. (1965) 'Toward a sociology of sport: a plea for the study of physical activity as a sociological and social psychological phenomenon', *Journal of Health, Physical Education, and Recreation*, 36: 24–5, 68–9.

Lazarsfeld, P. (1949) 'What is obvious?', *Public Opinion Quarterly*, 13: 378–80.

Loy, J. and Kenyon, G. (eds) (1969) *Sport, Culture, and Society*. Toronto, ON: Collier-Macmillan.

Maguire, J. (1999) *Global Sport: Identities, Societies, Civilizations*. Oxford: Polity.

Marx, K. (1852/1991) *The Eighteenth Brumaire of Louis Bonaparte*. New York: International Publishers.

Mittelstaedt, M. (2002) 'Smog linked to asthma in children', *Globe & Mail*, 2 February: A8.

National Forum on Health (1997) *Canada Health Action: Building on the Legacy*, 2 vols. Ottawa: Public Works and Government Services.

Novak, M. (1976) *The Joy of Sports*. New York: Basic Books.

Raphael, D. (2001a) 'Staying healthy in Canada: What's missing?' *Guelph Mercury*, 7 September: A8.

Raphael, D. (2001b) *Inequality is Bad for Our Hearts: Why Low Income and Social Exclusion are Major Causes of Heart Disease*. Report prepared for the North York Heart Health Network, Toronto, Canada. (*www.yorku.ca/wellness/heart*)

Rigauer, B. (1969) *Sport and Work*. New York: Columbia University Press.

Scott, J. (1971) *The Athletic Revolution*. New York: Free Press.

Thompson, K. and Tunstall, J. (eds) (1975) *Sociological Perspectives*. Harmondsworth: Penguin.

Vinnai, G. (1973) *Football Mania*. London: Orbach & Chambers.

Wacquant, L. (1992) 'The social logic of boxing in black Chicago: toward a sociology of pugilism', *Sociology of Sport Journal*, 9: 221–54.

Williams, R. (1977) *Marxism and Literature*. Oxford: Oxford University Press.

2

Politics, Power, Policy and Sport

BARRIE HOULIHAN

Overview

→ The scope of political science
→ Definitions of politics
→ Example 1: the National Stadium
→ Example 2: women's participation in the Olympic Games
→ Macro-level perspectives

The social sciences are differentiated primarily by their substantive concerns but also by their particular methodologies and associated methods. Psychology, for example, is concerned primarily with the study of individual behaviour and has developed methodologies that support the use of experimental methods largely derived from the natural sciences as well as methods more familiar in sociology such as observation. The substantive concern of sociology is the study of group behaviour and social institutions, such as the family and the school, and has developed a wide variety of methods for gathering information ranging from the collection of census data to the study of life histories and participant observation. By contrast the substantive concerns of political science are far less neatly

delineated, being focused on the sharply contested concept of power and its use in all its myriad forms. Nor does political science claim a distinctive methodology as it has tended to rely on the adaptation of methodologies developed in other social sciences.

THE SCOPE OF POLITICAL SCIENCE

Part of the difficulty of pinning down the focus of political science and its contribution to the study of sport is the diversity of fields of study that it encompasses. The major substantive fields within the discipline include government/public administration, policy analysis, political theory and international relations with each raising a

Table 2.1   *The scope of political science*

Field	Illustrative research topics	Illustrative research questions related to sport
Government/public administration	(a) Allocation of functions between central government departments and between central, local/regional government and semi-independent agencies (b) The influence of public officials on policy (c) The basis for successful policy implementation (d) The processes for protecting citizens' rights	(a) What are the consequences of responsibility for sport being given to a semi-independent agency (such as the various Sports Councils in the UK) rather than to a central government department? (b) How important are public officials (relative to political parties, ministers, media, sports lobby groups, etc.) in setting the agenda for sport policy making? (c) What administrative/ management factors affect the successful implementation of policies designed, for example, to increase participation in sport or the amount of time in the school curriculum devoted to PE and sport? (d) How, and with what impact, are the views of elite athletes, school children and sports fans, for example, conveyed to public administrators?
Policy analysis	(a) The process by which some private concerns become public policy issues and, maybe more importantly, some do not (b) Assessing the effectiveness of different combinations of policy instruments (incentives, sanctions and information) in achieving policy objectives (c) Assessing the impact of policy	(a) By what process did women's participation in sport, disability sport and drug use in sport emerge as public policy concerns in the form that they did and at the time that they did? (b) How effective have incentives such as leisure cards been in encouraging those on low incomes to use leisure facilities? (c) What evidence would be valid in demonstrating that involvement in sport reduces juvenile delinquency or that designation as a specialist sports college raised the self-esteem of pupils?

(Continued)

Table 2.1   *Continued*

Field	Illustrative research topics	Illustrative research questions related to sport
Political theory	(a) The changing conceptualisation of citizenship and its relationship to civil society (b) The role of the state in promoting individual liberty and social equality (c) The challenge to the division between the public and the private spheres	(a) Should access to sport and leisure be treated as a right and as an essential element of full citizenship? (b) Does state intervention to enhance access to sport (e.g. subsidies to leisure facilities) increase liberty or constrain liberty by influencing/directing the use of 'free time'? (c) To what extent is it the case that male participation in elite sport in the public sphere is only possible because of the exploitation of women in the private sphere of family life?
International relations	(a) Diplomacy between states (b) The development of international policy regimes (c) The role and importance of non-governmental international organisations	(a) Is sport an effective diplomatic resource? (b) What is the character and effectiveness of international policy regimes in dealing with issues such as doping in sport and the transfer of players between clubs? (c) Are international sports organisations such as the IOC independent actors in international politics?

distinctive set of questions relevant to the study of sport and politics. In addition, there is a rich diversity of macro-level perspectives and analytical frameworks from which these substantive fields may be studied, which includes Marxism, neo-Marxism, neo-pluralism, behaviourism, feminism and rational choice and a similarly broad range of middle range/meso-level frameworks associated with the analysis of policy such as advocacy coalitions, policy communities and policy networks. Table 2.1 illustrates both the scope of politics and also the range of issues related to sport that are raised.

As can be seen from Table 2.1 in addition to the concept of power, a further central thread in much political science is a concern with the role of the state either as a focus for policy or as a reference point for the analysis of concepts such as citizenship and civil society. Consequently, for many political scientists, politics is defined primarily in relation to the actions of the state and particularly the role of government and its authoritative use of power to make rules and laws that have precedence over rules from other sources in society (Moodie, 1984: 23). If this definition of politics is accepted, then attention would be directed towards, for example, the use of public funds to support sports policy, the location of responsibility for sport within the structure of government, and the way public policy for sport is determined and executed. Thus the decisions by UK governments to provide a subsidy of £120m for the construction of a national stadium on the site of Wembley Stadium, to make sport one of the beneficiaries of the National Lottery, and to establish a UK Sports Institute would all be examples consistent with Moodie's definition, as would (a) the decision by the United States government to legislate in 1978 to resolve the friction between the American Athletic Union, the National Collegiate Athletic Association and the United States Olympic Committee, (b) the licensing by the French government of sports clubs and coaches, and (c) the decision by the Australian government to underwrite the Sydney bid for the 2000 Olympic Games.

This conception of politics broadly confines attention to a limited range of institutions and forums such as parliaments, cabinets, ministries and courts. Power is conceptualised as largely a property of political institutions and a resource which enables 'power-holders' to achieve their particular goals. Consequently, the focus for study of sport and politics in the UK would include the decisions of ministers, the activities of the various sports councils, and legislation. However, while state institutions are clearly powerful, a second, more comprehensive and more subtle definition of politics requires that we look beyond the activities and outputs of the formal institutions of the domestic state and acknowledge the power wielded by non-state actors such as media businesses, commercial sponsors of sport and international sports federations, and by international governmental bodies such as the European Union and the Council of Europe. As Goodin and Klingemann (1996) suggest, politics is about the *constrained use of power*: 'It is the constraints under which political actors operate, and strategic manoeuvring that they occasion and that occurs within them, that seems to us to constitute the essence of politics.' This conceptualisation leads us away from an overconcentration on the formal institutions of the domestic political process and encourages an acceptance that power has sources not only within those institutions but also elsewhere.

A further implication of this broader view of sport politics is that not all decisions affecting sport will be made formally and publicly: many, even very important decisions are made in an ad hoc and far less

---

Box 2.1   Definition of 'policy'

There are many competing and overlapping definitions of policy. Hogwood and Gunn (1984) identify ten different uses of the term, including policy as a set of proposals, the decisions of government, a programme of action, and an aspiration or expression of general purpose. Heclo gives perhaps the most useful definition of policy as applying to 'something "bigger" than particular decisions, but "smaller" than general social movements. Thus, policy, in terms of level of analysis, is a concept placed roughly in the middle range.' (1972: 84)

explicit manner. For example, the intensity with which a government pursues the objective of drug-free sport may be determined informally and even implicitly as public officials interpret the minister's statements, or lack of comment, on the issue. Similarly, the balance of emphasis between elite achievement and mass participation in government sports policy might be determined by informal lobbying by national governing bodies, the national Olympic Committee and health interests.

However, while these processes may be informal, discreet or implicit and reflect an acknowledgement that power in the political system extends beyond the formal institutions of the state, they are nonetheless still largely centred on recognised state institutions and personnel. A third and significantly different definition is one that treats politics as an activity that takes place wherever there are disputes about objectives and how they might be achieved, and that power is a much more ambivalent and elusive concept than is reflected in conventional political science usage. This view suggests that attempting to maintain a distinction between the public and private spheres is misguided and indeed unsustainable in modern complex societies. Ponton and Gill, for example, argue that politics is about the arrangements for ordering social affairs and as a result the scope of study 'cannot, in principle, exclude the possibility of political activity in any sphere of human life at any level, from the smallest of groups, such as the nuclear family, to the activities of international organisations' (1993: 8). Thus politics is seen as a pervasive feature of modern life, inherent in all organisations whether public or private and common to all areas of human activity including sport.

While Moodie's more limited definition of the scope of politics is in marked contrast to that of Ponton and Gill, both share a common focus on institutions and a narrow view of power as a resource that can be acquired or lost, shared or monopolised, used or neglected and as such has much in common with Dahl's (1957) definition that X has power over Y if X is able to get Y to do something to the benefit of X which Y

Box 2.2   Definitions of 'the state' and 'government'

The state refers primarily to a territorial unity and to a collection of institutions. The term 'state' is often used to refer not only to government but also to a range of other distinct institutions including the military, the courts system, the police, the system of local administration and the school system. There is considerable debate about the boundary between the state and civil society with some arguing that even when voluntary organisations receive financial grants from government, they become part of the state. The 'state' as a territorial entity is easier to define as it refers to an area over which the state has unrestricted power. However, unrestricted power in modern global society is unlikely.

The term 'government' refers to the arrangements for making policy decisions that prevail at a particular time. While the state is a long-lasting or permanent entity, governments come and go. A state may therefore move from democracy to dictatorship and, within democracy, from a socialist to a conservative government.

would not otherwise have done. In recent years there have been attempts to refine our understanding of the concept of power with Lukes (1974), for example, identifying further dimensions to power, namely the capacity of interests, such as business, to keep issues off the policy agenda and the capacity to manipulate ideology to the extent that certain demands will not be articulated. More recently, theorists such as Laclau and Mouffe (1985) and Foucault (1978) have enhanced the subtlety of our understanding of hegemonic manipulation and the extent to which power is diffused beyond the institutions of the state. Foucault, for example, rejects the view of power as a phenomenon outside social relations in favour of a conceptualisation of power as diffused through all social relations. In particular, Foucault traces the broad variety of ways in which the state, working through a range of governmental and non-governmental, formal and informal institutions, seeks to exercise authority over citizens so that they remain 'disciplined', obedient subjects of the state.

The different interpretations of politics discussed above are summarised in Table 2.2, in which some of the implications for the study of sport politics are identified. The three interpretations are not exhaustive, but do indicate the variety of approaches within political science. Taken in conjunction with Table 2.1, political science can be seen to offer a conceptually and theoretically rich perspective from which to study sport which acknowledges the role and significance of the state, the international dimension to sport politics and policy, and the significance of ideological debates relating to values. Furthermore, by emphasising the centrality of the use of power, the various approaches direct our attention to questions such as: who holds power in sport at national and international levels, how is

that power utilised in pursuit of organisational objectives, and how do issues get on to the agenda of governments? All these questions are important to those of us who are concerned with the study of the public policy of sport, but they tend to direct our attention towards the input end of the policy-making process. In other words our attention is directed towards questions of access to the agenda of politics – how access is achieved and why certain issues capture the attention of key policy actors such as politicians, public officials, the media and major pressure groups while others languish at the margins. Although questions about access, input democracy and bias in agenda setting are clearly important, they can distract attention from the consequences of decisions or non-decisions on policy issues – the outputs of the policy process or, in Harold Lasswell's classic formulation 'Who gets what, when and how'. Lasswell's concern was with the distributional consequences of the use of power – who benefits and who loses out.

The insights provided by political science can be illustrated by reference to two current issues in sport, namely the choice of location for a national stadium and the participation of women in the Olympic Games.

WEMBLEY – THE NATIONAL STADIUM

A brief chronology of events

In the mid-1990s Sport England arranged a competition for the location of a national stadium which would be partly funded by the National Lottery. The Football Association, the Premier League, the Football League, the Rugby Football League and the British Athletic Federation were involved in the development of the project. In late 1996 Wembley was selected by Sport England as

Table 2.2   *Three definitions of politics and the implications for the study*
             of sportpolitics

Model	Politics	Power	Focus for analysis	Gender equity as an example of a focus for analysis
State institutional (Moodie, 1984)	Confined to the institutions of the state	A resource, the use of which is generally overt	Focus would be primarily on the decisions and activities of the sports ministry, state agencies and local authorities. Substantive concerns tend to be with the 'input' end of the policy process, i.e. the promotion and protection of interests within state institutions	Analysis of gender equity policies of the various sports councils, schools and other public bodies. Focus on implementation, e.g. through the use of inducements (access to National Lottery funding) and on measurement of impact, e.g. number of women visiting sports centres, joining sports clubs, or in the national Olympic squad
Universal institutional (Ponton and Gill, 1993)	An aspect of all institutions	A resource whose use is generally overt	Focus would extend to include the decision making of sports organisations, other organisations with an interest in sport such as television companies and sponsors, and also institutions such as the family Substantive concerns tend to be with the 'input' end of the policy process, i.e. the	The analysis would extend to include the media portrayal of male and female athletes, the attitudes of sponsors, the attitudes of parents to the participation of their male and female children in sport, the allocation of resources by clubs and governing bodies to support gender equity, and the interaction between these

(Continued)

Table 2.2   *Continued*

Model	Politics	Power	Focus for analysis	Gender equity as an example of a focus for analysis
			promotion and protection of interests within state institutions, but there is also a concern with the process of bargaining and negotiation between state and non-state actors	various non-state actors and the institutions of the state
Multi-dimensional power (Lukes, 1974; Foucault, 1978)	Ubiquitous and inherent in all social activity	Multi-dimensional ranging from the use of legislation and public finances to attitudes and values embedded in society. Power as manipulation and strategy	Focus on issues rather than institutions, with the aim being to trace the source, nature, utilisation and impact of power	The investigation of the construction of female and male identities; the development of patriarchal hegemony and its perseverance through a multiplicity of sites including the family, school and media as well as the sports club and the sports governing body

its preferred location and £120m was allocated from Lottery funds as a contribution to total costs.

Ownership lay with a trust, English National Stadium Trust (ENST) and a separate trust, Wembley National Stadium Limited, was established to raise the necessary finance to complete the project. The Football Association was the dominant partner in both trusts. By mid-1998 UK Athletics (the successor to the British Athletic Federation) had informed the ENST that none of its annual competitions would fill the stadium and that only two international athletics events would do so, namely the Olympic Games and the World Athletics Championships. Later the British Olympic Association admitted that Wembley was not necessarily the only centrepiece for any future bid for the Olympic Games. However, in January 2000 UK Athletics submitted a bid to host the 2005 World Athletics Championships in London with the rebuilt Wembley Stadium a clear possibility as the main venue.

Because of the weakness of support for the project from the BOA and UK Athletics, it was clear that it would be the FA that would take the long-term financial risk. In the meantime estimated costs for the project had risen from £136m to £334m. The growing uncertainty over the project was compounded by the government's increasing concern to achieve regeneration benefits for the local area from the national stadium project. In addition, problems were emerging with the design, especially regarding the cost and feasibility of incorporating an international competition standard running track.

By December 2000 the project had run into financial problems with the FA unable to borrow the revised estimate of £410m. By May 2001 the FA had announced that it was pulling out of the project, a decision which prompted the Home Secretary to appoint a working party to review the situation chaired by Patrick Carter. The Carter Report, published in September 2001, favoured Wembley over rival bids from Coventry and Birmingham, but did not make a firm recommendation. In late 2001 the government announced that while Wembley was the preferred option, a final decision was some way in the future.

According to Tony Banks, the then Minister for Sport, the development of a national stadium at Wembley was 'a project that we simply cannot allow to go wrong' (1997). Not only did the project 'go wrong' but it did so in spectacular style. The débâcle raised a large number of questions for the political scientist such as:

- Why was the government so keen to have a national stadium?
- Which nation was it to cater for?
- Which interests were involved in the decision making?
- What was the role of the Department of Culture, Media and Sport?

- Why was the government offering a subsidy to the richest sport in the UK?
- Why did the project go so badly wrong?

There is no obligation on a country to have a national stadium: although France has one, Italy, the US and Germany do not. It is possible that the British government was motivated simply by populism – a desire to curry favour with the electorate, or at least that large proportion of the electorate who are football supporters. Few politicians, especially in the Labour Party, can resist the opportunity to exploit the publicity that surrounds the 'people's game' and even Margaret Thatcher, who was both uncomprehending and contemptuous of sport, was photographed being given a kiss by Kevin Keegan, then captain of the England football team. While populism was probably one motive, there were certainly others. In recent years governments have become acutely aware of the regeneration potential of major sports infrastructure projects. In the United States building prestigious stadiums is a well-recognised form of city promotion or what is often referred to as 'civic boosterism'.

The decision to support Manchester's bid to host the 2002 Commonwealth Games was in large part motivated by the urban regeneration potential. With well over £80m of funding from the National Lottery, a cluster of sports venues (stadium, velodrome, indoor tennis centre and squash centre) have been built on the eastern side of the city in the hope that it will lead to a permanent boost to the local economy. The £120m that Sport England allocated to the Wembley national stadium project could be seen as part of a similar regeneration strategy for one of the less affluent London suburbs. According to the local authority, 'The multi-million pound regeneration proposals ... stemming from the new stadium development ... offer the best chance of reversing over two decades of economic decline in the Wembley area ...' (House of Commons 2000: Appendix 10 para. 1.2). The decision to support Wembley rather than Coventry or Birmingham was also partly due to an assumption that if Britain were to bid to host a major sports event such as the soccer World Cup or the Olympic Games, a London location was a requirement as the centrepiece for the bid.

The government of Tony Blair had made it clear that one of its objectives was to bring major international sports events to Britain partly because of the substantial contribution to the national economy, largely through tourism income, that can be gained from the hosting of sports events of global significance such as the Olympic Games, the football World Cup or the World Athletics Championships. Recent Olympic host cities, particularly Barcelona and Sydney, obtained substantial and, in the case of Barcelona at least, sustained increases in overseas tourist numbers which have been directly attributed to the publicity value of the Games. In Britain it is estimated that the annual value of sports tourism to the economy is £1.5bn, while it has been estimated that the Sydney Olympics will help reduce Australia's current account deficit by 1.25 per cent. For the city of Sheffield the first round matches of the Euro '96 football competition generated around £5.8m of expenditure with the 26,000 supporters who visited the city during the ten-day period, each spending between £50 and £100 per day. It is estimated by the Australian Tourist Commission that the country would attract an additional 2.1 million visitors between 1994 and the start of the Olympic Games in 2000 due to the city's raised profile and contribute over A$4bn to an aspect of the economy which already, in 1993, accounted for

11 per cent of Australia's exports. This expectation is based on assessments of Australia's previous experience in bidding for and hosting major sports events. For example, it was estimated that the hosting of the 1987 America's Cup generated expenditure of $464m and the equivalent of 9,500 full-time jobs. Even Brisbane's failed bid for the 1992 Olympic Games provided a significant boost to the local economy as it focused 'world-wide attention on Australia, its tourism potential, its excellent sporting facilities and its professional sports administration' (Department of Sport, 1987). Britain would dearly like to emulate Australia.

In addition to the fairly clear economic motives for supporting the idea of a national stadium, there is the far less specific, but nonetheless important notion of the identity politics of sport. For some countries, the development of a national stadium is an expression of collective identity and a way of asserting the vigour and vitality of the nation and, especially, its economy. Thus national stadiums can be seen as modern monuments fulfilling the same function as palaces in the eighteenth and nineteenth centuries and museums and 'sights' (such as the Eiffel Tower) in the nineteenth and twentieth centuries. Although some cultural monuments may be deemed expensive 'white elephants' at the time (e.g. the Millennium Dome in London) others, such as the Sydney Opera House or the Guggenheim Museum in Bilbao, can fulfil important symbolic functions for an entire community. However, the absence of a national stadium does not necessarily indicate a lack of sensitivity towards identity; rather, it may simply reflect the complexity of identity politics. For example, the absence of national stadiums in Germany, Spain and Italy may well reflect the strong political regionalism in these countries. Consequently, major sports events circulate throughout the country much in the same way that the Spanish monarch and court did in the seventeenth and eighteenth centuries. The absence of a national stadium thus allows symbolic national sporting events to fulfil the role of reinforcing national identity at the same time as acknowledging regional identities. The political dilemma for Britain is to decide which nation the national stadium is to represent. The Welsh have recently completed a new national stadium (the Cardiff Millennium Stadium), the Scots have long had a national stadium at Hampden Park, while Windsor Park in Northern Ireland fulfilled the same function, at least for the unionist community.

An analysis of governmental motives in relation to the national stadium provides rich opportunities to address a range of issues in sport politics, including how the regeneration potential of sports facilities and major events gained acceptability within government and the impact of the symbolic politics of identity on practical policy decisions. However, for a fuller understanding of the politics of the national stadium, the analysis of motives needs to be supplemented by an analysis of processes of decision making. A series of questions arise regarding how the agenda was set, who was involved and influential, and what were the motives, not just of government, but also of the other key players such as the various governing bodies, the commercial owners of the Wembley site, Brent Borough Council, the Greater London Authority and the British Olympic Association. In addition, attention might also be focused on the significance of the series of highly critical reports on aspects of the government's stadium policy by the House of Commons Culture, Media and Sport Select Committee. The analysis would also involve uncovering the sources of influence of key policy actors and the strategies adopted to exert influence.

Table 2.3 lists some of the organisations with an interest in the decision regarding the national stadium, but it is not exhaustive, with the most significant omission being the voice of the sports fan. However, as is routinely the case in many areas of public policy making, the public – whether as patients, tenants or sports fans – are confined to the margins of the policy process. As regards the role of the DCMS and especially of the Secretary of State, the latter seems to have had a potentially determining role, but one that appears to have been squandered, perhaps because of the lack of clarity of government objectives and indeed the incompatibility of objectives. The desire to construct a multi-sport national stadium as a centrepiece for bids for major international sports events conflicted with the desire to limit the commitment of public expenditure to the project, thus ensuring conflict with the Football Association who bore the brunt of the financial risk. In addition, the equivocal position of the British Olympic Association and the fragile financial position of both UK Athletics and the Rugby Football League left them at the margins of much of the debate. More significant from the standpoint of the DCMS was the virtual loss of any influence with the FA and its trust, WNSL, once the £120m of Lottery funding had been released for the purchase of the site.

Political scientists, especially those with a particular interest in policy, would find the national stadium episode a rich opportunity to analyse power in British sport policy making. There are important questions raised in each of the four broad fields of political science identified in Table 2.1. For example, the influence of public officials,

Table 2.3 *Motives of selected actors involved in the national stadium debate*

Interest/organisation	Motives/interests	Resources	Involvement
British Olympic Association	Consideration of a possible London-based bid to host the Olympic Games in 2012. Interested in the Wembley proposals but refused to commit to a Wembley-centred bid. Attracted by the possibility of an East London location and GLA support	(a) Support crucial to any future Olympic bid (b) No financial capacity to support a stadium project	(a) Significant influence over the DCMS Secretary of State regarding the acceptability of the various design options
UK Athletics	Concerned to host World Athletics Championships in either 2003 or 2005. Selected as host for the 2005 Championships by the IAAF	(a) Extremely limited, as predecessor body (British Athletics Federation) went bankrupt in 1997 there was no possibility of a financial contribution to the cost of the new stadium (b) No regular events that could make the use of an 80,000 seat stadium viable	(a) Increasingly peripheral from mid-1990s to 2000 (b) Sport England offered support for an alternative athletics stadium at Pickett's Lock in London to cater for the 2005 World Athletics Championships, but support was withdrawn due to cost in late 2001 with the result that the Championships were reallocated
Football Association	Seeking a replacement for Wembley, but daunted by the cost. Seeking to offset some of the cost by accepting the idea of a national stadium to cater for more sports than football	(a) The richest sport in England (b) Control major sporting assets, e.g. the England team and the FA Cup (c) The only sport that could guarantee capacity crowds for more than one or two events	(a) Wanted Wembley as the centrepiece of their subsequently unsuccessful bid to host the 2006 World Cup
Rugby Football League	Keen to retain access to a major venue for its flagship Cup and international matches	(a) No financial contribution to the cost of the stadium	
Sport England	Main supporter of the idea of a multi-sport national stadium, but also having to	(a) Controlled access to National Lottery funding	(a) Awarded £120m for the purchase of the Wembley site early in negotiations,

(Continued)

Table 2.3 *Continued*

Interest/organisation	Motives/interests	Resources	Involvement
	take account of regeneration potential of any investment. Strong supporter of a Wembley-based stadium		consequently had little leverage over the FA in later discussions
UK Sport	Concerned to attract major sports events to the UK	(a) No access to funding for capital projects (b) Ministerial advice (c) Responsible for attracting major sports championships to the UK	(a) Commissioned an independent review of the various stadium designs
Brent Borough Council	Regeneration in the Brent area	(a) Planning approval powers (b) Some financial capacity to contribute to infrastructure development	(a) Strongly involved in negotiating the 'planning gain', i.e. the regeneration benefits, in return for its support to WNSL
Greater London Authority	Regeneration in London	(a) Limited, but could 'spoil' the Wembley plans by offering the prospect of an East London stadium for a possible bid for the 2012 Olympic Games	(a) Negotiations with the BOA over an East London site for Olympic bid
Potential commercial lenders	Ensuring the security of, and an adequate return on, their investment	(a) Finance of approximately £350m	(a) Reluctant to lend to WNSL as they were not persuaded that the project could make an adequate return on capital
Department of Culture, Media and Sport	(a) Vaguely in favour of Wembley as the location for the national stadium.	(a) Strong influence over Sport England decisions (b) Control access to Treasury funding for bids for major events such as the soccer World Cup	(a) Strongly in favour of public/private financial partnerships rather than full public subsidy as was the case in France for the building of the Stade de France (b) A series of uncertain interventions which rarely clarified issues or moved the decision-making process forward

especially those within the quangos Sport England and UK Sport, is a recurring theme among specialists in public administration. Policy analysts may focus on the interplay between the various interests identified in Table 2.3 and be concerned to examine the resources possessed by each and the effectiveness of the negotiating strategy followed in pursuit of organisational interests. Political theorists might be interested in the implications for democratic accountability of the public/private financial partnership that underpinned the Wembley project. Or they might question spatial equity in relation to the location of a national stadium in London, when one of the three sports it is designed to cater for, rugby league, has only shallow roots in the south and when the main user, football, has roots in the north of England at least as deep as those in the London area. Finally, international relations specialists would focus on the growing influence of international non-governmental organisations such as the IOC and the major international federations, such as FIFA, in shaping, via the BOA and the FA, domestic sports policy objectives.

Not surprisingly, the events surrounding the decision to construct a national stadium gave a prominent place to state institutions and government as well as confirming the centrality of the concept of power – even if it is the power to obfuscate and prevaricate. The second example of sport politics, the participation of women in the Olympic Games, is very different in focus and context but, as will be shown, it is an issue that benefits considerably from political science analysis.

WOMEN'S PARTICIPATION IN THE OLYMPIC GAMES

The founder of the modern Olympics, Pierre de Coubertin, expressed the view in the late nineteenth century that 'the Olympic Games must be reserved for the solemn and periodic exaltation of male athleticism with … female applause as reward' (quoted in Coakley, 2001: 210). De Coubertin's views reflected the then dominant social Darwinist ideology that women possessed a limited quantity of energy for all functions – physical, social and intellectual – and that priority needed to be given to the physical function of reproduction and child rearing. This argument was used not only to justify the exclusion of women from education, but also their exclusion from participation in sport in general and the Olympic Games in particular. As Table 2.4 indicates, progress towards equality of participation in the Olympic Games has been slow and still has some way to go.

A political science analysis of the slow progress of women's participation in the Games would focus on a range of issues and questions including the following:

- the role and significance of ideology in shaping IOC policy and also in shaping the attitudes of governments towards the issue;
- the role and significance of women's pressure groups; and
- the attitude of individual international federations.

Hargreaves (1994) traces the interplay between broader changes in social attitudes towards women and the lobbying by women's organisations and their combined effect on the status of women in sport. In particular, she draws attention to the persistence of gender stereotyping throughout the history of modern Olympic sport which made women's participation in sports such as archery, tennis and figure-skating in the early part of the twentieth century more readily acceptable than their participation in athletics. Success in gaining acceptance for women's athletics was more the result of

Table 2.4   *Women's participation in selected summer Olympic Games*

Year	Location	No. of countries represented	No. of sports open to males/females (women's events as % of men's)	No. of male competitors	No. of female competitors	Female competitors as % of male competitors
1908	London	22	50/0 (0 %)	1,999	36	2
1932	Los Angeles	47	87/14 (16 %)	1,281	127	16
1964	Tokyo	93	115/32 (28 %t)	4,457	683	15
1980	Moscow	81	146/50 (34 %)	4,238	1,088	26
1984	Los Angeles	140	153/73 (48 %)	5,458	1,620	30
1988	Seoul	160	165/86 (52 %)	7,105	2,476	35
1992	Barcelona	170	171/98 (57 %)	7,555	3,008	40
1996	Atlanta	197	170/108 (64 %)	6,813	3,506	52
2000	Sydney	199	180/132 (73 %)	6,582	4,069	62

Sources: Coakley, 2001; IOC Report of the Sydney Olympic Games 2001

pressure from the Fédération Sportive Féminine Internationale which, in the 1920s, organised an alternative Women's Olympics in 1922 and a series of international competitions throughout the 1920s. The IOC has always been vulnerable to any threat to its self-perception as the organiser of the world's leading multi-sport festival. Consequently, the evidence of the growing popularity of the Women's World Games and the continuing shift in social attitudes resulted in the gradual acceptance by the IOC of women's participation in a steadily broadening range of sports events.

In addition to charting the interplay between changing cultural values and lobbying, Hargreaves also highlights a further recurring issue in the politics of women's sport, namely the choice between separate organisational development or assimilation into the existing male-dominated international federations. As the standard and popularity of women's sport increased, there was an understandable aspiration among many female athletes involved in Olympic sports to gain access to the Games. However, entry to the Games programme would mean losing their organisational independence and coming under the control of the existing male international sports federations. As Hargreaves comments, whereas 'women could more easily insulate themselves from opposition in the separate sphere of their own association; in a mixed association they were rendered weak and vulnerable' (1994: 214). The attitude of sportswomen in the 1920s and 1930s, when these debates were taking place, was split on the question of participation in the Olympics owing to differing

Table 2.5 *Percentage of women coaches in a selection of the ten most popular women's intercollegiate sports*

Sport	1977	1987	1997	2000	% point change 1977–2000
Basketball	79.4	59.9	65.2	63.3	−16.1
Volleyball	86.6	70.2	67.8	59.6	−27.0
Tennis	72.9	54.9	40.9	36.7	−36.2
Track	52.3	20.8	16.4	20.1	−32.2
Field hockey	99.1	96.8	97.6	99.4	+0.3
Soccer	29.4	24.1	33.1	34.0	+4.6

Source: Acosta and Carpenter, 2000, quoted in Coakley, 2001

attitudes towards the culture of male-dominated elite sport, the impact of commercialism on sport, and class attitudes towards many track and field events which were perceived to be low status. The relationship between women's sports organisations and the IOC and international federations on the one hand and the internal divisions between different groups of women on the other, demonstrates the importance of appreciating the internal politics of sport: 'power and control were fought over, not just between men and women, but between different groups of women' (Hargreaves, 1994: 215).

The question of assimilation or segregation remains a major current issue for women athletes, where it often appears to be the case that the price paid for increased opportunities for participation at the highest levels is a gradual loss of control over coaching and decision making within governing bodies (Houlihan and White, 2002; Coakley, 2001). While women's participation in the Olympic Games has steadily moved closer to that of men's, their involvement in the decision making of the Committee has increased far less rapidly and is still woefully inadequate. Of the 123 members of the IOC, only 11 are women, while of the 15 members of the powerful Executive Board of the IOC, only one is a woman. One of the few longitudinal studies of women's involvement in coaching, that by Acosta and Carpenter and reported in Coakley (2001), does not offer significant grounds for optimism. The passage into law of Title IX in 1972, which required that US colleges provide women with equal access to sports resources, resulted in many college athletics departments not only increasing the number of coaches to take account of the increased demand for coaching from female students, but also developing integrated coaching programmes. Both developments had the effect of reducing the proportion of female athletes receiving coaching from a female coach. It is also interesting to note that the two sports, soccer and field hockey, where the proportion of female coaches has remained steady are both sports where male participation is comparatively low.

The slow pace of change is also a reflection of the long-established informal power networks of male sports administrators, which create an informal 'male world' for sport which women find difficult to enter. The informal power network is reinforced by the formal power of sports federations which allocate resources – access to elite coaches, specialist training facilities and sports science expertise, television coverage, funding for travel and training, and competition opportunities – within their sport. The reluctance of boxing authorities to permit women's bouts, the frequent treatment of synchronised swimming and also long-distance swimming as being of secondary importance to diving and pool swimming, and the equivocal attitude of some football federations towards women's football all attest to the depth and abuse of male organisational power.

Although state power played only a limited role in shaping the early years of the modern Olympics, from about the mid-1960s onwards state sports agencies and governments became much more significant actors on the issue of gender equity and sport. In many developed countries in Europe and North America, legislation was used in an attempt to achieve greater gender equity with not always unequivocally positive results, as the example of the impact of Title IX in the United States demonstrated. However, in a significant number of mainly Islamic countries, state power has had an equally profound effect on women's participation in sport. As recently as 1996, over 30 Islamic countries sent male-only teams to the Atlanta Olympic Games. However, there are clear signs of change, albeit extremely gradual, as a number of Islamic countries, even some of the most traditional, are considering how to provide sports opportunities for their female population. For example, in 1993 Iran hosted the first Islamic Women's Games albeit with only an all-female audience permitted. More recently in 1998 the conservative country of Qatar hosted an IAAF Grand Prix II meeting at which male and female athletes were permitted to take part. These tentative signs of change are of particular interest to political scientists who, in seeking to explain the changed attitude towards women's participation in competitive international sport, might point variously to:

- the attraction of prestigious international sports events to rich though small states as a way of raising their international profile;
- the impact of lobbying groups such as those associated with the Brighton Declaration and Atlanta Plus, which have the aim of raising the issue of the exclusion of women from international sport; and
- the globalisation of ideas about universal human rights and their acceptance as an implicit condition of entry to the international political community represented by bodies such as the United Nations and the Olympic Movement.

This very brief review of one issue in the politics of women's sport shows the opportunities for the application of political science analysis, even vis-à-vis an issue in which state involvement is more recent and generally far less central and in which many of the key policy actors are independent organisations. Despite the less significant role for the state, the concept of power is central to much of the history of women's sport. At one level there is the power arising from the deeply embedded and male-dominated culture, which resisted change on the grounds of a stereotyped view of women as physiologically unsuited to vigorous exercise, of women's sport as vulgar, and more recently of women's sport as dull. Even the Olympic slogan of 'Citius, Altius, Fortius' (faster, higher, stronger) reflects a male conceptualisation of sport and one that embodies the militaristic and nationalistic context within which the modern Olympic movement emerged in the late nineteenth century. This concept is constantly reinforced by the modern media with their concern with drama, violence and excitement. How different would elite Olympic sport be if the slogan suggested by

Table 2.6 *Macro-level perspectives on sports politics and policy*

Key features	Neo-Marxism	Neo-pluralism	Liberal feminist	Radical feminist
Unit of analysis	Economic classes; social movements (ecological, feminist, anti-globalisation etc.)	Groups, though an acknowledgement that business is a particularly powerful group	Gender	Gender
Social dynamic	Class conflict in the workplace but also conflicts in other areas crucial to capitalist domination such as the media and culture, and also in conflicts over social issues such as the environment, racism and sexism	Competition for influence over policy between groups	Gender relations and the advocacy and pressure group activity of social interests including those of women's organisations	Patriarchy and the resistance to patriarchal oppression by feminist activism
Role of the state	Dominated by the capitalist class but itself a site of class conflict. However, any victory for anti-capitalist interests will only be short term as in the last instance the state will defend capitalist interests	Both an arena for group competition and also an important independent policy actor	An arena for gender equity activism and a target of gender equity lobbying	Both a reflection of the patriarchal nature of society and an important source of the maintenance of patriarchy
Perception of sport	An element of contested cultural terrain may be exemplified by conflicts between fans and corporate interests for control over football clubs	A policy area around which cluster a number of interest groups which compete for the attention and resources of the state	An important arena in which to pursue gender equity	A highly visible reflection of patriarchal hegemony. When women's sport is permitted, it is done on terms dictated by male-dominated governing bodies and in ways that confirm male perceptions of appropriate sport for women

(Continued)

Table 2.6 *Continued*

Key features	Neo-Marxism	Neo-pluralism	Liberal feminist	Radical feminist
Case studies: illustrative concerns				
The national stadium	Emphasis on the impact of commercial banking interests in shaping the project and furthering the commodification of sport, but also on the motives of the government in incorporating sport into its management of national identity	Focus on the interplay of competing interests, including those whose main concern is with profit, regeneration benefits, bidding for international sports events and the promotion of national identity	Further evidence of the skewing of resources for sport towards facilities primarily used by sportsmen	The stadium is a monument to male conceptualisations of sport and an important symbolic element in the reproduction of patriarchal hegemony
Women's participation in the Olympic Games	Concerned with the significance of feminist activism as a non-class social movement. Also concerned with the role of the Games in reproducing patriarchal relations that are necessary to the continuing success of capitalism	Focus on the interplay between women's rights campaign groups and the major sports institutions	Assessing progress towards equality of access to all levels of sports competition and to all other functions within sport such as coaching and management	Concerned with the compromises required from women as a condition of participation in the patriarchal hegemony that is contemporary sport

Won, Young Shin (2001) of 'More vividly, more harmoniously, more beautifully' were adopted?

Many of the concepts employed to analyse the two cases are drawn from middle-range theories of decision making and policy analysis which tend to emphasise institutional processes, pressure group activity, bargaining and the political behaviour of policy actors. While this level of analysis can be insightful, macro-level theorising not only provides a challenge to middle-level analysis but also raises analytical issues concerning the fundamental structuring of the social formation, as Table 2.6 indicates. As such, political science offers the student of sport a variety of levels of analysis and also a range of macro-level perspectives, which illuminate different facets of an issue and provide alternative formulations of the issue and alternative avenues of enquiry and scholarship.

CONCLUSION

The two examples of sport politics discussed above illustrate the value and centrality of key political science concepts such as power and the state in developing a comprehensive understanding of the social significance of sport in contemporary society. They also illustrate the range of application of political science analysis, encompassing not just politics *of* sport but also politics *in* sport. The study of the politics *of* sport draws attention to the identification and analysis of the motives for government and broader state involvement in sport and the process by which sports policy is formulated. In democracies attention would focus on the interplay between the institutions of the state (including parliaments, the civil service, the courts and schools) and non-state sports organisations (including governing bodies, media companies and sponsors) in shaping sports policy. By contrast, a concern with politics *in* sport accepts that the capacity to affect the distribution of sports opportunities is not just possessed by the state but is also evident in sports clubs, governing bodies and media businesses. According to this view, the power to 'act politically' is derived from control over a wide variety of resources such as expertise, money, organisational capacity and moral authority. By acknowledging the insights that may be derived from the study of politics of sport and politics in sport, political science offers an important complement to the analyses provided by the other major social sciences.

Chapter summary

- Political science offers a number of subfields through which to approach the analysis of sport.
- Power is a central concept in political science whether the focus is on the actions of governments and public agencies or private sports organisations.
- The two contrasting examples of the national stadium and women's participation in the Olympic Games illustrate the range of interests involved in sports decision making and the scope for the application of perspectives in the analysis of the use of power.
- While much political science analysis of sports policy involves the application of middle-range theories and concepts the use of macro-level theories such as neo-Marxism, neo-pluralism and feminism offer valuable additional insights into the source, utilisation and consequences of power.

Further reading

Goodin and Klingemann (1996) provide a clear introduction to the scope and potential of political science, while Hogwood and Gunn (1984) and John (1999) provide a similarly valuable introduction to policy analysis. Coakley applies, both directly and indirectly, concepts and theories of political science to a range of issues in sport. The volume edited by Sugden and Tomlinson (2002) investigates the concept of power in sport from a number of different perspectives. Hargreaves (1994) uses many concepts from political science in her analysis of women in sport. Houlihan (1994) and Riordan and Krüger (1999) provide political analyses of international sport. Houlihan (1997) provides a comparative analysis of sports policy and Houlihan and White (2002) provide an analysis of sports development policy in the UK.

REFERENCES

Acosta, R.V. and Carpenter, J. (2000) *Women in Intercollegiate Sport: A Longitudinal Study – Twenty-three Year Update, 1977–2000*, mimeo. Brooklyn, NY.

Banks, T. (1997) *House of Commons* debates, 3 March, col. 500W.

Coakley, J.J. (2001) *Sport in Society: Issues and Controversies*. 7th edn. Boston, MA: Irwin, McGraw-Hill.

Dahl, R. (1957) 'The concept of power', *Behavioral Science*, 2: 201–15.

Department of Sport (1987) *Recreation and Tourism*, Annual report 1986–87, p. 49.

Foucault, M. (1978) *The History of Sexuality, Vol. 1*. New York: Pantheon.

Goodin, R.E. and Klingemann, H.-D. (1996) 'Political science: the discipline', in *A New Handbook of Political Science*. Oxford: Oxford University Press.

Hargreaves, J. (1994) *Sporting Females: Critical Issues in the History and Sociology of Women's Sports*. London: Routledge.

Heclo, H. (1972) 'Policy analysis', *British Journal of Political Science*, 2: 83–108.

Hindess, B. (1996) *Discourses of Power: from Hobbes to Foucault*. Oxford: Blackwell.

Hogwood, B. and Gunn, L. (1984) *Policy Analysis for the Real World*. London: Oxford University Press.

Houlihan, B. (1994) *Sport and International Politics*. Hemel Hempstead: Harvester-Wheatsheaf.

Houlihan, B. (1997) *Sport, Policy and Politics: a Comparative Analysis*. London: Routledge.

Houlihan, B. and White, A. (2002) *The Politics of Sports Development: Development of Sport or Development through Sport?* London: Routledge.

House of Commons (2000) The Culture, Media and Sport Select Committee, 4th Report, *Wembley National Stadium*, Session 1999–2000, Cm. 4686. London: HMSO.

John, P. (1999) *Analysing Public Policy*. London: Pinter.

Laclau, E. and Mouffe, C. (1985) *Hegemony and Socialist Strategy: Towards a Radical Democratic Politics*. London: Verso.

Lukes, S. (1974) *Power: a Radical View*. London: Macmillan.

Moodie, G.C. (1984) 'Politics is about government', in A. Leftwich (ed.), *What is Politics? The Activity and its Study*. Oxford: Basil Blackwell.

Ponton, G. and Gill, P. (1993) *Introduction to Politics*. Oxford: Basil Blackwell.

Riordan, J. and Krüger, A. (1999) *The International Politics of Sport in the Twentieth Century*. London: E & F.N. Spon.

Sugden, J. and Tomlinson, A. (eds) (2002) *Power Games ... a Critical Sociology of Sport*. London: Routledge.

Won, Young Shin (2001) 'Reconsidering the Olympic motto relating to socio-cultural changes and the variations of the events in the 21st century! More vividly, more harmoniously, more beautifully'. *Proceedings of the First World Congress of Sociology of Sport*. Yonsei University, Seoul, Korea.

3

History and Sport

MARTIN POLLEY

When J.K. Rowling created Hogwarts Academy as a supernatural version of a private school for her Harry Potter novels, she gave it a distinctive sport. Quidditch is a ball game played by teams on broomsticks. It is used in Hogwarts to teach loyalty and teamwork. In recognition of the parallels with real school sports, Rowling created a history for Quidditch, which her characters were meant to know about:

[Hermione] had … lent him [Harry] *Quidditch through the Ages*, which turned out to be a very interesting read. Harry learnt that there were seven hundred ways of committing a Quidditch foul and that all of them had happened during a World Cup match in 1473. (Rowling, 1997: 133)

Under a pseudonym, Rowling subsequently wrote *Quidditch through the Ages* as a charity spin-off from her novels (2001). Successful satire always tells us much about the subject being satirised. What Rowling did through Quidditch was to draw attention to an important feature of all sports' cultures: that each sport's distinctive past matters to the people who play and follow it in the present.

Some of the ways in which this can be seen are worth considering before we analyse the ways in which history can contribute to sports studies. The related cults of record keeping and record breaking demonstrate a symbiotic relationship between past and present: Matthew Webb's Channel swim in 1875, Roger Bannister's 1954 sub-four minute mile, and Geoff Hurst's World Cup final hat-trick of 1966, are just a few examples of superlative performances which become learnt by generations of each sport's followers. Rules and styles of play are not reinvented on a daily basis: they are inherited from the past, and adapted when new situations arise. The sporting calendar is heavily based on historical circumstances: the use of Saturday afternoons for team games is linked to the working patterns established in nineteenth-century cities, for example, while longer-term traditions around Christmas and Easter are still evident in the timing of some sports (Brailsford, 1991). The names of many events can be linked to particular moments: the 12th Earl of Derby's patronage of a horse race at Epsom in 1780, and the diffusion of a version of football out of Rugby School during the nineteenth century, are two examples of the roots of sporting names still in use. The ways in which sports are scored are linked to the past: for example, real tennis's traditional usage of a clockface has given us the point sequence in lawn tennis. The use of terminology from certain languages links sports to their roots: the widespread use of French in fencing, or of Japanese in judo, are explicable only historically.

Clubs in many sports also care about the past; and another way of seeing how the past matters in contemporary sport is to look at certain features of their cultures. The practice of naming grounds, or parts of grounds, after famous players is one way in which we can see this, evident, for example, in the Sir Tom Finney Stand at Preston North End FC's Deepdale, or in NEC Harlequins RFC's Stoop Memorial Ground. The erection of statues to significant individuals from a club's or a city's past is another form of this, as evidenced by that of Billy Bremner in Leeds and of Reg Harris at the National Cycling Centre in Manchester. The proliferation of sports museums, and the promotion of sports sites as tourist attractions also bear witness to this trend. Wimbledon and Lord's include historical elements in their guided tours, for example; while specific sports are catered for by such museums as the River and Rowing Museum at Henley-on-Thames and

the National Horseracing Museum at Newmarket (Vamplew, 1998). A sense of the past clearly matters to many sports' and clubs' followers whenever change is debated, whether it be the movement of a club to new premises, or a change in format or timetable. The former can be exemplified by the words of a Reading FC supporter recalling Robert Maxwell's 1983 attempt to merge this club with Oxford United: 'When will these petty despots realise that messing about with a football club is a dangerous business? The locals, wherever they are, will not go quietly' (Kirkpatrick, 2001). Indeed, this attitude can be seen in many Rugby League enthusiasts' resistance to the restructuring of the sport for the 1995–96 season (Kelner, 1996: 146–72). A large part of the sports publishing sector is devoted to non-academic historical materials such as amateur club histories, statistical records and personal histories after *Fever Pitch* (Hornby, 1992).

Any present-centred analysis of sport needs to remember that the past figures strongly. Moreover, any study of past societies can show that sport has mattered. Sport has taken people's attention, time and money in many historical settings, and any history that ignores them is missing something. With these strands in mind, it is clear that the historical study of sport is an academic exercise that can contribute to the interdisciplinary field of sports studies. By going to the past, we can learn both what sport was in different times, and how contemporary sports developed as they did. This chapter aims to explore and analyse some of the ways in which historians can make that contribution.

HISTORIANS AND SPORT

To understand how history can contribute to the study of sport, we need first to consider some general points about what historians do. No sports historian comes to sport without some form of wider historical training. Thus, no sports historian treats sport in isolation, or comes to it without a wider sense of how history can be studied.

Historians' approaches to the past vary enormously, but some common disciplinary features unite them: 'history takes an interest in the past in its own right rather than using it as a source to explain the present' (Holt and Mason, 2000: ix). However, there are limitations on what historians can study, which gives us the second common disciplinary feature: they can study only parts of the past that left evidence behind, and for which evidence has survived. The dominant type of evidence has been documentary: government archives, private papers, newspapers and published materials have long been the most consulted forms of sources. The range has recently broadened, and many historians are now happy to use artefacts, buildings, visual evidence, oral testimony, and many other non-written sources (Brivati et al., 1996: parts III–VII). Without such evidence, historians cannot function. So all studies of history are driven by the discovery of evidence from the period being studied, and its analysis and interpretation. Historians aim to be able to describe what happened, explain how and why it happened, and link past events to wider contexts and to the passage of time.

This requirement for evidence from the period being studied has helped to create something of an anti-theoretical strand in some historical writing. Generations of historians have been trained to find evidence, interpret it, and then come to a conclusion. In this setting, many practitioners have avoided overtly theoretical approaches in favour of empiricism. In the second half of the twentieth century, uncontested empiricism became less prevalent, particularly under the influence of Marxism, feminism, psychoanalysis and structuralism. Moreover, Collingwood's *The Idea of History* (1946) and Carr's *What Is History?* (1961) encouraged historians to think critically about the nature of their evidence, the decisions involved in choosing subject matter and sources, and how the historian's autobiography influences the way in which s/he approaches the past (Collingwood, 1994; Carr, 1990). These influences, allied to the scepticism towards great narratives raised by postmodernism, have made many historians critical of the things that their predecessors took for granted. In this setting, 'the removal of "objective truth" as a meaningful goal is counterbalanced by a perceived need for many different accounts of the past – none claiming any special privilege, but each providing some illumination from its own perspective' (Southgate, 1996: 8). A consideration of these issues can help us to understand how historians approach their subject matter.

A final characteristic that we need to note is that historians' approaches to the past change over time. All historians live and work in their own present, and however much a historian may immerse him or herself in the period under investigation, that present will be evident in what gets written. The topics chosen for study vary with time and are influenced by contemporary concerns and personal ideology: for example, very few historians investigated women's history before the growth of feminism (Holloway, 1998). The sources historians use do not remain static, as new materials may be discovered or made available. This is most obvious in the annual release of government archives under the 30 year rule in the British system (Cox, 1996). The methodologies used vary with time and technology, seen most obviously in the recent growth of computer-based projects.

Historians are linked to their own time and place through the media in which their work is disseminated: mass-produced books, academic journals, websites and television documentaries are four media in which historians currently work, none of which has been available for all historians who have ever lived. Finally, the historian's vocabulary will link the historian to the time and place of research and publication, a point illustrated in this chapter by the use of subjective pronouns that are not gender specific.

These examples illustrate the observation that the historian's agenda is set by a combination of past and present: the events and issues that mattered at the time being studied meet the attitudes, ideologies, techniques, language and hindsight of the historian's own day. Historians can work around these constraints by avoiding anachronistic treatment of their periods. Holt and Mason's model is one to aspire to here. Writing in the late 1990s about British sport in the immediate post-Second World War period, they justified the themes covered in their book in historical rather than contemporary terms:

We have tried to piece together what mattered *then* rather than what matters now. Women, ethnic minorities and the disabled are more important in the 1990s than they were in the 1950s and we try to explain this. But the 1950s cannot be understood simply in terms of the absence of disadvantaged groups. Post-war sport had its own agenda which has to be understood in its own terms. (Holt and Mason, 2000: ix. Emphasis in original)

However, despite historians using these criteria as part of their basic approach, the links between the past and the historian's present are ultimately unavoidable. We can see this very clearly in Collins's *Rugby's Great*

Split, his 1998 monograph on the development of Rugby League. He starts by asking 'Why are there two forms of rugby?': 'given the profound changes which both rugby league and rugby union are currently undergoing, the question now has an importance which transcends mere historical curiosity' (1998: xi). For our purposes, the keywords here are 'currently' and 'now'. Only a historian writing in the late 1990s, who had witnessed the development of professionalism in Rugby Union and the league code's restructuring, could have approached the subject in this way. We must keep this relationship between the time of writing and the historiography in mind if we are to understand the ways in which historians have approached sport.

Once we accept this relationship, then we can put sports history into a disciplinary context. Historians have not always been interested in sport as an area of analysis. Up until the late 1960s, sport was largely ignored, despite the fact that history by that time encompassed many political, social, economic and cultural subjects. In 1963, James highlighted the anomalies involved in historians' ignorance of sport when he argued in favour of cricket's inclusion in social history books:

A famous Liberal historian [Trevelyan] can write the social history of England in the nineteenth century, and two famous Socialists [Postgate and Cole] can write what they declared to be the history of the common people of England, and between them never once mention the man who was the best-known Englishman of his time. I can no longer accept the system of values which could not find in these books a place for W.G. Grace. (James, 1963: 157)

By the end of the 1960s, as Baker (1983) has shown, only a few books had attempted to bring sport into academic history, most notably Brailsford's *Sport and Society* (1969). This pioneering work, driven by the assumption that sport was related to the society in which it took place, was expanded in the 1970s and 1980s by a new generation of sports historians, including Holt, Mangan, Mason and Vamplew. By the late 1980s, the subject was being taught at universities, while new research was being fostered by journals (such as *The International Journal of the History of Sport*), monograph series (such as that by Manchester University Press) and by the British Society of Sports History (BSSH) (Cox, 2000; Holt, 1996; Polley, 1998: 166–71; Vamplew, 2000). The expansion of the subject matter was acknowledged by Holt in 1989 in the introduction to *Sport and the British*. His attempt to 'explain the nature of sport in modern Britain in terms of change in society, politics, and culture' had been made possible by the changing academic climate: 'It is only as a result of the appearance of a substantial body of new research in the history of sport itself and in the wider realm of social history that such a survey can be attempted at all' (1989: vii). Holt's declaration was a clear sign that an academic historiography of sport had emerged.

In the 1990s, these trends continued, but with some notable developments helping to establish sports history as a branch of historical study. Higher education institutions' willingness to support postgraduate studies in the field created a training structure for sports historians. Undergraduate courses also proliferated. These developments helped to create markets for more books, for which academic publishers such as Frank Cass and Routledge have catered. Cass's series 'Sport in the Global Society' showed history's place in the mainstream of the socio-cultural study of sport. Alongside works rooted in sociology (such as Finn and Giulianotti, 2000), the law (such as Greenfield and Osborn, 2000), and politics (for example, Booth, 1998) were books based firmly in history, notably Beck's *Scoring for Britain* (1999) and Williams's *Cricket and England* (1999). The BSSH continued to grow, broadening its constituency in the late 1990s by promoting both non-British and postgraduate research (BSSH, 2001). British sports historiography's coming of age was neatly summarised by Beck. When comparing an unpublished early 1980s version of his research on football with his 1999 monograph, he noted that 'whereas previously I included a whole chapter justifying the historical study of sport, today such a rationale seems superfluous' (1999: vii). So, despite the 'suspicions of those who drift slowly along what is left of the old historical mainstream' (Lowerson, 1998: 201), British sports history by the start of the twenty-first century has become a vital and dynamic area of historiography. It has an increasingly diverse gaze, taking in the global and the local, the general and the specific, and the paradigms of class, gender, ethnicity and physical ability. Moreover, British sports historians have established good links with colleagues in many other disciplines, and with sports historians working in other parts of the world, particularly through such organisations as the North American Society for Sport History (NASSH). These characteristics enable it to make a distinctive contribution to the wider study of sport in society, one that complements and supplements the approaches of the present-centred disciplines.

WHAT HISTORY CAN CONTRIBUTE

What, then, has sports history told us about sport? What can sports studies gain from a consideration of historiography? Any attempt to synthesise the historiography is bound to be selective, so we shall concentrate on a number of areas in which historians' insights benefit any other social science or humanities-based enquiry into sport.

The first theme that has emerged is an obvious one: that sport has been played differently in different settings across time. From this starting point a great deal of analysis of the nature of sport, and of the nature of its relationship with its contexts, has flowed. It is easy to assume that the models on which our sports are based embody eternal values. As Guttmann noted after introducing classical sport to his sociology students, the fact that 'the sports festivals of the ancient Greeks took place without significant quantification and without the modern obsession with the sport record is ... a great surprise' (1990: 239). Sports history can help us to refine our vocabulary and our assumptions. To begin with, the term 'sport' itself is shown up as historically variable and relative. Up until the mid-nineteenth century, 'sport' was usually taken to entail hunting, shooting and fishing. The term was appropriated for team games and individual physical activities after that; and it is now fluid, as activities as wide-ranging as Building, Antennae, Span, Earth (BASE) jumping, freestyle, and ballroom dancing bid for categorisation as sports. Historical study can allow us to get above emotive and absolute positions in such debates, and recognise that meanings change in relation to contextual change.

Beyond semantics, historical study shows us that the use of current sports names can be misleading if they are applied uncritically to past physical activities. Records of activities called 'football' exist from at least the fourteenth century (Russell, 1997: 5),

but none of the games played under that name in the early twenty-first century can claim a simple linear relationship over seven hundred years. Association, Australian rules, gridiron, Rugby League, Rugby Union, for example, all have structural features in common with the many local and regional versions of the pre-industrial period. They are all invasion games involving varying amounts of handling, kicking and running.

To trace lineage is far harder than noting basic similarities, however, as the diffusion routes are extremely complicated. This can be illustrated through the example of Rugby Union in Wales. The Rugby School version of football was introduced to Wales by old Rugbeans through Llandovery College and St David's College, Lampeter. The Rugby version itself drew on various local traditions, while the areas in West and South Wales exposed to the Rugby/Lampeter/Llandovery version had their own traditions. By the 1870s, the modern form had emerged under the name of rugby football, which went on to become the major male team sport of the area (Smith and Williams, 1980). Counter this complicated route, which has come to light through historical research, against a simplistic account of how 'football' in Welsh villages in the sixteenth and seventeenth centuries was a direct forerunner of modern Rugby Union. So, instead of approaching the development of sport from the present, and looking for patterns in the obvious folk games appearing in all sports' genealogies, sports history encourages us to judge the past by its own standards. It may be convenient to claim that 'ancient Central and South American civilizations played a form of basketball, which they called pok-tapok', but it cannot be accurate: the people playing pok-tapok could not have conceptualised their activity as 'a form of basketball'

(Cox and Physick, 2000: 31). So the first point to emerge from sports historiography – that sports have been played in different ways at different times – can teach us to avoid anachronism.

The second theme that we can isolate is linked to a basic concept in the present-centred study of sport: that all sports are linked to the contexts in which they are played. If we are to understand how sports have developed, and how sport in the present inherits features from the past, then we need to think about the wider contexts in which sports are played. Historians of the British Isles have tended to divide that area's history into three broad periods: pre-industrial, industrial and post-industrial, with the first running up to the mid-eighteenth century, the second running into the twentieth century and the latter emerging from approximately the 1930s. These models are problematic. In particular, applying the points about anachronism made above should stop us from using the phrase 'pre-industrial', since the people living then could not have known what was coming next. However, the periodisation does work as a useful model for examinations of social, economic and cultural activity. This three-part model has been attractive to many historians who have wanted to contextualise sport.

The assumption at work here is that the predominant characteristics and 'core features' (Horne et al., 1999: 2) of the given society will be evident in the sports that it played. There are two linked elements to this. First, that the contexts within which sport is played provide historically relative opportunities and constraints for those involved; and second, that the form the play itself takes – its level of physicality, its degree of regulation, its timespan and so on – is linked to shared characteristics of the people playing at that moment in time.

The opportunities and constraints model has proved very useful for historians wanting to understand the relationship of any sport with its society. Much of the analysis in this area has been centred on social class, a detail which we can link to the early academic sports historians' research agendas, influenced as they were by 'history from below' (Lowerson, 1998: 201). Malcolmson's *Popular Recreations in English Society 1700–1850*, Mason's *Association Football and English Society, 1863–1915*, and Bailey's *Leisure and Class in Victorian England* set an agenda which has remained relevant in sports history (Malcolmson, 1973; Mason, 1980; Bailey, 1978; Jones, 1986; Collins, 1998; Holt, 1989; Holt and Mason, 2000; Polley, 1998). While the bulk of this work has been on working-class sport, Lowerson (1993), Holt (1989, 1996), and others have shifted attention to the middle classes. Subsequent work has kept class in focus, but has also taken other contexts into account: gender, ethnicity, politics and group identities have all been brought in as important contextual issues.

A few examples will suffice here. Brailsford's work (1969) on leisure in the early modern period showed how educational precepts and religious beliefs set limitations on the amount of sport that could be played, and on its timing. The puritans' objections to recreational sabbath-breaking, for example, and their suppression of sports and games that were redolent of Catholicism, placed constraints on what could be played. For the nineteenth century, Bailey (1978) and others have shown how the provision of sport in various areas was linked to wider socio-economic settings, and to the political and social concerns of the providers. Hargreaves's *Sporting Females* (1994) brought together much of the pioneering work on women's sport, and showed how contexts based in gender relations influenced which sports could be played by women. The influence of political contexts on sporting opportunities and constraints can be seen in Beck's work (1999) on the relationships between sport and British diplomacy. Domestic political contexts were explored in Jones's work (1988) on the role of trade unions and the Labour Party in lobbying for more time and sports facilities during the interwar period, and the role of communist and socialist organisations in promoting alternative sporting events. The influence of wider senses of identity on sport can be seen in Cronin's work on Ireland (1999), where widespread discourses of nationalism, republicanism and unionism have all influenced people's access to sport. It has also been explored through many regional and local studies of sport, of which Hill and Williams's collection of essays on *Sport and Identity in the North of England* (1996) stands as an excellent example. These are illustrations of the wealth of work that has been done in this area. The contexts outlined here show that we need to look beyond the basic model of a sport's socio-economic setting. It is only through a holistic approach to contexts that we can get a clear picture of why certain sports flourished in certain settings.

When we come to the relationship between the historical context and the form that sports have taken, historians have been particularly influenced by two models, developed by Guttmann (1978) and by Dunning and Sheard (1979). Guttmann developed his model by defining 'seven characteristics of modern sports': secularism; equality; specialisation; rationalisation; bureaucracy; quantification; and records (1978: 54). These were 'likely to be taken for granted and to be thought of as self-evidently "natural"' (1978: 15). His model became historical in its exploration of the sports of different periods, from primitive to modern. He checked his seven characteristics off against the sports of these settings. For example, he found that classical Roman sport had much in common with modern sport, with only the importance of religion, limited equality of access and limited quantification marking it as different. His analysis of how sports were performed in different settings established a useful model. However, it can be problematic because of its apparently present-centred approach: it appears to account for change over time by showing what sport was moving towards (that is, the modern model), rather than what players in the past were 'moving away from' (Struna, 2001). Nevertheless, his sociological and anthropological insights did much to focus historians' attention on how the forms of sport embody wider values, best illustrated in his overarching model of how the rise in the quantification of sports performance ('record') has been related over time to the decline of sport's religious significance ('ritual'):

When we can no longer distinguish the sacred from the profane or even the good from the bad, we content ourselves with minute discriminations between the batting average of the .308 hitter and the .307 hitter. Once the gods have vanished from Mount Olympus or Dante's paradise, we can no longer run to appease them or to save our souls, but we can set a new record. It is a uniquely modern form of immortality. (Guttmann, 1978: 55)

Because of Guttmann's wide-ranging periodisation, and the fact that British sport was not central to his work, his model for explaining the forms of sports in historical context has been less influential in British sports historiography than Dunning and Sheard's more specific model. Working within figurational sociology, they developed a schema for understanding sport in historical context for their study of rugby football, *Barbarians, Gentlemen and Players* (1979). They took the basic periodisation of 'pre-modern' and 'modern', which they linked to socio-economic and cultural characteristics, and identified certain features that were present in the team games of each period. Their table, 'The structural properties of folk games and modern sports', listed 15 characteristics common to each type of game, paired in oppositional terms to allow comparison over time. For example, the lack of 'fixed limits on territory, duration, or numbers of participants' of folk games were placed alongside the 'spatially limited pitch with clearly defined boundaries, within fixed time limits and with a fixed number of participants' of modern sports. This scheme synthesised historians' findings on how pre-industrial and industrial Britain had played, and fitted into figurational sociology's wider interest in uncovering cultural aspects of the 'civilising process'.

This approach has been very influential in all British sports historiography. For a decade, it was the orthodox description of the dramatic changes that occurred in sport during the nineteenth century. Its influence is still evident, as seen in Horne et al.'s reproduction of the table in their *Understanding Sport* (1999: 9). However, further historical research has shown up some of its limitations as an attempt to explain development. The key challenge, summarised by Holt, lies in the fact that many 'traditional' or 'folk' sports survived industrialisation and modernisation: the emphasis on change disguises the continuities of historical experience. Holt gives the cameo of Jerry Dawson to illustrate this. In the early twentieth century, Dawson played one of the modernised versions of football – Association Football – to a high standard, playing in goal for Burnley and England. Alongside this, he was 'a champion at

knur-and-spell', a traditional sport played on moorland in Lancashire and Yorkshire. As Holt notes, the continuities and co-existence of 'new and old sports' can be missed if we 'set up a rigid and precise distinction between traditional and modern forms' (1989: 68).

This trend has also been shown in Murfin's coverage of football in Workington. A traditional form of football, matching all of Dunning and Sheard's characteristics as a folk game, was played from at least 1775. It involved teams of unequal sizes playing across meadows, streets, the beach and the river, with the 'goals' a mile apart. This game increased in frequency to three times a year in the late nineteenth century, at a time when such sports were supposed to be dying out. Alongside this, Workington also developed a number of organised Association Football teams. The most successful one, Workington Town FC, was formed in 1884, two years after the third Easter match was probably instituted. The club and the folk game co-existed, suggesting that both versions were meaningful to their players and followers regardless of the changing context (Murfin, 1990: 110–15).

The 'rigid and precise distinction' also misses the fact that a number of sports became highly organised before industrialisation. Horse-racing, cricket and golf had widely accepted rules, decision-making bodies and high levels of national organisation by the mid-eighteenth century. Indeed some of the clubs involved – the Jockey Club, Marylebone Cricket Club and the Royal and Ancient Golf Club at St Andrews – remain influential. Evidence also exists of multi-sport events, requiring high levels of organisation, which took place in various parts of the British Isles in the seventeenth and eighteenth centuries. Furthermore, the modernisation model clearly cannot be applied to all parts of the

British Isles at the same time. It may work for the ports, textile and mining towns of the industrial period, which became the heartlands of male team sports of football and Rugby League; however, it had far later relevance for such areas as mid-Wales, rural Scotland, the bulk of Ireland and south-western England. Beyond these historical examples, the survival of such a blatantly pre-modern sport as fox hunting into the twenty-first century also shows up the model's limitations beyond team sports. The model of pre-modern and modern sports has thus been an influential one in focusing historians' attention on how, when and why sports change in relation to wider socio-economic change. However, the ways in which many historians have attempted to apply it critically serve as a neat illustration of the theory/empiricism clash evident in much historical work. Despite these debates, the key point remains that work on the history of sport has shown up ways in which sports in the past have been linked to wider contexts, both through the opportunities and constraints that fenced the events, and through the exact forms that sports took. We cannot hope to understand sports in the present unless we explore this aspect of their past.

Our third theme – that of origins – is linked to the wider issue of contexts, but is worth studying on its own. This is because it is an area of the past which, if left to individual sport's apologists, would remain mythologised. It is difficult to ascribe a precise moment of origin to any sport. Organised forms tended to evolve out of various local and regional versions, with diffusion routes and wider contexts of technology, patronage and the media playing their parts in shaping the new versions. However, the quest for origins is one that interests historians in many areas. In researching sport and play, historians have encountered many problems in their attempts to identify the first recognisable form of a particular sport. Young, in his *History of British Football*, noted that 'a historian knows that to speak of any phenomenon as being the first of its kind is either impossible, or impolitic, or both' (1968: 3). The evidence of forms of organised play from all societies for which we have records bears this out. However, many sports establishments have worked hard to promote a straightforward heritage for their sports, a heritage designed to stress both antiquity and legitimacy. MacLennan gives us an extreme example of this in his work on shinty *(Camanachd)*. He quotes from *The Book of the Club of True Highlanders* of 1881, which notes:

[I]t is said, and, no doubt, with great truth, that the game of *Camanachd*, or club playing, was introduced into the Green Isle [Great Britain] by the immediate descendants of Noah. On such authority we may rationally conclude that it was played by Noah himself; and if by Noah, in all probability by Adam and his sons. (Quoted in MacLennan, 1998: 4)

While no one would dispute that ancient peoples played games, the attempt to trace a linear history from biblical to modern times needs to be treated critically.

The quest for origins has not gone exclusively to the ancient world: in many sports specific 'origin myths' have been located in the modern period. Dunning et al. (1993) have drawn attention to two such events that are often cited as specific moments of birth: the 'Doubleday myth' of 1839 in baseball, and the 'Webb Ellis story' from 1823 in Rugby Union. Claiming that belief in these myths is 'a kind of sports equivalent of the belief in the tooth fairy or Father Christmas', the authors draw our attention instead to the political and social reasons why certain groups wanted to promote such specific myths (1993: 1). Going beyond this, historians have confirmed the truth of Young's comments, and accepted that games based on invasion principles, or striking/fielding principles, cannot be simplistically linked to modern sports with those structural similarities. Indeed, the wide variety of modern sports which do share such similarities – such as cricket, baseball, rounders and stoolball, or the many versions of football – warns us against any belief in linearity. The specific 'origin' of any one of them needs to be linked to local and regional issues, and to the power relations of the individual game's promoters, rather than any moment of invention.

It is this type of origin, rather than mythical moments of birth, that has exercised historians, who have been involved in studying how specific sports emerged by name, and under some kind of control, at different points in history. It is the attention to the organised and standardised nature of these events for which primary evidence is available that has been evident in the historiography. Collins (1998) has done this in an exemplary way in his account of the splits within rugby football in the 1880s and 1890s that led to the formation of the northern rugby union, which, in 1922, took on the name of Rugby League. Similarly, Mason (1980) examined the gradual formalisation of rules and practices between different football clubs in the 1850s and 1860s which led to the formation of the Football Association in 1863. So, while the subject of origins has rightly occupied many historians, they have tended to approach it critically and empirically rather than tracing any sport's pedigree back to Genesis. Here we can see the historian's insistence on evidence shaping the way in which s/he approaches the past, and the attendant scepticism towards mythologised views of the past.

These are some of the key themes that have emerged from sports historiography. Taken together, they show up the richness and complexity of sport in the past, while also demonstrating the problems involved in taking too narrow an approach to how sport developed. While sports historians recognise the value of looking at sport in the past as a way of understanding sport in the present, their work shows that sport in the past needs to be understood on its terms.

LINKS WITH OTHER DISCIPLINES

Academic sports historians have not been the only people to explore sport's past. Non-academic historians, who have come to the subject out of enthusiasm and interest, have also worked in this area. These historians, typically devoted to individual clubs or institutions, 'often deal with their topic without reference to the wider issues' (Vamplew, 2000: 179). Holt noted that the historiography they produced was 'little more than the book of Chronicles or the book of Numbers' (1989: 2). However, the particular contribution that this literature makes is becoming recognised by academics: Vamplew, for example, has praised the way in which such work can provide 'empirical evidence needed to test academic hypotheses' (2000: 179).

Another group to have made a contribution to the understanding of sport in the past has been sports sociologists, particularly those working within the tradition of developmental or figurational sociology after Elias. Dunning, Maguire, Jarvie and others have gone to sport's pasts in order to trace the development of forms over time, always linking change and continuity in sport to 'structured processes that occur over time and space. Emphasis is placed on probing how the present has emerged out of the past' (Jarvie and Maguire, 1994: 132). Under this academic flag, useful work has been done which has illuminated how sports have emerged. As we have seen, concepts and models from this approach have influenced the approaches of many historians. Indeed, many of the individuals involved work comfortably in both history and sociology camps, exemplified best by Grant Jarvie. A sociologist by training, Jarvie was the Chairman of the BSSH from 1997 until 2001, while his publications range from a co-authored survey of the main issues in sports sociology through to an analysis of the development of Highland Games (Jarvie and Maguire, 1994; Jarvie, 1991). Hargreaves's work also illustrates this linkage, most obviously in her seminal *Sporting Females* of 1994. However, it is worth noting that there are some genuine differences between the approaches of historians and sociologists, despite the success with which some individuals have balanced the disciplines:

Sociologists frequently complain that historians lack a conceptual framework for their research, whilst historians tend to feel social theorists require them to compress the diversity of the past into artificially rigid categories and dispense with empirical verification of their theories. (Holt, 1989: 357)

The debates that this can lead sports analysis into are neatly summarised and exemplified by Horne et al. (1999: 73–94). Their claim that 'history without adequate conceptualisation or theorisation can be little more than a form of antiquarianism' (1999: 77) is a useful rejoinder to some historians' anti-theoretical stances.

Sociology has also been influential in getting historians to interview people who took part in the events being analysed. The development of oral history in the 1960s borrowed from qualitative sociology the idea that ordinary participants' accounts could contribute to our understanding of an event or phenomenon. It clearly has limitations for any historian: the survival of witnesses, the reliability of their memory

and the role of hindsight all influence the process. However, many historians have been happy to use it as a way of getting factual information about events that may not have been recorded in other sources, and as a way of bringing to life the culture that surrounded these events. These aspects have been obvious in, for example, Duval's work (2001) on women's athletics, in which interviewees talked not just about participation, but also about the social life that surrounded the sport. This approach is now becoming commonplace.

While sociology may be the most obvious discipline to complement sports history, it is not the only one. A few examples must suffice. Whannel's work on sport and the media, particularly *Fields in Vision* (1992), includes coverage of television's historical relationship with sport, as well as models for analysis of media texts that historians can use. In cultural studies, Blake's work on sport, alongside his work on literature and pop music, has analysed sport's cultural place over time, with an emphasis on such aspects as its language, and on the ways in which the sporting body has been displayed (1996). The influence of cultural studies on sports historians is becoming notable as a number of them apply models from linguistic theory to their primary sources. Hill (1998) has been influential here. His reading of the 'legend' of footballer and cricketer Denis Compton is characterised by an emphasis on narratives and mythologies within the texts written about him. Through this approach, we can learn not just what happened, but what sport meant to its players, followers and administrators, and how it fitted into their world views. Geography is another discipline with some links to sports history, best seen in Bale's work on sporting landscapes and townscapes, notably in *Landscapes of Modern Sport* (1994). In all of these areas, and many more, a fascinating cross-fertilisation has gone on between sports historians and sports analysts based in other disciplines.

CONCLUSION

This chapter has outlined some of the approaches taken by sports historians to provide us with a detailed picture of how sports were in the past. Sports historians, and their colleagues in other disciplines, have demonstrated and exemplified the links between sports and their various contexts, and have shown how both continuity and change across time have given us the sports we play in the present. As sports history has developed into a subdiscipline of history, it has attracted more academics, many with new questions to ask of old material, or with wholly new research agendas. This is also demonstrated by the growth of works of synthesis, which is always evidence of the health of a discipline. The fact that mainstream historians writing general texts on periods of British history now routinely include some sporting material is another sign of the discipline's importance, as seen in Marwick's *British Society since 1945* (1996). Moreover, while academic journals catering exclusively for sports history develop and thrive, notably *The International Journal of the History of Sport* and *The Sports Historian*, other journals continue to pick up on the subject: the *Journal of Contemporary History* and *History Today* are among those that have encouraged research on sport.

This suggests that the discipline of history is now taking sports history seriously. Sports studies is also taking sports history seriously. The inclusion of historical chapters in many key texts in the field stresses the fact that sports studies students need to know about the past: Cashmore (2000), Coakley (1998) and Horne et al. (1999) all deploy history as a necessary area for any understanding of the subject. It is within this tradition that this essay has been offered. While it has been acknowledged that a knowledge of sports history is an important part of any study of sport, emphasis has also been placed on how to deal with the material that historians write. Without engaging with the culture within which historians work, and without looking at the common interests and themes running through much of the diverse historiography, it is easy to use historians' writings simply as a storehouse for factual information. While sports historiography must fulfil this purpose, it is about more than this: it is about our interest in roots and origins, and our desire to know what happened and why.

Chapter summary

- Historians aim to describe what happened, explain why it happened, and link past events to wider contexts and to the passage of time.
- Although largely ignored by social historians until the late 1960s, sports history is now a vital and dynamic area of historiography.
- Sports history encourages us to judge the past by its own standards and to understand sport in the context in which it is played. In particular, sports history highlights the effect of political and social context on what sport is played, by whom and in what way.
- There has been a mutually enriching dialogue especially between historians and sociologists, but also with geographers and students of the media.

Further reading

Dennis Brailsford's 1969 text remains a key introduction to the scope, methods and potential of sports history. Alan Guttmann (1978) and Dunning and Sheard (1979) also provide contrasting, but highly stimulating and wide-ranging historical analyses of sport. Jarvie's 1991 study of the Highland Games, Whannel's 1992 study of sport and the media, and Hargreaves's 1994 study of women's sport all demonstrate the insight that can be derived from sports history in the study of particular aspects of sport. Finally, Struna (2001) and Vamplew (2000) discuss some of the methodological issues that sports historians face.

REFERENCES

Bailey, Peter (1978) *Leisure and Class in Victorian England: Rational Recreation and the Contest for Control, 1830–1885*. London: Routledge & Kegan Paul.

Baker, William (1983) 'The state of British sport history', *Journal of Sport History*, 10 (1): 53–66.

Bale, John (1994) *Landscapes of Modern Sport*. Leicester: Leicester University Press.

Beck, Peter (1999) *Scoring for Britain: International Football and International Politics, 1900–1939*. London: Frank Cass.

Blake, Andrew (1996) *The Body Language: the Meaning of Modern Sport*. London: Lawrence & Wishart.

Booth, Douglas (1998) *The Race Game: Sport and Politics in South Africa*. London: Frank Cass.

Brailsford, Dennis (1969) *Sport and Society: Elizabeth to Anne*. London: Routledge & Kegan Paul.

Brailsford, Dennis (1991) *Sport, Time, and Society: the British at Play*. London: Routledge.

British Society of Sports History (BSSH), official website. *http://www.umist.ac.uk/sport/index2.htm*

Brivati, B., Buxton, J. and Seldon, A. (eds) (1996) *The Contemporary History Handbook*. Manchester: Manchester University Press.

Carr, E.H. (1990) *What Is History?* London: Penguin.

Cashmore, Ellis (2000) *Making Sense of Sports*. 3rd edn. London: Routledge.

Coakley, Jay (1998) *Sport in Society: Issues and Controversies*. 6th edn. Boston, MA: Irwin McGraw-Hill.

Collingwood, R.G. (1994) *The Idea of History*. Revised edn. Oxford: Oxford University Press.

Collins, Tony (1998) *Rugby's Great Split: Class, Culture and the Origins of Rugby League Football*. London: Frank Cass.

Cox, Nicholas (1996) 'National British archives: public records', in B. Brivati, J. Buxton and A. Seldon (eds), *The Contemporary History Handbook*. Manchester: Manchester University Press, pp. 253–71.

Cox, Richard (2000) 'British Society of Sports History', in Richard Cox, Grant Jarvie and Wray Vamplew (eds), *Encyclopedia of British Sport*. Oxford: ABC-Clio, pp. 48–9.

Cox, Richard and Physick, Ray (2000) 'Basketball', in Richard Cox, Grant Jarvie and Wray Vamplew (eds), *Encyclopedia of British Sport*. Oxford: ABC-Clio, pp. 31–3.

Cronin, Mike (1999) *Sport and Nationalism in Ireland*. Dublin: Four Courts Press.

Dunning, Eric and Sheard, Kenneth (1979) *Barbarians, Gentlemen and Players: a Sociological Study of the Development of Rugby Football*. Oxford: Martin Robertson.

Dunning, E., Maguire, J. and Pearton, R. (1993) 'Introduction: sports in comparative and developmental perspective', in E. Dunning, J. Maguire, and R. Pearton, (eds), *The Sports Process: a Comparative and Developmental Approach*. Champaign, IL: Human Kinetics, pp. 1–18.

Duval, Lynne (2001) 'The development of women's track and field in England: the role of the athletic clubs, 1920s–1950s', *The Sports Historian*, 21 (1): 1–34.

Finn, Gerry P.T. and Giulianotti, Richard (eds) (2000) *Football Cultures: Local Contests, Global Visions*. London: Frank Cass.

Greenfield, Steve and Osborn, Guy (eds) (2000) *Law and Sport in Contemporary Society*. London: Frank Cass.

Guttmann, Allen (1978) *From Ritual to Record: the Nature of Modern Sports*. New York: Columbia University Press.

Guttmann, A. (1990) 'Teaching "sport and society"', in D.L. Vanderwerken (ed.), *Sport in the Classroom: Teaching Sport-Related Courses in the Humanities*. London: Associated University Press, pp. 237–47.

Hargreaves, Jennifer (1994) *Sporting Females: Critical Issues in the History and Sociology of Women's Sport*. London: Routledge.

Hill, Jeffrey (1998) 'The legend of Denis Compton', *The Sports Historian*, 18 (2): 19–33.

Hill, Jeff and Williams, Jack (eds) (1996) *Sport and Identity in the North of England*. Keele: Keele University Press.

Holloway, Gerry (1998) 'Writing women in: the development of feminist approaches to women's history', in William Lamont (ed.), *Historical Controversies and Historians*. London: UCL Press.

Holt, Richard (1989) *Sport and the British: a Modern History*. Oxford: Oxford University Press.

Holt, Richard (1996) 'Sport and history: the state of the subject in Britain', *Twentieth Century British History*, 7 (2): 231–52.

Holt, Richard and Mason, Tony (2000) *Sport in Britain 1945–2000*. Oxford: Blackwell.

Hornby, Nick (1992) *Fever Pitch: a Fan's Life*. London: Victor Gollancz.

Horne, John, Tomlinson, Alan and Whannel, Garry (1999) *Understanding Sport: an Introduction to the Sociological and Cultural Analysis of Sport*. London: E. & F.N. Spon.

James, C.L.R. (1963) *Beyond a Boundary*. London: Stanley Paul.

Jarvie, Grant (1991) *Highland Games: the Making of the Myth*. Edinburgh: Edinburgh University Press.

Jarvie, Grant and Maguire, Joseph (1994) *Sport and Leisure in Social Thought*. London: Routledge.

Jones, Stephen (1986) *Workers at Play: a Social and Economic History of Leisure 1918–1939*. London: Routledge & Kegan Paul.

Jones, Stephen (1988) *Sport, Politics and the Working Class: Organised Labour and Sport in Interwar Britain*. Manchester: Manchester University Press.

Kelner, Simon (1996) *To Jerusalem and Back*. London: Macmillan.

Kirkpatrick, Jeff (2001) 'Reading', *Guardian Unlimited*, 21 February 2001. http://football. guardian.co.uk/fanzines/story/0,8507,441097,00. html, accessed April 2001.

Lowerson, John (1993) *Sport and the English Middle Classes*. Manchester: Manchester University Press.

Lowerson, John (1998) 'Opiate of the people and stimulant of the historian? Some issues in sports history', in W. Lamont (ed.), *Historical Controversies and Historians*. London: UCL Press, pp. 201–14.

MacLennan, Hugh Dan (1998) 'Shinty's place and space in the world', *The Sports Historian*, 18 (1): 1–23.

Malcolmson, R.W. (1973) *Popular Recreations in English Society 1700–1850*. Cambridge: Cambridge University Press.

Marwick, Arthur (1996) *British Society since 1945*. 3rd edn. Harmondsworth: Penguin.

Mason, Tony (1980) *Association Football and English Society, 1863–1915*. Hassocks: Harvester.

Murfin, Lyn (1990) *Popular Leisure in the Lake Counties*. Manchester: Manchester University Press.

Polley, Martin (1998) *Moving the Goalposts: a History of Sport and Society since 1945*. London: Routledge.

Rowling, J.K. (1997) *Harry Potter and the Philosopher's Stone*. London: Bloomsbury.

Rowling J.K. (as Kennilworthy Whisp) (2001) *Quidditch through the Ages*. London: Bloomsbury.

Russell, Dave (1997) *Football and the English: a Social History of Association Football in England, 1863–1995*. Preston: Carnegie.

Smith, Dai and Williams, Gareth (1980) *Fields of Praise: the Official History of the Welsh Rugby Union 1881–1981*. Cardiff: University of Wales Press.

Southgate, Beverley (1996) *History: What and Why? Ancient, Modern, and Postmodern Perspectives*. London: Routledge.

Struna, Nancy (2001) 'Reframing the direction of change in the history of sport', *International Journal of the History of Sport*, 18 (4): 1–15.

Vamplew, Wray (1998) 'Facts and artefacts: sports historians and sports museums', *Journal of Sports History*, 24 (2): 268–82.

Vamplew, Wray (2000) 'History', in Richard Cox, Grant Jarvie and Wray Vamplew (eds),

Encyclopedia of British Sport. Oxford: ABC-Clio, pp. 178–80.

Whannel, Garry (1992) *Fields in Vision: Television Sport and Cultural Transformation.* London: Routledge.

Williams, Jack (1999) *Cricket and England: a Cultural and Social History of the Inter-war Years.* London: Frank Cass.

Young, Percy (1968) *A History of British Football.* London: Stanley Paul.

Part Two   *Structuring Opportunities in Sport*

4

Social Exclusion from Sport and Leisure

MICHAEL F. COLLINS

Jesus is recorded as saying *the poor you will have among you always, and you can help them whenever you like* (Mark 14.7, Revised English Bible)

Overview

→ Introduction: What is social exclusion?
→ Citizenship, class and social capital
→ Class differences in sport and how they exacerbate other factors
→ Race, gender, disability, age, sexuality and geography
→ Case studies: combating poverty and exclusion in sport and leisure
→ The costly parameters of social inclusion

INTRODUCTION: WHAT IS SOCIAL EXCLUSION?

Rowntree in York and Booth in London undertook the first serious studies of poverty in nineteenth-century England. They described, as did Dickens *'absolute poverty'* – people 'on the breadline'. These were people without the basics of life: adequate, warm shelter, nutritious food, education and life-supporting work. However, by the mid twentieth century, life was seen as more than survival, and included aspects of enjoyment and involvement in society,

encompassing culture, art and sport. The absolute definition of poverty was gradually replaced by a relative definition of poverty measured in relation to what was customary for the standard of living and style of life in the country. This definition was adopted in the 1990s in the European Union Poverty Programmes I and II.

But social exclusion is a process, and is described much more widely in terms of access, or lack of it, to four basic social systems, namely democracy, welfare, the labour market, and family and community (Commins, 1993). The term 'social exclusion' was first used by a French welfare minister in 1974, but is now everyday EU-speak. With the return of the New Labour government in 1997, tackling social exclusion became a high priority and a 'cross-cutting' theme of first central, and soon local government. The new Social Exclusion Unit (1998) in the Cabinet Office used a description, rather than a definition in *Bringing Britain Together*, as

a shorthand label for what can happen when individuals or areas suffer a combination of linked problems such as unemployment, poor skills, low incomes, poor housing, high crime environments, bad health and family breakdown.

(Cabinet Office,
www.open.gov.uk/co/seu/more.html)

The EU's, and indeed, Tony Blair's main weapon against exclusion and in support of social insertion is to fit people for work and encourage the economy to produce jobs. As I shall point out, this will not meet everyone's needs.

Exclusion and poverty, and sport and leisure

I argue elsewhere (Collins et al., 1999; Collins, 2003) that poverty is the core of exclusion: a few people who are not poor may be affected by other dimensions in which exclusion can be expressed (such as sexuality, gender, age, ethnicity, disability or location, as discussed below), but few poor people are not excluded in some way. So, who is poor in Britain? Before the 1970s the postwar welfare state had ensured that the poor fell overwhelmingly into two overlapping groups: the elderly who had no personal pension provision and the chronically sick. But now the poor are more heterogeneous:

- 24% of adults are receiving and 30% of children are in families that are receiving under half the average male wage (which is the measure of poverty used by the EU)
- 75% of disabled people who depend on benefits (which at UK levels of payment makes them poor automatically)
- most of those not in work comprising the following categories:

  - 35% of the chronically sick/disabled
  - 46% of single parents
  - 57% of ethnic minorities
  - 65% of the over-50s

compared to 33% of the population. But many of those in work are on low/insecure pay, and need income support.

The battle with poverty had been waged throughout the postwar years and by 1979 only 7 per cent of adults were classed as poor. But in the UK, in common with all countries of the OECD including the USA, the gap between the richest and poorest social groups has been widening over the last 20 years, especially in countries with neo-liberal governments. However, while the gap is narrower in countries such as Scandinavia and The Netherlands, where benefits and pay rates are higher, the gap has still grown. By 1994, 24 per cent of adults in the UK were poor. Recent improvements in child allowances and lower unemployment have reduced the figure, but below-inflation rises in pensions, income support and disability benefits offset some of this improvement. Consequently, the figure for the number in poverty remained high at 23 per cent in 2001. Poverty restricts leisure spending, and the disparities between the richest and poorest groups become even more exaggerated, as is evident from Table 4.1 which indicates that the richest 10 per cent have 6.7 times the

Table 4.1   *Household and leisure expenditure*

Expenditure	Top 10 per cent of population	Bottom 10 per cent of population
Total weekly household expenditure	£ 849.00	£ 126.70
Total weekly leisure expenditure	187.50	20.20
	(22 per cent)	(16 per cent)

Source: 2001 Family Expenditure Survey data, reported in the *Guardian*, 24 Jan. 2002, p. 8.

income of the poorest but spend 9.8 times as much on their leisure.

CITIZENSHIP, CLASS AND SOCIAL CAPITAL

If, following Commins (1993), citizenship is defined as the ability to take part fully in all aspects of society, then the cultural sphere including sport must be included. Taking part for the individual requires confidence, skills, knowledge, ability to manage time and relationships, and having a group of supportive friends and companions, including some who share the same desire to take part. This is what Bourdieu called social capital, and which I call personal social capital, to distinguish it from the communal sort discussed below. Bourdieu (1985) argued that the social capital of different strata of society varied according to the *habitus*, or social, economic, environmental and psychological milieu in which they were brought up and lived, and the associated values and meanings. Surveys show that social groups ABC1 – middle- and upper-class people with higher incomes, higher educational attainment, their own cars (often personal rather than one shared by the household), and a wide-ranging social network – spend more on sport and leisure and have a wider range of interests.

The second form of social capital is a shared one; this I call communal capital. Putnam, studying American society, defined

this as: shared values; social control and order; reduced financial inequalities; confidence in institutions and leaders in society; participation in political, social and cultural networks (including playing sport and belonging to sports clubs); and trust in and support from one's friends, neighbours and close kin – the social glue, as it has been called. In *Bowling Alone* (Putnam, 2000), he reported finding that in contemporary America all these forms of social involvement and commitment were in steep decline, with more and more individualised, consumerised activity, relying on others to provide high-quality goods and services, but with no commitment in the transaction other than ephemeral customer satisfaction.

Others have made similar claims regarding the decline in social cohesion. Fukuyama, for example, argued that since the fall of European communism, one form or another of liberalism has become the dominant political ideology. This analysis led him to assert 'the end of history' in so far as history lies in active political contention about how society should be ordered. From a different perspective, Beck (1992) argued that in a postmodern, individualised society, the concept of class is terminally crumbling, and will be replaced by individual values and behaviours centred around consumption. How an individual country defines the boundaries of individual classes lies in its own social history, though the UK has been held up as the epitome of a strongly socially stratified society, from elite and aristocracy to meanest labourer. Roberts concurred with Beck's view, arguing that 'money is now at the root of the main differences between the use of leisure in different social strata, and the leisure differences between them are basically and blatantly inequalities rather than alternative ways of life' (1999: 87).

Others contend that this view is mistaken. Adonis and Pollard argued strongly that 'Britain's class system separates its people as clinically today as it did half a century ago – far from diminishing, class divisions are intensifying as the distance between the top and bottom widens and the classes at both extremes grow in size and identity' (1997: ix) and that 'far from leisure being in the vanguard of the classless society, the way we live our lives is a daily, hourly testament to our place in Britain's class structure' (1997: 244). Kew (1997: 149) agreed, and wrote of Bourdieu providing 'compelling evidence for the saliency of social class in structuring if not determining a person's choice and preferences in sport'. Horne et al. (1999), Jarvie and Maguire (1994), and Sugden and Tomlinson (2000) also concur, the latter summarising Bourdieu's perspective that:

sport acts as a kind of badge of social exclusivity and cultural distinctiveness for the dominant classes; it operates as a means of control or containment of the working or popular classes; it is represented as a source of escape and mobility for talented working class performers ... it articulates the fractional status distinctions that exist within the ranks of larger class grouping. (Sugden and Tomlinson, 2000: 319).

Sport has been seen in different ways as part of citizenship. In 1975 a Labour government White Paper, *Sport and Recreation*, called it part of the fabric of the social services, which Coalter et al. (1986) termed *recreation as welfare* (of participants). Thereafter it became an instrument of economic policy (in job creation and regeneration), youth control (as a result of rising youth crime, unemployment and urban unrest) and health promotion (as much by the commercial fitness industry as by government), which the same authors labelled *recreation for welfare*. The widening poverty gap, and attempts to increase efficiency in public leisure services under Mrs Thatcher, especially through Compulsory Competitive Tendering, led to 'good', middle-class citizens being able to access such services and being effectively subsidised by poorer taxpayers (Audit Commission, 1989). As Ravenscroft noted, the 'politics of choice' had been replaced by the 'politics of means' (1993: 42). Glyptis (1989: 42) and Coalter both commented on the dualism of policies for welfare and for promoting participation, the latter arguing that there was a 'lack of a coherent philosophy or politics of 'recreational welfare' with which to resist consumerist definitions and managerialist practices' (1989: 127). Of course, in a post-industrial society, consumption is necessary to sustain employment – Tony Blair encouraged people to go on spending to avoid the depression afflicting Japan, the USA and Germany in 2001–2. Coalter (2000) accused leisure students of neglecting and despising consumption as shallow, passive and meaningless in contrast to active participation (especially in 'serious' leisure) which they value as deep in meaning and constructive for the individual and society.

CLASS DIFFERENCES IN SPORT AND HOW THEY EXACERBATE OTHER FACTORS

Poverty exacerbates other forms of exclusion mentioned above, and one group thus

Table 4.2   *The effect of disability, ethnicity and class in sports participation*

	Disabled	Ethnic minority
Males		
100	59	78
(65)	*(35)*	*(46)*
Females		
73	41	53
(45)	*(35)*	*(46)*

Note: Figures in italic in parentheses represent semi- or unskilled groups' (DE) participation within the main groupings.

affected that has become a policy target is at-risk disaffected youth. This can be demonstrated by Sport England's (2001a) Sport Equity Index of participation, which benchmarks participation for each group against the group with the highest participation (for example, males with no disability have a participation rate of 60.3% = 100). Thus in Table 4.2 the separate effect of disability and ethnicity can be seen, and (in italics) the additional effect of being in the semi- or unskilled groups.

How does this affect sport? Box 4.1 identifies the impact of class on different levels of participation ranging from children's to that of the elite squads of selected sports:

- *Item 1* shows the great difference in take-up of starter and performer schemes between affluent and deprived areas of Nottinghamshire.
- *Item 2A* shows that the gap in adult participation has not closed over the decade. It had started to do so in the early 1990s but in the recent recession, the leisure expenditure of poorer people was cut and the gap began to widen.
- *Item 2B* shows that over the last generation, visiting leisure centres has become much more concentrated among upper social strata, in part the result of above-average price increases and the marketing policies pursued in the public sector due to budget pressures and CCT.

- *Item 3* makes it equally clear that there is a strong gradient in joining sports and fitness clubs, the latter in particular with a strong gap in quality and price between budget and premium brands. It also shows the combined advantage enjoyed by full-time students who have access to facilities and clubs which are often subsidised and who come disproportionately from social groups ABC1.
- *Item 4* shows that the class gap carries through into elite sport. The AB social groups were over-represented by 100% while the DE social groups were 60% under-represented. Only Rugby League was near to the average. The cost of supporting elite participants is such that even swimming, Rugby Union and cycling have 83%, 69% and 50% respectively in AB groups.

The classic argument for the value and operation of the unfettered market is that these non-sporting folks are choosing something else from the wide leisure menu available. This is just not so, as Table 4.3 shows.

Large differences in participation as measured by social groups exist in relation to foreign and adventure holidays, visiting libraries, museums and galleries, and reading books. Smaller, but still significant gaps in participation exist in relation to domestic holiday-taking, visiting theatres, cinemas and countryside, and in buying books. Only

Box 4.1   Social gradients in forms of sports participation

1   Children's take-up in youth sports schemes, Nottinghamshire

	% Less deprived areas	% Deprived areas
Champion Coaching beginners	87	13
Go for Gold beginners	92	8
Performance Resources squads	92	8
Notts population	71	29

Source: Collins and Buller, 2000, forthcoming

2A   Adult (aged 16+) participation, at least once a month (%)

	1987	1996
Professional	65	63
Unskilled	26	23
Difference	39	40

Source: UK Sport/Sport England, 1999

2B   Adult visits to sport and leisure centres (%)

	1960s	1990s
Professional	20	40
Unskilled	7	8
Difference	13	32

Source: UK Sport/Sport England, 1999

3   Adult membership of sports clubs, 1996 (%)

	Health/fitness	Sport
Professional	6	16
Unskilled	1	4
Difference	5	12
Student	4	18

Source: UK Sport/Sport England, 1999

4   Adult participation in twelve elite national squads (%)

	National squads	GB population	Difference
Professional/managerial AB	38	19	**19**
Low/unskilled DE	10	25	**15**
Difference	28	6	

Source: English Sports Council, 1998

Table 4.3 *Social inequalities in participation across the leisure spectrum*

%	Holidays				Advent.	Pub	Library	Theatre	Pop music	Gall.	Books		Cinema	Day vis.	Tourist	GB pop.
	GB	Abroad	Air char.	Coach							Buy	Read				
AB	76	65	31	7	63	24	79	34	26	47	32	69	17	23	32	22
C1	73	51	36	10	59	29	75	33	34	31	31	61	19	30	33	27
C2	70	41	40	9	54	38	51	18	22	23	18	44	11	21	20	23
D	69	36	47	8	49	34	57	16	18	15	19	41	10	26	15	28
E	60	26	37	9	33	24	49					46	2			
Diff. AB–DE	16	35	+2	+2	30	0	30	18	8	32	13	23	15	−3	17	N/a

in going to pop concerts, pubs and coach holidays does the gap narrow. Slightly more people from social groups D and E make day visits to the countryside than ABs, but this includes going to the coast and village pubs and shops. This is not evidence of a different leisure lifestyle, only of a much narrower one. Smith (2001) graphically showed how some 40 per cent still do not take a holiday, most for cost, health and social reasons rather than choice. Smith also highlighted how the English Tourism Council did not see how it could promote inclusion policies because it believed the market to be too fragmented.

Finally, is the same strength of class differences exhibited in other countries? De Knop and Elling (2001) found a similar pattern of social difference in Flanders and The Netherlands, as did Nagel and Nagel (2001) in Germany, while Van der Meulen et al. (2001) found the same gap for Dutch performance sports groups. More (1999) explained exclusion of lower-income groups from outdoor recreation from US state and national parks in terms of the same financial pressures on authorities as in the UK, which led to increasing prices to users to raise income.

EXCLUSION IN SPORT AND RACE, GENDER, DISABILITY, AGE, GEOGRAPHY AND SEXUALITY

Other authors in this volume deal with three factors traditionally associated with exclusion through societal/structural effects, namely gender, race and disability. Tess Kay suggests that *the history of women's involvement in sport is one of substantial exclusion*, on medical, aesthetic and social grounds – that most forms of sport are unsuited or even especially hazardous to women's bodies, unpleasing in presenting women as athletes, or inappropriate to

women's roles in society (see also Kay's chapter 6 in Collins, 2003). This structural and limiting masculinity is evidenced clearly from primary school onwards (Sport England, 2000) to the international boardroom and medal podium, in playing, coaching, administering and making policy in sport. Only recently, after hard lobbying and the lonely efforts of pioneers, under the umbrella of the Brighton Declaration (Sports Council, 1994a) are these attitudes changing. But Kay shows that change will only come when the institutions become less male dominated and move to empower women. The slowness to do this, from the IOC to local clubs, is testimony to the fact that the importance of change is only grudgingly accepted.

Carrington and McDonald deal with race in sport as part of wider social and political discourses, and show how the 1970s saw the Labour government adopt affirmative action through programmes like Action Sport, but allied it with images of urban decay and criminality. This set up what they call a *racialised discourse* through the 1980s which problematised cultural differences. This was partly redressed by the Sports Council's (1994b) policy paper and English Sports Council's (1997) guide for local authorities. However, concurrently the Major government's policy priority in *Sport: Raising the Game* (DNH, 1995) shifted to excellence, and did not mention ethnic issues. Action was left to the governing bodies of professionalised team games, notably in soccer (*Kick It* [racism] *Out*), Rugby League (*Tackling Racism*) and cricket (*Hit Racism for Six*). The Blair government has shown more sensitivity to the issue with two Social Exclusion Unit reports on ethnicity in urban renewal and labour markets (Cabinet Office, 2000, 2001).

Carrington and McDonald criticise the DCMS, however, for ignoring the issues of unequal power in institutions, even after the establishment of the organisation Sporting Equals. A catalyst for addressing this issue might be the publication of the Cantle Report on community cohesion in the wake of the 2001 riots in Bradford, Oldham and Blackburn, which commented that fragmentation and segregation had developed to the point where 'many communities operate on the basis of parallel lives [that] do not seem to touch at any point, let alone overlap and promote any meaningful interchanges' (Home Office, 2002a: 9). Despite little evidence, a parallel report by MPs (Home Office, 2002a: 28) asserted that 'sporting and cultural opportunities can play an important part in re-engaging disaffected sections of the community, building shared social capital and grassroots leadership through improved cross-cultural interaction'.

Recent Sport England national statistics (Rowe and Champion, 2000) confirmed that people of South Asian origin have markedly lower participation rates than other minorities or the indigenous population. The Cantle Report remarked on the notably poor provision of leisure for youth in most multicultural areas. Of course it has to be remembered that first-generation minorities settling into a new land and new communities worry first about obtaining employment and housing; the second generation strive to achieve a good education for their children; often it is only the third generation who seek to adopt or adapt in cultural terms. Many of the South Asian groups settled later than others and may not have passed through these transitions.

Thomas describes how the medical model of disability prevailed for many decades, individualising the problem and blaming the victim (Barnes et al., 1999), especially in terms of their ability to undertake paid work – 75 per cent of disabled people depend on welfare, and by definition are poor, which limits their ability to afford transport and sport and leisure activities. In the last decade and a half the social model suggests that disability in society (and in sport) is socially constructed by common values and by institutions. I suggest elsewhere (Collins, 2003) that recent events demand a further model – of empowerment – to be offered. A new broad 1995 Act of Parliament makes any form of discrimination illegal, and Thomas describes how establishing a new (1998) English Federation of Disability Sport is an attempt to weave together two disparate threads of organisations (of provision by form of disability and by type of sport) into a stronger, unified institutional fabric.

How these factors produce differences in sports participation are summarised in Box 4.2. Gender role differences are evident at primary school level and become more pronounced in secondary school (Item 1). Although the gap in overall adult participation is closing, it is doing so very slowly and a gap still exists in sports club membership (Items 2a and 2b). However, the growth of aerobics, dance, aquarobics and general fitness activities, has led to women becoming the noticeable majority of sports centre users (Item 2c). So far as ethnic differences are concerned, only the African group comes close to the level of participation of indigenous whites. The participation rate of South Asian minorities is notably low, and particularly so amongst the women. So far as disability is concerned, Sport England national survey data were due in 2002, but those published already for children clearly show them to be markedly disadvantaged, even when many are enrolled/'mainstreamed' in ordinary schools.

Discrimination by gender, race and disability has resulted in anti-discrimination legislation, the allocation of public expenditure

Box 4.2   Variations in sports participation by gender, race and disability

Gender

1a   Sport at school (no. of sports played 10 or more times a year)

	Boys	Girls	Difference
Played in primary school	3.3	3.5	+0.2
Played outside primary school	10.1	9.5	−0.6
'I am a sporty person' (%)	60	47	13
Played in secondary school	3.7	4.0	+0.3
Played outside secondary school	4.8	3.6	−1.2
'I am a sporty person' (%)	52	28	22

Source: Sport England, 2000

2a   Adults participating in sport once a month or more (%) (excl. walking)

	Men	Women	Difference
1987	57	34	−23
1990	58	39	−19
1993	57	39	−18
1996	54	38	−16

Source: UK Sport/Sport England 1999

2b   Club membership in the last 4 weeks

	Men	Women	Difference
Health/fitness club	3	4	+1
Sports club	13	4	−9

Source: UK Sport/Sport England, 1999

2c   Visiting sport and leisure centres

	Men	Women	Difference
1960s	71	29	−42
1970s	68	33	−36
1980s	55	45	−10
1990s	42	58	+16

Source: Sport England, 1999

Ethnicity

Participating in one or more activities in the last 4 weeks (%) (excl. walking)

	White	Minority groups	Difference
1990	48	43	−5
1993	48	38	−10
1996	46	41	−5

(Continued)

Box 4.2 Continued

	White	Caribbean	African	Indian	Pakistani	Bangladeshi
1999–2000	46	39	44	39	31	30
Difference		7	2	7	15	16

Source: UK Sport/Sport England, 1999; Rowe and Champion, 2000

Disability and children

	Disabled, 2000	All, 1999	Difference
Not playing any sport 10+ times a year	26	6	20
Less than 3 hours a week secondary PE	20	53	23
1 hour or none in summer holiday	32	10	22

Source: Sport England, 2001b

and the establishment of promotional/ lobbying organisations. These types of discrimination have also attracted significant media attention, as reflected in the coverage of the London Marathon and the Sydney Olympics and Paralympics which raised the level of public awareness.

Other forms of exclusion have received much less coverage and attention. Ageism, for example, has received far less attention in Europe (Collins, 2003) than in North America, where greater affluence and consumer confidence among older people have perhaps made it a higher-profile issue. There was a flurry of activity in Britain in the 1970s with Bernard's (1988) and Midwinter's (1992) studies on leisure and age and the Sports Council's '50+ and All to Play For' campaign. Despite the ageing of the population in Britain, the proven benefits of physical activity in maintaining body functions in older people, and the potential savings on health and social budgets of sustained mobility and independence, Sport England and DCMS have remained steadfastly silent on the issue. Other European countries as in Belgium and Scandinavia

(see UK Sport 1999) have achieved greater participation of people over 50.

As regards the geography of exclusion, far more attention has been directed towards issues of access in urban than in rural areas, despite the levels of poverty being almost the same (see Coalter et al., 2000). More area-based initiatives for urban renewal and sports promotion have been focused on inner cities than the countryside despite evidence of only modest benefits, as shown by Robinson (n.d.), for example, in his assessment of the City Challenge programme over five years on Tyneside. The small number of programmes designed to overcome rural exclusion have, arguably, to address a more daunting series of barriers to participation including greater distance, poor and costly transport, and also the problems of meeting capital costs or providing a threshold population to support services and facilities in sparsely populated areas (Slee et al., 2001).

Perhaps the least understood and acknowledged aspect of exclusion is that of sexuality. It is clear that the masculine ethos of most sport has created an aura of

Table 4.4   *Local authorities with leisure and loyalty cards, 1999*

| Authority | No. of leisure/loyalty cards | | | |
	No. (% of group total)	Incl. sport	Incl. arts	Incl. commercial
London boroughs	22 (27)	22	8	11
Metropolitan districts	30 (100)	30	13	9
Unitary authorities	30 (88)	33	15	15
Non-metropolitan districts	131 (70)	129	39	41
Welsh unitary authorities	13 (68)	13	3	1
Total	226 (76)	227	78	77

Source: CIPFA, 1999

homophobia, and homosexuals and lesbians have for years kept quiet rather than risk homophobic stereotyping and abuse. Recently homosexual and lesbian sportspeople have 'come out'; homosexual clubs and teams have appeared; and Gay Games have been launched (Clarke, 1998). Few governments or national sports bodies have tackled this issue: the Dutch Ministry of Welfare, Public Health and Culture had Hekma (1998) undertake a review, and its national Olympic Committee has included sexuality in its anti-discrimination code since 1994.

Now we look at two case studies of attempts to break the barriers of cost and access: the first concerns the use of leisure cards and the second a local project, the Nottinghamshire's Sports Training Scheme, designed to widen access to youth sport.

CASE STUDIES: COMBATING POVERTY AND EXCLUSION IN SPORT AND LEISURE

Anti-poverty strategies and leisure cards

In the 1980s local authorities, especially those that were Labour controlled and in large cities, became concerned to combat the growth in poverty. By 1995 a third had

developed formal anti-poverty strategies and some had also begun producing leisure passports or cards, which offered discounts for a broad range of services rather than discounts limited to particular locations or activity. Collins and Kennett (1999) described them as a tool that enabled improved targeted marketing without the problem of 'free riders', while aiming at social and specifically inclusionary objectives. This made them acceptable to Tory managerialists as well as welfarist or egalitarian liberal and Labour politicians. Collins and Kennett discovered 50 per cent adoption in their national survey in 1996–7, but aspirations for this to increase to 80 per cent in 3–5 years. Authorities with corporate anti-poverty strategies were three times as likely to have a leisure card scheme. Some schemes offered a standard discount to targeted populations while others had two tiers, with one tier offering a discount to all citizens and a second tier offering more substantial discounts to target groups. The most recent data on the adoption of leisure cards is shown in Table 4.4.

It can be seen that by 1999, 77 per cent of authorities had a leisure or, aping supermarkets and DIY centres, a loyalty card. While all but one of these offered municipal sport, only 34 per cent offered municipal arts, and the same share offered private sector leisure, retail, taxis, etc. Limiting

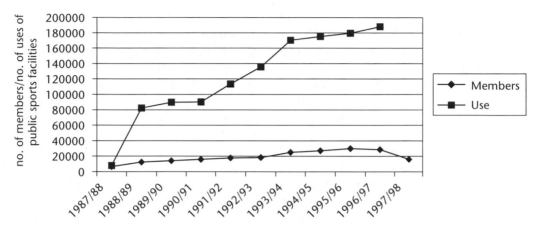

Figure 4.1   Use of Leicester leisure pass compared to membership totals

offers to sport is a sure way of limiting take-up, since it will miss a large number of children, women and men who do not see themselves as sporty (about 38 per cent according to the Allied Dunbar National Fitness Survey, 1991), and most older people. A Leicester City officer said that to be attractive cards should provide 'from veg to Verdi'.

Despite the widespread adoption of the card scheme, the evidence – which is admittedly fragmented – of their success in overcoming social exclusion is weak:

- Apart from a few authorities that reach 25–30 per cent of their target groups, many have low take-ups of between 5 and 15 per cent.
- Owing to financial pressures, many local authorities reduced the discounts they offered to levels that were unattractive to people with little disposable income.
- Most schemes were severely under-resourced, with one-third having no budget, and a quarter having no staff dedicated to marketing/managing their cards. Leicester City Council, a pioneer

whose card reached 30,000 citizens and incorporated many arts, retail and other commercial services (see Figure 4.1), recently cut its marketing staff and lost 10,000 holders in two years.

- Only a minority of local authorities had active outreach marketing (roadshows/ sessions in job centres, ethnic/women's/ disabled/senior citizens' clubs, etc.); the rest depended on passive/shotgun methods of marketing (e.g. posters, on-site leaflets, leaflet drops) which had very low success rates of only 1–2 per cent.

For most local authorities, the judgement must be that as a contribution to combating social exclusion, leisure/loyalty cards are an act of tokenism. There seem to be three major areas of weakness, the first of which is the clear under-investment in the management of the card schemes, particularly to enable the exploitation of new technology. Second, too few schemes are public/private partnerships. Leisure/loyalty cards must be a public/private patrnership otherwise more and more private sector initiatives will erode the more attractive parts of the package.

One very successful scheme is in the City of Nottingham which has 79,000 leisure card-holding residents, and 29,000 with concessions to use a wide range of public and private outlets. The addition of several thousand teenage holders of the DFES's Connexion card will swell these numbers significantly. Third, card schemes need professional marketing. Put simply, most local authorities have not invested sufficiently in knowing, serving and retaining their customers by comparison with companies such as the David Lloyd chain of fitness clubs.

Starting young: Nottinghamshire Sports Training Scheme (NSTS)

Most European countries have specialist primary PE teachers, the UK does not; similarly, many countries provide two hours a week or more of PE and sport, whereas the UK does not. Furthermore, there was no professional and co-ordinated training of coaches until the National Coaching Foundation started work in the 1980s. The weakness of primary school PE teaching and the lack of well-qualified coaches were frequently cited as explanations for the poor foundation of sports skills among the young and the large post-school drop in sports participation. In response to this problem, Nottinghamshire County Council, which has often pioneered developments in sport, decided in 1989 to promote a county-wide Nottinghamshire Sports Training Scheme (NSTS) to encourage more youngsters to participate in sport. Using clubs and governing bodies linked to PE teachers, the Scheme provided starter courses which led to improver and advanced courses. The NCF's nationwide Champion Coaching scheme, introduced in 1991, was incorporated into the NSTS, as was a Performance

and Excellence element (later called Performance Resources), to provide links to county squads or higher-level competitive clubs. Champion Coaching was organised through the governing bodies of sport. From 1993 the County Council organised, in conjunction with the district councils, a pre-Champion Coaching course called 'Go for Gold'.

The City and southern county has enjoyed a buoyant economy, but coal mining in north Nottinghamshire has almost disappeared, and textiles and other industries have suffered cuts in jobs. Collins and Buller (2000, forthcoming) used postal, telephone and interview surveys to examine children's take-up of Champion Coaching and relate it to indicators of deprivation, levels of satisfaction with the programme, and children's involvement in sport. The surveys showed a high degree of enjoyment and satisfaction of both children and parents with the organisation and delivery of the coaching courses (around 90 per cent). Between a quarter and a third had joined local sports clubs, and found those helpful and supportive. There were two big caveats to this success. First, two in five of the children claimed that they were not told about 'exit routes' into clubs and squads, and second, the take-up of all three sets of courses was socially selective. As the figures in Box 4.1 and Figure 4.2 show, affluent areas produced a disproportionate number of entrants. There is no obvious explanation for the low take-up of places on Champion Coaching by children from poorer areas. The NSTS, of which Champion Coaching was a part, was well publicised and cheap (fees were waived on request if they were problematic for families). There still seemed to be a fear, on the part of parents on low incomes, of not being able to keep up even the low payments. It is less

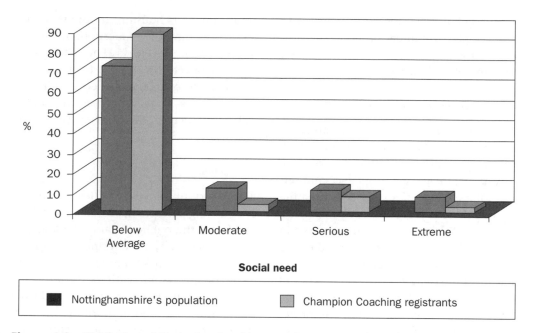

Figure 4.2   Distribution of Champion Coaching participants in Nottinghamshire

easy to explain why teachers in schools in such areas were not proposing their interested or gifted pupils to NSTS.

This case study shows that even in a well-resourced and managed scheme, there is as much reproduction of existing structural disadvantage as there is breaking of barriers. Sport England has demonstrated considerable awareness of exclusion issues, as indicated by its high-profile Active Sports programmes in schools, clubs and communities, through 45 county partnerships, and through well-funded schemes targeted at places of concentrated deprivation via Sport Action Zones and Priority Areas. However, there is not much evidence of a detailed strategy for implementation to ensure the breaking of the powerful and persistent social barriers to participation. Although there is guidance for national governing bodies of sport on tackling social

exclusion due to race, gender and disability, there is little guidance regarding the more pervasive factor of poverty (Sport England, 2001c).

THE (COSTLY) PRINCIPLES OF EFFECTIVE INCLUSION POLICY

Everyone is looking for good practice with which to respond to the government's concern for social inclusion. Nonetheless there is hardly any serious research or evaluation of schemes (Collins et al., 1999), and while some schemes look to have good short-term effects (DCMS, 1999; Coalter, 2001), it is too soon to say these are lasting or significant outcomes as it is estimated that programmes need to operate for between five and ten years in order to overcome such strong long-term barriers (Brodie and Roberts, 1992).

If successful social inclusion policy is to be developed, a number of factors need to be acknowledged and issues addressed, including the following:

Excluded people face multiple constraints

Some constraints are societal and can rarely be overcome by the agency of an individual; some are personal and can only be overcome by good self-image, self-confidence and settled values; other constraints, mediating between these two groups, need the action of intermediaries, such as managers and policy-makers. Table 4.5, synthesised by the author from a large number of studies, indicates the strength of different types of constraints. Particularly in relation to the unemployed, disabled, ethnic minorities and young delinquent groups, the removal of one constraint leaves a number of others firmly in place. As can be seen from the rows of the table, some constraints affect several groups, like poor transport systems and all non-car-owners, which is patently difficult to grapple with now privatisation has dispersed control of provision on rail or buses. Attention to such constraints therefore helps many people in several groups like aids to mobility for the physically disabled, which also benefit the frail and elderly, parents with children in prams and shoppers laden with bags and bundles.

Joined-up policies

The multiplicity of constraints is what justifies the Blair government in advocating proper linkage between the separate policies and departments of central and local government when they affect the same people and areas. It is not easy to overcome political *amour-propre*, bureaucratic empire-building, or different priorities, timescales, styles and philosophies of delivery between departments responsible for education,

environmental, housing, transport, leisure services, community education, and sometimes social services. The 'brigading' together of services in both town hall and Whitehall into large, multi-service administrative units may simply mean higher walls and deeper ditches between larger ministries.

Partnerships

A corollary of joined-up policies is that of establishing partnerships for delivery which cut across the public, commercial and voluntary sectors. Sport England is trying to make this the basis of its Active Sports development system, with local authorities, county governing bodies of sport and their clubs, and education authorities and their schools having to co-operate before they can have Exchequer funding for a partnership manager or apply for Lottery funding for facilities and programmes. Sport cannot 'go it alone', but it has to be recognised that partnerships or networks are not always amongst equals (and sport may often be a minor partner in redevelopment projects, for example), and partnerships can be fragile. One of the new Sport England showcase projects has 39 partners; satisfying so many can be a managerial nightmare, if not an impossibility.

Sustained policies and longer time spans

Every new politician or chief executive feels the pressure to do and *be seen to do* something new; consequently there is in sport and leisure, from Sport England and DCMS in particular, a constant stream of new programmes and new or changed grant conditions. This 'initiativitis' is compounded by a reliance on short-term programmes, often of three years' duration, which is nowhere near long enough to yield outcomes of significant social change. The PAT 10 report

Table 4.5 *Multiple constraints and exclusion in sport and leisure*

Constraint/ exclusion factor	Youth			Poor/ unemployed	Women	Poor people	Ethnic minorities	People with disabilities/ learning difficulties
	Children	Young people	Young delinq.					
Structural factors								
Poor phys./soc. environ.	+	+	++	++	+	+	++	+
Poor facilities/ community capacity	+	+	++	++	+	+	+	++
Poor support network	+	+	++	++	+	+	+	++
Poor transport	++	++	++	++	++	++	+	++
Mediating factors								
Managers' policies/attitudes	+	+	++	++	+	+	++	++
Labelling by society	+	++	+++	+	+	+	+++	++
Lack of time structure	+	+	++	+++	+++	+	+	+
Lack of income	+	+	++	+++	+	++	++	++
Personal factors								
Lack of skills/personal social capital	+	+	+++	+++	+	+	++	++
Fears of safety	++	++	++	++	+++	++++	++	++
Powerlessness	++	++	+++	+++	++	++	++++	++
Poor self/body image	+	+	++	++	+	+	++	++

Key: The number of + shows the severity of constraints for particular groups

(DCMS, 1999) advocated that programmes should last at least five years, and more programmes of this length are being established.

Tighter focus of both people and place policies

There is a political temptation when drawing up policies targeted at places to take in as many people as possible. However, given that even in the most deprived areas the majority of people are not poor and excluded, it is not easy to ensure that benefits get to those who need them most. One of the strengths of leisure card schemes was the capacity to reach target groups efficiently and effectively, and with no outward stigma. The new Sport Action Zones range in size from 1,100 people in south Leicester through 88,000 living in Lambeth and Southwark to 480,000 in the whole of Cornwall, and 852,000 in South Yorkshire. Given that each receives the same modest budgets and has one professional manager, it is difficult to see how work in such large areas as the latter two can be more than token in the face of the problems that they face.

Involving the citizens and building social capital

Giddens (1994) foresaw the development of a more active, clever, individualised citizenry, with each citizen seeking his/her own networks, which Ellison described as 'new solidarities across a range of putative "communities" as a form of defence against social changes which continually threaten to frustrate such ambitions' (Ellison, 1997: 714). Sports clubs as a form of social capital are a classic example of self-help, and their voluntary work has been crucial to sport in every country in the world. Indeed no country, even those with the most *dirigiste* command economy, has been able to manage without them. The particular contribution of voluntary organisations has been clearly recognised by the Blair government which would like to see community organisations taking a greater role in shaping society. Many departmental and lottery grants are predicated on voluntary organisations, including sports clubs, being partners in, and agents of, change. Yet the pressures of time, the demands for coaches and administrators to be as knowledgeable and skilled as those who are paid, combine with the attractions of playing until a greater age and a myriad of other leisure interests to threaten their future. A recent international survey found that in all the countries studied, the volunteer force was ageing and struggling to meet new demands (Heinemann, 1999).

Unfortunately, we know very little about the UK's approximately 150,000 sports clubs except that, with on average 43 members, they are much smaller than their European counterparts. The small size of clubs intensifies the pressures on volunteers, yet requires the duplication of roles like chair, secretary, treasurer, etc. for small numbers of members. Thus they constitute a fragile resource base for preparing capital funding bids, and for meeting the needs of target population groups such as disabled people or ethnic minorities. Yet the small scale of many clubs often indicates that they have deep local roots and strong social ties. The government, Sport England and the Central Council of Physical Recreation need to know much more about these clubs (as the Germans do with their quadrennial survey, e.g. Heinemann and Schubert, 1994) before adding to the tasks and challenges already thrown out to them in Active Sports, World Class programmes, Sport Action Zones, flagship schemes and other programmes. For all that, communal social capital in the form of sports clubs seems in a stronger state in Britain (Hall, 1999) than found by Putnam in the US, but still not as strong as in Norway (Rothstein, 2001).

A final point under this heading is that on the whole it is better to bolster and revive existing sports clubs than to let struggling ones die and then to have to create successors. For example, the Coal Industry Welfare clubs in villages and suburbs whose mining industry disappeared between the 1970s and 1990s often provided the best, if not the only, sports facilities in their communities. Despite urging from the Sports Council, many CISWO clubs were lost leaving many communities with few sports facilities. Currently, the government is using Lottery funding to support sports development officers to work in these ex-mining communities with one of their key tasks being to encourage community development and club formation – a task that is proving extremely slow and difficult.

CONCLUSIONS

The Blair strategy for tackling poverty and exclusion is based on a principle that everyone has a right to participate in society and the opportunity to reach their full potential (DSS, 1999) through:

- tackling the main cause of poverty – worklessness, and providing security for those for whom work is not always an option;
- providing support at all points in the life cycle through improving housing, education, health facilities, obtaining

work skills, reducing discrimination, and removing the 'benefits traps' that discourage working; and
- investing in individuals and communities, getting away from the old single-policy, top-down approaches, to delivering policies in a way that is relevant to people's lives. (DSS, 1999: 30–1)

What is quite clear is that a good proportion of the socially excluded from sport and other aspects of a good society will not be able to be helped by training and work (e.g. those too old, too sick or too disabled). However, they *will* require social investment. Some of all excluded groups will require affirmative and concentrated action to overcome their doubts, based on past experience, about the truth of the promises and the reality of the help offered by politicians and managers: 'we've heard it all before' is a litany that kills social policy all too often.

The lessons from this chapter are that the three-sector (public, commercial and voluntary) sports system is evolving, but that the public and voluntary sectors, despite the plethora of policy statements and initiatives, are struggling. They have made and could yet make substantial contributions to the deeply rooted issue of social exclusion, independent of other services such as social housing, economic development or welfare: after all, *mankind shall not live by bread alone* (Bible, Matthew 4.4). However, to release the potential of sport as a vehicle for achieving greater social inclusion, we need to know more than the relatively scattered, and small-scale existing research tells us about both sport and social exclusion, otherwise much of our scarce and hard-won investment of both money and ideas will benefit the already well-supplied or will wither on the vine.

Chapter summary

- Social exclusion may be defined as the lack of access to one or more of four basic social systems, namely democracy, welfare, the labour market, and family and community networks of support.
- While sport has increasingly been used as a tool of social engineering, it is generally acknowledged as an important element of welfare.
- Social class is at the heart of social exclusion from sport, with those in social classes D and E having markedly lower levels of participation, as in most other forms of active leisure.
- Inequalities in terms of social class are often compounded by other social characteristics such as race, ethnicity, gender, (dis)ability, age, geography and sexuality.
- Public agencies have introduced policies, such as discount cards, aimed at overcoming social exclusion from sport. Successful schemes need to take account of a number of factors, including the multiple nature of constraints and the need for a precise focus on target groups.

Further reading

The Social Exclusion Unit (1998) provided a description of the conditions that contribute to social exclusion and Adonis and Pollard (1997) explored the relationship between social class and opportunity. Collins (2002) explores social exclusion in more detail in relation to sport.

There are many studies which examine the impact of particular factors affecting participation in sport: Glyptis (1989) looked at the relationship between unemployment and leisure; Hekma (1998) explored sexuality and sports participation; and Slee et al. (2001) examined social exclusion from countryside recreation.

REFERENCES

Adonis, A. and Pollard, S. (1997) *A Class Act: the Myth of a Classless Society*. London: Hamish Hamilton.

Audit Commission (1989) *Sport for Whom?* London: The Audit Commission.

Barnes, C., Mercer, G. and Shakespeare, T. (1999) *Exploring Disability: a Sociological Reader*. Oxford: Polity Press.

Beck, U. (1992) *Risk Society: Towards a New Modernity*. London: Sage.

Bernard, M. (ed.) (1988) *Positive Approaches to Ageing: Leisure and Lifestyle in Older Age*. Stoke on Trent: Beth Johnson Foundation.

Bourdieu, P. (1985) *Distinction: A Social Critique of the Judgement of Taste*. London: Routledge.

Brodie, D. and Roberts, K. (1992) *Inner City Sport: Who Plays, What are the Benefits?* Culembourg: Giordano Bruno.

Cabinet Office (2000) *Minority Ethnic Issues in Social Exclusion and Neighbourhood Renewal*. London: Cabinet Office.

Cabinet Office (2001) *Improving Labour Market Achievements for Ethnic Minorities in British Society: a Scoping Note. www.Cabinet-office.gov. uk/info/2001/ethnicity/scope.shtml*, accessed 13 Aug. 2001.

Chartered Institute of Public Finance and Accountancy (1999) *Leisure Service Charges.* London: CIPFA.

Clarke, G. (1998) 'Queering the pitch and coming out to play: lesbians in physical education and sport', *Sport, Education and Society*, 3 (2): 145–60.

Coalter, F. (1989) 'Leisure policy: an unresolvable dualism?' in C. Rojek (ed.), *Leisure for Leisure.* Basingstoke: Macmillan, pp. 115–29.

Coalter, F. (2000) 'Public and commercial leisure provision: active citizens and passive consumers?', *Leisure Studies*, 19: 163–81.

Coalter, F. (2001) *Realising the Potential of Cultural Services: the Case for Sport.* London: Local Government Association.

Coalter, F., Duffield, B. and Long, J. (1986) *The Rationale for Public Sector Investment in Sport.* London: Sports Council/ESRC.

Coalter, A., Allison, M. and Taylor, J. (2000) *The Role of Sport in Regenerating Deprived Urban Areas.* Edinburgh: Scottish Central Research Unit.

Collins, M.F. (2003) *Sport and Social Exclusion.* London: Routledge.

Collins, M.F. and Buller, J.R. (2000) 'Bridging the post-school institutional gap: Champion Coaching in Nottinghamshire', *Managing Leisure*, 5: 200–21.

Collins, M.F. and Buller, J.R. (in press) 'Social exclusion from high performance sport?', *Social Issues in Sport.*

Collins, M.F. and Kennett, C. (1999) 'Leisure, poverty and social exclusion: the growing role of passports in leisure in Great Britain', *European Journal for Sports Management*, 6 (1): 19–30.

Collins, M.F. et al. (1999) *Sport and Social Exclusion.* Report to Policy Action Team 10, DCMS. London: DCMS.

Commins, P. (ed.) (1993) *Combating Social Exclusion in Ireland 1990–94: a Midway Report.* Brussels: European Commission.

De Knop, P. and Elling, A. (eds) (2001) *Values and Norms in Sport.* Aachen: Meyer & Meyer Sport.

Department of Culture, Media and Sport (DCMS) (1999) *Policy Action Team 10 Report: Sport, Arts and Social Exclusion.* London: DCMS.

Department of National Heritage (DNH) (1995) *Sport: Raising the Game.* London: DNH.

Department of Social Security (DSS) (1999) *Opportunity for All: Tackling Poverty and Exclusion.* DSS 1st Annual Report. London: DSS.

Ellison, N. (1997) 'Towards a new social politics; citizenship and reflexivity in late modernity', *Sociology*, 31 (4): 697–717.

English Sports Council (1997) *Working Towards Racial Equality – a Good Practice Guide for Local Authorities.* London: ESC.

English Sports Council (1998) *The Development of Sporting Talent, 1997.* London: ESC.

Giddens, A. (1994) *Beyond Left and Right: the Future of Radical Politics.* Oxford: Polity Press.

Glyptis, S. (1989) *Leisure and Unemployment.* Milton Keynes: Open University Press.

Hall, P.A. (1999) 'Social capital in Britain', *British Journal of Politics*, 29: 417–61.

Heinemann, K. (ed.) (1999) *Sports Clubs in Various European Countries.* Cologne: Club of Cologne.

Heinemann, K. and Schubert, M. (1994) *Der Sportverein* [The sports club]. Schorndorf: Verlag Karl Hofmann.

Hekma, G. (1998) '"As long as they don't make an issue of it" … gay men and lesbians in organised sports in the Netherlands', *Journal of Homosexuality*, 35 (1): 1–23.

Home Office (2002a) *Community Cohesion: Report of the Review Team chaired by Ted Cantle.* London: Home Office.

Home Office (2002b) *Building Cohesive Communities: A Report of a Ministerial Group.* London: Home Office.

Horne, J., Tomlinson, A. and Whannel, G. (1999) *Understanding Sport: An Introduction to the Sociological and Cultural Analysis of Sport.* London: E. & F.N. Spon.

Jarvie, G. and Maguire, J. (1994) *Sport and Leisure in Social Thought.* London: Routledge.

Kew, F. (1997) *Sport: Social Problems and Issues.* Oxford: Butterworth Heinemann.

Midwinter, E. (1992) *Leisure: New Opportunities in the Third Age.* Dunfermline: Carnegie UK Trust.

More, T.A. (1999) 'Reconceiving recreation policy in an era of growing social inequality', *Proceedings of NE Recreation Research Symposium.* US Forest Service, pp. 415–19.

Nagel, M. and Nagel, S. (2001) *Social Background and Top Performance Sports.* Paper presented to ECSS Congress, 24–28 July, Cologne.

Putnam, R.D. (2000) *Bowling Alone*. New York: Simon & Schuster.

Ravenscroft, N. (1993) 'Public leisure provision and the good citizen', *Leisure Studies*, 12: 33–44.

Roberts, K. (1999) *Leisure in Contemporary Society*. Wallingford, Oxon: CABI Publishing.

Robinson, T. (n.d.) *The City Challenge Programme in South Newcastle*. Newcastle upon Tyne: Newcastle University Press.

Rothstein, B. (2001) 'Social capital in the social democratic welfare state', *Politics and Society*, 29 (2): 207–41.

Rowe, N. and Champion, R. (2000) *Sports Participation and Ethnicity in England – National Survey 1999–2000. Headline Findings*. London: Sport England.

Slee, W., Curry, N. and Joseph, D. (2001) *Removing Barriers, Creating Opportunities: Social Exclusion in the Countryside Leisure in the UK*. Cardiff: Countryside Recreation Network.

Smith, R. (2001) 'Including the forty per cent: social exclusion and tourism policy', in G. McPherson and M. Reid (eds), *Leisure and Social Exclusion: Challenges to Policy and Practice*. Publication no. 73. Eastbourne: Leisure Studies Association.

Social Exclusion Unit (1998) *Bringing Britain Together*. London: Cabinet Office.

Sports Council (1994a) *The Brighton Declaration on Women and Sport*. London: Sports Council.

Sports Council (1994b) *Black and Ethnic Minorities in Sport: Policy and Objectives*. London: Sports Council.

Sport England (1999) *Survey of Sports Halls and Swimming Pools in England*. London: Sport England.

Sport England (2000) *Young People and Sport in England, 1999*. London: MORI, for Sport England.

Sport England (2001a) *Sports Equity Index*, available on *www.sportengland.org.uk*

Sport England (2001b) *Young People with a Disability and Sport: Headline Findings*. London: Sport England.

Sport England (2001c) *Making English Sport Inclusive: Equity Guidelines for Governing Bodies*. London: Sport England.

Sugden, J. and Tomlinson, A. (2000) 'Theorising sport and social class', in J. Coakley and E. Dunning (eds), *Handbook of Sports Studies*. London: Sage, pp. 309–21.

UK Sport (1999) *Compass 1999: Sports Participation in Europe*. London: UK Sport.

UK Sport/Sport England (1999) *General Household Survey: Participation in Sport in GB, 1996*. London: UK Sport/Sport England.

Van der Meulen, R., Kraylaar, G. and Utlee, W. (2001) *Lifelong on the Move: an Event Analysis of Attrition in Non-elite Sport*. Paper to ECSS Congress, 24–28 July, Cologne.

5

Sport and Gender

TESS KAY

Contemporary sport is a truly global phenomenon, bringing shared experiences to a worldwide audience – yet sport is not universally inclusive. It can also be a powerful mechanism for delivering a divisive version of society – one that promotes white above black, male above female, physical prowess above alternative qualities, certain body types above others. And because of its pervasive presence, the divisions that arise through sport carry a social significance that reach far beyond sport itself. The very fact that sport appears to be outside the bounds of 'real life', and thus outside real social relations, heightens its power in constructing an extreme notion of the social order as a hierarchy based on difference.

This chapter examines the relationship between sport and gender. Its focus is on the significance of sport in contributing to the gender order – that is, the social relations between males and females. Here we are concerned with two things – how gender relations are evident within contemporary sport, and also how sport itself influences contemporary gender relations. Our primary concern is to gain an understanding of how gender is played out within sport, by examining the extent to which one sex (male) is more powerful, more influential and simply more present within sport than the other (female), and the processes through which this occurs. However, we shall also look beyond sport, to consider the broader social significance of the uneven gender relations that are constructed within it.

The scale and visibility of modern sport make it an extraordinarily significant social institution, and one that is well positioned to transmit its values and ideologies. A core value within sport is its construction of a form of masculinity that elevates male experience over female. A wide range of scholars have depicted sport as a particularly powerful setting for the construction of masculinity (e.g. Birrell and Theberge, 1994a, 1994b; Bryson, 1987, 1990; Connell, 1987; Hall, 1993; Hargreaves, 1994; Messner and Sabo, 1990; Willis, 1982). Whitson (1990) described sport as one of the central sites in the social production of masculinity, while Connell (1987) considered it to be the institution that most systematically promotes images of ideal masculinity. The close identification of sport with masculinity places 'non-masculine' groups at the margins of sport, and in doing so, undermines their position in a society in which sport is highly valued.

THE FEMALE EXPERIENCE OF SPORT: A HISTORY OF EXCLUSION

This section explores the rationales for women's exclusion from sport; the history of opposition to women's sports participation; how gender discrimination is embedded in the structures of sport; and the contemporary significance of this historical legacy.

Throughout the world, there is a lengthy history of sport being seen as incompatible with feminine qualities. Three rationales have been given for opposing women's participation:

1 *the medical rationale*, that women are physiologically unsuited to sporting activity and may be damaged by it;
2 *the aesthetic rationale*, that women engaging in sport are an unattractive spectacle; and
3 *the social rationale*, that the qualities and behaviours associated with sport are contrary to 'real' femininity.

The history of women's involvement in sport is therefore one of substantial exclusion: through formal or informal means, women have been debarred from equitable access to sports experiences.

Change has clearly taken place: few people would today argue that it is 'unnatural' for women to take part in sport. In Britain the slow acceptance of women into sporting activity became evident from the late nineteenth century, when the development of sport within educational institutions lent impetus to women's participation in sport and physical recreation. By the outbreak of the First World War, there was scarcely a sport that women had not tried; nonetheless, participation was still considerably limited by prevailing definitions of femininity, and sport remained an unusual, almost extraordinary activity for women to engage in (Theberge, 1990).

Progress came slowly in the face of opposition both within and beyond sport. In France, the churches formally opposed women taking part: 'Even the Pope spoke against women's participation in some competitive sports events' (McPherson et al., 1989: 227). The sports establishment itself displayed substantial resistance to women's involvement. Pierre de Coubertin, founder of the modern Olympics and influential in international sport, publicly opposed women's participation in competitive sport well into the 1930s, arguing that women should be expelled from the Olympic Games, and even claiming that their Olympic participation was illegal (McPherson et al., 1989). Opposition to women's participation in the Olympics was not helped by some unfortunate displays when women participated in the Games in events in which they appeared to have little experience. The inaugural Olympic women's 800 metre race in 1928 was a débâcle:

Both of Canada's entries in that 800 metres event finished the race, and this in itself was quite an achievement. It was the first time that such an event had been held for women, and most of the entrants were not prepared for the gruelling distance. Of the eleven starters, only six finished, and most of those collapsed at the end of the race. (Schrodt, 1976: 40)

De Coubertin's efforts to remove women from the Olympics more than 20 years after they had been admitted gives some indication of the strength of feeling on the issue. Although primarily concerned with women's exclusion from public competitive sport, De Coubertin's argument that their participation was unaesthetic and contrary to the Laws of Nature went further. His ultimate view was that women's function within sport was not to compete themselves, but to applaud the male competitor: 'At the Olympic Games their primary role should be, as in the ancient tournaments, to crown the victor with laurels' (De Coubertin, 1935; in McPherson et al., 1989: 227).

Attitudes to women's involvement in sport have become more receptive as expectations about their position in society have become less restrictive, but traditional notions of what is 'appropriate' are still influential. Many sports continue to be seen as less suitable for women than men, and female participation in the types of activities in which women have traditionally participated (e.g. tennis, swimming, gymnastics) is generally seen as more compatible with femininity than their participation in 'male' sports (e.g. football, rugby, cricket). It is men rather than women who feel most strongly about this, however: they hold more conventional views about how suitable different sports are for each sex. This has a special significance in view of the widely recognised male dominance of the power structure of British sport.

The masculinity of sport is a product of the way in which sport has been institutionalised and developed, rather than a reflection of the intrinsic qualities of sporting activity. In itself, sport is no more ideally suited to men than to women (Coakley, 1990), but has been comprehensively masculinised through its history of male control. Throughout history men have controlled sport, used it for their purposes, and shaped it to fit their abilities. The simple legacy of this is that gender inequities are inherent in sports structures today. They are most evident on the international stage, where women not only still compete in smaller numbers than men, but face specific restrictions on the events in which they are allowed to take part. The sports establishment's reluctance to remove increasingly anomalous restrictions on women's competitive sport has shown just how resistant sport can be to the supposed attitudinal shift of the late twentieth century.

In comparison with earlier times, women's involvement in sport has undoubtedly increased – but historical comparisons can be flattering. What is at issue today is not how women's sports involvement compares with that of previous generations of females, but how it contrasts with that of the contemporary male. The current situation certainly demonstrates 'improvement' vis-à-vis earlier eras, but pro-feminist analyses of sport of the 1980s and 1990s suggested that 'the female in sport is still considered a woman in a man's territory' (Birrell, cited in Boutilier and San Giovanni, 1983: 80). We now turn our attention to the evidence of women and girls' current relationship to sport, and the issues that arise from it.

THE FEMALE EXPERIENCE OF SPORT: THE CONTEMPORARY PICTURE

Sports participation by women and girls is lower than participation by men and boys in virtually every country in the world. The differential between the sexes varies from country to country, and there are now a handful of countries in which the differences are only marginal. In most, however, they are marked, and in some cases, quite extreme. The overall pattern is unequivocal: females do not participate in sport on the same scale as males, and in most countries there is a wide gap between the sexes.

In Britain, differences in sports participation between the sexes begin to emerge in secondary school years. Initially the differences are not great – young people in Britain generally have high levels of sports participation, and during school years the gap between the sexes is only about 3 per cent. However, school sport appears artificially to inflate girls' 'natural' sports participation levels: outside school, girls are much less likely to take part in sport than are boys. Girls are less likely than boys to be frequent participants in sport, more likely than them to be non-participants, and more likely to give up sport when they leave school.

These and other differences lay a pattern that becomes even more marked in adulthood. Throughout their lives, women are less likely than men to take part in sport; women who do participate, on average participate less frequently than men, and the range of sports in which women engage is narrower than that for men. There are also

qualitative differences in the type of sports participation, for girls and women show a preference for less structured forms of sport, and are less likely than males to take part in competitive sports – especially 'traditional' team sports. The areas that do attract women, and have shown marked increases in the last 20 years, are exercise and keep-fit activities with a strong body-shaping component.

It is therefore unsurprising that taking part in sport on a regular basis is a minority activity for British women. In 1996, only 39 per cent of women aged 16 or over had participated in sport on at least one occasion in the four weeks prior to interview, compared to 58 per cent of men (Office for National Statistics, 1998). Women's sports participation also declines more quickly with age than does that of men, and is much more susceptible to the impact of family and household responsibilities than men's. There is a particularly strong impact on women's sports participation when their household contains a child under the age of 5, while men's participation is much less affected. Women's social class also appears more significant for their sports participation than for men's: the gap between male and female participation rates widens going down the socio-economic scale; among manual workers, women's participation rate is only three-quarters of men's (Table 5.1). Overall, women's

Table 5.1   *Sports participation rates by sex and occupational group, 1996: % participation four weeks before interview*

Occupational group	Men aged 16+	Women aged 16+
Professional	78	85[1]
Employers and managerial	72	62
Intermediate and junior non-manual	78	63
Skilled manual	66	53
Semi-skilled manual	66	48
Unskilled manual	54	42

[1]This figure is an unexplained anomaly. It exceeded the forecast by nearly 20 per cent.
Source: ONS (1998; Table 13.13)

sports participation is more sensitive than men's to the impact of other social structural constraints, including age, social class, ethnicity and disability. It is only women who are relatively favourably positioned within the social structure who come close to closing the sports participation gap with men.

This pattern of female under-representation is even more acute in elite sport. Although female involvement at the top level of performance has been transformed over the last hundred years, stark inequalities remain. The number of sports in which women can compete is still lower than for men, and there are fewer single-sex sports for females. Overall, women continue to be a small minority of participants at the major international games, and there are still many countries which participate with no female representatives at all.

Women's relationship to contemporary sport is therefore a mixed picture. Comparisons with males appear discouraging, for there is little question that sport plays a smaller part in women's lives than in men's, and appears less accessible to them. Seen over time, however, there is little doubt that this situation is changing. In Britain, absolute levels of female sports participation have been rising since the 1970s, especially in health and fitness activities. There have also been rises in female participation in the sports that have traditionally been the preserves of males. Yet by most measures, women's participation remains low in absolute as well as relative terms: for example, despite the increased participation in fitness activities, most have physical activity levels below the threshold required for health benefits. Women and girls appear particularly distant from the commodified sports product of the contemporary global economy – the high-profile, competitive, commercial and professional world of sport that dominates the media. We now move on to examine the barriers that appear to inhibit full access to sport by females.

CHOICE OR CONSTRAINT? EXPLANATIONS FOR FEMALE UNDER-REPRESENTATION IN SPORT

It has long been recognised that women and girls are under-represented in sport – but it was not until the late twentieth century that the assumption that sport is 'naturally' more suited to men came under sustained attack. Since then, the processes through which sport has been constructed as a determinedly masculine sphere have been subject to increasing scrutiny. The result has been a wealth of analyses of how women and girls are marginalised in sport; these address factors both within sport itself, and in the broader pattern of social relations in which sport is situated. In this section we examine both types of explanation and the interrelationship between them. We start with the broad picture – the social context of sport, and the societal pressures that contemporary patterns of gender relations exert on females.

Gender differentiation in social relations is a universal phenomenon which takes place within the contemporary patriarchy. In the public and private spheres, women lack the power, resources, autonomy and sense of self that males possess. This imbalance is a product of the gender relations between the sexes and strongly influences the sexes' differing experience of sport. As we have seen, women participate in sport less than men. Moreover they participate in different types of sport to men, although the range of sports in which women take part is broadening. However, for the most part, women participate in those conform to conventional notions of femininity. Furthermore, the areas of greatest growth in women's participation – i.e. fitness and exercise activities – are those which most obviously directly contribute to the attainment of the idealised female body image. The predominant pattern of female participation is therefore very much in line with traditional views on appropriate 'feminine' behaviour, suggesting that the female socialisation process continues to promote attitudes and values that influence women's and girls' relationship to sport.

Gendered expectations are instilled in children at a very early age. Parents, as a result of their own sex-role socialisation, transmit gendered values to their children that reproduce gender stereotypes (Greendorfer, 1983). The differences start almost from birth, when baby girls are more frequently touched, handled and talked to by their parents than baby boys, and are generally treated more protectively. Boys are allowed to be more adventurous and are more often allowed to explore their environment without intervention from their parents. This contributes to girls becoming less independent in their behaviour than boys, and as children's play behaviour develops, this sex typing becomes more marked. Girls are encouraged to play quietly like 'good' girls, and discouraged from taking part in activities that are rough or noisy. In contrast, parents may foster physically active play in boys and discourage more passive, 'girlish' behaviour. By the time they have reached school age, many children have learnt that physically active play is appropriate for boys, but less so for girls. A close association has been established between sport and masculinity, which also places it in opposition to supposedly 'feminine' behaviour.

In Britain it is during secondary school and adolescence that girls appear to turn away decisively from sport and to develop quite negative attitudes to it. There is a drastic decline in the proportion of girls who enjoy PE in school, which drops from 74 per cent at primary school age, to less than a third (29 per cent) by school-leaving age (Rowe, 1995). Some of the blame for this has been laid at the door of secondary school experiences of physical education, which are notably less successful at instilling a long-term interest in sport in girls than in boys. However, school experiences are only a part of a broader set of influences that affect adolescents. Many teenage girls simply do not associate sports activity with the femininity to which they aspire; in fact, sport and physical activity are more commonly seen as a distinguishing trademark of the 'unfeminine' girl.

Girls' dismissal of sport is in strong contrast to boys' affinity with it. The link between masculinity and sport is a close and enduring one: although most adult males give up active participation in sport as they grow older, they remain within the sports culture. The sports in which boys participate at school are those that are replicated and exalted in later life as major, prestigious, national and international institutions. Indeed, continued involvement in the world of sport is part of a rite of passage into a communal masculine adulthood. In contrast, girls' school experiences of sport tend to lack relevance to adult life: the activities traditionally offered to schoolgirls do not enjoy either the mass participation or elite status of boys' football, cricket and rugby, and role models are few. Sport is barely visible as a component of womanhood, and the transition to female adulthood is more likely to be seen as a time to leave sport behind than to continue with it.

This is reinforced as women reach adulthood and encounter widespread exposure to attitudes about their expected role. The need or wish to establish a heterosexual partnership as a central aspect of 'being female' encourages women to adopt behaviour deemed appropriate to attracting a male partner, combining 'good girl' behaviour with feminine sexuality expressed through an attractive appearance. The emphasis on female bodies as decorative and passive, rather than active and vigorous, draws women to leisure forms that reproduce these qualities and away from those, such as sport, that appear to contradict them.

The view that sport is contradictory to femininity has proved very persistent but is at odds with studies of women who do participate. Far from detracting from their personal development, sport appears to offer women substantial benefits. Those who take part in it experience little role conflict and report positive changes including increased self-esteem, personal development, physical power and well-being. Talbot (1989) has described the multiple benefits that accrued as allowing a woman to 'be herself through sport'. In fact, a number of authors have argued that this can contribute to a more general feeling for women of exercising control over their own lives and destinies (e.g. Deem, 1986). Participating in sport may therefore have broader implications for women's lives, and may nurture qualities that enable women to challenge their general subordination within a patriarchal society. Changes in the views of femininity may make such experiences more accessible to women; there is evidence that sport is being incorporated within models of femininity to some degree, with 'well-honed athletic female bodies now openly embraced as sexually

attractive according to heterosexual criteria' (Hargreaves, 1994: 169).

To a considerable extent, however, sporting qualities continue to be classed as 'masculine', with 'femininity' seen as the antithesis of sport. The influence of traditional notions of 'real' womanhood as heterosexual femininity thus remains very strong. Kay (2000) has suggested that it is especially influential on women's experiences of sport in countries and cultures where gender roles are most strongly differentiated. Kay drew on European sports participation data and analyses of international family-related social policy to explore the relationship between the two. She found substantial correlation: countries where social policy promoted strong gender differentiation in adult roles had the highest differentiation in sports participation, while those that made little distinction between the sexes, exhibited much smaller differentials in male–female sports participation rates (see Box 5.1).

Broad societal pressures are not the only factors that inhibit female presence in sport. We now examine the evidence that sport itself is a strongly masculine institution, and explore the implications this has for women's and girls' involvement.

GENDER INEQUITY IN THE PRODUCTION OF SPORT

Women's under-representation in the organisational and administrative structures of sport is a worldwide phenomenon. In comparison to men, women hold fewer positions of power in sport, and they hold positions of less power. In Britain they are under-represented across the full spectrum of sports provision, including the physical education profession, local government leisure services, sports governance, regional and

Box 5.1   Case study: How gender ideology influences sport

'Gender ideology' is a powerful, diverse, complex and pervasive phenomenon – but it is also remarkably hard to pin down. One way of doing this is to borrow the approaches that social policy analysts use to address gender issues.

Social policies are implemented by governments to respond to and influence social behaviour. For example, government legislation can make it relatively easy or hard for couples to divorce, depending on how much importance is attached to upholding 'traditional' families. Policies take account of public (electoral) opinion, and are therefore a broad indication of a nation's current consensus on its social institutions.

Family-related social policies contain assumptions about adult men's and women's roles, and can be used as a yardstick of a country's gender ideology. A key issue for policy analysts is the extent to which such policies encourage mothers to either stay at home to care for their children when they are young ('traditional' gender relations, with strong male–female differentiation) or to combine parenting with employment ('modern' gender relations: low male–female differentiation). We can use analyses that categorise countries on this basis, to see whether patterns of male–female sports participation seem to be related to broader gender differentiation in society.

The data in Table 5.2 show us that countries that support 'modern' gender roles, with relatively low gender differentiation, are also those where sports participation is most equal between the sexes. Countries that encourage mothers' employment have much smaller differentials in male–female sports participation rates than countries in which policy encourages mothers to remain at home to care for their children. In Finland and Sweden, low gender differentiation in social policy is reflected in sports participation: 'overall' sports participation rates are much less differentiated between men and women than in all of the 'high' countries, while 'regular' participation rates are marginally higher for women than men. At the other extreme, the two countries with the highest gender differentiation in social policy (Italy and the UK) also have the biggest differentials in overall participation rates for males and females, although not so markedly for regular participation. Overall, these patterns indicate a broad if imprecise correspondence between gender differentiation in sports participation, and broader gender differentiation in a country.

national policy-making organisations, and as representatives in international sports organisations. In this section we look at the gender bias in the structure of sport, and efforts to counter it through gender equity policies.

The sports structure

Whannel's (1983) suggestion that male dominance was built into the structure of British sport, in lasting form, fits well with the

Table 5.2 *Gender differentiation in social policy and sports participation*

A Gender differentiation in family-related policy		B Female sports participation rates (%)		C Female sports participation rates: difference over male (%)		D Female sports participation rates as % of male rate	
		All	Regular	All	Regular	All	Regular
Low	Finland	78	72	−5	+2	94	103
	Sweden	70	59	0	+1	100	102
Medium	Netherlands	61	27	−2	−9	97	75
High	Italy	15	9	−17	−4	47	69
	UK	60	21	−12	−13	83	62

Notes:

(a) The categorisation of countries' social policies (column A) is based on Gornick et al. (1997). The data used in columns B, C and D are based on Gratton (1999).

(b) The Compass project devised seven categories of sports participation. Here, 'regular' sports participation excludes 'irregular', 'occasional' and 'non-participant' participation.

(c) In column C, a positive figure (e.g. +2) indicates that the female participation rate is higher than the male; a negative figure (e.g. −5) indicates that the female participation rate is lower than the male.

evidence of women's under-representation in sports organisations. Until the 1990s no woman had been appointed to direct any of the Sports Council's national sports centres, only one had headed a Sports Council regional office, and only two out of the 14 senior positions at Sports Council headquarters had been held by women. The exception at national level was the National Coaching Foundation, whose Director was a woman. However, in coaching as a whole, women were greatly under-represented, especially at higher levels of responsibility. Women were even less visible in the sports media, particularly at management level, and were very much in the minority in sports-related research, where the use of concepts that did not incorporate the experiences of females risked judging females as marginal, deviant or comparative (Talbot, 1986). The one area where women

were better represented was sports development, a relatively new area of professional practice less bounded by traditions.

Female under-representation in the structure of sport is not only inequitable in its own right but has far-reaching consequences for women's involvement in sport as participants. This has been particularly evident at elite level, where women still face formal restrictions on their participation. Towards the end of the twentieth century, it looked as if these were disappearing: when the marathon became available to women in the 1984 Olympics, the argument that women's sport was limited by physiology appeared to have been laid to rest. Yet well into the 1990s, women continued to be excluded in the Olympics from the 3000 m steeplechase, 20 km walk, the 50 km walk and the pole vault, by a male sports hierarchy claiming to be acting protectively with women's best interests at heart (Coakley, 2001). Alongside this came the introduction in the 1980s of synchronised swimming and rhythmic gymnastics, which appeared to many to do more to reinforce the stigmas associated with women's sports than to challenge them (Theberge, 1990). By the end of the twentieth century it was clear that a male-dominated sports structure had failed to provide women with an equal basis for involvement. The advancement allowed to women had too often been grudging and piecemeal, coming only as a result of confrontation and struggle (Hargreaves, 1994), rather than fundamental attitudinal shifts within sport.

Rather perversely for an age of supposed gender awareness, the male stranglehold on sport seemed to be increasing. Although women's sports participation has risen, their involvement in sport as providers has dropped (Sports Council, 1992). In Britain, there has been a long-term decline in women's influence in physical education (Talbot, 1986), and considerable deterioration in women's representation elsewhere, for example on national governing bodies. The reasons lie in the increased professionalisation and bureaucratisation of sport, which has attracted men to newly salaried posts in women's sport that were previously filled on a voluntary basis by women. Further tensions have arisen between efforts to promote gender equity in sport, and initiatives to establish performance systems. Whitson and Macintosh (1990) found that in Canada, emphasis on high performance ultimately overrode the pursuit of equity-related objectives, despite these being explicit social goals of Sport Canada itself, and of the Canadian government. While traditional attitudes may be lessening, progress towards gender equity in sport faces renewed obstacles in the modernising forces that are driving the development of sport.

The overall pattern of women's involvement in sports production is therefore clear: women are under-represented in all areas, and their under-representation is most acute at higher levels of responsibility, including those for higher levels of performance. The resulting lack of female presence has not only been a disincentive to other women to become involved in sports production, but has led to isolation and relative powerlessness of those already involved. The lack of women involved in the provision of sport is regarded by feminist analysts as contributing to the 'maleness' of sport as a whole which alienates many females. It is this, rather than technical issues such as poor facilities and inappropriate programming, which most fully contributes to women's invisibility in sport. The institutional and organisational characteristics of sport are therefore central to the women and sport 'problem', and imply that women's access to sport requires their increased representation in all aspects of its provision.

Gender equity policies in sport

Many countries have now tried to address women's under-representation in sport by adopting formal policies to enhance their position. The USA predated most other nations in addressing female under-representation in sport through the use of Title IX of the 1972 Education Amendments Act. By the mid-1990s, Canada had implemented federal and provincial legislation to build gender equity into all levels of the structure of the Canadian Sport Coalition, established in 1992; while in Australia, programmes for promoting women's sports were operating in every state and territory by the early 1990s (Hargreaves, 1994). In Europe, the work of transnational institutions such as the European Sports

Conference and the Council of Europe has supported and encouraged gender equity efforts within individual nation states.

Over this period there has been significant development in the policy approaches adopted. Early policies tended to concentrate on the participation aspect of involvement, and came under criticism from feminist critics who argued that these were a superficial response to a deeply embedded problem. In Britain, 'top-down' policies that tried to 'get women into sport' were criticised by authors such as Green et al. (1990) as failing to recognise let alone address the fundamental issues affecting women. Above all, critics stressed that policies that focused on practical barriers to participation did little to challenge the underlying assumption that sport was an intrinsically masculine activity. They argued that the only effective strategy for addressing the root causes of women's alienation was to lessen sport's 'maleness' by giving women power within sport structures and organisations.

This was the approach underpinning the first formal British policy for Women and Sport, introduced in the early 1990s. The policy explicitly recognised female under-representation in sports organisations as a fundamental barrier to gender equity, and advocated women's equal involvement in all aspects and at all levels of sports participation, provision and management. It set detailed aims and objectives for major improvement in women's access to power and influence in the structure of sport, and was an explicit challenge to male power in the existing organisational and administrative structure of UK sport. The policy's successful implementation would result in far-reaching change within the sports establishment; however, it was dependent on voluntary action by the very organisations in which change is sought, and here it became evident that progress might be slow.

It is increasingly evident that in sport as elsewhere, formal policies do not guarantee effective action. The problem is well illustrated by the experience in the United States in the 1970s, when Title IX triggered a rapid professionalisation in women's sport that led to many men taking posts that had previously been held in an amateur capacity by women. Although female sports participation rates rose significantly, women's power within the sports establishment weakened rather than strengthened. Fasting (1993) reported another mixed picture when she reviewed European countries' progress towards the 'women and sport' goals adopted by the European Sports Conference in 1991. Although there was evidence of a generally receptive response, there was a considerable gap between intent and achievement: most countries (14 out of 24) had made progress in less than half of the agreed areas. McKay's (1997) in-depth analysis of resistance to 'affirmative action' initiatives in sports organisations in Australia, Canada and New Zealand confirmed these difficulties.

To date, policies to promote gender equity have too often foundered in the face of organisational and societal cultures in which gender differentiation was entrenched. We now turn to an institution that has a pervasive influence on this gendered construction of modern sport – the media.

GENDER AND THE SPORTS MEDIA

The way in which sport is portrayed is influential in limiting its appeal to women. Media coverage has been a major contributor to perceptions of sport's limited relevance to women. Inequality in the quantity and quality of coverage of male and female sport appears to have a long history. Lenskyj (1987) reviewed media views of physical activity for Canadian women between 1890 and 1930, and discovered that the media delivered distorted reports of women's athleticism. Rather than encouraging women to take up sport, some writers appealed to the growing interest in physical activity in reminding women of the health benefits of vigorous housework activities more commonly associated with the female role.

Both the media and women's involvement in sport have undergone profound changes in the last century; however, contemporary coverage of sport remains discriminatory and contains overwhelming masculine bias. Once again, the growing professionalisation and commercialisation of sport have encouraged this, fostering a portrayal of sport most likely to appeal to mass audiences. More coverage has been given to men's sport than to women's; there has been a general emphasis on sport's masculine characteristics; and coverage of women's sport has been highly selective, focusing on its most obviously feminine forms. As a result, women commonly receive less than 10 per cent of sports coverage, and often less than 5 per cent, with women's sport usually only being reported at the very highest levels of performance. Coverage of men's sport is not only more plentiful, but covers a wider range of performance levels and a wider range of sports. There are also differences in the tone of coverage: men's performance is more likely to be described in terms of 'strength', while women receive more attributions of weakness. News stories about women's sport also often focus on titillation and human interest rather than on performance and achievement. Moreover they emphasise sexual attractiveness, personal relationships and/or questions of sexuality.

A marked trend of recent years has been the increased coverage of non-sporting attributes of the more obviously attractive sportswomen, through features that focus exclusively on their appearance and personal life. One of the issues that arises from this is the extent to which female performers collude with, exploit and/or actively seek out coverage that capitalises on their non-playing attributes. As leading sports personalities of both sexes assume greater status as general media 'personalities' and derive a growing proportion of their earnings from their non-sporting activities, the attribution of responsibility for stereotypical coverage of sportswomen becomes more complex. The implications for women's sport as a whole are also hard to assess. On the one hand, these developments have increased the potential earning power of a select band of elite sportswomen. Set against this is the negative impact of coverage that many feel degrades and trivialises women's sport, and reinforces the very notions of restrictive femininity that involvement in sport can help women to challenge.

Media influence on sport is not confined to its sports-specific reportage. A wide range of media products contribute to the portrayal of sport as an element of men's and women's lifestyles and identities. Kay's (1999) study of the 'sport-related' content of 'general' magazines for men and women showed that sport was deeply embedded in the construction of maleness promoted in men's magazines, but had a minimal presence in the representation of femaleness in magazines for women. Where sport was presented to women, there was an overwhelming emphasis on body-shaping exercise activities which concurred with stereotypical notions of decorative femininity. There were also differences in the extent to which men and women's magazines featured sport as a cultural product for mass consumption. Men's magazines gave extensive exposure to the internationalised professional sports that dominate sports broadcasting and newspaper reportage; magazine coverage for women did not feature these sports at all. In some cases articles on fitness exercises went so far as to offer women 'sport-substitute' physical activities, to allow them to gain the benefits of sport without actually having to take part in it. The overriding message was that even in the late 1990s, 'real' sport was not for women.

The media play a significant part in the construction of the ideology of women's sport, and are a major contributor to perceptions of sport as a marginal activity for women. This reinforces notions that women's sport has less intrinsic value than men's, and that taking part in sport is only 'natural' for women when it involves activities that concur with conventional female gender-role images. The lack of coverage of women's sport at performance and excellence levels not only undermines women competing at these levels, but deprives all females of role models to counter these views.

CONCLUSION

Sport is fundamental to the contemporary construction of gender differentiation. In an era when sport is established as a global phenomenon with a global audience, the impact of co-opting sport for males and excluding women from full sports citizenship is all the greater. The particular significance of sport, however, is not that it is per se a site for gender difference, but that it is uniquely positioned to foster arguments that such difference is natural.

The significance of sport in naturalising gender difference, and thus legitimising gender relations that privilege men over women, lies in the extent to which sport reinforces widely held assumptions that

relationships of power between the sexes are based on 'natural' or biological factors (Birrell and Theberge, 1994a). Men's measurably superior performance in sports trials of strength and speed, and the construction of sports protocol around their physical aptitudes in more complex game-codes, 'proves' female inferiority. Sport therefore delivers 'apparently incontrovertible' evidence of men's superior command of highly valued and visible skills, and by implication depicts females as less skilful, less capable and of lesser value (Bryson, 1987). Women's social inferiority is seen not as a product of social processes such as gender stereotyping, but as a natural extension of women's traditional physical inferiority (Birrell and Theberge, 1994a). The cultural origins of patriarchal hegemony are thus obscured: 'An ideological view comes to be deposited in our culture as a commonsense assumption – of course women are different and inferior' (Willis, 1982: 130).

The particular power of sport in upholding gendered power relations lies in the closeness of sport to issues of men and women's embodiment and physicality. During the 1990s, theories of women's oppression have increasingly recognised how physicality and the control of women through the control of their bodies underpin the reproduction of inequitable gender relations (Birrell and Theberge, 1994b). Control of women's bodies, through the promotion of idealised standards of physical beauty and compulsory heterosexuality, is one of the primary mechanisms for control of women in patriarchal societies. However, the significance of gendered influences on men's and women's relationship with their own physicality often goes unrecognised: 'everyone has difficulty acknowledging the extent to which the body is a social construction' (Holmlund, 1994: 300). Bodies are, however, central to our sense of who we are and how we relate to the world (Whitson, 1990), and masculinising and feminising practices associated with the body lie at the heart of the social construction of masculinity and femininity. The maintenance of gender differentiation in sport is therefore instrumental in reinforcing the established structure of inequitable gender relations which sustains hegemony.

Theorists believe that sporting practices reinforce hegemony in the rest of society in a number of ways. Sport upholds the primacy of heterosexual men by linking maleness with highly valued and visible skills, and by sanctioning the male's use of aggression, force and/or violence (Bryson, 1987).

The paradox is that the exaggerated patterns of sex differentiation that occur within sport 'have a deceptive aura of common sense and naturalness' (Lenskyj, 1986: 144), and are more commonly recognised and accepted than contested and rejected. Sport is 'what boys and men naturally do, and what girls and women do not do, or do at peril to their own identities' (Birrell and Theberge, 1994b: 344). Sport therefore defines maleness as being in contrast to femaleness, and in this way makes a fundamental contribution to the construction of gender identities and gender relations that are based on assumptions of difference, which in turn perpetuate structures of disadvantage and exclusion.

Chapter summary

- Women's under-representation in sport has a long history and is closely associated with traditional views of gender relations. Historically women have faced formal and informal restrictions on their sports participation, and have played little role in the production of sport.
- Although social attitudes to men and women have become less restrictive, the modern female socialisation process continues to emphasise a form of femininity that gives little value to sport. At the start of the twenty-first century, women still occupy a marginal position in sport in virtually every country in the world.
- Societal disincentives for females to be involved in sport are reinforced by resistance within the sports establishment. Men dominate all areas of sports provision including the sports media, creating a masculine ethos that pervades sport. Policies that promote gender equity within sport can face considerable resistance, and may be negated by the stronger forces of professionalisation which characterise modern sport.
- The status of sport as a major social institution lends a special significance to women's subordinate position within it. Sport naturalises differences between men and women as biologically determined and thus contributes to the construction of discriminatory gender relations. Addressing gender discrimination within sport offers the potential to challenge gender disadvantage as a whole.

Further reading

The best study of gender and sport with substantial British coverage is by Jennifer Hargreaves (1994). This provides a stimulating, comprehensive and highly accessible account of women's relationship to sport which covers theoretical, historical and sociological perspectives, includes recreational and elite sport, and addresses both the participation and provision aspects of these issues. It is well complemented by Hargreaves (2000), which has a very different focus, being concerned with women from different places in the world and different cultures, and minority (lesbian and disabled) groups of women.

Several North American texts provide different levels of coverage of the topic. Of particular merit are Coakley (2001), Costa and Guthrie (1994) and Birrell and Cole (1994). Birrell and Cole's text has a fuller coverage of social science contributions including very detailed coverage of media dimensions; Costa and Guthrie's book includes sports science content.

REFERENCES

Birrell, S. (1983) 'The psychological dimensions of female athletic participation', in M.A. Boutilier and L. San Giovanni (eds), *The Sporting Woman*. Champaign, IL: Human Kinetics, pp. 49–92.

Birrell, S. and Cole, C. (eds) (1994) *Women, Sport and Culture*. Champaign, IL: Human Kinetics.

Birrell, S. and Theberge, N. (1994a) 'Feminist resistance and transformation in sport', in D.M. Costa and S.R. Guthrie (eds), *Women and Sport: Interdisciplinary Perspectives*. Champaign, IL: Human Kinetics, pp. 361–76.

Birrell, S. and Theberge, N. (1994b) 'Ideological control of women in sport', in D.M. Costa and S.R. Guthrie (eds), *Women and Sport: Interdisciplinary Perspectives*. Champaign, IL: Human Kinetics, pp. 341–59.

Boutilier, M.A. and San Giovanni, L. (eds) (1983) *The Sporting Woman*. Champaign, IL: Human Kinetics.

Bryson, L. (1987) 'Sport and the maintenance of male hegemony', *Women's Studies International Forum*, 10: 349–60.

Bryson, L. (1990) 'Challenges to male hegemony in sport', in M.A. Messner and D.F. Sabo (eds), *Sport, Men and the Gender Order*, Champaign, IL: Human Kinetics, pp. 173–84.

Coakley, J. (1990) *Sport in Society: Issues and Controversies*. St Louis: Times Mirror/Mosby College Publishing.

Coakley, J. (2001) *Sport in Society: Issues and Controversies*. 7th edn. New York: McGraw-Hill.

Connell, R.W. (1987) *Gender and Power: Society, the Person and Sexual Politics*. Cambridge: Polity Press in association with B. Blackwell.

Costa, D.M. and Guthrie, S.R. (eds) (1994) *Women and Sport: Interdisciplinary Perspectives*. Champaign, IL: Human Kinetics.

Deem, R. (1986) *All Work and No Play? The Sociology of Women and Leisure*. Milton Keynes: Open University Press.

Duquin, M.E. (1982) 'The importance of sport in building women's potential', *Journal of Physical Education, Recreation and Dance*, 53 (3): 18–36.

Fasting, K. (1993) *Women and Sport: Monitoring Progress towards Equality*. Oslo: The Norwegian Confederation of Sports Women's Committee.

Gornick, J.C. Meyers, M.K. and Ross, K.E. (1997) 'Supporting the employment of mothers: policy variation across fourteen welfare states', *Journal of European Social Policy*, 7 (1): 45–70.

Gratton, C. (1999) *Compass 1999: a Project Seeking the Co-ordinated Monitoring of Participation in Sports in Europe*. London: UK Sports Council.

Green, E., Hebron, S. and Woodward, D. (1990) *Women's Leisure, What Leisure?* London: Macmillan.

Greendorfer, S. (1983) 'Shaping the female athlete: the impact of the family', in M.A. Boutilier and L. San Giovanni (eds), *The Sporting Woman*. Champaign, IL: Human Kinetics, pp. 135–56.

Hall, M.A. (1993) 'Gender and sport in the 1990s: feminism, culture, and politics', *Sports Science Review*, 2: 48–68.

Hargreaves, J. (1994) *Sporting Females: Critical Issues in the History and Sociology of Women's Sports*. London and New York: Routledge.

Hargreaves, J. (2000) *Heroines of Sport: the Politics of Difference and Identity*. London: Routledge.

Holmlund, C.A. (1994) 'Visible difference and flex appeal: the body, sex, sexuality and race in the Pumping Iron films', in S. Birrell and C.L. Cole (eds), *Women, Sport and Culture*. Champaign, IL: Human Kinetics, pp. 299–315.

Kay, T.A. (1999) 'Gender ideologies in magazine portrayal of sport: King Eric v. the Billion $ Babe', *Journal of European Area Studies*, 7 (2): 157–76.

Kay, T.A. (2000) 'Leisure, gender and the family: the influence of social policy context', *Leisure Studies*, 19 (4): 247–65.

Lenskyj, H. (1986) *Out of Bounds*. Toronto: Women's Press.

Lenskyj, H. (1987) 'Canadian women and physical activity 1890–1930: media views', in J.A. Mangan and R. Park (eds), *From 'Fair Sex' to Feminism: Sport and the Socialisation of Women in the Industrial and Post-industrial Eras*. London: Frank Cass.

McKay, J. (1997) *Managing Gender: Affirmative Action and Organizational Power in Australian, Canadian and New Zealand Sport*. Albany, NY: State University of New York.

McPherson, B.D., Curtis, J.E. and Loy, J.W. (1989) *The Social Significance of Sport*. Champaign, IL: Human Kinetics.

Messner, M.A. and Sabo, D.F. (eds) (1990) *Sport, Men and the Gender Order*. Champaign, IL: Human Kinetics.

Office for National Statistics (1998) *Living in Britain: General Household Survey 1996*. London: HMSO.

Rowe, N.F. (1995) 'Young people and sport', Internal Sports Council Discussion Paper (unpublished).

Schrodt, B. (1976) 'Canadian women at the Olympic Games 1924–1972', *Canadian Association for Health, Physical Education and Recreation Journal*, 42 (4): 34–42.

Sports Council (1992) *Women and Sport: A Consultation Document*. London: Sports Council.

Talbot, M. (1986) 'Gender and physical education', *British Journal of Physical Education*, 17: 120–2.

Talbot, M. (1989) 'Being herself through sport'. Paper to the Leisure Studies Association Conference 'Leisure, Health and Wellbeing', Leeds.

Theberge, N. (1990) 'Women and the Olympics: a consideration of gender, sport and social change'. Paper presented to the International Symposium, 'Sport – The Third Millennium', Quebec, Canada.

Whannel, G. (1983) *Blowing the Whistle: the Politics of Sport*. London: Pluto.

Whitson, D. (1990) 'Sport in the social construction of masculinity', in M.A. Messner and D.F. Sabo (eds), *Sport, Men and the Gender Order*. Champaign, IL: Human Kinetics, pp. 19–30.

Whitson, D. and Macintosh, D. (1990) 'Equity versus high performance in Canadian amateur sport', *Canadian Association for Health, Physical Education and Recreation Journal*, May–June: 27–30.

Willis, P. (1982) 'Women in sport and ideology', in J.A. Hargreaves (ed.), *Sport, Culture and Ideology*. London: Routledge & Kegan Paul, pp. 117–35.

6

Sport and Disability

NIGEL THOMAS

Overview

→ Theorising disability
→ The emergence of disability sport
→ Physical education and youth sport
→ Organisational and policy development in the UK
→ Elite competition, classification and the Paralympics
→ Perspectives on disability sport
→ Conclusion

The Paralympic Games held in October 2000 provided an illustration of the quality and excitement in elite-level disability sport, and the significant advances in its development. In a short but rich history, disability sport has undergone substantial changes in its organisation, funding and public and political profile. However, there appears to be a paucity of literature that traces and evaluates these developments. This chapter seeks to fill this gap and provides a critical examination of the phenomenon of disability sport.

THEORISING DISABILITY

Those considered different from the physical, sensory or intellectual norm are considered abnormal and thus disabled in almost all societies. Being labelled as disabled has, at different times and in different cultures, led to reverence, pity, mockery, torture or death. In ancient Greece there was no place for women, non-Greeks and the physically or intellectually inferior; rather there was an obsession with bodily perfection. Greeks and Romans from 500 BC to AD 400 killed children that they considered to be disabled. The early Christians were compassionate to all but those with mental illness, who were considered as sinful and were often killed as a result. On the other hand, in the sixteenth and seventeenth centuries deaf people were deemed godly and superior to the hearing. It was not until the eighteenth century and the emergence of welfare and caring social policies, that disabled people were treated with more dignity. However, the ideology of caring in the late eighteenth and early nineteenth centuries marginalised disabled people, as illustrated by the proliferation of segregated institutions such as special schools and asylums for the mentally ill and the 'handi-capped' (Barnes, 1997).

Industrialisation in Britain exacerbated this segregation by creating social divisions between those who were deemed to be of use in the workplace and those who were not. Those not up to the physical and mental standards required for the work-place were thus considered useless. This is consistent with the dominant capitalist ide-ology which values individuals according to their productivity: from this perspective inability to produce results in low or no value. As Oliver suggests, disability is 'cul-turally produced through the relationship between the mode of production and the central values of the society concerned' (1990: 23). As a result, *disabled people are six times more likely to be out of work than non-disabled people* (DfEE, 2000).

DISABILITY MODELS

The way in which disability is defined helps to explain how sport for disabled people has developed. Definitions of disability gener-ally fall into one of two categories, medical or social.

The medical model or 'personal tragedy theory' perceives disability as an impair-ment owned by an individual, resulting in a loss or limitation of function. This implies the need for professionals to impose their own priorities on the lifestyles of disabled people, often relegating other personal or social needs to second place. This med-icalised perception of disability allows little leeway for the role of society in the construction of disability. Such definitions and understandings of disability are based on notions of normality or function, with little or no recognition of other cultural or personal factors. According to Stone (1995), individualised medical definitions and explanations of disability that ignore the wider aspects of disability are often deper-sonalised and insulting, treating disabled people as unfortunate, dependent, helpless and pitiable. Indeed, the obsession with bodily perfection, Stone suggests, is oppres-sive not just to those who are considered as disabled, but also to the non-disabled, as it alienates us all 'from our bodies'. Stone maintains that Westernised culture treats disability as a condition to be avoided, encouraging us to deny visible difference and aspire to the body perfect.

An alternative model of disability views disability as socially constructed, whereby *the responsibility for the disability lies with society rather than with the individual*. It is argued that society disables people by limit-ing their worth in society thus placing an additional burden on their own impairment, and isolating them unnecessarily from the rest of society. The central tenet of this model is that disability is created by non-disabled values, norms and beliefs, reducing it to a medical and individual problem.

There seems to be a general consensus among academics that, despite the accep-tance of environmental explanations, the medical model has dominated definitions of disability, and disabled people have been dominated by the medical professions (Drake, 1994; Oliver, 1990). Oliver (1990) argues that the ruling classes were domi-nant in the professions and acted as social controllers of the impaired. Furthermore, with disabled people under-represented in positions of authority, they have had little control over the organisations meant to serve them. For example, in an analysis of

British voluntary organisations, Drake (1994) found that (a) few of the influential positions were held by disabled people; (b) organisations run by non-disabled people had more resources and access to staff than organisations run by disabled people, and (c) organisations run by non-disabled people are more likely to receive financial support from the government.

The Disability Discrimination Act (DDA) was passed in 1996 to reduce the discrimination faced by disabled people. The Act states that disabled people should never be refused services or entry to places where the public can normally go because of their impairment. It has been criticised, however, for being too weak. Furthermore, whilst legislative changes, such as those detailed in the DDA, signify a challenge to the dominant non-disabled culture, typically, disabled people remain in subordinate, powerless positions and continue to be dominated by the predominant able-bodied hegemony.

THE NEED FOR A NEW MODEL

There has been growing support for the social model as it 'under-played the importance of impairment in disabled people's lives, in order to develop a strong argument about social structures and processes' (Shakespeare and Watson, 1997: 298). However, the social model has itself been criticised for failing to provide a definition and understanding of disability which acknowledge impairment and experience.

Hughes and Paterson (1997), for example, suggest that contrary to the beliefs of Shakespeare and Watson a necessary repositioning of the distinction between disability and impairment is required. They argue that both the medical and social models consider bodily impairment in similar ways,

that is, as discrete, physical and inert, 'pulled apart' from the social consequences of the impairment. Hughes and Paterson believe that if disabled people are to challenge effectively the political and economic structures that oppress and exclude them, they need to embrace body politics and accept the significance of the individual within the wider socio-political environment. In 2000 the World Health Organisation revised the 1980 International Classification of Impairment, Disability and Handicap (ICIDH-2). The ICIDH-2 was an acknowledgement of the criticisms made of the earlier definition, particularly by disabled activists and academics. The ICIDH-2 attempts to incorporate both the individual and the social models of disability by distinguishing between those limitations to activity that are best dealt with by medical intervention and those that are the cause and subject of social and environmental barriers. Bickenbach et al. (1999) claim that this model disabuses people of the notion that impairment is necessarily the prime disabler. Nevertheless the new classification has been criticised for continuing to classify difference in relation to prevailing social norms, thus perpetuating the stigmatising effects of labelling.

The literature indicates that:

1   disability has traditionally been defined as an individual loss or restriction;
2   the contemporary social explanation of disability, whilst perceived as an improvement, fails to embrace the individual experiences of impairment within the broader environmental explanation; and
3   in professional practices such as welfare and education, disabled people have been dominated by non-disabled officers and their medical understanding of disability.

Consequently, people with impairments continue to be disabled by a society dominated by the norms and values set by people without impairments.

THE EMERGENCE OF DISABILITY SPORT IN THE UK

Despite the intensification of debates on disability, relatively little attention has been paid, in the UK at least, by disabled activists to disability sport, perhaps because it provides such an overt and often visual illustration of the significance of impairment. Despite the long association between participation in sport and the development and maintenance of physical and mental health, the marginal status of disabled people has militated against their involvement in the dominant able-bodied sporting culture.

Where disabled people have been encouraged to participate in sport and physical activity, it has often been as a vehicle for physical or psychological therapy. For example, in the twentieth century the war injured were encouraged to use sport and recreational physical activity as a means of rehabilitation back into civilian life. This 'therapeutic recreation' concept became particularly well developed in America, where hospitals and schools have continued to use recreation as a form of therapy.

Whilst hospitals in the United Kingdom also embraced the American therapeutic recreation model, the concept of sport and competition specifically for disabled people, and in particular those with spinal cord injury, was first realised by Guttmann at Stoke Mandeville hospital in England. Although the initial rationale for his intervention was to provide therapeutic recreational activities, he soon recognised the wider potential of competitive sport. Consequently, Guttmann and the International Stoke Mandeville Games

Federation (ISMGF) which he then formed are acknowledged by many as instrumental in the inspiration and early development of disability sport in England. One of the earliest international competitive events for physically disabled people was held in 1948. Sports clubs and hospitals were invited that year to Stoke Mandeville, to coincide with the Olympic Games being held in London. According to Atha, President of the English Federation of Disability Sport, 'although Guttmann was a most remarkable pioneer, he was a single-minded autocrat and maverick, whose interest was limited to those with spinal cord injury and he would not entertain the involvement of other disabilities which I, as Vice-Chairman of the Sports Council, wished him to do' (interview, June 2000). Indeed, even though sport for blind and deaf people was, according to Price, Chairman of the British Paralympic Association and currently President of the European Paralympic Committee, established long before wheelchair sport, the inclusion of these disabilities was 'far removed from the consciousness of Guttmann (interview, 2000). Despite Guttmann's highly personal and distinctive views, few would deny his contribution to giving disability sport its early impetus.

Level of sports participation in the UK

There is scant empirical work which clearly demonstrates disabled people's low levels of participation in sport. The few studies that have been carried out tend to reflect similar patterns of participation. The Council for Europe (1987) found that while 30 per cent of non-disabled adults participated in sport, only 3 per cent of disabled people did so. Later studies in the UK found that 2.5 per cent of disabled people participated in sport (Williams and Newman, 1988) compared to 38.4 per cent for non-disabled men and 24.2 per cent for non-disabled women (Sports Council, 1988). Schmidt-Gotz et al. (1994) refer to a study in Germany in which 28 per cent of non-disabled people and 2.5 per cent disabled people were found to participate in sport. Sport England found from a recent nationwide survey that whilst the majority of disabled young people participate in sport both in and out of school time, the rate and frequency of participation are significantly lower than for the overall population. Only 14 per cent of disabled young people, compared to 45 per cent of the general population, take part in extracurricular sport.

As regards the range of sports played, Elvin (1994) found in a survey of 137 local authority leisure services that swimming was the most frequently mentioned programme of activity (94 per cent), weightlifting the most frequently run integrated activity (84 per cent) and short mat bowls the most frequently run segregated activity. While the shortage of data on participation is regrettable, its collection is fraught with practical and ethical problems:

1 It is very difficult to achieve agreement on definitions of impairment and disability.
2 It is difficult to estimate casual participation outside the club and national governing body structure.
3 The collection of such data may necessitate a labelling of 'people with impairment' and consequently perpetuate their social stigma.

Constraints on participation

Notwithstanding the paucity of empirical research, available evidence indicates that, however defined, disabled people take part in sport significantly less than their non-disabled peers. According to a recent Health Education Authority study (1999) involving 40 in-depth interviews and five focus groups, the significant causes of this lower participation in physical activity and sport include:

- lack of motivation and confidence;
- negative school experiences;
- no support from family and friends;
- lack of information on opportunities;
- transport problems;
- a lack of time and money; and
- poor physical access.

Sport England (2000) found from a recent survey that transport was a problem for 32 per cent of young people and that 21 per cent believed that staff at centres and sports clubs were not welcoming. The lack of time others have to supervise and support participation also seems to be a significant constraint, along with a lack of disabled role models. The most common barriers to participation in after-school sport were lack of money, ill health and unsuitability of sports facilities. Whilst the Disability Discrimination Act requires sports facility managers to take steps to ensure their facilities are accessible, facility design and the provision of adequate ramps and changing facilities is only a small part of the process of making a venue attractive for general use by disabled people (ISRM, 1999). A further factor which may contribute to low levels of participation is the poor media coverage of disability sport. Notwithstanding what may be perceived as the BBC's positive coverage of the recent Paralympic Games, the general coverage of disabled people in the mass media continues to medicalise, patronise and dehumanise disabled people, reinforcing stereotypes which 'form the bedrock on which the attitudes towards, assumptions about and expectations of disabled people are based' (Barnes, 1992: 39).

The socialisation process suggests that young people, influenced by socialising agents such as the media, family, peers, grow up adopting the values of their own society. Typically, these agents perpetuate and reinforce negative perceptions of disabled people in society and in sport. Thus, in society's system of social stratification, whereby individuals are ranked according to their contribution to society, disabled people are placed low in the social hierarchy and are therefore denied the power, prestige and life chances enjoyed by their 'superiors'. The lack of opportunity to take part in organised sport is just one consequence of this low status.

Compounding their low status in sport and in wider society is the homogeneous treatment disabled people are accorded, which assumes that they have similar lifestyles and experiences. For example, poor transport, unemployment and low self-esteem may be the key barriers for one group of disabled people while for another group the most significant constraint might be the lack of local sports provision. This heterogeneity of experience has consequently made it difficult for disabled people to form effective lobby groups. Indeed, it could be suggested that whilst many disability sport organisations have been formed since 1940, their multiplicity and differing concerns have made sustained and effective lobbying difficult.

PHYSICAL EDUCATION AND YOUTH SPORT

Special educational needs and integration

After the 1944 Education Act, pupils with disabilities were assigned to medically defined categories, including: the physically handicapped, blind, epileptic or educationally subnormal. Placement into special education was often a response to a medical or psychological assessment which placed pupils in predetermined categories of impairment and which did not, according to Halliday (1993), consider individual needs and competencies. The Warnock Report of 1978 abolished the previous set of medical categories and introduced the concept of special educational needs. One of the main reasons for this was to prevent the sharp distinction between two groups of children – the handicapped and the non-handicapped. The 1981 Education Act accepted the recommendations of the Warnock Report and defined a child as having a special educational need (SEN) if 'he has a significantly greater difficulty in learning than the majority of children of his age; or he has a disability which either prevents or hinders him from making use of the educational facilities of a kind generally provided in schools' (DES, 1981: 1).

The 1981 Education Act indicated that as many as 20 per cent of children have special educational needs, of which only 2 per cent are in special schools. It was also recognised that some children might not be deemed to have a special need in many curriculum areas, but might have such a need in physical education. Conversely, some children who have special educational needs in other academic subjects may not have a special need in physical education.

The Act encouraged what has been a gradual and partial transference of pupils from special to mainstream schools and thus to mainstream physical education. It has been partial inasmuch as the pupils mainstreamed into ordinary schools typically are those with less severe disabilities. Special schools still remain the traditional establishment for those with more severe disabilities.

PHYSICAL EDUCATION

Disabled children are typically considered to have a special educational need and their specific needs and types of provision are identified in a Statement. Despite the obligation on schools to meet these needs, disabled children regularly miss out on the range of physical education opportunities available to their non-disabled peers. In 1987 the Sports Council funded the Everybody Active Project in the North East of England (as one of the National Demonstration Projects) to investigate how to improve the physical education experiences and sporting opportunities of disabled young people (Stafford, 1989). Results of the study revealed that 96 per cent of the 51 mainstream schools in the survey excluded disabled pupils from specific activities. This massive structural inequality facing disabled people in sport was due to a low level of awareness of disability sport issues among leisure providers, poor knowledge of provision for disabled children among PE teachers, and poor PE training for teachers in special schools.

In 1992, the National Curriculum for Physical Education (NCPE) was introduced providing, for the first time, all pupils with an entitlement to a broad and balanced curriculum. Encouraging teachers to modify and adapt activities to suit pupils with special educational needs, the interim reports provided substantive support and advice on the planning and delivery of an accessible curriculum. However, a survey of 38 mainstreamed schools attended by disabled pupils found that despite 79 per cent of the PE department heads claiming to provide suitable PE activities, pupils with SEN, and in particular physically disabled pupils, did not have access to the full range of activities (Penny and Evans, 1995). For example, only 42 per cent provided dance and 56 per cent provided games for physically disabled pupils, although not always integrated with their peers. Games has been highlighted as the activity area in which it may

be most difficult to provide an appropriate experience for pupils with a disability in mainstream education. Furthermore, as Penny and Evans warn, since the publication of *Sport: Raising the Game* (DNH, 1995), the physical education curriculum has emphasised competitive team games, which coupled with the lack of flexibility in the guidelines, was unlikely to lend itself to a broad and balanced curriculum for pupils with SEN.

In a recent survey, Sport England found that 53 per cent of primary-aged disabled children and 41 per cent of 11–16-year-old disabled children spent less than one hour in physical education lessons and only 20 per cent of young disabled people spent two or more hours in PE lessons compared to 33 per cent of the overall school population. Moreover, the proportion of young disabled people taking part in after-school sport was 40 per cent compared to 79 per cent of the general school population.

In any case, according to Barton (1993), physical education for a disabled person is normally an adapted version of that originally designed for non-disabled people. Consequently, a pupil with SEN is likely to receive, at best, an inappropriate programme of activities, as it was originally intended for his/her able-bodied peers and has been adapted or amended in an attempt to meet his/her needs, taking no account of individual circumstances and after-school choices. It has been argued that these early experiences in physical education will have a profound effect on children's sporting careers.

ORGANISATIONAL AND POLICY DEVELOPMENT IN THE UK

The legacy of Ludwig Guttmann

The history of disability sport organisations in the UK has been short but turbulent. As well as the ISMGF, the British Paraplegic

Sports Society (BPSS) was also established in 1948 as a result of the Stoke Mandeville Games, initially to serve the sporting interests of those with spinal cord injury and, much later (when renamed the British Wheelchair Sports Foundation), to serve the sporting interests of other wheelchair users. In 1961 Guttmann inaugurated the British Sports Association for the Disabled (BSAD) which promoted itself as the national body with responsibility for providing, developing and co-ordinating sport and recreation opportunities for all people with disabilities. BSAD, supported by the Sports Council, sought to co-ordinate the plethora of organisations that were emerging to develop sport for disability groups other than those catered for by BPSS.

By the mid-1980s the Sports Council was playing a significant role in the policy development of sport for disabled people. In 1982 the Sports Council published *Sport in the Community: the Next Ten Years*, which recognised that for some groups, their vision of 'Sport for All' had not become a reality, and groups such as those with a physical or learning disability had substantial barriers 'to overcome' (Sports Council, 1982: 29). The promotion of sport for disabled people was acknowledged, but it formed no part of the national strategy, despite eight out of the nine regional Sports Councils identifying disability as a priority area within their regional strategies (1982: 31). However, during the 1980s the British Sports Council began to develop policy in the area of disability sport, although this rarely amounted to more than funding other organisations that were pursuing a more innovative and inclusionary vision of 'Sport for All'.

In 1988 the Sports Council published *Sport in the Community: Into the 90's* in which local authorities such as Northamptonshire, and governing bodies such as the Amateur Rowing Association, were cited as examples of organisations using innovative schemes to promote mass participation opportunities for disabled

people. More significantly, by 1988 the Sports Council was providing the British Sports Association for the Disabled with a grant of £100,000 a year. However, despite substantial Sports Council and commercial funding, it was perceived that the BSAD failed to provide either the effective unified voice for disability sport or an efficient organisational infrastructure for competition.

The 1989 government review

Despite BSAD's decision in 1987 to switch from being an umbrella to a membership organisation, dissatisfaction with the Association led to a gradual decline in BSAD membership and a weakening of the credibility of its claim to be the primary advocate on behalf of other disability sport organisations. According to Price,

the dual responsibility for membership (through BSAD's network of clubs) and national co-ordination (acting as an umbrella over all the NDSOs) had always been over-ambitious and misguided. As BSAD could not and did not claim exclusive responsibility for all disability groups, it could never adequately represent their interests vis à vis the Sports Council, but nor could it ignore that responsibility and invest its limited resources exclusively in its membership services. (Interview, 2000)

In 1989 Colin Moynihan, then Minister for Sport, initiated a review prompted in large part by criticisms aimed at BSAD by the other disability sports organisations and mainstream governing bodies. The disability sports organisations were accused of creating confusion and duplication by the Minister for Sport Review Group (1989). A key recommendation of the review called on governing bodies and other mainstream agencies to afford disabled people the benefits currently enjoyed by the non-disabled, as it was perceived that segregated disability sports organisations did not have the resources to support their athletes adequately.

Table 6.1   *Examples of national disability sports organisations (1948–98)*

Founded	Organisation
1930	British Deaf Sports Council*
1948	British Paraplegic Sports Association (later British Wheelchair Sports Association*)
1961	British Sports Association for the Disabled (later Disability Sport England*)
1976	British Blind Sport*
1978	British Amputee Sports Association (BASA)
1981	United Kingdom Sports Association for the People with Mental Handicap* (later, in 1995, the English Sports Association for People with Learning Disability*)
1981	Cerebral Palsy Sport*
1982	British Les Autres Sports Association (BLASA)
1989	British Paralympic Association
1990	British Les Autres and Amputee Sports Association* (merger of BASA and BLASA)
1998	English Federation of Disability Sport

*National disability sports organisations recognised by the Sports Council.

As a result of the perceived failure of BSAD to be an effective representative body, numerous organisations had been established, some with a remit to improve the range and quality of opportunities for one disability group in all sports, such as Cerebral Palsy Sport, and others to meet the sporting needs of all disability groups in one particular sport, such as the British Table Tennis Association for Disabled People. Table 6.1 shows that by 1989 there was a vast array of disparate autonomous organisations representing a range of disability and sporting interests.

Whilst at an international level disability specific organisations liaised with their own equivalent disability-specific international federations, e.g. British Blind Sport with the International Blind Sport Association, it was at the local, regional and national levels that BSAD was perceived as failing to develop competition and sports development structures to meet the specific needs of the disability groups in their remit. Whilst recognising the invaluable role BSAD played in the early development of disability sport, it failed to represent the breadth of disability sport interests. This failure became more pronounced as more disability-specific organisations were established and began to impose higher expectations for policy action and lobbying on BSAD. Notwithstanding these organisational shortcomings, Price claimed that the smaller NDSOs at times seemed envious of BSAD's position. 'They didn't have then, and haven't developed since, the network of grassroots clubs and regional organisations that even come close to BSAD's, nor did they enjoy the financial support of the Sports Council' (interview, 2000).

Box 6.1   The British Sports Association for the Disabled (BSAD)

In 1961 Guttmann inaugurated the British Sports Association for the Disabled (BSAD). BSAD, supported by the Sports Council, sought to co-ordinate the plethora of organisations that were emerging to develop sport for disability groups. The untenable dual responsibility of promoting participation for other organisations as well as developing its own sports club and event infrastructure, led to a gradual decline in BSAD membership and a weakening of the credibility of its claim to be the primary advocate on behalf of other disability sport organisations.

The mainstreaming of disability sport

As consequence of the publication of *Building on Ability* by the Minister for Sport Review Group in 1989, there occurred during the 1990s a gradual policy shift by the Sports Council towards the mainstreaming of disability sport. In 1993 the Sports Council published a policy statement *People with Disabilities and Sport*, in which they recommended that sport for disabled people was at a stage where 'having developed its own structures, [it should] move from a target approach to the mainstream' (Sports Council, 1993: 5). In other words, the Sports Council was recommending a gradual shift of responsibility for the organisation and provision of sport for disabled people, to move away from the NDSOs towards the mainstream, sports-specific national governing bodies. In doing so it highlighted those mainstream and disability sport agencies that were involved in the network of disability sport. However, whilst the National Disability Sport Organisations, regional sports forums, facility managers and teachers were all identified as being potential partners, no clarification was offered regarding the precise role of these groups. Elvin (1994), in an attempt to map the 'complex variety' of agencies involved in the provision of opportunities, found that despite the similarity in their objectives, many of the public and private sector organisations worked independently of one another. The National Disability Sport Organisations had, he believed, an important part to play but 'often lacked the resources and the facilities' to deliver programmes (Elvin, 1994: 325), and thus needed the co-operation of other agencies.

A new start

In recognition of the continued poor co-ordination between these agencies together with the wider political trend towards integration, the Sports Council convened a National Disability Sports Conference in 1996 to consider the future of disability sport in England. As a result of the conference, the Sports Council established a task force with the remit to 'facilitate the mainstreaming of disability sport in England by the year 2000' (Collins, 1997). In June 1997 the National Disability Sports Conference was reconvened to receive the task force recommendations and the results of the consultation exercise. Collins (1997: 1) reported that in contrast to earlier attempts at reform, there was now a unity of opinion on the future of disability sport policy, the main recommendation of which was the creation of an English Federation of Disability Sport (EFDS).

The EFDS was established in 1998 and, as indicated in Figure 6.1, plays a pivotal role in the co-ordination of opportunities provided and developed by disability sports organisations. It has a mission to:

- increase the choices for, and inclusion of, disabled people in all sporting communities;
- provide a professional first-stop shop service on all matters relating to sport for disabled people;
- increase the effectiveness of existing disability sport structures.

Atha (President of EFDS) suggests that the EFDS provides 'a much needed united voice for disability sport in England' which combines the 'specialist expertise of the NDSOs, thus enabling the EFDS 'powerfully [to] demonstrate that disabled people have a right to access sport as a matter of common

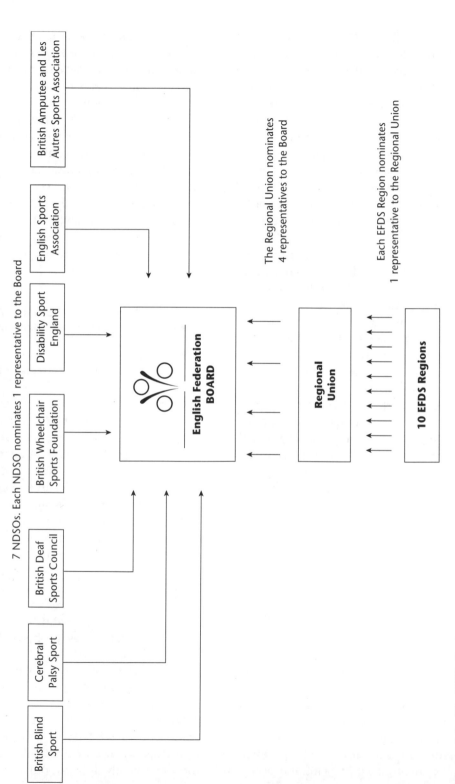

COMPOSITION OF BOARD OF DIRECTORS

7 NDSOs. Each NDSO nominates 1 representative to the Board

British Blind Sport

Cerebral Palsy Sport

British Deaf Sports Council

British Wheelchair Sports Foundation

Disability Sport England

English Sports Association

British Amputee and Les Autres Sports Association

English Federation BOARD

The Regional Union nominates 4 representatives to the Board

Regional Union

Each EFDS Region nominates 1 representative to the Regional Union

10 EFDS Regions

Figure 6.1 The EFDS structure

practice' (EFDS, 1999). The success of the EFDS will depend upon a diverse range of factors, including its capacity to retain the respect of disability sports organisations. Whilst the ability of the EFDS to represent the interests of the regions and the NDSOs is largely within the control of the EFDS, government funding of sport, government and local authority policies on sport and school physical education and the media coverage of disability sport for example, are all factors outside their control but which may be crucial to its success.

The establishment of the EFDS provided a sharp insight into the policy environment within which disability sports organisations operate. It can be argued that the slow progress towards the development of an effective organisational lobbying focus for disability sport was due in part to two factors: first, the reluctance of mainstream sports governing bodies to acknowledge disability sport as a significant issue and, second, the unwillingness of the non-disabled administrators in existing disability organisations to relinquish what Price suggests had become for many a personal crusade. Indeed Derek Casey, former Chief Executive of Sport England, Price and Atha concur that the attractions of working in elite disability sport had encouraged the retention of roles better served by different and possibly mainstream organisations. Price claims that a significant opportunity to improve sport for disabled people has been missed and is disappointed by the current organisational arrangements. The relationship between Sport England and EFDS seems reminiscent of that between BSAD and the former Sports Council, with Sport England, like the Sports Council before it, seeming to prefer a single outlet for all disability needs and interests. This is not to ignore the gradual, and welcome, increase in the involvement of NGBs and others in

the mainstream of sport at the elite end of the spectrum; simply to express disappointment with the slow pace of movement in that direction and apparent lack of emphasis on the involvement of mainstream providers closer to the grassroots (Price, personal communication). Atha is generally more optimistic and contends that the disability sports organisations, currently under the direction of EFDS, should retain control and power, as the mainstream NGBs 'will never take on disability fully so we will need disability sports organisations well into the foreseeable future and quite possibly always' (Atha, interview).

ELITE COMPETITION, CLASSIFICATION AND THE PARALYMPIC MOVEMENT

The Paralympic movement

The first summer Paralympic Games were held in 1960 immediately after the Olympic Games in Rome. However, as Doll-Tepper (1999) highlights, the term Paralympic is a recent title replacing the previous disability or organisationally defined nomenclature such as the Paraplegic Games. Advocates within the Paralympic movement emphasise that whilst the Paralympics were once exclusively for paraplegics, the 'Paralympics' is so called to reflect its 'para-llel' status to the Olympics. It should also be noted that the deaf are not a part of the Paralympic movement, instead providing elite competition in a 'World Games for the Deaf'.

The Paralympic Games are now significantly larger than they were in 1960, in terms of the number of athletes, administrators and countries represented. In Sydney 2000, over 4,000 athletes from 123 countries competed in 18 sports. Although the Paralympic Games were initially developed for the spinally injured only, they now

Table 6.2   *The summer Paralympics, 1952–2000*

Year	Olympics venue	Paralympics venue	No. of countries	No. of athletes	Disablity groups	GB position
1952	London	Aylesbury, England	2	130	SCI	n/a
1960	Rome, Italy	Rome, Italy	23	400	SCI	n/a
1964	Tokyo, Japan	Tokyo, Japan	22	390	SCI	2nd
1968	Mexico City, Mexico	Tel Aviv, Israel	29	750	SCI	n/a
1972	Munich, Germany	Heidelberg, Germany	44	1,000	SCI	4th
1976	Montreal, Canada	Toronto, Canada	42	1,600	SCI, VI, LA	5th
1980	Moscow, USSR	Arnhem, Netherlands	42	2,550	SCI,VI, AMP, CP	5th
1984	Los Angeles, USA	New York, USA Aylesbury, UK	42	4,080	SCI, VI, AMP, CP	2nd 6th
1988	Seoul, Korea	Seoul, Korea	61	3,053	SCI, VI, AMP, CP, LA	3rd
1992	Barcelona, Spain	Barcelona, Spain	82	3,020	SCI, VI, AMP, CP, LA	3rd
1996	Atlanta, USA	Atlanta, USA	103	3,195	SCI, VI, AMP, CP, LA, MH	4th
2000	Sydney, Australia	Sydney, Australia	127	4,500	SCI, VI, AMP, CP, LA, MH	2nd

Key:

SCI	spinal cord injury	CP	cerebral palsy
LD	learning disability	LA	les Autres (the others)
AMP	amputees	VI	visually impaired and blind
MH	mental handicap		

include amputees, people with cerebral palsy, people with an intellectual disability, the visually impaired, wheelchair users and les autres (the term used to cater for those with other forms of physical impairment). Table 6.2 summarises the development and expansion of the Paralympic Games.

The increase in links between the Olympics and the Paralympics is mirrored by the increase in standards, events, spectators, hospitality, technology and sports science. The increase in standards is often exemplified by the diminishing divide between Olympic and Paralympic world records. For example, Nigerian amputee Ajibola Adoeye set a Paralympic record of 10.72 seconds for the 100 m, less that one second slower than the Olympic record.

The Great Britain team have achieved significant success in the Paralympic Games. Recent performances have earned them third position in 1992 at Barcelona and fourth position at Atlanta in 1996. However, the success in Barcelona, at least according to the Sports Council (1993), was in spite of the 'minimal support' offered by the formal organisational structures. Notwithstanding what the Minister for Sport described, in 1989, as a 'long history of fragmentation and dissatisfaction within the UK disability sports organisational structure', recent changes to the funding for both Olympic and Paralympic development have significantly enhanced the opportunities for athletes and their coaches. In particular, the formation of the British

Paralympic Association (the first national Paralympic Committee) and the introduction of the National Lottery World Class Performance Plans have provided athletes with a higher quality of training and event preparation. The result of this support is illustrated by the success of the 2000 Games in Sydney, where Great Britain finished in second position, with a total of 131 medals, only 18 less than the triumphant host nation.

Classification

Classification is a central characteristic of competitive disability sport, as it is the method that groups athletes into the categories which enable 'fair' competition. Initially athletes were classified in groups according their impairment, for example: 8 classes for CP athletes, 3 for visually impaired athletes, 7 for wheelchair athletes, 9 for amputees, 6 for les autres and 1 for LD. Since 1992, sport-specific classification systems have been introduced in which an individual is grouped according to their functional ability in the sport rather than their clinical impairment, which reduces the number of classes and improves the standard of competition. Whilst classification provides the vehicle by which disabled people compete, concerns surrounding the fairness of classification systems have abounded.

Integration and the Paralympics

As standards of performance have increased, it is argued that the original rehabilitation purpose through sport has given way to sport for sport's sake and competition for competition's sake. Furthermore, as part of the IPC's commitment to increase the integration of disabled athletes into mainstream sporting structures, demonstration Paralympic events have been held within the Olympic schedule, a primary rationale for which is to provide athletes with sports science support and afford elite-level athletes a similar status to that enjoyed by their Olympic counterparts. However, Tim Marshall (a recent member of the board of Sport England), for example, holds the view that the IPC should stop trying to gain access to the Olympic Games but should encourage the IOC to provide the Paralympic Games with similar services to those provided to the Olympic Games.

There is also some debate about 'reverse integration', which is the inclusion of non-disabled athletes in disability sport events. While, on the one hand, this might be a worthwhile educational experience for non-disabled people and could also increase the opportunities available to disabled athletes, on the other hand, the practice might lead to unequal and unbalanced competition, resulting in the marginalisation of disabled people from the events that were meant to serve them.

PERSPECTIVES ON DISABILITY SPORT

Dominant perspective: sport as a form of therapy/socialisation

Sport is a phenomenon that reflects wider cultural values within society; thus in a similar way to women, blacks and homosexuals, disabled people have been excluded from both mainstream society and sport. Whilst there is rich discourse on sport as a predominantly white, male, middle-class hegemony, discussions on disabled people's marginalisation in sport are not so common. Administrators and athletes in disability sport have striven, however, for greater recognition and in doing so have tended to emphasise the extent to which sport can be of physical and psychological benefit, and a vehicle for social acceptance. This approach supports the notion that sport is a form of therapy, used to rehabilitate individuals into mainstream society. This is illustrated by Steadward's suggestion that the Paralympic movement 'provides a tremendous inspiration for people around the world to overcome adversity' (1996).

The Health Education Authority (1999) found that the existence of disability sports clubs in the UK provided a motivation for disabled people to be involved in regular physical activity. However, others believed that the emphasis by disability sports organisations on competition may serve to discourage rather than encourage participation. Nonetheless, it seems reasonable for those considering themselves as disabled to seek the benefits of sport in a similar way to their non-disabled peers, that is, to develop friendships, release stress, and improve health and fitness. Guttmann (1976) believed that sport was:

invaluable in restoring the disabled person's physical fitness, i.e. his strength, co-ordination, speed and endurance ... restoring that passion for playful activity and the desire to experience joy and pleasure in life ... promoting that psychological equilibrium which enables the disabled to come to terms with his physical defect, to develop activity of mind, self-confidence, self-dignity, self-discipline, competitive spirit, and comradeship, mental attitudes ... to facilitate and accelerate his social re-integration and integration. (Guttmann, 1976: 12–13)

According to Brasile et al. (1994), disabled people's motives for participation are similar to those of non-disabled people, for example, using after-sport social activities to seek acceptance from others. Whilst Taub and Greer (1998) concur, their interviews with disabled athletes revealed that the non-disabled respond to disabled people's participation in sport with disbelief about their physicality and with a clear lack of knowledge about their physical capability. One interviewee with cerebral palsy said, 'they [non-disabled people] want to be so nice to people, but they don't really know what they're doing. So they give you the wrong kind of support, either paternalistic or the wrong type of information' (Taub and Greer, 1998: 290). They found that disabled athletes did not internalise these negative responses, believing that sport made them feel (a) more capable and (b) that they had not yet reached their full physical potential.

In summary, disability sport may simply provide the opportunity for acceptance and normalisation, maintaining society's equilibrium by providing positive opportunities and rehabilitative benefits for those whose impairment has disrupted society's balance. A wheelchair user, for example, may be disabled by the steps and kerbs of a shopping centre but the same individual may enjoy the benefits of, and not be disabled by, a game of wheelchair basketball in an accessible sports centre. Whilst recognising the sporting excellence of disabled athletes, and the potential for shifting perceptions away from a therapeutic to a recreative model, disabled people's participation in sport may still be as much about therapy as it was in the 1950s.

Challenging the dominant perspective

Emulating able-bodiedness

The overall treatment of sport and disability has been largely descriptive, atheoretical and uncritical (Williams, 1994; Barton, 1993) and policy and practice have been dominated by a medical, individualised approach to disability. Consequently, Oliver (1990) argues that the dominant perspectives of policy-makers and researchers perpetuate disabled people's subordination. Using Gramsci's analysis of culture, the following section offers alternative explanations to the functionalist positions implicit in much of the literature concerning the involvement of disabled people in sport.

The relationship between disability and sport has been described by Steadward (1996) as 'contradictory and complex', as disability is associated with individual weakness, whereas sport is associated with strength, aggression and power over an opponent – characteristics rarely attributed to disabled people. This perspective helps to explain Hahn's (1984) suggestion that disabled people's participation in sport is an attempt to emulate non-disabled values and an example of disabled people's struggle for acceptance in a predominantly able-bodied world.

Concurring with this argument, Barton (1993) asserts that disability sport is merely an imitation of non-disabled sport in which disabled people are encouraged to accept a set of non-disabled values. Hahn (1984) suggests that much of the literature surrounding the study of sport for disabled people has focused on the attempts to adapt non-disabled people's activities for individuals with impairments. It seems that physical education and sport for a disabled person are normally adapted versions of those originally designed for non-disabled people. However, to start from the premise that sport should be adapted and made appropriate for the disabled individuals confirms and reinforces the hegemony of able-bodied sport.

High cost – low gain

A second reason for questioning the dominant perspective on sport for disabled

people lies with the disproportionate efforts and costs that disabled people have to make to achieve what may be perceived as equality in sport. As Hahn suggests, disabled men and women seemingly can seek to approximate equality only through 'the exertion of almost superhuman effort' (Hahn, 1984: 6). This concept of equality is consistent with the experiences of other minority groups and ignores the additional economic, physical and emotional price that disabled people may need to pay in order to reap the same benefits as their non-disabled peers.

Moreover, there is little evidence to suggest that disabled people's participation in sport, however successful, has made any impact upon the broader social, political and economic environment in which disabled people live. For example, disabled people are still less likely to be in paid employment. That is not to say that participation in sport by disabled people may not produce many personal benefits, indeed for some it may now be a career. However, for the majority of the disabled population, it seems that sport has done little to challenge the dominant able-bodied hegemony and advantage the wider disabled community. Furthermore, it seems that disabled people are traditionally offered opportunities in special or separate settings segregated from the mainstream community, thus reducing any impact such performances may have on non-disabled people, and detracting from the important social, economic and environmental barriers facing disabled people. For example, an unintended consequence of the Paralympic Games could be that the exclusively able-bodied culture of the Olympics remains unchallenged, thus maintaining and perpetuating disabled people's inequality.

The oppression and marginalisation of disadvantaged groups through the medium of sport are well documented. According to

Hahn (1984), similar to blacks in the ghettos of America, disabled people by participating in sport are encouraged to strive for goals that are both unattainable and less important than the wider and more important political, social and occupational goals.

Exclusivity of able-bodied sport

It is accepted that sport is a valued cultural practice and, as such, is significant in the lives of disabled people. Sport has the capacity therefore to play what Hahn (1984) calls a gatekeeping role, whereby those who are able to participate in the commonly recognised sports will be accepted into wider society and those who do not possess these physical capabilities may be denied the benefits of this membership. Even participation in adapted versions of recognised sports does not ensure acceptance into wider society. Furthermore, society's increasing concern with physicality, health, fitness and the 'body beautiful' provides the disabled population with the opportunity to challenge and clarify the values that these preoccupations project. Greek males were expected to compete both individually and collectively in the pursuit of physical and intellectual excellence in gymnasiums, amphitheatres, and of course the Olympic Games (Barnes, 1997). It could be argued that the most significant gatekeeping role that sport plays is in the context of the aesthetic screening for physicality, with only some movements deemed as graceful and only some types of sporting bodies as attractive. The institution of sport gives priority to certain able-bodied forms of human movement (Barton, 1993); this means that the sports disabled people may wish to play, and the way they participate, may not be deemed attractive according to non-disabled values. Moreover, even within the disability sport and Paralympic sport

movement, there appear to be some impairments that are considered less acceptable than others.

CONCLUSION

Despite considerable change since the formation of BSAD in 1961, it is clear that the organisational structure of sport for disabled people is still in a state of transition. Over the last 40 years or so a wide range of disability-generic, sport-specific and local organisations have developed sport at all levels but have worked predominantly in isolation from the mainstream sports bodies. Now enjoying better financial and political support, some disability sports organisations, encouraged by Sport England, are striving to co-ordinate their efforts, provide a united voice for disability sport, and build relations with mainstream sporting agencies. Unfortunately, the level of organisational coherence among disability sports organisations is still poor and the links between disability sports organisations and mainstream governing bodies are weak.

In recent years mainstream governing bodies of sport have begun to consider issues related to disability sport, often stimulated by Sport England funding. However, the response has been varied. While some national governing bodies of sport have embraced disabled people's needs within their existing national and regional structures, others have allied themselves to new disability, sport-specific governing bodies, and others have encouraged the traditional generic disability sports organisations to retain responsibility. The pattern of response reflects the varying levels of expertise, confidence and commitment within mainstream governing bodies of sport.

The current emphasis within Sport England on mainstreaming is problematic.

The rationale for mainstreaming, that is providing access to services typically provided by, and generally only available to, able-bodied people, seems to be (a) that resources controlled by mainstream sports organisations are greater, and (b) that able-bodied sport is the norm to which disabled athletes should aspire. With regard to the latter, it seems that the policy and practice of sport for disabled people are primarily concerned with the extent to which we can, or should, integrate groups or individuals who are considered as outside of the main body of society, into the mainstream. In most cases the discussions of mainstreaming are based on an implicit assumption that integration is necessarily desirable. This perspective is logical in so far as it is mainstream non-disabled society that has constructed definitions and public perceptions of disability. However, if integration is about equality, it can be argued that integration can only be achieved by deconstructing what is considered as 'normal'. That is, rather than categorising people into normal and abnormal groups, and then seeking to integrate the disabled or abnormal in with the non-disabled or normal, perceptions of what is 'normal' may need to change.

Chapter summary

- Competing models of disability – the medical and the socially constructed – shape the way in which disability sport has developed and shape the nature of current policy debates.
- Disability sport developed substantially within a medical model of disability that treated sport primarily as a vehicle for physical and/or psychological therapy.
- Low levels of participation by disabled people have been explained with reference to a variety of factors, including negative school experience, lack of motivation and confidence, lack of support from family and friends, transport problems and poor physical access.
- Britain has a complex pattern of organisations providing sports opportunities for the disabled, some defined by sport and others by type of disability.
- A key and highly controversial debate within British sport is whether disability sport should be organised separately from mainstream governing bodies.

Further reading

Barnes (1997), Oliver (1990) and Hughes and Paterson (1997) provide rich points of entry to the politics of disability in general. Stone (1995) provides a challenging critique of 'body politics' and disability. For an examination of the development, current context and politics of disability sport, Doll-Tepper (1999) provides a European perspective. Steadward (1996) explores the politics of integration within the Paralympic movement and Barton examines the provision for children with disabilities within the Physical Education curriculum and schools.

REFERENCES

Barnes, C. (1992) *Disabling Imagery and the Media. An Exploration of the Principles for Media Representations of Disabled People.* Halifax: The British Council of Disabled People and Ryman Publishing.

Barnes, C. (1997) 'A legacy of oppression: a history of disability in western culture', in L. Barton and M. Oliver (eds), *Disability Studies, Past, Present and Future.* Leeds: The Disability Press, pp. 45–61.

Barton, L. (1993) 'Disability, empowerment and physical education', in J. Evans (ed.), *Equality, Education and Physical Education.* London: The Falmer Press, pp. 43–54.

Bickenbach, J.E., Chatterji, S., Badley, E.M. and Ustun, T.B. (1999) 'Models of disablement, universalism and international classification of impairments, disabilities and handicaps', *Social Science and Medicine*, 48: 1173–87.

Brasile, F.M., Kleiber, D.A. and Harnisch, D. (1994) 'Analysis of participation incentives among athletes with and without disabilities', *Therapeutic Recreation Journal*, Jan.–March: 18–33.

Collins, D. (1997) *Conference Report.* National Disability Sport Conference. London: Kings Fund Centre.

Council for Europe (1987) *European Charter for Sport for All: Disabled Persons.* Strasbourg: Council for Europe.

Department for Education and Employment (DfEE) (2000) *Key Facts and Figures Feb. 2000 Disability Briefing* (2000) Labour Force Survey Autumn 1999 Great Britain. DfEE 14/3/2000 Feb. 2000. *www.disability.gov.uk.*

Department for Education and Science (DES) (1981) *The Education Act.* London: HMSO.

Department of National Heritage (DNH) (1995) *Sport: Raising the Game.* London: DNH.

Doll-Tepper, G. (1999) 'Disability sport', in J. Riordan and A. Kruger (eds), *The International Politics of Sport in the Twentieth Century.* London and New York: E. & F. N. Spon, pp. 177–90.

Drake, R.F. (1994) 'The exclusion of disabled people from positions of power in British voluntary organisations', *Disability and Society*, 9: 461–90.

Elvin, I.T. (1994) 'A UK perspective in the development and management of sport for people with a disability', in H.V. Coppenolle, Y. Vanlanderwijck, J. Simons, P. Van de Vliet and E. Neerinckx (eds), *First European Conference on Adapted Physical Activity and Sports: a White Paper on Research and Practice.* Leuven, Belgium: ACCO.

English Federation of Disability Sport (EFDS) (1999) *Building a Fairer Sporting Society.* Sport for Disabled People in England. A Four Year Development Plan 2000–2004. Crewe: EFDS.

Guttmann, L. (1976) *Textbook of Sport for the Disabled.* Oxford: HM & M Publishers.

Hahn, H. (1984) 'Sport and the political movement of disabled persons examining non-disabled social values', *Arena Review*, 8 (1): 1–15.

Halliday, P. (1993) 'Physical education within special education provision – equality and entitlement', in J. Evans (ed.), *Equality, Education and Physical Education.* London: The Falmer Press.

Health Education Authority (1999) *Physical Activity in Our Lives. Qualitative Research among Disabled People.* London: Health Education Authority.

Hughes, B. and Paterson, K. (1997) 'The social model of disability and the disappearing body: towards a sociology of impairment', *Disability and Society*, 12 (3): 325–40.

Institute of Sport and Recreation Management (ISRM) (1999) *Disability in Sport: the Legal Framework. The Disability Discrimination Act 1995.* Melton Mowbray: ISRM. Ref. 188:12/99.

Minister for Sport Review Group (1989) *Building on Ability.* Leeds: HMSO for Department of Education, the Ministers' Review Group.

Oliver, M. (1990) *The Politics of Disablement.* Basingstoke: Macmillan.

Penny, D. and Evans, J. (1995) 'The National Curriculum for physical education: entitlement for all?', *The British Journal of Physical Education.* Winter: 6–13.

Schmidt-Gotz, E., Doll-Tepper, G. and Lienert, C. (1994) 'Attitudes of university students and teachers towards integrating students with disabilities into regular physical education classes', *The Physical Education Review*, 17 (1): 45–57.

Shakespeare, T. and Watson, N. (1997) 'Defending the social model', *Disability and Society*, 12 (2): 293–300.

Sports Council (1982) *Sport in the Community: The Next Ten Years.* London: Sports Council.

Sports Council (1988) *Sport in the Community: Into the 90's. A Strategy for Sport 1988–1993.* London: Sports Council.

Sports Council (1993) *People with Disabilities and Sport. Policy and Current/Planned Action.* London: Sports Council.

Sport England (2000) *Young People with a Disability and Sport.* London: Sport England.

Stafford, I. (1989) 'Everybody active. A Sports Council national demonstration project in England', *Adapted Physical Activity Quarterly*, 6: 100–8.

Steadward, R. (1996) 'Integration and sport in the Paralympic movement', *Sports Science Review*, 5 (1): 26–41.

Stone, S. (1995) 'The myth of bodily perfection', *Disability and Society*, 10 (4): 413–24.

Taub, D.E. and Greer, K.R. (1998) 'Sociology of acceptance revisited: males with physical disabilities participating in sport and physical fitness activity', *Deviant Behaviour*, 19: 279–302.

Williams, T. (1994) 'Sociological perspectives on sport and disability: structural-functionalism', *Adapted Physical Activity Quarterly*, 17 (1): 14–24.

Williams, T. and Newman, I. (1988) 'Initial research on integration and involvement in community sport and recreation', *Working Papers of the Everybody Active Demonstration Project No. 4*, Sunderland Polytechnic.

7

The Politics of 'Race' and Sports Policy

BEN CARRINGTON AND IAN McDONALD

Overview

→ The emergence and development of sports policy and 'race'
→ Sports policy, community and multiculturalism
→ From anti-racism to managing racial inequalities
→ Contemporary developments and issues in sports policy and 'race'
→ Working towards racial equality?
→ Bureaucratic managerialism: the new discourse of anti-racism?
→ Conclusion

Writing about the growing body of literature on racism and ethnicity in critical studies of social policy, Ian Law noted that although 'issues of racism and ethnicity remain topical and there is a steady growth in research and writing which engages with these issues across the varied fields of social policy, there is a noticeable underdevelopment in areas such as health and sport and leisure' (1996: x). As a corrective to this neglect, this chapter will, first, give a chronological and thematic overview of key developments in government sports policy and 'race' since the 1970s and, second, provide a social and political analysis of these developments. Although sports policy has its own set of concerns and has a degree of autonomy from other social fields, it does not exist within a social and political vacuum. Therefore, we pay particular attention to how the specific concerns and issues within sports policy are refracted through other policy agendas. Our approach is to locate the analysis of 'race' and ethnicity in sports policy within broader social and political discourses. In this way, we avoid two dangers of policy analysis. We avoid a reduction of the analysis to formal or stated policy commitments by the government and sporting bodies on 'race' and ethnicity. Policy is interpreted processually as a complex and dynamic course of action or inaction involving contingently constructed social networks in which particular goals may be as much implicit and unintended as explicit and intended. In short, the policy *text* is decentred and the policy *context* prioritised. In this way, we can talk of a de facto government sports policy for 'race' and ethnicity that both precedes and transcends the formal and stated aim of policy. The substantive significance of particular policy interventions is derived from their constitutive role as part of broader social and political discourses. This guards against the second danger of policy analysis, namely of overplaying the fecundity of policy statements and underplaying the political meaning of policy implementation.

THE EMERGENCE AND DEVELOPMENT OF SPORTS POLICY AND 'RACE'

The racialisation of sports policy discourse

The first sports policy intervention on 'race' and ethnicity was framed within a discourse of equality, expressed in the slogan of 'Sport for All'. Although always more an aspiration than a specific policy goal, 'Sport for All' signalled a belief amongst an incipient sports policy community in the early 1970s that access to participation opportunities in sport was a right of citizenship in mature liberal democracies.

The early to mid-1970s was a propitious time for the development of sporting opportunities with two factors in particular being important in raising the levels of participation. First, the formation of an executive GB Sports Council in 1972 meant that a strategic approach to the development of sport was possible. Second, the restructuring of local authority administrative boundaries in 1974 resulted in the creation of discrete and often large leisure and recreation departments with a higher political

profile and dedicated budgets (Houlihan, 1991). In 1973/4 alone, 137 sports centres and 190 swimming pools were built (Henry, 1993: 117). Coalter et al. (1988) refer to this period as 'recreational welfare', reflecting the consensus that sport and recreation played a legitimate function in terms of an expansive welfare state improving the quality of life for those unable to access opportunities in the private sector. During this period, 'race' and ethnicity were not identified as areas requiring specific intervention. It was considered evident that levels of participation amongst all under-represented groups would benefit from the general expansion in facilities. This was a viewpoint that was proven later to be naïve and unrealistic.

No sooner had the concept of 'recreational welfare' been established, than it was subjected to a series of initially subtle but, over a period of time, fundamental changes. 'Recreational welfare' was a philosophy that depended on a buoyant economy with generous levels of public spending on sports facilities. Yet the mid-1970s saw Britain enter a period of profound economic crisis. Recreational welfare was, according Coalter et al., 'conceived in affluence, born in uncertainty and ended in austerity' (1988: 22). Faced with a severe economic crisis, the Labour government abandoned its Keynesian approach to economic management, and embraced a monetarist position. This resulted in cuts in public expenditure, hastening a reduction in the levels of welfare services available to the most needy and vulnerable in society, and inevitably feeding into the increasing levels of poverty and alienation in many parts of the country (Cliff and Gluckstein, 1988). The deteriorating social fabric of the inner cities increasingly became a central policy concern of government and a source of wider public anxiety.

The slide into economic crisis provided the backdrop for the racialisation of political debates about urban policy and social policy that developed from the late 1960s, with black youths being linked in popular and political discourse to social instability and crime. As Solomos notes, it was during the 1970s that, 'the imagery of violence and decay became synonymous with those inner-city localities in which black migrants had settled and established themselves' (1993: 135). An important influence on the process of criminalisation was the media-produced moral panic about 'mugging' in the early 1970s, which was constructed as a new 'black juvenile' crime, and perceived by the public as constituting a major social problem (Hall et al., 1978). However, in response, there was a growing sense of frustration within black communities, and an increasingly antagonistic relationship between black youths and the police, reflecting 'a deep crisis in the relationship between these communities and the state, especially the police' (Witte, 1996: 59). These tensions would eventually explode in the summer of 1981, with the riots in Brixton, Toxteth, Moss Side and many other cities and towns across Britain. Although white and black youth were involved in the riots, they were construed in popular and political discourse as 'race riots', thus feeding the imagery of inner cities as havens of black criminality.

Unwilling to address the structural nature of the problems caused by mass unemployment and reduced welfare spending, the Labour government had already laid the basis for sport to be used as one of its more affordable and politically expedient options. A number of official government reports, including the White Papers on *Sport and Recreation* (DOE, 1975), *A Policy for the Inner Cities* (DOE, 1977a) and the *Recreation and Deprivation in Urban Areas* (DOE, 1977b)

document, had delineated the role of sport as a tool of urban social control. It meant, in effect, a racialisation of sports policy discourse as 'equality of opportunity was ... abandoned and resources were henceforth concentrated more on the problems of "deprived areas", that is, on preventing vandalism and delinquency, dealing with the consequences of unemployment and doing something about the plight of ethnic minorities' (Hargreaves, 1986: 187).

At the same time as the Labour government was pressing for a shift in sports policy towards targeting deprived areas, a consensus was emerging in the sports policy community that a facility-based strategy for reducing the unequal patterns of sport participation was ineffective. As Ian Henry noted:

> While 'sport for all' might be the avowed goal of sports policy, with a particular emphasis on reaching disadvantaged groups, research evidence throughout the latter half of the 1970s increasingly indicated a failure on the part of the public sector services to attract ethnic minorities, the unemployed, the elderly, women, the disabled, and low-income groups. (Henry, 1990: 46)

Accordingly, the Sports Council encouraged local authorities to move away from the building of large prestigious sports centres and towards the development of locally accessible centres (Henry, 1993: 118). The paternalism of traditional facility-based management approaches thus gave way to a community-development approach based on the principle of 'empowering' disadvantaged members of the local community. This new emphasis in Sports Council strategy was confirmed with the publication of its strategic document in 1982, *Sport in the Community: the Next Ten Years*, which argued for the need to 'target' recreationally disadvantaged groups, such as women, the disabled, the elderly and ethnic minorities. However, which groups would actually be targeted was to be dictated by the pressing political concern with the perceived social breakdown in the inner cities. So while Houlihan (1991: 99) noted that 'Sport For All slowly became "sport for the disadvantaged" and "sport for inner-city youth"', Hargreaves argued that in practice this meant a preoccupation with youth, especially black youth: 'It is clear that the main concern is with the potentially troublesome – the unemployed, young white working-class males, and young working-class blacks' (1986: 189). The first significant programme to use the new target-group approach were the 15 Action Sport projects that were piloted in inner-city locales in London and Birmingham from 1982 to 1985 (Rigg, 1986). Action Sport was a project-based initiative that revolved around a sports worker going into particular communities to set up activity sessions and programmes. These first Action Sport programmes can be interpreted partly as a result of deliberations within the sports policy community, and partly as a response to the riots. So, despite the long list of Sports Council target groups, Action Sport focused predominantly on the perceived protagonists of social disorder, namely urban black youth and young working-class males.

Thus, the specific intervention to increase the opportunities for participation by ethnic minority groups was ambiguous. It was 'positive' to the extent that those in the sports policy community recognised that, in effect, affirmative action was required to redress the structural imbalances in participation. However, the racialisation of political discourse with its constructions of black criminality and inner-city decay ensured that the implementation of Sports Council policy agendas reinforced stereotypes about

black physicality and intellectual deficiency, therefore performing 'ideological work at reproducing blacks' subordinate position' (Hargreaves, 1986: 197). If the riots of 1981 elicited a physical response by the state to regain social control of the inner cities, then there is an argument for interpreting the role of sports policy as a form of 'soft' policing, ensuring in Foucauldian terms the main-tenance of social control by involving perceived problematic groups in sporting activities.

SPORTS POLICY, COMMUNITY AND MULTICULTURALISM

Although, predictably, there was strong condemnation of the riots in 1981 from the Thatcher government, there was also acknowledgement in subsequent state-sponsored investigations that racism in the police, along with problems of social deprivation and alienation, were contributory factors in producing such disorder (Solomos, 1993; Witte, 1996). Such conclusions paved the way for a growth of racial equality strategies mainly from local rather than central government, where anti-racist policies based on the concept of multiculturalism were most vigorously pursued. Multiculturalism was welcomed by many people as an advance on assimilationist models of 'race relations' in the embrace rather than the denial of cultural diversity. However, the doctrine of official multiculturalism is problematic as it fails to break out of the discourse of 'race'. In the context of what Barker (1981) called the New Racism – which shifted the discourse of racism from biology to ethnicity and culture – a new form of racial stratification emerged based on stereotypical notions of absolute ethnic difference. Ethnicity was intended by advocates of multiculturalism to be conceived of as a dynamic and fluid process of cultural self-identification and conceptually distinct from the objectifying and static category of 'race' (cf. Hesse, 2000). However, under the new racism, multiculturalism and ethnicity often rearticulated the old meanings of 'race' within a new socio-political discourse of inherent difference. Ethnicity became an imposed, fixed and immutable category, a cultural prison from which those it embraced could rarely escape – what Gilroy (1987) called ethnic absolutism.

Much of the focus for the Sports Council during the 1980s lay with working alongside local authorities in promoting sport in the community. As we have seen, its strategic document *Sport in the Community: the Next Ten Years* identified a number of target groups requiring specific policy interventions. However, the political climate of the early part of the decade dictated that black (male) urban youth were prioritised. However, as the memory of the riots faded, so the Action Sport projects incorporated other designated target groups, in particular Asian women. Though many of these projects were worthy and well intended, they tended to conform to an ethnic absolutist discourse of multiculturalism. For example, a number of projects in Manchester based on swimming, badminton and keep-fit, which were set up in 1987–8 and targeted at Asian women (and cited as an example of good practice by the Sports Council), reveal a tendency to view 'Asian women' as a culturally homogeneous 'other': 'Unlike the men, many Asian women living in Old Trafford had no social life outside the family. The strict constraints on young women, which they readily accepted, had to be understood and respected by project workers' (Sports Council, n.d.). Stereotypical perceptions of Asian women as socially isolated and passive, colluding in their

subordination to a patriarchal domesticity, abound in the evaluative project report.

The problem with adopting the target group approach is that it tended not to recognise the cause of the estrangement felt by many black and Asian people towards sport. The emphasis on 'cultural constraint' or 'difference' led policy-makers and sport development officers to problematise the target groups in question. In asking what it was about 'their culture', 'their religion', that needed to be understood in order for opportunities in sport to be made available, it allowed 'our sports' and 'our structures' to be left unexamined. Therefore, the persistent 'problem' of relatively low levels of participation amongst many ethnic minority groups is inadvertently blamed on 'them', whilst at the same time legitimating a presumed 'normal' level of sporting participation based on unacknowledged sporting practices of white, middle-class males. Fleming, whose research among Asian male youths showed that sport could be used as a tool by the white ethnic majority for excluding minority South Asian communities, argued that 'the preoccupation with cultural difference is a diversion and a distraction from the most fundamental issue – the pervasive impact of racism in all its guises' (Fleming, 1994: 172).

So the early Action Sport projects were geared towards black youth, but were located within a problematic law and order framework, whilst the attempt to relate to other ethnic minority groups was premised on the notion of cultural disadvantage and otherness. Furthermore, there was little evidence that such policies were succeeding in 'evening out' the differential levels of sport participation. Black and ethnic minority groups were still less likely to participate in sport than their white counterparts (McIntosh and Charlton, 1985; Verma and Darby, 1994). Such stubborn patterns of inequality in levels of participation demanded a different strategic focus, from one that treated 'race' and ethnicity as static variables that had to be overcome by sport *animateurs*, to one that saw 'race' and ethnicity as relations of power.

FROM ANTI-RACISM TO MANAGING RACIAL INEQUALITIES

During the early 1990s, fan-based football groups became increasingly successful at challenging popular images of all football fans as racist hooligans. They argued that although crude and overt forms of racism were still a problem on the terraces, they were restricted to a minority of fans who, in the absence of an anti-racist initiative, could attract much larger numbers behind them. They succeeded in persuading a number of bodies to come together to launch the 'Let's Kick Racism Out of Football' campaign in 1993. Sponsored initially by the Commission for Racial Equality (CRE) and the Professional Footballers' Association (PFA), with support from the Football Trust, the campaign soon gained the backing of all the main football bodies. It aimed to ensure that all those who go to see or play football could do so without fear of racial abuse or harassment. After the initial focus on fan racism in the professional game, it has since broadened its priorities to include amateur football, the dearth of professional South Asian players, the issue of racism in European football, and the continuing forms of discrimination from the boardrooms and managerial positions off the field of play (Back et al., 1996, 2001; Bains and Johal, 1998; Garland and Rowe, 2001). The significance of this campaign is that it has shifted the debate about 'race' and ethnicity away from the 'cultural peculiarities' of ethnic minorities towards the perpetrators of racism, whilst developing a more complex understanding of the articulation of racism beyond forms of 'race hate', and placed the responsibility for action on the relevant authorities.

The Sports Council accepted this shift of emphasis at a seminar organised in 1992, which was confirmed in its 1994 policy document on *Black and Ethnic Minorities and Sport*. It recognised that disadvantage and discrimination caused racial inequality and that positive action was required to address the causes of racism, rather than just its effects. It stated:

> The Sports Council recognises that racism is present in sport and can appear in many forms. We define racism to be all actions (or inactions), policies and practices of individuals or organisations, whether deliberate or not, which create or sustain racial inequality ... Because many people in sport have understood racism to consist only of overt and deliberate forms of discrimination, more subtle and unintentional racism is often not even detected. (Sports Council, 1994: 17)

The authors of the document argued that a combination of, and complex interplay between, socio-economic status, cultural lifestyle and racism accounted for the position of black and ethnic minorities in sport. It recognised the failings of previous approaches which did little:

> to challenge the underlying causes of this inequity ... A majority of decision-makers have little understanding of the sporting needs and aspirations of black and ethnic minorities. They are not aware of how disadvantage and discrimination restrict access to sport. (Sports Council, 1994: 18)

The report recommended that sports organisations inspect their own procedures and practices, and develop proactive policies to ensure equity within their own structures.

In addition, it advocated community development interventions to support and develop not only levels of participation but also self-management of projects.

Black and Ethnic Minorities and Sport was an analytically sound, realistic and constructive document. Its publication suggested that a more progressive approach to sport and racial inequality might be adopted. However, no sooner had the document been published than the Conservative government launched a major new policy for sport in 1995 which privileged the development of excellence in Britain's traditional team sports. Outlined in the policy document, *Sport: Raising the Game*, the new policy not only omitted any discussion of racism, but embraced a wholly traditionalist approach to sport that completely erased equality as a serious or central issue. Furthermore, the strategic emphasis on top-level sport, with its evidence of black athletic success, had the effect of denying the existence of racial barriers to progression in sport. In addition, in rejecting its responsibility towards sport in the community, it could also ignore the problems of racism in non-elite sport.

The campaign for racial equality in sport continued in football, and on a smaller scale in other sports, as evidence of racist practices intermittently emerged, leading to varied attempts to address the problem. For example, in 1996, the launch of the 'Tackle Racism in Rugby League' campaign – a joint venture from the CRE and the Rugby Football League (RFL) – was a response to research that demonstrated that racism was 'a small but significant' issue in the sport (Long et al., 1995; see also Long et al., 1997a). The campaign aimed to make Rugby League clubs take positive action to eradicate all racist abuse from their grounds, and to develop the game among ethnic minority communities in the clubs' local areas.

In cricket, a year earlier in 1995, issues of racism in sport hit the headlines when the reputable *Wisden Cricket Monthly* magazine published an article arguing that black and other foreign-born players should not play for England as they apparently would not try as hard as their white team-mates (Henderson, 1995). The spurious evidence provided for these claims owed more to nationalistic prejudices against 'non-white' cricketers than it did to any serious discussion about nationality and sport (Marqusee, 2001). In the wake of this and other evidence of racism in cricket, the campaign to 'Hit Racism for Six' (1996) was established to lobby the England and Wales Cricket Board (ECB) to address racism in the game.

The ease with which the analyses and recommendations contained in *Black and Ethnic Minorities and Sport* could be marginalised by the Sports Council – and sport governing bodies – so soon after its publication, suggests that a commitment to anti-racism had yet to be cemented in the organisation, and that the nuanced understanding of 'race' and ethnicity was probably restricted to those responsible for producing the report.

CONTEMPORARY DEVELOPMENTS AND ISSUES IN SPORTS POLICY AND 'RACE'

Social exclusion and racial equality under New Labour

It was expected that the election of a Labour government would herald a broader approach to sports policy – one that would be as concerned with increasing mass participation as raising levels of excellence (Labour Party, 1997; English Sports Council, 1997). However, as Houlihan argues, in office Labour have enthusiastically embraced the quest for international sporting success:

Despite rhetorical flourishes about reinvigorating the concept of Sport for All, it is the extent of continuity between the in-coming Labour government and its predecessors that has been most striking over the last two years ... in many ways the Labour Party sought to outshine the Conservatives in its commitment to competition and elite achievement. (Houlihan, 2000: 175)

Notwithstanding Houlihan's comments, within their shared commitment to national success, there are important policy distinctions between the two governments. Unlike *Sport: Raising the Game*, the publication of Sport England's National Lottery Strategy, *Investing for Our Sporting Future* (1999) and the subsequent government policy documents *A Sporting Future for All* (DCMS, 2000) and *The Government's Plan for Sport* (DCMS, 2001) contain significant references to the issue of equality. Sensitive to charges of favouring the elite levelled at their predecessors, Labour have emphasised that they are as much concerned with developing opportunities for a broader range of the population. This is expressed in policy commitments that see sport as a regenerative resource in deprived urban areas, and in the belief that diverse social groups should not be discriminated against and disenfranchised in the sporting sphere (DCMS, 2000). New Labour's use of sport to press its claims for a more just society is framed within the concept of 'social exclusion' and the political philosophy of the Third Way.

The starting point of the Third Way is that the failure of both state socialism and the unrestrained free market demonstrates the necessity for political discourse to move beyond the old language of Left and Right.

Tony Blair set out his Third Way approach to politics at a seminar in 1999, by citing the following points:

That human capital, people and their skills now matter more than money or equipment to economic success. That markets work best, but are fallible and need regulation – they cannot provide health, education or welfare. That how a government spends taxes, and what services it funds, is as important as how much it spends. *That the foundation of a modern welfare state is work for those who can and security for those who cannot. That strong civic society rests on responsibilities as well as rights ...* (White, 1999; emphasis added)

Of particular interest here is the Third Way position on poverty and equality. For advocates of the Third Way, the cause of poverty is seen less in structural terms and more in the failure or inability of people to access the 'networks of opportunity' (Dean and Woods, 1999: 10) that are assumed to exist within society to all its members. In a useful discussion of the concept of social exclusion under New Labour, Bennington and Donnison (1999: 64) point out that 'the concept of social exclusion is used to signify a shift in focus away from the poor and the state of poverty, towards the processes, policies and institutions which cause or reinforce poverty by excluding people'. Therefore what is required is not a redistribution of income, but a promotion of the means to ensure that individuals are included in the labour market and within the wider community. In short, people who are 'socially excluded' need a 'hand-up' not a 'hand-out'. Social exclusion rather than poverty is the scourge of modern liberal democracies.

Giddens has suggested that no rights without responsibilities is 'a prime motto for the new politics' (1998: 65). In response,

Lindsey German writes (1999: 11) that '[t]he accompanying talk of "rights and responsibilities" claims that rewards in society come from taking a responsible part in society'. She argues that the logic of the Third Way is ultimately to place the burden of responsibility on the individual for lifting themselves out of poverty. If, despite the state's efforts, people remain stubbornly unemployed, then this is their own fault and reflects their own personal inadequacies and/or failure to take the 'new opportunities' they have been offered. 'In this', concludes German, 'they represent a return to Victorian liberalism' (1999: 11). In her critique of the Third Way, Chantal Mouffe (2000) has also drawn attention to how the analysis of poverty, unemployment and poor education is abstracted from the wider structures of power in society, most notably in the economic and political spheres. She comments that:

By redefining the structural inequalities systematically produced by the market system in terms of 'exclusion', they eschew any type of structural analysis of their causes and sidestep the fundamental question of what needs to be done to tackle them. (Mouffe, 2000: 122)

Before we turn our attention to how the discussion of social exclusion and inclusion relates to sports policy and 'race', we need to clarify further how the terms are used. In political discourse, social exclusion and social inclusion are seen as binary opposites: so that in tackling social exclusion, the desired political goal of social inclusion will be achieved (Giddens, 1998). Although often used this way within sports policy, it is important to recognise that Sport England refers to social inclusion in an additional way, that is, as the conceptual framework to promote equality in terms of gender, 'race' and disability in sport. Social inclusion is the *principle* under which all sports organisations are asked to ensure that no barriers exist towards the increased participation of disabled people, women and ethnic minorities in sport. When used in this sense it is distinct from the use of social exclusion/inclusion in political discourses of poverty and lack of opportunities within deprived communities. Social exclusion has been very precisely operationalised in policy discourse: it occurs as a consequence of high unemployment, high rates of crime, poor health and low educational achievement. Where sport is part of this discourse, the concern is with how sports – along with other activities such as the arts, community projects and regeneration programmes – can be used to tackle social problems and thereby assist in the process of developing social cohesion (DCMS, 1999).

Sport England's Active Communities programme, which is aimed at providing participation and coaching opportunities in areas of social deprivation, has perhaps most relevance to the social exclusion agenda. In referring to the regenerative remit of sport, the social exclusion agenda at best implicitly relates to ethnic minorities inasmuch as they are part of the designated deprived communities. However, if the critics are correct that absent from the discourse of exclusion is the determining effect of structural relations of power, then the impact of racism in perpetuating discriminatory treatment will not be recognised. So, while 'race' is recognised as a social factor in patterns of social exclusion, the significance of *racism* is rarely treated as a contributory factor. Hargreaves's (1986: 198) prescient remark that 'the social structure is conjured away and what is left are individuals with their problems' remains as pertinent to New Labour's approach in the first decade of the twenty-first century, as it was about the individualistic ideology of the Conservative government throughout the 1980s and early 1990s.

Whereas the social exclusion agenda disavows the significance of racism, Sport England's principle of social inclusion leaves open the possibility for a discourse of racial discrimination and therefore of anti-racism. Indeed, there has been a flurry of activity, predominantly at the level of policy formulation, in recent years around the issue of social inclusion, racial equality and sport. A number of political factors coalesced to put racial equality on the political and sporting agenda. Not least of these were the high-profile inquiries and court cases relating to the murder of Stephen Lawrence, and the subsequent Macpherson Report published in February 1999. The definition of institutional racism contained in the report was taken up as the benchmark against which all public organisations should measure themselves. It defined institutional racism as:

The collective failure of an organisation to provide an appropriate and professional service to people because of their colour, culture or ethnic origin. It can be seen or detected in processes, attitudes and behaviour which amount to discrimination through unwitting prejudice, ignorance, thoughtlessness and racist stereotyping which disadvantage minority ethnic people. (Macpherson, 1999)

The changing political climate was reflected in the legislative amendments to the 1976 Race Relations Act. The Act was changed to make it unlawful for any public authority (private or voluntary bodies as well as statutory bodies) to discriminate on racial grounds when it is carrying out public functions. Further, and of greater significance for sports policy, it is now a duty of all public authorities to work towards eliminating racial discrimination and promoting racial equality in carrying out their functions. The second of these changes has potentially huge implications for sports governing bodies and clubs in placing the responsibility on them to be proactive in eliminating racial inequalities. It is the political space opened up by the Macpherson Report, and the legislative changes made in its wake, that have allowed significant policy developments to occur.

WORKING TOWARDS RACIAL EQUALITY?

Until recently, the analysis of patterns of racial inequality in sports participation has relied on small-scale and localised surveys, or information derived from the General Household Survey. The results of the first ever large-scale quantitative survey into the relationship between sports participation and ethnicity conducted by the Office for National Statistics on behalf of Sport England, is therefore of particular interest in that it confirms the existence of racial inequalities (Sport England, 2000). The survey found that the overall participation rate for ethnic minority groups in sport was 40 per cent compared with a national average of 46 per cent. Clearly, there are significant differences in rates of participation when the figures are broken down by gender and ethnicity. For example, black African men have a higher participation rate than the national average for all men, while Bangladeshi women had participation rates well below the national average for women.

The survey revealed that a large proportion of individuals from all ethnic groups say they would like to take part in a sport in which they currently do not participate, demonstrating a positive attitude to sport. However, also revealed was the fact that the main reasons for individuals not participating in sport were related to home and family responsibilities, work demands and lack of local facilities. The report concluded that while there is clear evidence of racial inequality in sport, this appears to have little to do with racism. Such a conclusion has to be treated with caution and may be largely a function of the quantitative methodology employed. As we have argued, racism works in increasingly complex and subtle ways: racial inequalities are often achieved and maintained while eschewing a language of 'race' and racism. It may be that more qualitatively inclined methodologies are better suited to eliciting the dynamics of racial ideologies buried beneath alternative explanations. In reflecting on his experience of conducting research into racism in sport with Asian and black athletes, Jonathon Long concluded that 'had we not been doing qualitative interviews, we may not have uncovered their experiences of racism' (Long, 2000: 129).

While uncovering levels of participation in sport lends itself to a quantitative approach, understanding the subjective experiences of individuals in sport demands a theoretically informed interpretative approach. It will be necessary for Sporting Equals, a body created by Sport England and the CRE in 1998, to work with governing bodies to develop policies for racial equality and to achieve a sophisticated understanding of the dynamics of racism in sport if it is to make progress. The evidence from a survey by Sporting Equals to gauge the approach of governing bodies to racial equality indicated a general resistance to discuss these issues. Of 62 national governing bodies surveyed, half did not respond, while 50 per cent of those that did claimed that racial discrimination was not a problem in their sport.

In producing a Racial Equality Charter for Sport (see Box 7.1), Sporting Equals appears to recognise that patterns of racial inequality in terms of participation, management and support are intimately related to a culture of racism that permeates British sporting establishments. As Box 7.1 reveals, racial inequality is not seen as being divorced from racial discrimination and, in a novel departure for policy-makers, representation in aspects of sport apart from participation is recognised.

Box 7.1 The Racial Equality Charter for Sport

Governing bodies and sports organisations will:

- Make a public commitment to challenge and remove racial discrimination and to achieve racial equality in sport.
- Encourage people from all communities to become involved in sport.
- Welcome employees and spectators from all communities, and protect all employees and spectators from racial abuse and harassment.
- Encourage skilled and talented individuals from all communities to become involved at all levels of sports administration, management and coaching.
- Develop the best possible racial equality policies and practices, and to review and update them regularly.
- Celebrate cultural diversity in sport.

(Sporting Equals, 2000)

Signatories to the Charter include the Chief Executives of Rugby Football League, Rugby Football Union, UK Athletics, England and Wales Cricket Board, English Basketball, Amateur Swimming Association and the National Coaching Foundation (Sporting Equals, 2000). In December 2000, Sporting Equals published *Achieving Racial Equality: a Standard for Sport* (2000). It encouraged governing bodies and organisations to provide evidence that they were working towards race equality objectives by developing Race Equality Action Plans and by monitoring the people who are taking part in the sport by age, gender, disability and ethnic origin. It also provided a means to measure the outcomes of its policies and action plans. Sporting Equals has devised a three-tier 'quality mark' scheme – preliminary, intermediate and advanced – which indicates the level of achievement by the organisation. This is intended to be incorporated in Sport England's criteria for National Lottery funds.

It is apparent then that racial equality is increasingly accepted at the level of policy formulation, although the situation is far more uneven amongst particular governing bodies. The chief mechanism for encouraging national governing bodies and sports organisations to integrate racial equality objectives into their strategic development plans is to link it to National Lottery funding criteria (DCMS, 2000). However, framing the quest for racial equality within the concept of social exclusion raises problems. In the final part of this chapter, we look at recent initiatives in cricket to illustrate some of these problems.

BUREAUCRATIC MANAGERIALISM: THE NEW DISCOURSE OF ANTI-RACISM?

Arguably, the sport that has made the most progress in developing a strategy for racial equality is cricket. The first half of the 1990s saw cricket officials and commentators promoting an inward-looking and racially exclusive form of nationalism (Marqusee, 1998). This invoked an imperial conception of Englishness prevalent in political discourse in the 1980s and 1990s, which actively sought to exclude 'non-white' citizens from the national imagined community (Carrington, 1998). However, by the end of the 1990s, the main debate centred on the need for cricket to tackle racism and to embrace its 'non-white' players, especially those from the Asian communities.

Such a dramatic shift can be seen as the result of a number of factors:

- the combination of anti-racist lobbying (Hit Racism for Six, 1996, 1998) and research (Long et al., 1997b; McDonald and Ugra, 1998);
- a recognition that traditional notions of Englishness may be detrimental to the performance of the national team (Hughes, 1999; Engel, 1999);
- the pressure to respond to the challenges set out by the Macpherson Report;
- the vigour with which Sport England promoted equity; and
- the contribution of the Asian communities to ensuring that the Cricket World Cup in 1999 was a commercial and sporting triumph (Crabbe and Wagg, 2000).

In 1998 the ECB created a Racism Study Group to compile a report that would outline the extent of racism in the game, based mainly on a quantitative survey of players and officials, and to produce a set of recommendations on how to tackle racism and ensure racial equality. The report was published in the autumn of 1999 and, according to Terry Bates of the ECB, was 'comprehensive and conclusive' (ECB,

1999: 5). After the racial controversies that had embroiled cricket for much of the 1990s, the report was widely received as a welcome step forward for this most tradition-bound of sports.

Unfortunately, the report failed to address the most fundamental issue on whether and how racism exists in cricket. It would only go as far as saying that their survey revealed that 58 per cent of respondents (of whom only a minority were 'non-white') *believed* that racism exists in English cricket. Accordingly, the report recommended 'that the ECB accepts and acknowledges ... that there is definitely, at least, *perceived racism* in cricket' (ECB, 1999: 43 [emphasis in the original]). However, in formulating the recommendation in this way, it allowed the ECB to sidestep the question of whether it accepted that racism was a real, rather than just a perceived, problem in the game. If the problem was one of perception, then it was that, rather than structural change, that needed to be managed. Furthermore, the report also stated that 'this survey did not establish that there is institutional racism in English cricket, as only 12 per cent thought that racism was ingrained in English cricket' (ECB, 1999: 43). This is a *non sequitur* as the measurement of institutional racism is not dependent purely on the beliefs of individuals covered by the survey. The report was silent on whether it accepted the conclusions of two separate academic reports based on Yorkshire (Long et al., 1997b) and Essex and East London (McDonald and Ugra, 1998) that a culture of racial exclusion is endemic within the structure of cricket.

If the report was weak analytically, then at least it came up with some measured and practical proposals to tackle racism and embrace the black and Asian cricket communities. However, many of the most significant proposals have not been implemented. For example, in the wake of the carnival atmosphere brought to the World Cup by many South Asian fans, it was recommended that the ban on banners, flags, placards and musical instruments in One Day Internationals and Test Matches be lifted for sections of the stands. The ban remains in force at certain grounds. It was recommended in the report that a number of tickets for these matches be reserved for sale on match days at affordable prices, which would give better access to more people from the black and South Asian community. This has been rejected on 'commercial' grounds. The report also recommended the establishment of a national forum to discuss the progress of anti-racism policies and the development of black and Asian cricket. This forum has yet to be created. Mike Marqusee, author of the widely acclaimed *Anyone but England: Cricket, Race and Class* (1998), dismissed the report as 'an empty, cynical document, offering little more than lofty declarations and skirting all the difficult questions' (Marqusee, 2000; for a more optimistic reading of the report see Williams, 2001).

The document illustrated how a governing body can be compelled to address the issue of 'race' and investigate issues of racial inequality, but will tread far more circumspectly around the issue of racism, especially where it might be implicated as a perpetrator. While the publication of *Clean Bowl Racism* illustrated how the ECB may appreciate the importance of 'race' as an issue, and while they are clearly sensitive to widespread perceptions of racism in the game, there is no evidence in the report that they accept that these perceptions may be reflecting the reality of racism in cricket. The problems facing black and Asian cricket teams is, according to the ECB, more a question of poor facilities and lack of coaching opportunities than racial discrimination. Yet, even on the question of investment in inner-city cricket, which would have a dramatic effect in widening the participation base of the group amongst all ethnic groups, the report had little of import to say. During the same period as the publication of *Clean Bowl Racism*, the ECB launched its Inner-city Community Cricket Project, amidst much publicity and government support. However, in an evaluation of the project in East London, Miller found that they were insufficiently funded and planned, and after the initial publicity, poorly supported by the ECB. He concluded that the commitment from the ECB to developing cricket in the inner cities 'represents little more than rhetoric' (Miller, 2001: 58).

The report can be seen as a bureaucratic managerialist response by the ECB. That is, on paper the ECB now has a clear anti-racism strategy and a commitment to improve the opportunities for ethnic minority cricket communities, which are predominantly located in inner-city areas. The ECB is also one of the signatories to the Sporting Equals' Racial Equality Charter. However, in practice, as we have outlined, the policy declarations have had little impact in affecting the culture of cricket or the relations of power with regard to control of the game. The general point is that unless policy documents are supported by analytical rigour, political commitment, financial support and systematic development, they will have little impact in reducing racism in sport and they will have a negligible effect on the social exclusion of ethnic minority groups.

CONCLUSION

In this chapter we have provided a critique of the relationship between 'race' and ethnicity and the development of sports policy since the 1970s. Our approach has been to locate sports policy within its social and political context in order to elicit a fuller understanding of how 'race', ethnicity and anti-racism are implicated in the policy process. We have argued that a concern with 'race' has been a constituent, if complex and ever-shifting feature of national sports policy since the 1970s. We have been guided in providing a critique by the advice of Michael Hill (1997: 22) to be: 'wary of taking policy-makers too seriously [*or too literally – text added*]. Policies may be intended to improve social conditions, but examining whether this is the case should be part of the object of enquiry rather than the assumption of research.'

A critical perspective is especially pertinent in the area of 'race' and ethnicity as governments in liberal democratic regimes rarely declare that their intention is to worsen or maintain poor social conditions, or contain the anger and disaffection of disadvantaged ethnic minorities. Yet despite the plethora of policy documents produced over the past 20 years, which have declared their intention to improve the opportunities for black and ethnic minorities in sport, patterns of racial inequality persist in participation, while many governing bodies still obstinately refuse to discuss 'race' issues within their own organisations. Those governing bodies that do, as we have illustrated with the case of cricket, prefer a managerialist approach that permits a discussion of 'race', encourages the signing of charters, and embraces policy pledges. Unfortunately, they are often reluctant to pursue policies that require significant investment of resources or that threaten entrenched interests. In this context we would argue that it is necessary for *all* governing bodies to take proactive steps in seeing the policy process as a framework that enables intervention and change both within their sports and within their own structures (see Table 7.1).

Table 7.1   *Racialisation in sport: a framework for policy intervention*

Arena	Context	Forms of racialisation	Policy response
Sporting institutions	• Administration, ruling bodies and decision making • Players' associations • Club ownership and committee control	• Racial inequality in terms of access to decision-making forums • Racial exclusion in relation to membership	• Increasing access and representation of Asian and black people within the administrative and ruling bodies of the sport • Challenging the normalised nature of whiteness in sport environments, representation through the media and the economics of ownership
Sporting practices	• Scouting and patterns of recruitment • Players' culture • Management and coaching • Administration and marketing • Representation/ experiences of black and Asian fans	• Connection between racialised attributes, sporting capacity and professional competence • Racialised forms of abuse within the playing/coaching/ spectating arenas	• Awareness within sport of racial stereotyping • Building a consensus against racialised common sense • Tighter adherence to codes of practice for players and coaches • Priority to developing Asian and black coaches/ scouts • Where appropriate, action against racist activity

Source: Adapted from Back et al. (2001: 214).

Meanwhile, the opportunity to develop sport in disadvantaged and deprived communities (a strong policy theme over the last 30 years) has been compromised by its justification within a problematic social control and empowerment rationale. While it may be overstating the case to assert that the conditions of black and ethnic minority communities in sport have not improved as a result of policy initiatives over the past 30 years, we cannot simply accept the underlying premise of these initiatives that sport improves 'race relations'. A more critical understanding of the changing nature of the politics of 'race' and sport would be aided if social policy analysts who have examined 'race' and racism began to take sport more seriously than they have up until now, and similarly if sports policy theorists paid greater attention to the centrality of 'race' and racism within their own analyses of the politics of sport and leisure.

We have argued elsewhere that inequalities and discrimination continue to structure the reality of sport for black and ethnic minorities in Britain in complex and often contradictory ways (Carrington and McDonald, 2001). Nonetheless, it is important to recognise the progress that has been made within sports policy, at least in terms of defining the problem. For example, the discussion in the sports policy community has shifted away from problematising minority groups and towards adopting a reflexive positioning regarding their structures of provision. Furthermore, the legitimacy of tackling racism and working towards racial equality is increasingly accepted, if not necessarily adequately understood, within the higher echelons of the sports policy community, notably the Department of Culture, Media and Sport, Sport England and Sporting Equals. Although a deep culture of racism may permeate sport in Britain, it is a still a contested cultural space. As such, the goal of creating a socially inclusive sporting world, which is both necessary and realistic, cannot be solely a matter of the right policy. If racism and racial inequality in all aspects of sport are to cease to be of significance, and if the promise of Sport for All is to be realised, then the analysis of policy needs to be related to broader relations of power in the culture of sport and society.

Chapter summary

- Policy on 'race' and ethnicity and sport needs to be analysed within the context of broader changes in social policy.
- 'Sport For All' reflected the discourse of equality dominant in the 1970s and early 1980s and which was replaced in the 1980s with a discourse that targeted potentially disruptive social groups such as black male urban youth.
- The policy of targeting problematised the target group rather than focusing on structural barriers and constraints on participation in sport.
- In the 1990s there was a move away from the policy of focusing on the 'cultural peculiarities' of ethnic minorities towards a concern with the perpetrators of racism.
- The impact on sport of changes in social policy has been to support a series of initiatives aimed at overcoming barriers to participation, and challenging racism at sports events and in sports organisations.
- While recognising the progress that has been made, it is still the case that inequalities and discrimination continue to structure the reality of sport for blacks and ethnic minorities.

Further reading

Law (1996) provides an introduction to the interrelationship between 'race' and ethnicity and the evolution of social policy, while Solomos and Back (1996) focus on the issue of 'race' and racism in Britain. There are a number of studies that explore racism in particular sports such as soccer (Back et al., 2001), cricket (Williams, 2001) and Rugby League (Long et al., 1997a). There are also studies (e.g. Bains and Johal, 1998) that focus on racism as experienced by particular ethnic groups. Carrington and McDonald (2001) provide a comprehensive examination of 'race' and sport in Britain.

REFERENCES

Back, L., Crabbe, T. and Solomos, J. (1996) *Alive and Still Kicking*. London: Advisory Group Against Racism and Intimidation and the Commission for Racial Equality.

Back, L., Crabbe, T. and Solomos, J. (2001) *The Changing Face of Football: Racism, Identity and Multiculture in the English Game*. Oxford: Berg.

Bains, J. and Johal, S. (1998) *Corner Flags and Corner Shops – the Asian Football Experience*. London: Victor Gollancz.

Barker, M. (1981) *The New Racism*. London: Junction Books.

Bennington, J. and Donnison, D. (1999) 'New Labour and social exclusion: the search for a Third Way – or just gilding the ghetto again?', *Social Policy Review*, 2: 45–70.

Carrington, B. (1998) '"Football's coming home" But whose home? And do we really want it? Nation, football and the politics of exclusion', in A. Brown (ed.), *Fanatics! Power, Identity and Fandom in Football*. London: Routledge, pp. 101–23.

Carrington, B. and McDonald, I. (eds) (2001) *'Race', Sport and British Society*. London: Routledge.

Cliff, T. and Gluckstein, D. (1988) *The Labour Party: a Marxist History*. London: Bookmarks.

Coalter, F., with Long, J. and Duffield, B. (1988) *Recreational Welfare: The Rationale for Public Leisure Policy*. Aldershot: Avebury.

Crabbe, T. and Wagg, S. (2000) 'A carnival of cricket? The cricket world cup, 'race' and the politics of carnival', *Culture, Sport and Society*, 3 (2): 70–88.

Dean, H. and Woods, R. (1999) 'Introduction', *Social Policy Review*, 2: 7–27.

Department of Culture, Media and Sport (DCMS) (1999) *Policy Action Team 10. A Report to the Social Exclusion Unit*. London: DCMS.

Department of Culture, Media and Sport (2000) *A Sporting Future for All*. London: DCMS.

Department of Culture, Media and Sport (2001) *The Government's Plan for Sport*. London: DCMS.

Department of the Environment (DOE) (1975) *Sport and Recreation*. London: HMSO.

Department of the Environment (1977a) *A Policy for the Inner Cities*. London: HMSO.

Department of the Environment (1977b) *Recreation and Deprivation in Urban Areas*. London: HMSO.

Department of National Heritage (1995) *Sport: Raising the Game*. London: HMSO.

Engel, M. (ed.) (1999) *Wisden Cricketer's Almanack*. Guildford: John Wisden & Co.

England and Wales Cricket Board (ECB) (1999) *Clean Bowl Racism: 'Going Forward Together': a Report on Racial Equality in Cricket*. London: ECB.

English Sports Council (1997) *England, the Sporting Nation: a Strategy*. London: English Sports Council.

Fleming, S. (1994) 'Sport and South Asian youth: the perils of false universalism and stereotyping', *Leisure Studies*, 13: 159–77.

Garland, J. and Rowe, M. (2001) *Racism and Anti-racism in Football*. Basingstoke: Palgrave.

German, L. (1999) 'The Blair project cracks', *International Socialism: a Quarterly Journal of Socialist Theory*, 82: 3–37.

Giddens, A. (1998) *The Third Way: the Renewal of Social Democracy*. London: Polity.

Gilroy, P. (1987) *There Ain't No Black in the Union Jack*. London: Hutchinson.

Hall, S., Critcher, C., Jefferson, T., Clarke, J. and Roberts, B. (1978) *Policing the Crisis: Mugging, the State, and Law and Order*. London: Macmillan.

Hargreaves, J. (1986) *Sport, Power and Culture*. London: Polity.

Henderson, R. (1995) 'Is it in the blood?', *Wisden Cricket Monthly*, July: 9–10.

Henry, I. (1990) 'Sport and the state: the development of sports policy in post-war Britain', in F. Kew (ed.), *Social Scientific Perspectives on Sport*. Leeds: BASES/NCF.

Henry, I. (1993) *The Politics of Leisure Policy*. Basingstoke: Macmillan.

Hesse, B. (ed.) (2000) *Un/Settled Multiculturalisms: Diasporas, Entanglements, Transruptions*. London: Zed Press.

Hill, M. (1997) *The Policy Process in the Modern State*. 3rd edn. London: Harvester Wheatsheaf.

Hit Racism for Six (1996) *Hit Racism for Six: Race and Cricket in England Today*. London: Wernham Press.

Hit Racism for Six (1998) Submission to ECB Racism Study Group, *HR46 Website. http://www-uk.cricket.org/ECB_SUBMISSION.html*.

Houlihan, B. (1991) *The Government and Politics of Sport*. London: Routledge.

Houlihan, B. (2000) 'Sporting excellence, schools and sports development: the politics of crowded policy spaces', *European Physical Education Review*, 6 (2): 171–93.

Hughes, S. (1999) 'Talking cricket: ethnic minorities in search of a level playing field', in *Electronic Telegraph*, 28 August 1999. *http:// www.telegraph.co.uk/.html*

Labour Party (1997) *Labour's Sporting Nation*. London: Labour Party.

Law, I. (1996) *Racism, Ethnicity and Social Policy*. London: Prentice Hall.

Long, J. (2000) 'No racism here? A preliminary examination of sporting innocence', *Managing Leisure*, 5 (3): 121–33.

Long, J., Tongue, N., Spracklen, K. and Carrington, B. (1995) *What's the Difference? A Study into the Nature and Extent of Racism within Rugby League*. Leeds: Leeds Metropolitan University/The Rugby Football League/Leeds City Council.

Long, J., Carrington, B. and Spracklen, K. (1997a) '"Asians cannot wear turbans in the scrum": Explorations of racist discourse within professional rugby league', *Leisure Studies*, 16: 249–60.

Long, J., Nesti, M., Carrington, B. and Gilson, N. (1997b) *Crossing the Boundary: the Nature and Extent of Racism in Local League Cricket*. Leeds: Leeds Metropolitan University.

McDonald, I. and Ugra, S. (1998) *Anyone for Cricket? Equal Opportunities and Changing Cricket Cultures in Essex and East London*. London: University of East London Press.

McIntosh, P. and Charlton, V. (1985) *The Impact of Sport for All Policy, 1966–1984, and a Way Forward*. London: Sports Council.

Macpherson, Sir W. (1999) *The Stephen Lawrence Inquiry: Report on the Inquiry by Sir William Macpherson of Cluny*. Cm. 4262. London: HMSO.

Marqusee, M. (1996) *War Minus the Shooting: a Journey through South Asia during Cricket's World Cup*. London: Heinemann.

Marqusee, M. (1998) *Anyone but England: Cricket, Race and Class*. London: Two Heads Publishing.

Marqusee, M. (2000) 'English fans priced out as ECB sidesteps race equality', in *http://thewicket. com/2000_08_01/sub_story3.asp*

Marqusee, M. (2001) 'In search of the unequivocal Englishman: the conundrum of race and nation in English cricket', in B. Carrington and I. McDonald (eds), *'Race', Sport and British Society*. London: Routledge.

Miller, N. (2001) 'Cricket, racism and identity: a critical analysis of English cricket in the 1990s'. Unpublished MA dissertation, University of Surrey, Roehampton.

Mouffe, C. (2000) *The Democratic Paradox*. London: Verso.

Rigg, M. (1986) *Action Sport: an Evaluation*. London: Sports Council.

Solomos, J. (1993) *Race and Racism in Britain*. 2nd edn. London: Macmillan.

Solomos, J. and Back, L. (1996) *Racism and Society*. Basingstoke: Macmillan.

Sport England (1999) *Investing for Our Sporting Future: Sport England Lottery Fund Strategy 1999–2009*. London: Sport England.

Sport England (2000) *Sports Participation and Ethnicity in England: National Survey 1999–2000*. London: Sport England.

Sporting Equals (2000) *Achieving Racial Equality: a Standard for Sport*. London: Sport England/ CRE.

Sports Council (n.d.) *Action Sport: Selected Case Studies*. London: Sports Council.

Sports Council (1982) *Sport in the Community: the Next Ten Years*. London: Sports Council.

Sports Council (1994) *Black and Ethnic Minorities and Sport*. London: Sports Council.

Verma, G. and Darby, D. (1994) *Winners and Losers: Ethnic Minorities in Sport and Recreation*. London: Falmer Press.

White, M. (1999) 'Blair hails middle class revolution' *Guardian*, 15 January. *http:// www.guardianunlimited.co.uk/Archive/Article/. html*

Williams, J. (2001) *Cricket and Race*. Oxford: Berg.

Witte, R. (1996) *Racist Violence and the State*. London: Longman.

8

Sport, Physical Education and Schools

DAVID KIRK

Overview

→ A genealogy of physical education
→ Physical education as a contested concept
→ The practice of physical education: what have we learned from research?
→ Issues and trends in physical education

This chapter provides an introduction to the study of physical education as a topic of social research. It begins with a genealogy that shows physical education to be an essentially contested concept that has been the subject of acrimonious debate and struggle for over a century and a half. The role of educational philosophers in contributing to the conceptual confusion surrounding physical education is examined and their epistemological approach is challenged. Social epistemology is introduced as an approach to the study of knowledge that allows researchers to investigate empirically the social conditions of knowledge production. Social epistemology proposes that physical education may be defined by the practices that take place in its name.

This approach is used to frame a diverse range of research on the practice of physical education. Research on teaching and teacher education, the social construction of gender, curriculum policy and practice, and student perspectives, participation and learning is overviewed selectively to demonstrate the complexity of the practice of physical education and the difficulty of providing simple definitions. The chapter concludes with a discussion of four issues that may be key to physical education's future.

A GENEALOGY OF PHYSICAL EDUCATION

The earliest forms of physical education to appear in government schools, somewhere between the 1860s and 1880s in Britain, were commonly referred to as drill. Drill involved a combination of marching and other military manoeuvres and exercises drawn from one or more of the many systems of gymnastics that existed at the time. By the time of the publication in 1909 of the official government syllabus for schools, the system of free-standing exercises devised by the Swede Per Henrick Ling had won out over earlier military versions of drilling and exercising. Around this time, just before the First World War, the term 'physical training' began to be used in schools to describe the Ling system. The adoption of the Ling system was viewed as progressive at this time since it was based on a therapeutic rationale, despite being delivered in a militaristic way.

Meanwhile, boys and girls in the fee-paying schools had been playing sports and games since at least the 1850s, and these activities effectively formed the basis of their 'physical education', although this term itself did not come into common usage until after the Second World War in 1946. By then, the Ling system of gymnastics had been almost completely replaced in government schools by a form of physical education based on educational gymnastics and dance, and another based on sports and games. These forms of physical education, new to the expanding government secondary schools system during the 1950s and 1960s, formed the basis of physical education programmes in operation today.

If this brief history suggests a smooth and seamless progression towards more enlightened forms of physical education over time, then it is misleading. Far from being smooth, the emergence of forms of physical education over the 150-year period was marked by conflict, contestation and struggle. For example, the choice of a military form of drilling and exercising for young primary school children in the 1880s was based in large part on the view that these children had to be controlled and disciplined (Kirk, 1998). The requirement by law that all children attend school was new in the 1880s, and school authorities were keen to extract the maximum benefits from the state's investment in the education of the masses. They saw military drilling and exercising to be ideal for controlling the behaviour of allegedly unruly and undisciplined working-class children (Smith, 1974).

When in the early 1900s it became clear that these exercises were unnecessary, inappropriate and in some cases harmful for young children who were actually less likely to riot than their upper-class peers, there was pressure to change. However, the militarists from all sectors of society were set against any change and believed military drill to be essential to law and order in schools and in society more broadly (Penn, 1999). The new Ling system was implemented against a backdrop of ferocious debate and much acrimony, and it took a long time to shake off the military style of presentation.

The shift from Lingian to educational gymnastics provides another example of contestation over which form of physical education should be taught in schools. The main body of qualified physical education teachers between 1890 and 1946 were women trained in private single-sex colleges (Fletcher, 1984). By the 1930s, some of these teachers began to feel the Ling system was too regimented for children and, influenced by the work of Rudolf Laban in particular, they began to practise a looser and more creative form of gymnastics. The traditionalists fought this development tooth and nail, and it took over 20 years for educational gymnastics to become established as the main form of physical education for younger children and older girls. Ironically, just as this happened in the early 1950s, men began to enter the physical education profession in large numbers. They didn't like the look of educational gymnastics at all, and championed instead a form of physical education based on sports, games and fitness activities. Before long, the mainly female educational gymnasts were fighting a rearguard action (Kirk, 1992). By the end of the 1960s, the male form of physical education was widespread and dominant (Whitehead and Hendry, 1976).

All of this is to demonstrate that the form physical education has taken at any point in its modern history has been the outcome of fierce battles between rival individuals and groups. Physical education is, quite literally, an essentially contested concept.

PHYSICAL EDUCATION AS A CONTESTED CONCEPT

Perhaps owing to this history of conflict, since the 1970s it has become part of the conventional wisdom among physical educators that there is no consensus within their profession on the aims and content of their subject. Textbook writers point to the many definitions of physical education that have proliferated over the past 30 years as proof that there is no established definition. Even though physical educators as a profession seem to disagree about the nature of their subject, they are usually quick to point out to anyone who will listen that physical education and sport are not the same thing. This claim confuses a lot of people in the sport community as well as members of the general public, since sport seems to form a very large and increasing part of what physical educators have been teaching in schools since the end of the Second World War.

This apparently confused state of affairs was arguably made worse by a group of philosophers of education, who in the 1970s and 1980s attempted to clarify the meaning of physical education through epistemology, which is the study of knowledge. Epistemological studies had formed one major strand of the philosophy of education since the 1960s. In Britain early pioneers were Richard Peters (1966) and Paul Hirst (1974), while in the United States the work of Philip Phenix (1964) was influential. Peters, Hirst, Phenix and the other scholars who followed them were interested in the meaning of the concept of education. This work was informed by the language analysis approach of philosophers such as Wittgenstein.

The educational philosophers of the 1960s and 1970s were interested in how an analysis of the concept of education and other related ideas might inform educational policy making and practice. Their approach found particular application in the troublesome issue of what subject matter should be taught to children in schools. In countries such as Australia and Britain, Peters's notion of 'worthwhile activities' and Hirst's 'forms of knowledge' thesis were very influential in shaping policymakers' views on those subjects that should be a required part of the school curriculum and those that should be optional or excluded (Lawton, 1983).

This line of epistemological study in the philosophy of education had serious implications for physical education. According to the Peters/Hirst perspective, physical education did not qualify as an educationally worthwhile subject. It could not then be regarded as part of the 'core curriculum' of schools. At best it was consigned to the role of elective or at worst to the extracurricular programme of the school. By the early 1970s, philosophers such as David Best (1978) and Bob Carlisle (1969) had joined the debate over physical education's educational status. While they found ingenious ways of affirming physical education's educational worth within the terms of the arguments proposed by Peters and Hirst, few questioned the appropriateness of the language analysis approach to analysing key concepts. The outcome of physical educationists' uncritical acceptance of this approach was a seemingly endless, circular and self-referential debate with little actual progress in schools and by government in terms of recognition of the educational value of physical education. Significantly, they also made little progress in understanding the aims, content and pedagogy of physical education.

There is some irony here, as educational philosopher David Aspin (1976) on more than one occasion has pointed out. In his *Philosophical Investigations*, Wittgenstein (1953) proposed that in the absence of tight definitions of words, another way to discover the meaning of words or concepts is to explore their family resemblance and to investigate their 'meaning-in-usage'. Even though this implies empirical investigation and contextualisation of word usage, none of the philosophers of education moved much beyond their armchairs. The result was the examination of the meaning of words and concepts *in the personal experience* of the philosopher.

However, the tools with which to mount such a critique, as Aspin (1976) demonstrated, had been available to philosophers prior to the 1970s. This critique emerged from another direction however. In 1971, Michael F.D. Young edited a volume of papers entitled *Knowledge and Control*. The 'new directions' sociology of education signalled in the book's subtitle was concerned broadly with the social construction of school knowledge. A key interest of contributors such as Esland, Bernstein, Bourdieu and Young himself was to examine the social conditions of knowledge production. This work had enormous implications for

the epistemological studies of Peters, Hirst and philosophers in physical education, since it became possible to locate their work within the social contexts in which it was produced. This led, among other things, to an ability to ask questions about vested interests, power and ideology – themes that were picked up with a curriculum focus by US authors such as Michael Apple (1979) and Henry Giroux (1981).

This work did not enter the English-language literature in physical education until Evans edited a collection of sociological studies that appeared in 1986. However, neither Evans nor his contributors at this time applied the tools of new directions sociology of education in a critical appraisal of the language analysis approach.

Building on new directions sociology of education, the curriculum history research of Goodson (1988) and others, it was now possible to examine the question of the definition and purpose of physical education from a social epistemological perspective. In contrast to previous epistemological studies in education that were concerned with the meaning of concepts according to the philosopher, social epistemology is concerned with the empirical study of the meaning-in-use of concepts and the practices that are undertaken in the name of such notions as physical education. Such an approach retains the focus of earlier studies of knowledge forms in terms of understanding the meaning of words and concepts. In social epistemology, such inquiry is grounded in specific sites, during designated periods in time, and attempts to understand the meaning-making activities of individuals and groups within complex configurations of social forces, institutions and cultural forms.

So in order to understand the essentially contested concept of physical education, we need to look closely at what people do in the name of physical education. These practices effectively constitute physical education; they define physical education (Kirk, 1992). In order to do this, we need an overview of what is already known from research about these practices. What becomes immediately evident from this overview is that physical education is not easily defined because the practices constituting it are varied and complex.

THE PRACTICE OF PHYSICAL EDUCATION: WHAT HAVE WE LEARNED FROM RESEARCH?

Since the late 1960s, an emerging and diverse literature has sought to investigate the practice of physical education. Evans and Davies (1986) provide an excellent overview of this early research. The focus here is on what we have learned from research studies since the mid-1980s. The majority of research has been concerned with teaching and teacher education, the social construction of gender, curriculum policy and practice and students' perspectives, participation and learning.

Teaching and teacher education

The study of teachers and teaching makes up a substantial category of research on the practice of physical education. Within this research programme, socialisation into teaching has been a central organising concept. This research has been influential in steering researchers towards an interest in teachers' lives and careers. Researchers have also turned their attention to teachers' work and to their interpretations of the forces that operate on the routine, day-to-day aspects of their work.

The cyclical process of recruitment of physical education teachers, their acquisition of the knowledge, values and practices of the profession during pre-service teacher education courses, their induction into the workplace and their subsequent career paths have been subject to much critical scrutiny by researchers. They have conceptualised this process as one of socialisation into physical education teaching. In two important collections of research studies edited by Templin and Schempp (1989) and Stroot (1993), socialisation is considered to be a dialectical process involving the dynamic interplay between self-identity and collective practices of physical educators which results in the production of professional identities. Research into each of these key stages of the socialisation process has been overviewed by the authors contributing to the Stroot (1993) collection, and some of the key findings summarised.

Recruitment into teaching

At the recruitment stage, the early work of Lawson (1983) and Dewar and Lawson (1984) reported that the subjective warrant for entering a career in physical education teaching included the prospects of continuing association with sport and physical activity at which prospective student teachers had already excelled, opportunities to work with people and offer a service to the community, and the promise of good working conditions. More recent research reported by Hutchinson (1993) suggests that these and other orientations formed before entry to the field are likely to persist throughout and beyond a teacher education course. In a critical analysis of the recruitment phase, Dewar (1989) argued that a prospective recruit's experience of school physical education has a significant influence on the early formation of beliefs about the work of teachers of physical education.

Teacher education

Professional preparation has been recognised as an agent of socialisation into teaching (Graber, 1989). Templin and Schempp (1989) report that as a consequence, considerable attention has been directed to the structure of pre-service teacher education courses. However, Doolittle et al. (1993), in their consideration of the effects of teacher education programmes on altering the entry beliefs of student teachers, suggest that pre-service courses typically have a low impact on these beliefs. This claim is supported by Rovegno (1992, 1993), who has shown that pre-service teacher education can only, with some difficulty, assist student teachers to overcome cultural templates and adopt a socially critical perspective on teaching physical education. Doolittle and Schwager (1989) and Tinning et al. (1996) have made tentative claims that inservice teacher education can make a positive contribution to altering teachers' beliefs and values.

Entry into the workforce

Stroot et al. (1993) provide an overview of the research on the induction of physical education teachers into the workforce. They note that young teachers experience reality shock, role conflict, isolation and a washout effect during the first year of teaching. Macdonald has extended this research by reporting on factors contributing to a high attrition rate among newly qualified teachers of physical education. These factors include a trend towards the de-professionalisation of teaching within the context of the rise to prominence of other vocational applications of the field of human movement studies such as exercise management and prescription, and close surveillance of new teachers' private and public lives (Macdonald and Kirk, 1996; Macdonald, 1995; Macdonald et al., 1994).

Teachers' work, lives and careers

An emerging programme of research has begun to attend increasingly to teachers' work, building on Lawson's (1989) framework for understanding workplace conditions (Stroot and Lawson, 1993). Additional research by Armour and Jones (1998), Sparkes et al. (1993) and Squires and Sparkes (1996), has used a life history approach to teachers' lives and careers, and has produced explanations of teachers' motivations for and interests in remaining in or leaving teaching. Supplemented by interview and survey-based research (e.g. Evans and Williams, 1989; Macdonald and Kirk, 1999), these studies suggest that gender, social class and religion play key roles in the formation of teachers' professional identity and teachers' abilities to access opportunities to enhance promotion prospects. Ennis and her colleagues (Ennis and Chen, 1993; Ennis, 1992) developed a research programme centred on the investigation of teacher value orientations for teaching physical education and the effects of value orientations on teaching practices and programme development.

The social construction of gender

As a professional body of physical educators began to emerge in the first half of the twentieth century, they were strictly segregated in their training according to 'the sex of the individual' (Kirk, 1992). Owing to this single-sex training, gendered forms of physical education have vied with each other for a dominant place in school programmes. In the last 30 years, a form of physical education sponsored principally by male physical educators with competitive team games at its core has come to dominate school programmes in Australia, Britain and parts of North America. Fletcher's historical sociology of the female tradition in English physical education has shown that progressive desegregation of courses from the mid-1960s resulted in the marginalisation of a distinctly female version of the subject, best exemplified by activities such as modern educational dance and educational gymnastics (Fletcher, 1984). In this historical context, a significant research programme has developed around the topic of the social construction of gender in and through physical education, focusing particularly on girls' and women's experiences of physical education and physical education teacher education.

Griffin utilised ethnographic methods in a study of gender in co-educational middle school physical education (Griffin, 1984, 1985). She noted that patterns of interaction between students, and subsequent opportunities to learn, were heavily influenced by the sex of the students. While she noted considerable variation in participation styles within the sexes, much of the boys' conduct was characterised by overtly physical and aggressive forms of behaviour and public clowning, while girls' behaviour was characterised by co-operation and verbal communication. She noted that girls were regularly hassled by boys to give up equipment or for taking an activity seriously, and that boys often delimited the range of their own potential learning experiences by ridiculing as 'sissy' or for 'wimps' some forms of physical activity. As a result of these studies, Griffin (1989) argued that gender is a key socialising agent in physical education and a major mediating factor in student learning.

Scraton's (1992) study of gender and girls' physical education sought to locate girls' experiences of physical activity in schools within a broad framework of women's oppression within a patriarchal society. She also intended to contribute to feminist theory at a time when there was little serious

attention being paid to 'the physical' by feminist scholars. Scraton showed how images of femininity and gender-appropriate behaviour were constructed and legitimated through girls' experiences of physical education. Methodologically, Scraton attempted to examine together the structures of power, the ideological positions represented within them, and their instantiation within school practices. Her research had political purposes, and sought to outline possibilities in and through physical education for the emancipation of women (Scraton and Flintoff, 1992).

Given the long history of sex segregation in physical education teacher education, studies by Flintoff (1993) and Dewar (1990) have been particularly important. Both studies, again utilising ethnographic methods, examined the social construction of gender and the reproduction of gender inequalities at a time when physical education teacher education institutions were required through legislation to move towards de-segregated, co-educational arrangements both in Europe and North America. In both studies, the researchers found that women were forced to negotiate forms of gender and sexual identity that were regarded as appropriate to the dominant masculinist ethos of the institutions. In Dewar's study, for example, women negotiated identities within the physical education teacher education peer group that could be categorised as a 'prissy' ultra-feminine identity, a 'jock' identity that involved women displaying strongly masculine behaviours, and a 'dyke' identity of lesbian students. Flintoff's and Dewar's studies hold important implications for school physical education and suggest that physical education teacher education faces serious future challenges in addressing the social construction of gender.

Wright's study of teacher talk and its contribution to the construction of gendered subjectivity in physical education is one of the few sociological studies of physical education to employ the analytical tools of social semiotics utilising audio and video recordings of lessons in addition to standard ethnographic methods (Wright, 1993, 1997; Wright and King, 1991). Her findings supported those of Griffin and Scraton to the extent that girls were represented through teacher talk as being in deficit of qualities the teachers valued, such as skilfulness, perseverance, application and toughness. The language teachers used to communicate with students revealed deeply entrenched expectations of appropriate gendered behaviour of girls and boys, lending support to Martinek's (1981) earlier research on the Pygmalion effect.

Feminist studies of girls and the construction of femininity remain the predominant form of research on gender within the physical education research literature (e.g. Williams and Bedward, 1999; Lyons and Lyons, 1998). While boys have been included in some studies of gender, such as Griffin's, and Lyons and Lyons's (1998), their participation in physical education tended not to be conceptualised as a means of the social construction of masculinity. An emerging line of research has now begun to examine boys' experiences of physical education and sport (Gard and Meyenn, 2000; Walker, 1988; Wright, 2000) and outdoor adventure activities (Humberstone, 1990) in the making of masculinities.

Curriculum policy and practice

A third substantial programme of research in physical education has been concerned with curriculum policy and practice. These two points of focus have sometimes been treated as distinct topics of study. However, Penney and Evans (1999) have proposed

that they form a continuum of activities in which policy is made in a range of sites, including the offices of specialised curriculum developers and policy-makers, and also in school and classroom practice. Much of this research has tended to focus on specific contemporary curriculum developments and their impact on school practices, and this has led some researchers to examine explicitly the processes of change in physical education, both within specific sites such as schools, and across sites and systems.

The combined results of research studies of contemporary practice since the mid-1980s demonstrate accelerating curriculum development in physical education as a result, in some cases, of shifts in social values and in others, of system-wide changes to education in a number of countries.

The emergence of health-based forms of physical education has been a widely investigated development. Studies by Tinning and Kirk (1991), Kimiecik and Lawson (1996), Cale (1997) and Harris (1998) have utilised data from surveys, document analysis and teacher and student interviews to locate these developments within a new health consciousness among the middle classes of many Western countries. Some studies report that a typical outcome of health-based developments has been a narrowing of programme goals and content to focus almost exclusively on improving the physical fitness of children through exercise, while ignoring or reducing the importance of other potential educational outcomes for physical education. Others suggest that in Britain particularly, health-related issues tend to be dispersed through the curriculum resulting in time pressure and marginalisation.

A second and more recent development of major significance has been sport education. According to Siedentop (1994), sport

---

Box 8.1   Sport education

Siedentop (1994) identifies six features of sport education that resemble the forms of sport practised in the community.

1   *Seasons* are one key characteristic of Siedentop's model and represent the macro unit of time around which sport is organised. Seasons include periods of practice and competition.
2   *Affiliation* relates to players' identification with their team, to their sense of membership and belonging. In sport education, individuals usually remain in the same team throughout the season.
3   *Formal competition* is a third, and defining, characteristic of sport. As such, it must be present in sport education, even though the nature of the competitive experience for children is carefully regulated according to their developmental levels and the teachers' intended educational outcomes.
4   *The culminating event* provides a focus for the season and a motivator for players to work hard.
5   *Record keeping* provides feedback and incentives for individuals and teams.
6   *Festivity* adds an important social element to sport for its participants.

---

education models competitive sport, including the allocation of roles such as player, coach, administrator and reporter and competitions between teams and leagues played within seasons. This model of sport education has now been trialled extensively. Research and development projects have been carried out in the USA, mostly in primary schools (Siedentop, 1994). Complementing this focus, much of the work in New Zealand by Grant and his colleagues (Grant et al., 1992), and in Australia by Alexander and his colleagues (1996), has been in secondary schools.

These studies and others that have followed have reported findings in relation to student learning outcomes and teacher professional development. These studies have shown that sport education provides a more meaningful experience of physical education for young people than the traditional, multi-activity model, and higher levels of identification with school physical education (e.g. Grant, 1992; Alexander et al., 1993; Bennet and Hastie, 1997). Hastie (1996, 1998) has shown that sport education delivers improvements both in the development of techniques and in tactical decision making, and also improves young people's understanding of games through their participation in a range of roles such as umpire, manager, scorekeeper, and so on. Grant et al. (1992) and Carlson and Hastie (1997) suggest that sport education provides opportunities to develop the student social system in classes, such as higher levels of peer support, while other researchers have shown that it enhances learning experiences for all categories of students, including 'lower-skilled' young people (Carlson, 1995; Hastie, 1998; Alexander and Luckman, 1998). Studies suggest this model provides teachers with more opportunities to interact with students on a one-to-one basis (Hastie, 1998), delivers quality professional development opportunities to teachers (Alexander et al., 1996) and in primary schools provides opportunities for curriculum integration (Alexander and Luckman, 1998).

A third curriculum development has been Teaching Games for Understanding (TGfU). Following Bunker and Thorpe's (1982) advocacy for a tactical approach to games education, TGfU attracted growing interest among physical and sport educators through the 1980s and from researchers in the 1990s. Much of this research has taken the form of experimental studies that have compared TGfU with the forms of games teaching it is assumed to replace, traditional technique-based approaches that typically manipulate some form of whole/part/whole learning of skills (e.g. Griffin et al., 1997; Lawton, 1989).

Rink et al. (1996) noted that research on TGfU has reported positive learning outcomes for students. They also noted that these studies have been unable to provide conclusive support for TGfU over technique-based approaches. The most powerful finding across these studies is that students who have been taught from a tactical perspective tend to perform better on tests of tactical knowledge than those who have been taught from a technique-based perspective. Some studies have suggested that a tactical approach may be perceived by students to be more enjoyable than the technique-based approach, and so students may be more highly motivated to participate. On most other measures, there appear to be few differences between approaches in terms of student learning.

Physical educators' attempts to respond to system-wide changes in education have also been widely researched. In Australia, Fitzclarence and Tinning (1990) found considerable resistance from teachers to the

development of a new form of physical education in conjunction with the Victorian Certificate of Education for Years 11 and 12 students. Macdonald and Brooker (1997) studied the trialling of a new Senior School Syllabus in Physical Education in the Australian state of Queensland. They concluded that a strength of the syllabus, based on Arnold's model of learning in, through and about physical activity, was its integration of 'theoretical' and 'practical' work and its challenge to the mind/body dualism that often characterises thinking about physical education.

Evans and his colleagues (1996) have focused much of their research since the late 1980s on the effects of the Educational Reform Act (ERA) of 1988 in England and Wales on the provision of physical education and sport in schools and on the implementation of a National Curriculum for Physical Education (NCPE). This research programme has produced an analysis of the ideological forces shaping the government's positioning of physical education within the school curriculum, which has tended towards a conservative, traditional orientation celebrating masculine values and competitive sport (Evans, 1990).

It has also produced a thorough examination of the interdependent roles of government agencies such as Sport England, local education authorities and schools in constructing a delimited range of forms that physical education might take, restricted predominantly to performance in sport and games. Penney and Evans (1999) argue that as a result of the interactions between these levels of policy creation and implementation, serious inequities remain in terms of children's access to a broad and balanced experience of physical education that the ERA was intended to assure. Penney and Evans (1999) also suggest that the NCPE accorded teachers a high degree of ownership of, and flexibility in, curriculum

---

Box 8.2   The National Curriculum for Physical Education (NCPE)

The NCPE has been revised twice in 1995 and 1999 since its first appearance following the Educational Reform Act of 1988. In its current form, the NCPE requires schools to use six categories of activities (games, gymnastics, athletics, dance, outdoor and adventurous activities, and swimming and water safety) to facilitate learning in the following four key aspects: acquiring and developing skills; selecting and applying skills, tactics and compositional ideas; evaluating and improving performance; knowledge and understanding of fitness and health. Requirements for the type of activities that must be offered vary for each key stage, with the latest revision streamlining the number of activities to be offered at KS 1 and 2.

---

development, albeit within important frames, but that teachers largely failed to exploit the potential for such development. They suggested that teachers have been constrained by both conservative official texts and by contexts that offer little incentive or support for the development of innovative ideas. They concluded that the development of the NCPE has not resulted in the emergence of new or diverse discourses in physical education but rather the consolidation of marginality and the reinforcement of established discourses in both 'policy' and 'practice'.

Student perspectives, participation and learning

The study of school students has appeared somewhat erratically in the physical education literature. Researchers have conducted three forms of research that have included students: studies of participation; studies of attitudes and identity; and studies of learning.

The majority of research on students has involved surveys of participation. Research using surveys usually require students to self-report their participation levels and various likes and dislikes in relation to school physical education and sport. This form of research tends to conceptualise participation and attitudes as indicators of the effects of physical education programmes. Surveys by the Australian Sports Commission (1991) and Mason (1995) are good examples of this genre of research. Participation results from individual studies are by themselves difficult to interpret. One of the few significant patterns to emerge from these studies is that levels of participation begin to taper significantly along with positive attitudes towards physical education, disproportionately among girls, with the onset of adolescence. Another finding that emerges regularly from such surveys is that young people in the main have positive attitudes towards participation in physical activity but are often discouraged by over-competitive attitudes among peers, teachers and other adults.

In the case of the focus on attitudes and identity, much of this research is dispersed throughout the research literature and linked to other topics such as gender (Wright, 2000), drop-out from sport (Robertson, 1988) and student alienation (Carlson, 1995). Biddle (1999) among others has conducted a range of studies concerned with the measurement of young people's motivation for participating in physical education. This psychological research suggests that some motivational profiles are more desirable than others in terms of the nature of young people's engagement in physical education and physical activity more generally.

Another emerging line of research has been concerned with learning in physical education. The interest in learning presents a challenge to physical education researchers. The challenge is that learning within the physical domain remains poorly understood, particularly in schools settings (Rink et al., 1996). Progress has been made in measuring cognitive processes in physical activity settings (Solmon and Lee, 1997), while developments in motor learning theory have assisted researchers' understanding of the ecological dimensions of learning (Abernethy, 1996). However, dualistic assumptions about learning and knowledge development in physical education remain pervasive (e.g. McMorris, 1998).

One aspect of the research programme on learning has investigated children's conceptions of games play, often linked to initiatives such as TGfU and HRE. This research has sought to understanding children's alternative conceptions of playing games compared with adult and expert conceptions. It has suggested that these alternative conceptions are highly influential in determining what children learn in school physical education (Griffin et al., 1999; Placek et al., 1998).

From this concern for what young people learn in physical education there has emerged a call for research to focus on the relationship between learning, instruction and subject matter (Metzler, 2000). Rink (1999) suggests that all instructional strategies need to be based on learning theory. This is because instructional approaches that

are not rooted in a clear understanding of learning are unlikely to produce desired learning outcomes. Rovegno (1999) argues that learning must be understood in relation to the subject matter of physical education. According to Rovegno, research that has sought to identify generic features of quality instruction provides little assistance in teaching specific content. Kirk and Macdonald (1998) claim that a neglect of learning may account for many of the failures of curriculum reform in physical education. They advocate situated learning theory as an underpinning rationale for curriculum development so researchers can assess the influence of specific sites and socio-cultural milieu on young people's learning.

ISSUES AND TRENDS IN PHYSICAL EDUCATION

We can see from the brief selective overview of research that the practice of physical education is far from simple to describe. Perhaps it is now easier to understand why individuals and groups have contested physical education over time; what counts as physical education is varied and complex. There are nevertheless some pressing themes that emerge from the research on physical education which provide some signposts for future developments. This chapter concludes with a brief examination of four prominent issues: the marginal educational status of physical education; physical education versus sport; girls and gender; and the relationship between research, practice and change.

The marginal educational status of physical education

The educational philosophising of Peters, Hirst and others in the 1960s through to the

1980s reinforced already existing prejudices within the educational policy and teaching communities that physical education should not be included in the core curriculum of schools. Despite valiant attempts by some philosophers to defend physical education on Peters's and Hirst's own territory, the flawed assumptions on which this form of epistemology rests made it difficult for physical educators to overturn existing prejudices. Significantly, there was very little support for this kind of philosophical argumentation from the grassroots of physical education teaching, where practitioners with interests in biophysical science found the arguments too esoteric and abstract to fit the pressing concerns of school practice.

The health-related exercise (HRE) movement that began in Britain in the early 1980s seemed to some physical educators to offer much more solid arguments for physical education's place in the curriculum than perhaps the epistemological waffling of the philosophers. HRE does indeed make a sound case for physical education's contribution to young people's health. However, if only health-related activity were to be included in physical education, then many potentially worthwhile and valued sports and games might be excluded.

Another earlier hope for physical educators that developed from L.P. Jacks's (1931) book *The Education of the Whole Man* was that physical education could claim a place in the curriculum on the grounds that it complemented, rather than contributed to, the academic and intellectual development of pupils. While this view has retained widespread intuitive appeal for physical educators, it may give too much ground to critics who argue that this rounded quality in education can be developed through other, less expensive means than physical education.

So physical educators have still to address satisfactorily the central issue, which is the extent to which children acquire and develop socially valued knowledge through their subject. In order to make a case for the educational value of physical education on a par with other school subjects, physical educators have begun to attend more closely than ever before to how children learn to play games and sports and to participate effectively in a range of physical activities. In order to do this, physical educators need to be able to provide evidence of what children learn as a result of their school physical education programmes and the progress they make in the course of their school careers.

The dramatic growth in examinations in physical education in countries such as Australia, England and Wales, Ireland and Scotland has forced this issue to the fore in secondary schools. New curriculum developments such as the NCPE 2000 in England and Wales has similarly required teachers to address the assessment of learning in, about and through the physical. The satisfactory resolution of these issues will play a central role in determining whether physical education will become more mainstream or remain marginal to the educational purposes of schools.

Physical education versus sport

Physical educators often become agitated when sport is used in place of physical education as a label for their subject. They point out that the aims of physical education are different from the aims of sport and that to confuse the two fails to do justice to the educational mission of physical education. From what we have learned so far in this chapter, this is a very odd argument indeed, since physical educators openly acknowledge that there is no one agreed definition of their subject, and no consensus on what the subject might achieve in educational terms. We have also learned that physical educators never thought much of the philosophers' efforts on their behalf, and favoured arguments that are more concerned with the biology of health and the psychology and ethics of personality development and good citizenship than with core educational issues of learning. And we know that since the end of the Second World War, for over 50 years, physical educators have increasingly used sport as the main and sometimes sole vehicle for teaching their subject. It is for these reasons that the hostility of physical educators to being associated with sport makes little sense.

It is also the case that provision for children's and youth sport has developed dramatically since the 1980s compared to previous decades. As younger and younger children have been drawn into adult organised sport, sports themselves in Britain and elsewhere have begun to adopt more pedagogically sound, developmentally appropriate and ethically defensible practices (Australian Sports Commission, 1994). In other words, for at least the last decade it has been increasingly recognised that sport for young people needs to be underpinned by most of the principles that inform school physical education.

Some physical educators would also point out that not everything that they do in physical education is sport. This objection has some validity, since physical education could and sometimes does include dance, outdoor adventure activities and other non-competitive activities such as exercise for health. These activities have tended to be devalued, however, where physical education is viewed primarily as the foundation of a sport development continuum where the sports stars of the future are introduced to fundamental sport skills (Kirk and Gorely, 2000). While schools certainly can play a role in sports development, it is too restricting of school programmes and too limiting of the opportunities offered to young people for this to be the primary purpose of school physical education. This is simply because not all young people will become sports performers beyond school. The pyramid structure that underpins thinking about sports development, where increasing numbers of people are excluded as performers ascend to higher and higher levels, actually works against lifelong sports participation.

Box 8.3   The relationship between school physical education and sports performance

Kirk and Gorely (2000) examine the relationship between school physical education and sports performance. They criticise traditional ways of thinking about this relationship (e.g. pyramids, foundation stones and trickle-down effects). They suggest that these ways of thinking are problematic in their logic, their exclusionary nature and their positioning of physical education. Kirk and Gorely present a more inclusive way of thinking about the relationship. The alternative model is based on four components: clearly articulated pathways; the use of modified games and sports; teacher and coach education; and policy development. The researchers argue that this alternative model brings physical education and sport performance into a sensible and productive relationship which meets the needs of the general population for quality physical education while at the same time meeting the needs of sport performance across the lifespan.

Some key challenges remain for physical educators in their relationship to sport and the sports development community. For physical educators to deny their intimate relationship with sport is perhaps unwise, given the massive appeal sport has for the general public. At the same time, physical educators do not want to work solely in the cause of producing elite sports performers, a role that is in any case more properly the province of the club system. The development of sport education as a way of teaching sport as part of physical education may be one possible resolution to this issue, since sport is presented in an explicitly educational form and mirrors the real world of sport more closely than most multi-activity physical education programmes.

Girls and gender

Even if physical educators can get to grips with their marginal educational status in schools and their relationship to sport, there remains the pressing issue of girls and gender. As we learned earlier in this chapter, sport in general and the physical education profession more specifically have been rooted in gender difference for over 150 years. As one researcher observed in the mid-1980s, sport has been a 'male preserve' for much of this time (Theberge, 1985). There is a common view among physical educators that girls now have equal opportunities with boys to participate in sport and other physical activities. However, several recent studies in Britain have shown that this is not the case and that gender inequity remains a serious and pervasive problem (Lyons and Lyons, 1998; Williams and Bedward, 1999; Institute of Youth Sport, 2000). On the basis of almost three decades of research on this topic, we now understand that the problem of girls'

declining interest in physical education is not girls themselves so much the social construction of gender.

In order to feel feminine and to be viewed by others as feminine, many girls choose not to participate in many of the activities offered in physical education programmes since these activities emphasise masculine qualities such as physicality, aggression and strength. A key issue for physical education is to offer forms of physical activity that are acceptable to girls and that equip them to lead active and healthy lives. More than this, physical educators need to develop anti-sexist pedagogies that also challenge hypermasculine practices. It is these practices that contribute to girls' concerns about participating in physical activity since they underpin unacceptable forms of behaviour by men and boys, including ridicule and sexual harassment. The Nike/Youth Sport Trust Girls in Sport Partnership project developed in 1999 and 2000 suggested some ways in which physical educators might move forward on this issue. However, the project also showed how much work remains to be done before girls are able to enjoy quality physical education tailored to their individual and collective needs.

Research, practice and change

This chapter has demonstrated that there now exists a substantial body of research on many dimensions of physical education in schools. However, this growing body of knowledge seems to have had little impact on improving practice. This issue is not unique to physical education since it is commonplace in other subject areas. But physical educators seem particularly resistant to change and to using research as a means of learning more about their subject and their pupils, as the literature on girls, gender and physical education demonstrates clearly (IYS, 2000). Given the complexity of the practice of physical education, a reluctance to engage with the literature may be understandable, but it is nevertheless unfortunate and probably unacceptable.

Of course, teachers are easy targets for writers, politicians and policy-makers. The problem is not teachers any more than it is researchers or any other single group. The issue is the lack of a process that makes it possible and desirable for all parties to support and use good research to inform good practice. Higher education institutions, professional associations and a range of other agencies undoubtedly could do more to create

and sustain a process. A better understanding of the policy-making process would itself assist in the development of such a process (Houlihan, 2000). However, the main responsibility for fusing research and practice to promote change for the better in school physical education seems to lie with government agencies and departments. Organisations such as the Youth Sport Trust, the British Association of Advisers and Lecturers in Physical Education, and the Physical Education Association of the UK have begun to develop close relationships with government. Researchers need to be part of these partnerships if progress is to be made.

Chapter summary

- Physical education is a contested concept that has been the subject of acrimonious debate for over a century and a half.
- The gradual shift within state schools from drill to physical training, and more recently to physical education, was shaped by a range of factors including the perceived need to control potentially unruly working-class children.
- It is possible to challenge effectively the view of Peters and Hirst that physical education does not qualify as an educationally worthwhile subject by examining closely what people do in the name of physical education.
- Recent research has provided rich insight into the socialisation of physical education teachers, the role of physical education in the social construction of gender, and the politics of physical education curriculum development.
- Current issues and trends in physical education include the continuing marginal status of physical education in the curriculum, the tension between physical education and sport, and the significance of the social construction of gender for girls' participation in physical education.

Further reading

Kirk (1992, 1998) identifies and traces the interplay between the competing discourses that have shaped the history of physical education. Evans and Davies (1986) and Stroot (1993) provide excellent analyses of the practice of physical education and the process of socialisation into the profession respectively. The role of physical education in gender socialisation is dealt with by Griffin (1989), while Scraton (1992) and Penney and Evans (1999) examine the politics of physical education reform.

REFERENCES

Abernethy, B. (1996) 'Basic concepts of motor control: psychological perspectives', in B. Abernethy, V. Kippers, L.T. Mackinnon, R.J. Neal and S. Hanrahan (eds), *Biophysical Foundations of Human Movement*. Melbourne: Macmillan, pp. 295–311.

Alexander, K. and Luckman, J. (1998) 'Teachers' perceptions and uses of the sport education curriculum model in Australian schools'. Paper presented to the British Sports Council's Seminar on Sport Education, Loughborough University, November.

Alexander, K., Taggart, A. and Medland, A. (1993) 'Sport education in physical education: try before you buy', *The ACHPER National Journal*, 40 (4): 16–23.

Alexander, K., Taggart, A. and Thorpe, S. (1996) 'A spring in their steps? Possibilities for professional renewal through Sport Education in Australian schools', *Sport, Education and Society*, 1 (1): 23–46.

Apple, M. (1979) *Ideology and Curriculum*. London and New York: Routledge.

Armour, K.M. and Jones, R.L. (1998) *Physical Education: Teachers' Lives and Careers*. London: Falmer Press.

Aspin, D. (1976) '"Knowing how" and "knowing that" and physical education', *Journal of Philosophy of Sport*, 3: 97–117.

Australian Sports Commission (1991) *Sport for Young Australians*. Canberra: Australian Sports Commission.

Australian Sports Commission (1994) *National Junior Sports Policy*. Canberra: Australian Sports Commission.

Bennet, G. and Hastie, P. (1997) 'A sport education curriculum model for a collegiate physical activity course', *Journal of Physical Education, Recreation and Dance*, 68 (1): 39–44.

Best, D. (1978) *Philosophy and Human Movement*. London: Allen & Unwin.

Biddle, S.J.H. (1999) 'Adherence to sport and physical activity in children and youth', in S.J. Bull (ed.), *Adherence Issues in Exercise and Sport*. Chichester: John Wiley, pp. 111–44.

Bunker, D. and Thorpe, R. (1982) 'A model for the teaching of games in the secondary school', *Bulletin of Physical Education*, 10: 9–16.

Cale, L. (1997) 'Physical activity promotion in schools: beyond the curriculum', *Pedagogy in Practice*, 3 (1): 56–68.

Carlisle, R. (1969) 'The concept of physical education', *Proceedings of the Philosophy of Education Society of Great Britain*, 3.

Carlson, T.B. (1995) 'We hate gym: student alienation from physical education', *Journal of Teaching in Physical Education*, 14: 467–77.

Carlson, T.B. and Hastie, P.A. (1997) 'The student social system within sport education', *Journal of Teaching in Physical Education*, 16 (2): 176–95.

Connel, R.W. (1989) 'Cool guys, swots and wimps: the interplay of masculinity and education', *The Oxford Review of Education*, 15 (3): 291–303.

Dewar, A. (1989) 'Recruitment in physical education teaching: toward a critical approach', in T.J. Templin and P.G. Schempp (eds), *Socialization into Physical Education*. Indianapolis: Benchmark, pp. 39–58.

Dewar, A. (1990) 'Oppression and privilege in physical education: struggles in the negotiation of gender in a university programme', in D. Kirk and R. Tinning (eds), *Physical Education, Curriculum and Culture*. Lewes: Falmer, pp. 67–100.

Dewar, A. and Lawson, H.A. (1984) 'The subjective warrant and recruitment into physical education', *Quest*, 36: 15–25.

Doolittle, S. and Schwager, S. (1989) 'Socialization and inservice education', in T.J. Templin and P.G. Schempp (eds), *Socialization into Physical Education*. Indianapolis: Benchmark, pp. 105–22.

Doolittle, S.A., Dodds, P. and Placek, J.H. (1993) 'Persistence of beliefs about teaching during formal training of preservice teachers', *Journal of Teaching in Physical Education*, 12 (4): 355–64.

Ennis, C.D. (1992) 'The influence of value orientations in curriculum decision making', *Quest*, 44: 317–29.

Ennis, C.D. and Chen, A. (1993) 'Domain specifications and content representativeness of the revised Value Orientation Inventory', *Research Quarterly for Exercise and Sport*, 64: 436–46.

Evans, J. (1990) 'Defining the subject; the rise and rise of the New PE', *British Journal of Sociology of Education*, 11 (2): 155–69.

Evans, J. and Davies, B. (1986) 'Sociology, schooling and physical education', in J. Evans (ed.), *Physical Education, Sport and Schooling: Studies in the Sociology of Physical Education*. Lewes: Falmer, pp. 11–40.

Evans, J. and Williams, T. (1989) 'Moving up and getting out: the classed and gendered career opportunities of physical education', in T.J. Templin and P.G. Schempp (eds), *Socialization into Physical Education*. Indianapolis: Benchmark, pp. 235–50.

Evans, J., Penney, D., Bryant, A. and Hennick, M. (1996) 'All things bright and beautiful? PE in primary schools post the 1988 ERA', *Educational Review*, 48 (1): 29–40.

Fitzclarence, L. and Tinning, R. (1990) 'Challenging hegemonic physical education: contextualising physical education as an examinable subject', in D. Kirk and R. Tinning (eds), *Physical Education, Curriculum and Culture*. Lewes: Falmer, pp. 169–92.

Fletcher, S. (1984) *Women First: the Female Tradition in English Physical Education, 1880–1980*. London: Athlone.

Flintoff, A. (1993) 'Gender, physical education and initial teacher education', in J. Evans (ed.), *Equality, Education and Physical Education*. London: Falmer, pp. 184–204.

Gard, M. and Meyenn, R. (2000) 'Boys, bodies, pleasure and pain: interrogating contact sports in schools', *Sport, Education and Society*, 5 (1): 19–34.

Giroux, H.A. (1981) *Ideology, Culture and the Process of Schooling*. London: Falmer.

Goodson, I.F. (1988) *The Making of Curriculum: Collected Essays*. London: Falmer.

Graber, K.C. (1989) 'Teaching tomorrow's teachers: professional preparation as an agent of socialization', in T.J. Templin and P.G. Schempp (eds), *Socialization into Physical Education*. Indianapolis: Benchmark, pp. 59–80.

Grant, B.C. (1992) 'Integrating sport into the physical education curriculum in New Zealand secondary schools', *Quest*, 44: 304–16.

Grant, B., Tredinnick, P. and Hodge, K. (1992) 'Sport education in physical education', *New Zealand Journal of Health, Physical Education and Recreation*, 25 (3): 3–6.

Griffin, P. (1984) 'Girls' participation patterns in a middle school team sports unit', *Journal of Teaching in Physical Education*, 4 (1): 30–8.

Griffin, P. (1985) 'Boys' participation styles in a middle school team sports unit', *Journal of Teaching in Physical Education*, 4 (2): 100–10.

Griffin, P. (1989) 'Gender as a socializing agent in physical education', in T.J. Templin and P.G. Schempp (eds), *Socialization into Physical Education*. Indianapolis: Benchmark, pp. 219–34.

Griffin, L.L., Oslin, J.L. and Mitchell, S.A. (1997) *Teaching Sports Concepts and Skills: a Tactical Games Approach*. Champaign, IL: Human Kinetics.

Griffin, L., Dodds, P., Placek, J.H., Carney, M.C., Tremino, F., Lachowetz, T. and Raymond, C. (1999) 'Middle school students' conceptions of soccer: their solutions to tactical problems', *Research Quarterly for Exercise and Sport*, 70 (1) Supplement: 89.

Harris, J. (1998) 'Health related exercise: rationale and recommendations', *British Journal of Physical Education*, 15 (1): 11–12.

Hastie, P. (1996) 'Student role involvement during a unit of sport education', *Journal of Teaching in Physical Education*, 16: 88–103.

Hastie, P.A. (1998) 'Skill and tactical development during a sport education season', *Research Quarterly for Exercise and Sport*, 69 (4): 368–79.

Hirst, P.H. (1974) *Knowledge and the Curriculum*. London: Routledge & Kegan Paul.

Houlihan, B. (2000) 'Sporting excellence, schools and sports development: the politics of crowded policy spaces', *European Physical Education Review*, 6 (2): 171–93.

Humberstone, B. (1990) 'Warriors or wimps? Creating alternative forms of PE', in M. Messner and D. Sabo (eds), *Sport, Men and the Gender Order*. Champaign, IL: Human Kinetics, pp. 201–10.

Hutchinson, G.E. (1993) 'Prospective teachers' perspectives on teaching physical education: an interview study on the recruitment phase of teacher socialization', *Journal of Teaching in Physical Education*, 12 (4): 244–54.

Institute of Youth Sport (IYS) (2000) *Girls in Sport Project: Final Report*. Loughborough: IYS.

Jacks, L.P. (1931) *The Education of the Whole Man*. London: University of London Press.

Kimiecik, J. and Lawson, H.A. (1996) 'Toward new approaches for exercise behaviour change and health promotion', *Quest*, 48 (1): 102–25.

Kirk, D. (1988) 'Ideology and school-centred innovation: a case study and a critique', *Journal of Curriculum Studies*, 20 (5): 449–64.

Kirk, D. (1990) 'School knowledge and the curriculum package-as-text', *Journal of Curriculum Studies*, 22 (5): 409–25.

Kirk, D. (1992) *Defining Physical Education: the Social Construction of a School Subject in Postwar Britain*. London: Falmer.

Kirk, D. (1998) *Schooling Bodies: School Practice and Public Discourse, 1880–1950*. London: Leicester University Press.

Kirk, D. and Gorely, T. (2000) 'Challenging thinking about the relationship between school physical education and sports performance', *European Physical Education Review*, 6 (2): 119–33.

Kirk, D. and Macdonald, D. (1998) 'Situated learning in physical education', *Journal of Teaching in Physical Education*, 17: 376–87.

Lawson, H.A. (1983) 'Toward a model of teacher socialization in physical education: the subjective warrant, recruitment and teacher education', *Journal of Teaching in Physical Education*, 2 (3): 3–16.

Lawson, H.A. (1989) 'From rookie to veteran: workplace conditions in physical education and induction into the profession', in T.J. Templin and P.G. Schempp (eds), *Socialization into Physical Education*. Indianapolis: Benchmark, pp. 145–64.

Lawton, D. (1983) *Curriculum Studies and Educational Planning*. London: Hodder & Stoughton.

Lawton, J. (1989) 'Comparison of two teaching methods in games', *Bulletin of Physical Education*, 25: 35–8.

Lyons, S. and Lyons, K. (1998) 'An investigation into girls' attitudes to and participation in physical education and sport in the London Borough of Barking and Dagenham', unpublished report, July.

Macdonald, D. (1995) 'The role of proletarianization in physical education teacher attrition', *Research Quarterly for Exercise and Sport*, 66 (2): 129–41.

Macdonald, D. and Brooker, R. (1997) 'Moving beyond the crisis in secondary physical education: an Australian initiative', *Journal of Teaching in Physical Education*, 16 (2): 155–75.

Macdonald, D. and Kirk, D. (1996) 'Private lives, public lives: surveillance, identity and self in the work of beginning physical education teachers', *Sport, Education and Society*, 1 (1): 59–75.

Macdonald, D. and Kirk, D. (1999) 'Pedagogy, the body and Christian identity', *Sport, Education and Society*, 4 (2): 131–42 .

Macdonald, D., Hutchins, C. and Madden, J. (1994) 'To leave or not to leave: health and physical education teachers' career choices', *The ACHPER Healthy Lifestyles Journal*, 41 (3): 19–22.

McMorris, T. (1998) 'Teaching games for understanding: its contribution to the knowledge of skill acquisition from a motor learning perspective', *European Journal of Physical Education*, 3 (3): 65–74.

Martinek, T. (1981) 'Pygmalion in the gym: a model for the communication of teacher expectations in physical education', *Research Quarterly for Exercise and Sport*, 52: 58–67.

Mason, V. (1995) *Young People and Sport in England, 1994: a National Survey*. London: Sports Council.

Metzler, M.W. (2000) *Instructional Models for Physical Education*. Boston, MA: Allyn & Bacon.

Penn, A. (1999) *Targeting Schools: Drill, Militarism and Imperialism*. London: Woburn Press.

Penney, D. and Evans, J. (1999) *Politic, Policy and Practice in Physical Education*. London: E. & F.N. Spon.

Peters, R.S. (1966) *Ethics and Education*. London: Allen & Unwin.

Phenix, P. (1964) *Realms of Meaning*. London: McGraw-Hill.

Placek, J.H., Griffin, L.L., Dodds, P. and Briand, J. (1998) *Children's Views of 'Bunching Up': A Field Study of Naïve Conceptions in Soccer*. American Education Research Association Special Interest Group: Research on Learning and Instruction in Physical Education Conference Proceedings, 29.

Rink, J.E. (1999) 'What do students learn in physical activity and how do they learn?' Keynote presentation to the AIESEP Conference, Besançon, France, April.

Rink, J.E.R., French, K.E. and Tjeerdsma, B.L. (1996) 'Foundations for the learning and instruction of sport and games', *Journal of Teaching in Physical Education*, 15: 399–417.

Robertson, I. (1988) *The Sports Drop-out: a Time for Change?* Belconnen: Australian Sports Commission.

Rovegno, I. (1992) 'Learning a new curricular approach: mechanisms of knowledge acquisition in preservice teachers', *Teaching and Teacher Education*, 8: 253–64.

Rovegno, I. (1993) 'Content knowledge acquisition during undergraduate teacher education: overcoming cultural templates and learning through practice', *American Educational Research Journal*, 30: 611–42.

Rovegno, I. (1999) 'What is taught and learned in physical activity programs: the role of content'. Keynote presentation to the AIESEP Conference, Besançon, France, April.

Scraton, S. (1992) *Shaping up to Womanhood: Gender and Girls' Physical Education*. Buckingham: Open University Press.

Scraton, S. and Flintoff, A. (1992) 'Feminist research and physical education', in A.C. Sparkes (ed.), *Research in Physical Education and Sport: Exploring Alternative Visions*. London: Falmer, pp. 167–87.

Siedentop, D. (ed.) (1994) *Sport Education: Quality PE through Positive Sport Experiences*. Champaign, IL: Human Kinetics.

Smith, W.D. (1974) *Stretching their Bodies: the History of Physical Education*. London: David & Charles.

Solmon, M. and Lee, A. (1997) 'Development of an instrument to assess cognitive processes in physical education classes', *Research Quarterly for Exercise and Sport*, 68 (2): 152–60.

Sparkes, A.C. (1990) *Curriculum Change and Physical Education: Towards a Micropolitical Understanding*. Geelong: Deakin University Press.

Sparkes, A.C., Templin, T.J. and Schempp, P.G. (1993) 'Exploring dimensions of marginality: reflecting on the life histories of physical education teachers', *Journal of Teaching in Physical Education*, 12 (4): 386–98.

Squires, S.L. and Sparkes, A.C. (1996) 'Circles of silence: sexual identity in physical education and sport', *Sport, Education and Society*, 1 (1): 77–102.

Stroot, S.A. (ed.) (1993) 'Socialization into physical education'. Special issue, *Journal of Teaching in Physical Education*, 12 (4).

Stroot, S.A. and Lawson, H.A. (1993) 'Footprints and signposts: perspectives on socialization research', *Journal of Teaching in Physical Education*, 12 (4): 437–46.

Stroot, S.A., Faucette, N. and Schwager, S. (1993) 'In the beginning: the induction of physical educators', *Journal of Teaching in Physical Education*, 12 (4): 375–85.

Templin, T.J. and Schempp, P.G. (eds) (1989) *Socialization into Physical Education*. Indianapolis: Benchmark.

Theberge, N. (1985) 'Towards a feminist alternative to sport as a male preserve', *Quest*, 37: 193–202.

Tinning, R. and Kirk, D. (1991) *Daily Physical Education: Collected Papers on Health Based Physical Education in Australia*. Geelong: Deakin University Press.

Tinning, R., Macdonald, D., Boustead, J. and Tregenza, K. (1996) 'Action research and the professional development of teachers in the health and physical education field', *Journal of Educational Action Research*, 4 (2): 391–406.

Walker, J.C. (1988) *Louts and Legends*. Sydney: Allen & Unwin.

Whitehead, N. and Hendry, L. (1976) *Teaching Physical Education in England – Description and Analysis*. London: Lepus.

Williams, A. and Bedward, J. (1999) *Games for the Girls: the Impact of Recent Policy in the Provision of Physical Education and Sporting Opportunities for Female Adolescents*. Summary report of a study funded by the Nuffield Foundation.

Wittgenstein, L. (1953) *Philosophical Investigations*. Oxford: Blackwell.

Wright, J. (1993) 'Regulation and resistance: the physical education lesson as speech genre', *Social Semiotics*, 3: 23–56.

Wright, J. (1996) 'Mapping the discourses of physical education: articulating a female tradition', *Journal of Curriculum Studies*, 28 (3): 331–52.

Wright, J. (1997) 'A feminist poststructuralist methodology for the study of gender construction in physical education: description of a study', *Journal of Teaching in Physical Education*, 15 (1): 1–24.

Wright, J. (2000) 'Bodies, meanings and movement: a comparison of the language of a physical education lesson and a Feldenkrais movement class', *Sport, Education and Society*, 5 (1): 35–50.

Wright, J. and King, R.C. (1991) '"I say what I mean", said Alice: an analysis of gendered discourse in physical education', *Journal of Teaching in Physical Education*, 10: 210–25.

Young, M.F.D. (ed.) (1971) *Knowledge and Control: New Directions for the Sociology of Education*. London: Collier-Macmillan.

Part Three

The Impact of Commercialisation

9

The Business of Sport

LEIGH ROBINSON

Overview

→ The commercialisation of sport
→ A trend towards sport spectating
→ Changing technologies, increasing competition and the professionalisation of sports management
→ The structure of the sport industry
→ Sports sponsorship and sports betting
→ Conclusion

In 2000 the American basketball player Shaquille O'Neal signed a contract with the Los Angeles Lakers that was to earn him £52m in the following three years. Also in 2000 sportswear giant Adidas-Salomon reported sales of £3bn and the English Premier Football Club, Manchester United, signed a £28m deal with communications company, Vodafone. Research carried out by Van Puffelen et al. (1988) showed that income from sports and sports events amounted to 1.8 per cent of gross national product of The Netherlands, while Davies's (2000) study of Sheffield in the UK provided evidence of revenue from sport amounting to nearly 5 per cent of the city's GDP. Sport is a big business.

The Olympic Games is perhaps the clearest example of the direction that sport has taken in the last few decades. A fundamentally different event from its amateur beginnings, the Sydney 2000 Olympics accommodated over 15,000 athletes and support staff from 199 nations; hosted 17,000 media representatives and co-ordinated a workforce of more than 100,000, including 62,000 volunteers. The total bill for staging the Games was £2.4bn; however, it has been estimated that the Games will reduce Australia's current account deficit by 1.25 per cent of GDP. The event had 103 sponsors and providers, including IBM, Coca-Cola and Visa. More than 91 per cent of all tickets were sold for the Games with an average price of £50, although seats for the opening/closing ceremonies ranged from £210–576. An estimated 6–7 million people watched the Games in person, with billions more worldwide following the competition on television. NBC paid £415m for the US television rights and the worldwide television rights were sold for £782m. The magnitude of the changes that have occurred in the sport business led Wilson (1988: 7) to claim that 'those who still believe, as the founder of the modern Olympics proclaimed, that the most important thing is not to win but to take part, belong to another world'.

It is not, however, only the major events and professional sports that have been affected. National governing bodies, the organisations that run sport, are required to produce business plans to ensure continued state funding; in turn, they expect the same from affiliated clubs and associations. There are an increasing number of paid professionals employed to develop and promote sport, such as sports managers, sports agents and development workers. It is obvious that sport is no longer a pastime, organised and run by amateurs. It is a business that competes for scarce consumer resources, requiring a 'business' approach to its management, utilising professional management techniques. This chapter considers the reasons why sport has become a business and then goes on to discuss three of the key sectors of the industry: professional sport, sports sponsorship and sports betting.

THE COMMERCIALISATION OF SPORT

In the past two decades, sport has moved from being a pastime to a business as a result of the process of commercialisation, which has led sports managers and organisations to become concerned with business principles. This commercialisation process has led sports organisations to be described as 'business-like' as they become market orientated, pursue operational strategies that maximise profit or revenue, and become responsive to the needs of customers.

This commercialisation of sport has two aspects. The first has been an increase in the truly commercial operations of sport. Sports organisations have become focused on maximising revenue, using this principle as the underlying rationale for decision making and strategy development. As a result, expenditure on sponsorship, television rights, players' salaries and sports betting has risen markedly in the past few decades as sports organisations have sought to optimise their opportunities to generate revenue by adopting a business approach to the management of sport. The second aspect of commercialisation has occurred within not-for-profit or state sports organisations. These organisations have undergone substantial cultural and operational change within the last decade, as managers have moved towards a business-like approach in the management of their organisations. This led to changes in the basis for decision making in these organisations which have come to reflect those of commercial organisations, also reflected in organisational strategies.

The increase in the commercial operations of sport has primarily been caused by a growth in the number of professional sports and sports teams. For example, the number of professional football clubs in Germany increased 128 per cent in the 1990s (Zimmerman, 1997), Rugby Union turned professional, and swimmers, cyclists, sailors and athletes are now paid to train. The true value of sport, however, as a business is perhaps most obvious in those spectator sports with a worldwide audience, such as football or Formula One.

The commercialisation of the not-for-profit or state sports organisations has been primarily a result of a push towards efficiency, effectiveness and quality and this,

---

Box 9.1   The business of car racing

Today's Formula One car is at the cutting edge of technology. The sport is often likened to a 'miniature space programme', and for this reason Formula One consumes large amounts of capital. Sponsors pay the teams between £9m and £35m per year, for their company's livery to appear on the cars. The commercial attraction of the sport is so great that two sponsors, Benetton and British American Tobacco, have purchased teams. Companies are prepared to pay such large amounts because of the enormous television audience that Formula One attracts worldwide. Billions of viewers tune in to watch the FIA Formula One Championship; in terms of worldwide audiences it is second only to the summer Olympic Games and the soccer World Cup (*Guardian*, 11 March 1997). All of those involved in Formula One are becoming richer. In 1996, Michael Schumacher signed a deal with Ferrari worth a reputed £14m a year, which was later increased to £18m. Notably, in 2000, Bernie Ecclestone, the man primarily credited with the commercial development of Formula One, in particular the worldwide audience, was named Britain's richest man. He sold half of the holding company for Formula One and made £617m. (Source: Monk, 2000)

---

alongside the increasingly competitive sports market (discussed below) led these organisations to adopt the same strategies and techniques as profit-orientated organisations. The most obvious example of this is the International Olympic Committee (IOC), ostensibly a not-for-profit organisation that manages one of the most desirable sports 'products' in the world. In the recent past, staging the Olympic Games was guaranteed to cost the host city millions, making countries reluctant to host the Games. As a result of the efforts of Juan Antonio Samaranch, President of the IOC and strong advocate of commercialisation, the Olympic Games is a much sought-after product and subject to intense competition between sponsors.

Even at a local level, Robinson (1999) has provided evidence of a substantial culture shift in the management of UK public sports facilities, highlighting how the use of commercial management techniques and practices were now commonplace within this sector of the sports industry. Similarly, in the voluntary sector, Slack and Hinnings (1992) in their study of change in Canadian national sports organisations, noted how such organisations had moved towards a more professional and bureaucratic structure. Thus, the commercialism of the sport industry has not just been confined to commercial organisations; indeed it could be argued that there is little difference in the management techniques used to run sports organisations, whether commercial, state or not-for-profit in many Western, industrialised countries. Robinson's (1999) research certainly suggests that the traditional differences in management between the commercial, state and voluntary sectors of the sport industry are no longer obvious.

The commercialisation of sport has been condemned as an undesirable process, as it has been argued that commercialism takes away from the 'essence' of sport. Robinson

(1999) has argued that professionalism and specialism have undermined the community and recreational focus of sport, while Vamplew (1988) discussed at length how commercialism of sport has encouraged cheating, gambling and violence. However, the money made by professional players and teams, the trend towards professionalisation of traditionally amateur sports, such as Rugby Union, and the increasing amount of money being paid for the right to televise sport, suggests that while the *desirability* of the commercialisation of sport can be contested, the actual process of commercialisation cannot be debated.

It is apparent that commercialisation has been the driving force behind the development of sport as a business, resulting in an industry that provides revenue for national and local economies through event revenue, taxes, employment, tourism and sponsorship. This commercialisation has been brought about primarily by the actions and interactions of the following four factors: a trend towards sport spectating; changing technologies; increasing competition; and the professionalisation of sports management.

A TREND TOWARDS SPORT SPECTATING

There is evidence of a growing trend towards sport spectating. In the USA, Major League Baseball (MLB) finished the 2000 season with the highest single-season total in history of 72,748,970 recorded attendances (MLB, 2000). In the UK, Mintel (1999a) found that three-quarters of British adults had watched live sport in 1998, which is considerably more than those who claimed to have taken part. This trend is supported by evidence of increases in televised sport coverage in the UK, of nearly 45 per cent between 1996 and 1998 (Mintel, 1999a).

The value of spectator sport is perhaps most clearly demonstrated by the cost of the television rights for the Summer Olympic Games. In 1960, the US television rights for the Summer Olympics cost £231,000. Twenty years later, they cost £51m and in 1984, the Summer Games carried a £132m price tag, while the Sydney 2000 cost the NBC £415m. This is just the cost of the rights, it does not include production costs (Parks et al., 1998).

This trend towards spectator sport has commercialised sport in two main ways. First, given the sums of money involved in sponsorship, gate receipts and television rights, sport needs to be managed as a business venture. Second, in return for revenue, spectators and sponsors have high expectations of the occasion that sport provides. When discussing the reasons for the trend towards sport spectating, Chelladurai claimed that:

the total package is quite attractive indeed. Because it involves large sums of money, and because excellence is projected in spectator sport, people in general tend to be attracted to it. It is exciting and fashionable to talk about the millions of dollars an athlete makes or the billions of dollars involved in sport sponsorship. (Chelladurai, 1997: 9)

It is not enough simply to play the game; there needs to be opening and half-time entertainment, additional commentary, match analysis, catering facilities and merchandising. Spectator sport is entertainment and needs to be managed as such.

CHANGING TECHNOLOGIES

In the last few decades, technological changes have radically altered the face of sport and the most significant of these technologies has been television. Wilson (1988) argued that TV has transformed the lives of all of those who play, organise and promote sport, as television has provided greater income for established sports and an opportunity for exposure for minority sports. He outlined how:

Nothing was too much to ask of sports desperate to catch television's eye. Traditions, even rules, were tossed aside at the merest hint that by doing so they would please the one-eyed god they had come to worship. Cricket created a new one-day competition for it, and played in pink shirts with a yellow ball under floodlights. Tennis introduced the tiebreaker into its scoring system and moved Wimbledon's men's final to a Sunday. Golf dropped its random draw, and the International Olympic Committee moved the cycle of Winter Olympics by two years. Squash even rebuilt its courts in glass and painted yellow stripes on its ball. (Wilson, 1988: 9)

The impact of TV on sport has been significant and has forced the commercialisation of sport by requiring sports providers to develop the business practices necessary to deal with the demands placed on their sport by spectators requiring entertainment. It is, however, a two-way relationship. Although sport has changed to suit the needs of television, television has recognised this; it has accommodated the trend towards spectating by increasing televised sport, as outlined earlier. The potential this offers for additional viewing rights, sponsorship and thus more revenue for sport, is enormous. The TV market is also highly competitive. The advent of satellite, cable and digital TV, alongside increases in the number of terrestrial channels, has had the consequence of further increasing the value of sport, as major broadcasting organisations compete to televise popular events. In addition, the advent of 'pay as you view' television technology, where TV companies can charge viewers to watch particular events, means that the relationship between sport and television will become even stronger, reinforcing the need for a business approach to the management of sport.

Although television will continue to have a major impact on sport, other technological changes are beginning to have a significant effect. In 2000, at a Rugby Union test between England and Australia, spectators could purchase head sets to listen to the referee's comments; the England manager was able to watch replays and access match statistics on his own interactive TV monitor; and the final decision awarding the game to England was made by the video referee. The use of video referees to assist officials in Rugby League is commonplace, as is the technology used in tennis to detect faults. Cricket umpires are told, via technology, when there is not enough light to continue play and there are currently discussions about the introduction of video referees into the sport. The use of such technologies has been introduced into sport as the subjective nature of human decision making is no longer considered appropriate for such a profitable and professional business as sport.

Internet technology has also become increasingly important. The sports betting industry is likely to change fundamentally as a result of online technology that allows punters to bet on any sport, anywhere in the world, thus increasing the business opportunities for the sports betting industry. It has been claimed that the sale of Internet rights has the potential to generate Europe's top football clubs more than $1bn in revenue in the next decade (SportBusiness, 2000a). In the US, sports leagues are using the new media to create a greater affinity with fans, as the technology allows more personal communication. The National Basketball Association, the National Hockey League and the National Football League view the ability of online technology to allow interaction with fans to be 'the greatest invention ever for a sport league' (SportBusiness, 2000b: 50).

INCREASING COMPETITION

Although sport is still considered one of the biggest links between people, it is clear that sports organisations are operating in an increasingly competitive market, with competition coming from other sports and leisure providers, both at home and abroad. Luker (2000: 48), in his analysis of the sports industry, stated that 'a changing marketplace, new technology and fresh competition for the public leisure time and dollars means that old assumptions have to be challenged ... It's no longer about getting people to say yes to your sport – it's about getting people not to say no.'

The increasingly competitive market for sports business is primarily due to improvements in technology. First, technological advances in means of travel have made customers of sports events far more mobile, allowing them to buy sports services in other cities, countries or even hemispheres. Second, modern communications have shrunk the sports world to little more than a village. It is possible for people to view events all over the world, place bets on the outcome and have as their 'local' team, a sports team in another country.

Competitiveness becomes even more prominent when one considers that sports organisations compete for discretionary expenditure. Thus, managers are not only competing within the industry, but are also competing with other ways of using discretionary income. This requires a business approach to the delivery of sports products in order to ensure business survival in an increasingly competitive industry.

PROFESSIONALISATION OF SPORTS MANAGEMENT

One of the main consequences of the commercialism that has occurred in sport over the past three decades has been the increasing professionalisation of those who have been and are involved in managing sports organisations. When discussing the consequences of commercialisation upon sporting organisations, Boucher (1991: 517) noted how:

The 1990s find the administration of sport, athletics and recreation in a state of veritable transition. With the proliferation of sport opportunities and the commercialisation of many forms of sport during the 1970s and 1980s, notions of how to manage a sports organisation efficiently and effectively have undergone marked and profound changes.

The presence of strategic planning, human resource strategies and marketing plans, discussed by Boucher, have led to improvements in professional practice. This professionalisation has been brought about by two main factors. First, there has been a growing programme of education and training for those who wish to become sport managers. Over 200 universities in North America offer degree programmes in sport management and it is one of the fastest-growing areas of study in American universities (Chelladurai, 1997). The picture is the same in the UK, where there are over 1,000 higher education courses offered that contain 'sport' or 'leisure' in the title. Professional bodies have also had a role to play: Japan has two organisations catering for professionals and academics, as does the UK.

There is a European Association for Sport Management, the North American Society for Sport Management and the Recreation Association of New Zealand. All of these organisations have contributed to the increasing professionalism of those involved in sport management.

Second, the academic study of sport management has initiated and carried out research aimed at analysing and evaluating the management of sports organisations, in order to establish best practice. Research in this area has considered all aspects of management, such as organisational design, marketing, sponsorship, the management of people, quality management, ethics and equity. There are several scholarly and trade journals which disseminate the findings of such research to an international audience.

The main consequence of these two factors has been the emergence of a management culture based on the belief that good management practice is the solution to organisational survival. Inherent in this culture is the belief that good management reflects business-like management, which has driven the commercialisation of sport management, and thus sport, in all industry sectors. Evidence of this new culture can be seen in tighter financial controls, the decentralisation of management responsibility, and an emphasis on the attainment of concrete goals (Farnham and Horton, 1996). Smith and Stewart (1999) noted the importance of personal and people skills and good generic management skills, while Craig (1995) identified the increasingly common presence of performance indicators within sports organisations. In addition, the use of quality management techniques, strategic planning and marketing is widespread within the industry, introduced into sports organisations by sports professionals. It is therefore clear that the professionalisation of sports managers has contributed to the increased commercialisation of the sports industry.

THE STRUCTURE OF THE SPORTS INDUSTRY

The sports industry is arguably one of the most complex to be found, as it incorporates the voluntary, public and private sectors and can be broken down into manufacturing, retailing, entertainment and service segments, each containing specialised subfields. Chelladurai (1994) and Parks et al. (1998) have argued that the sports industry should be segmented along the lines of the products (goods and services) that are produced by the sports organisation. Chelladurai (1994) has suggested that sport can be divided into several key segments, which have further subsegments. He believes that the main segments are the provision of sport for participation and spectating, and also considers sponsorship services to be the fastest-growing segment of the sports industry. Participation services can subdivided on the basis of participants' motives, which could be the pursuit of pleasure, excellence, skill or health and fitness. Spectator services are primarily offered by team sport which provide either commercial entertainment (professional sport) or non-commercial entertainment (sport promoting excellence, such as intercollegiate sport). Alternatively, Parks et al. (1998) divide the sports industry into three key segments: sport performance, sport production and sport promotion. It is clear from both of these proposed structures for the sports industry that the industry is fragmented and complex, made up of a variety of products. In addition, each segment contains organisations from the public, voluntary and private sectors, highlighting the complex structure of the sports industry, as can be seen in Figure 9.1.

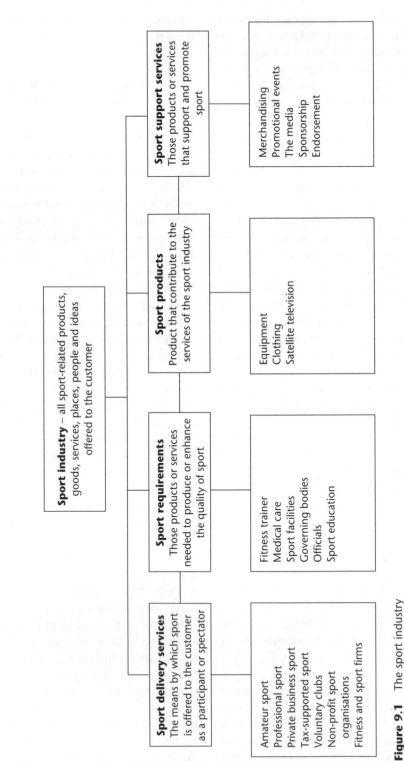

Figure 9.1   The sport industry

Source: Adapted from Parks et al., 1998

This chapter goes on to consider the three aspects of the sports industry which are considered to exemplify the dynamism, breadth and diversity of the business of sport. The first of these is professional sport, which has the primary purpose of making a profit for teams and leagues and which generates income for players. The second of these is sport sponsorship, which is arguably the fastest-growing sector in the business of sport. The sports betting industry is the final sector to be considered: not only is it purely commercial in its operations, but it has also raised public awareness of the management of some sports.

PROFESSIONAL SPORT

Professional sports, as packaged events, provide considerable entertainment and pleasure for spectators as well as providing revenue for players and owners. The main purpose of professional sport leagues is to make a profit through the provision of sport as entertainment, while the primary purpose of a professional sports person is to make a living from playing sport. As a result, professional sports are the most obvious example of business in sport.

Professional sport has its origins in Ancient Greece, where a class of professional sportsmen known as 'athletai' existed. These men were well paid, recruited from mercenary armies and trained exclusively for brutal competition. Having said this, it was not until the nineteenth century that professional sport began to develop in earnest, with boxers, jockeys and runners being routinely paid for their efforts. Baseball was the first team to employ professionals and formed the first professional league in 1871. In the UK, football began to pay players illicitly in the mid-1880s and in 1885 the Football Association legitimised

professionalism, which led to the multi-million pound business that football is today, at the beginning of the twenty-first century.

Chelladurai (1994) has suggested that there are three main reasons why professional sports are considered entertainment. First is the notion of 'the contest', where competition and the unpredictability of results are considered to be key elements in sporting entertainment. He argues that an essential ingredient in the 'contest' is the level of excellence achieved by the contestants – the higher the excellence, the greater the entertainment value. This is why professional sport is more attractive to watch than amateur sport. Second, Chelladurai (1994) outlines how professional sport is a 'spectacle'. Although the contest is the core of the event, there is usually a spectacle associated with the event, such as opening and closing ceremonies of the Olympic Games or the parades and half-time shows associated with rugby, football and basketball. For some, these are more important than the contest itself, as demonstrated by the opening and closing ceremonies of the Sydney Olympics being completely sold out and having the highest television viewing figures of the Games. Finally, Chelladurai considers that sport as entertainment offers a social venue where people can come together, not only for the contest and spectacle, but also for social purposes. This is particularly obvious in team sports that encourage fan identity, such as football, baseball, basketball and rugby, where watching the spectacle often forms an important social occasion for spectators.

THE UNIQUE NATURE OF PROFESSIONAL SPORT

It is apparent therefore that the package associated with professional sport is paramount for its continued commercial success and as such requires professional management. However, although professional sport is a commercial enterprise, sport is not simply another business. Smith and Stewart (1999) have outlined the following eight features as making sport distinctive from other forms of business.

- *Irrational passions*: Sport and typical businesses operate within difference behavioural parameters. The major concern of profit-centred businesses is efficiency, productivity and responding quickly to changing market conditions. Sport, on the other hand, is typified by strong emotional attachments that are linked to the past by nostalgia and tradition. For example, a proposal to change training or playing venues may fail simply because of an attachment to a traditional venue. In addition, predictability and certainty – valued in business – are not always valued by sports fans. Fans are more attracted to a game where the result is problematic, than to one where the winner is virtually known in advance.

- *Profits or premierships*: The most significant difference between professional sporting organisations and private business is the way in which they measure performance. The main objective of typical businesses is to optimise profits; however, while this is increasingly important to professional clubs, profits are usually less important than their position in competitive leagues. This is clearly demonstrated by the poor financial performance of some of the English football Premier League clubs, whose expenditure on players to assist with winning the Premiership has caused financial losses.

- *Designing a level playing field*: Business success is often measured by market domination; however, continued domination

of a sporting event or league may be self-defeating. Highly predictable outcomes often lead to reduced attendances and waning interest. In order to combat this, some sports have introduced rules to distribute playing talent equally between teams. For example, in an attempt to make teams more evenly matched, in the US, Major League Baseball has a complex set of rules which regulates the draft or purchase of players based on the previous year's performance and strict eligibility criteria.

- *Variable quality*: Sport is one of the few products or services that depends on unpredictability for its success. With this unpredictability, however, comes variable quality, brought about by many factors such as the weather, injuries, the quality of the opponents or even the crowd. For example, spectators attending an Olympic swimming session may see several close races or even new Olympic records or they may see a number of races which contain neither of these qualities. The price of the session remains the same no matter what the quality of the performances. This makes sport very different from other businesses, where consistency and reliability are highly valued.

- *Collaboration and cartels*: Team sports depend upon the continued commercial viability of their opponents. Indeed, there is little incentive to see rivals fail as this would reduce the number of clubs or teams involved in competition and thus the number of games and associated gate receipts. In addition, at the most basic level, opponents must co-operate with their rivals in order to deliver an attractive sporting experience to fans or customers. This collaboration can take several forms, such as the cross-subsidising of less successful teams, as occurs in the Six-Nations Rugby Tournament, where a proportion of income from television is divided equally among the countries who participate. In this respect, the sports business is fundamentally different from other businesses, where collaboration is relatively rare.

- *Product and brand loyalty*: On the whole, sport engenders a high degree of loyalty at both the product (sporting competition) level or the brand (team) level. At the product level, there is a low degree of substitutability between sports, i.e. the satisfaction that comes from one sport will not easily transfer to another. For example, if a supporter's rugby team was playing away and the match wasn't televised, it is unlikely that the supporter would watch a hockey match as an alternative. At the brand level, club affiliation is very strong. Fans invest an enormous amount of personal energy in their chosen team and this can create lifelong attachments. For example, 83 per cent of English Premier League supporters have always supported their chosen club. In contrast, if a consumer purchases electronic equipment and is dissatisfied with it, they are likely to change providers.

- *Vicarious identification*: The identification that fans have with sports and teams often spins off into their relationships with family and friends, into the choice of sporting heroes and sporting behaviour. The selling of team kit is a clear example of the way that people identify with their chosen sporting team, with sales of sport kit in the UK, rising from £80m in 1994 to £210m in 1998. In addition, identification with sporting heroes will lead many supporters to emulate their behaviour in clothing; a fact recognised by Nike and their sponsorship of Tiger Woods. It is difficult to imagine such vicarious identification occurring among consumers of electrical goods.

- *Fixed supply schedules*: Although most typical businesses can usually increase production to meet increased demand, sports clubs have fixed or highly inelastic production curves for their products (excluding the sale of membership and memorabilia). Clubs can only play a certain number of times during a competition or season and although the venue can be changed to allow increased attendances, the organising body cannot usually decide to play the game twice.

Sports managers, spectators and players must appreciate these special features of sport. Viewing sport simply as a commercial enterprise loses sight of the key qualities that give sport its identity – the passion and emotional support of spectators. At the same time, because of its special features, it requires the use of professional management techniques in order to ensure that it is an effective business. In support of this, Smith and Stewart (1999: 21) concluded their discussion of the unique features of sport by arguing that 'anyone who intends to manage sport as if it is somehow culturally privileged and immune from business influences is destined to fail'.

SPORTS SPONSORSHIP

Sports sponsorship is arguably the fastest-developing business in sport. Gratton and Taylor (2000: 177) claimed that:

sport sponsorship is a $20 billion global industry, dominated by the USA, which accounts for a quarter of the total. It is estimated to be growing at an annual rate of 10 per cent, fuelled by escalation in the sponsorship fees for major events and professional team sport.

In the UK expenditure on sports sponsorship, in 1993, was estimated at £242m climbing to £290m by 1996 (Mintel, 1994). By 1999, sports sponsorship in Britain amounted to £350m in contract fees (Cassey and Finch, 2001), with an anticipated rise to £500m by 2002 (Kolah, 1999). In 2000, sponsorship of sport in the UK grew by 6 per cent.

Meenaghan (1991) has attributed this growth in sponsorship to the following reasons:

• *Government policies on tobacco and alcohol.* Changing government policies on advertising of alcohol and tobacco have caused manufacturers of such products to seek alternative promotion media. Continued sponsorship by such companies is, however, debatable with many governments having banned tobacco sponsorship of sporting events. For example, a European Union directive imposing a ban on all tobacco advertising and sponsorship began in 2001 and will achieve full coverage in 2006.

• *Escalating costs of advertising media.* Part of the attraction of sponsorship is the belief that it provides a highly cost-effective marketing communications tool, compared with traditional advertising. This is particularly the case when a brand becomes associated with an event, such as the Whitbread Round the World Race and the Embassy Professional World Snooker Championships.

• *The proven value of sponsorship.* It is often difficult to be certain about the benefits of sponsorship; however, there is increasing evidence of the success of sponsorship in raising the profile of a business and generating sales. One such example is the £7m invested in the 1989/90 Whitbread Round the World Race by

Lion Nathan breweries of New Zealand. Their yacht *Steinlager 2* won the race and gained an estimated £35m in free advertising around the globe. Sales of Steinlager went up by 24 per cent in the United States and by 21 per cent internationally.

• *New opportunities due to increased leisure activity.* The range of activities being pursued in leisure time is greater now than it has ever been, thus providing increased opportunities for sponsorship involvement.

• *Greater media coverage of sponsored events.* Media coverage of sporting events has extended greatly, increasing the opportunity for sponsorship. Not only has television coverage of sport increased markedly, but also new technologies, such as the Internet, have increased the types of media outlets available.

• *Inefficiencies in traditional media.* A large part of the attraction of sponsorship has been its potential role in overcoming the inefficiencies of traditional advertising media. For example, many viewers tend to switch channels during advertisements, decreasing the actual audience for television advertising. Sponsorship is seen as a way of gaining more television time. Research carried out by Performance Research (1991) found that 70 per cent of golf enthusiasts could recall the sponsors of events, whereas only 40 per cent could remember the commercials aired during the events.

THE BENEFITS OF SPONSORSHIP TO SPORT

Defined by Meenaghan (1991: 36) as 'an investment, in cash or in kind, in an activity, in return for access to the exploitable commercial potential associated with that activity', sponsorship of sport can take many forms. Mann (1993) has argued that anything is available for sponsorship, providing it has linkages with the sponsor's objectives. Nevertheless, the following six categories can be considered the main areas of sport sponsorship.

- *Event specific*, e.g. Whitbread Round the World Race.
- *Individual specific*, e.g. Nike's sponsorship of Tiger Woods.
- *Team specific*, e.g. Vodafone's sponsorship of Manchester United.
- *Competition specific*, e.g. Embassy World Snooker Championships.
- *Ground specific*, e.g. The Reebok Stadium – Bolton Football Club.
- *Coaching scheme specific*, e.g. Kellogg's sponsorship of swimming development in the UK.

The benefits of sponsorship to sport are two-fold. First, sport requires financing and even those sports and events that can be considered to be commercial welcome the additional income generated by sponsorship activity. Sponsorship has become the second most important source of revenue for the Olympic Games; it has provided a lifeline for governing bodies and has allowed elite players to earn salaries that are the envy of most other occupations.

Second, sport seeks media exposure and publicity. As this is also what sponsoring companies seek, they are likely to take steps to improve publicity for the sponsoring event and thus increase awareness of both the event and the company. To assist with this, Cook (1993) has described how it has become common for sponsors to provide a journalist to cover an event to ensure that they gain the maximum exposure from reporting the event. An example of success of this type is outlined by Gratton and Taylor (2000), who described how the joint publicity of sport and sponsors led snooker from being a low-interest sport with little media coverage, to becoming the fourth most televised sport in Britain.

It is not, however, all positive and Gratton and Taylor have outlined two important costs of sponsorship to sport. First, as sponsorship is essentially a commercial activity, sponsors expect a commercial return on their investment, often leading to their requiring some control over the events and competitors whom they sponsor. For example, top competitors are often subject to excessively crowded schedules in order to meet the demands of the sponsors.

Second, Gratton and Taylor (2000) have argued that sponsors are normally only interested in major events and elite performers, which creates several problems. First, conflict can arise between sponsors and the rules of sport federations on the amateur status of competitors, such as occurred in Rugby Union in the early 1990s. Second, there is often a lack of continuity to much sponsorship activity. Sponsors often withdraw from a sport with little notice, leaving sports with a shortfall of income. Finally, the focus on elite events and participants creates a division between sports. For example, the relationship between television and sport determines the attraction of a sport to sponsors. The major sports with their guaranteed TV coverage have no difficulty in finding sponsors – it is the minor sports, potential elite athletes and youth schemes, that have problems. In addition, this division is occasionally seen within sports. Sponsorship of men's football is phenomenal; sponsorship of women's football is practically non-existent.

THE BENEFITS OF SPORT TO SPONSORS

Crompton (1996) has suggested that there are four reasons why organisations sponsor sport. The first of these is image enhancement. Sport creates a positive image and business organisations, identifying the value of this image to their brands or products, have increasingly sought to build an association with sporting activity. By associating elite performers with the product, the aim is to create an elite image for the company. Another 'image' motivation for sponsorship is to change the perceived image of a company or product, as was the goal of Silk Cut's sponsorship in the Whitbread Round the World (Yacht) race (see Box 9.2).

A second reason for sponsorship is to increase awareness of the company and/or of a product. One such company that successfully used sport sponsorship to raise its profile is Cornhill Insurance who sponsored Test cricket in the UK from 1977 to 2000. Cornhill estimates that an increased annual premium income of £10m can be attributed to the sponsorship. Cornhill has recently ended its sponsorship of cricket as it felt that due to decreasing spectator numbers, it was not getting value for money for its support.

A third reason for sponsorship is the potential for hospitality opportunities and many organisations regard these opportunities for entertainment as a key motive for sponsorship. This is particularly the case for blue chip events such as Formula One, golf championships, tennis Grand Slam tournaments and Rugby Union internationals. Not only do these events provide an opportunity to entertain clients, but they also suggest that the company is a major player in industry as they have access to such events. Finally, sponsorship of sport provides the opportunity to trial products or to make sales opportunities. Sport events, leagues and competitions provide product sampling opportunities, while the sale of sponsors' merchandise is commonplace at sporting events.

Sponsorship of sport has reached such levels that those sports and athletes fortunate to attract sponsorship are now receiving unprecedented levels of income. Many sports would not survive without it, a situation also facing many professional athletes. Although the positive impact of sponsorship

---

Box 9.2   Changing images: the value of sports sponsorship

Karen Earl Ltd (London-based sponsorship consultants) were briefed to find a sponsorship that would change the female-oriented perception of the Silk Cut cigarette brand within the UK market. Having considered several options, it was decided to sponsor the British entry in the Whitbread Round the World Race. This generated coverage of the brand from sailing journalists. The second part of the strategy was to design the yacht as a shark and add a creative element to crew clothing and branding. The rugged imagery of the design brought a huge amount of interest from consumer and lifestyle magazines, particularly from men's lifestyle magazines. The end result in the UK was worth three times the overall media spend. (Source: Glendinning, 2000)

on sport is undeniable, a major problem is its volatility and unpredictability, as sponsors are quick to change sports if results are not forthcoming. This requires sport managers and participants to adopt a business-like approach to their sport, as sponsors have, in effect, become employers in the business of sport.

SPORTS BETTING

The sports betting market, originally developed out of a passion for horse racing, has expanded in recent years to take account of a growing demand for the opportunity to gamble on the outcome of a wide range of sports events. In 1998, the worldwide turnover for betting and gaming increased by 30 per cent (Mintel, 1999b). In Australia, the market has experienced growth of approximately 12 per cent a year since the mid-1990s, and similar growth has been experienced in New Zealand (Australian Bureau of Statistics, 1999). In the UK, 16 per cent of the population had bet on sport in the last two years and Mintel (1999b) estimate a growth of 9 per cent in the gross betting market over the years 1999–2004.

Although sports betting realises little legitimate income for professional sport teams and athletes (with the exception of funding via national lotteries), the sports betting industry impacts on professional sport in two ways. The first of these is arguably positive, encouraging increased spectating and following of sport via the opportunity to make money on outcomes. The sports betting market comprises bets placed on course, in betting shops, over the telephone and on the Internet, with off-course betting making up the largest proportion of bets. Mintel (1999b) have estimated that, in the UK, the off-course betting stakes for 1999/2000 were worth £7.2m, with most of

this money coming from betting on horse racing. There is also a large amount of illegal betting which Mintel estimated inflates the figures by 15–20 per cent.

The way forward, however, appears to be online. The online revolution began with Gibraltar-based Victor Chandler's betting operation in May 1999, and in 2000, William Hill, UK bookmakers, became the first major player to offer duty-free betting. In 2000, the first dedicated worldwide football betting Internet service was launched. VIPsoccer.com offers tax-free betting and accepts bets from anywhere in the world on games in leagues across the world. In the UK, the Hilton Group committed £100m to provide betting on the Internet, through interactive television and mobile telephones. The US betting company Autotote have aligned with Arena Leisure, operators of six UK racecourses, to create an international web-based betting business founded on horse racing.

Online betting has been able to gain market share quickly, by offering tax-free or reduced tax betting to punters, as operators have either absorbed the cost of the tax deduction or have based their operations offshore. In response to this, the UK government recently abolished betting tax, replacing it with the requirement for bookmakers to pay 15 per cent of their gross profits directly to the government.

The second impact of sports betting on professional sport is much less positive, as the opportunity to earn large sums of money from gambling has raised many concerns among other sectors of the industry. Sports gambling has always been justified on the basis of the revenue it supplies to governments through taxation and in the UK; indeed, the betting levy raised more than £61m in 1999. It is, however, impossible to ignore the ethical issues surrounding sports betting, with the following being key concerns:

Sports betting is likely to:

- increase attempts by players and coaches to influence the outcome of scores;
- create suspicion by fans who feel that the outcome was influenced;
- increase costs spent on monitoring and policing the league to preclude game fixing and point shaving;
- change the nature of sport, focusing not on the beauty of competition, but on the 'points spread';
- encourage and promote gambling;
- increase personal health problems associated with gambling. (Davis, 1994)

Although all of these concerns are clearly important, it is the first three that are of greatest concern to those who run the business of sport. Marco Pantani, 1998 winner of the Tour de France was, in 2000, the first sportsperson to be found guilty under civil law of trying to manipulate the result of a sporting event by the use of banned drugs. In the UK, the government has recently established the Independent Football Commission to watch over the game. More obviously, recent events in cricket, outlined in Box 9.3, demonstrate how sports betting can undermine sport and sport events.

Box 9.3   The scandal of cricket

The year 2000 was a bad one for cricket. Allegations of match 'fixing', which originated in India, spread throughout the cricketing world, resulting in lifetime bans for Pakistan's Salim Malik and South Africa's Hansie Cronje. In addition, the investigative report released by India's Central Bureau of Investigations implicated other key past and present players from Sri Lanka, New Zealand, Australia, England and the West Indies in the scandal. These players were accused of either accepting sums of money for 'information' about pitch conditions, tactics or team morale, or more serious, for 'fixing matches by underperforming in batting and fielding'.

The scale of the match-fixing allegations was so widespread that it was argued that

the integrity of the game, so accepted that it is a figure of speech, has been dealt a heavy blow. The revelations have undermined the enjoyment of a generation of cricket fans. Every unexpected result, each thrilling comeback against impossible odds, now looks suspect. (*Independent*, 2000)

Betting on cricket, on a major scale, started after India won the World Cup in 1983. Betting on cricket matches has been on the upswing ever since live telecasts of cricket matches started on a regular basis and has spread throughout the country. The use of computers and mobile phones promoted and supported the spread of betting until betting on cricket is now considered to be the biggest organised racket in India, in terms of monetary turnover and volume of transactions.

(Continued)

Box 9.3   Continued

The CBI Report (2000) claimed that 'with a large amount of money at stake in the betting racket on cricket, it makes sense for both bookies and punters to manipulate results of cricket matches'.

The investigation of the named players continues, by the anti-corruption unit that was established in the wake of the India scandal. The damage to the reputation of cricket is indubitably enormous and provides a clear example of the problems associated with sport betting. It appears, however, that the lesson will be learned slowly, as in November 2000 the England and Wales Cricket Board set up a lucrative online betting contract to enable the board to cash in on a Test series between England and Pakistan.

CONCLUSION

Commercialism has been apparent in sport since the expansion of professional sport in the nineteenth century. What makes the contemporary sport industry so different is that all sectors of the industry are concerned with a business approach to sport. The emergence of sport as a business has been the result of the actions and interactions of a number of factors. Increasing customer expectations of service quality, value for money and entertainment have forced managers of sports organisations to become increasingly innovative, efficient and customer focused. This, alongside increasing competition and advances in technology, has led to a commercial approach to the management of all types of sports organisations – sport managers have become business-like in their operations. It is the money to be made from sport though, which above all makes it a business. Income from sales of sports clothes, equipment and merchandising,

gate receipts and concessions make sport a commercial viability. Income from sponsorship and broadcasting rights make sport an attractive business.

Watt (1998) has suggested that sport is a key sector of the national economy, an argument supported by Gratton and Taylor (2000) and Davies (2000). Indeed, sport has become so significant in the economy that it is becoming subject to the same legislation and operating principles as all other industries. This is apparent in the European Union's decision not to consider football as a 'special case'; ruling against it remaining exempt from the employment legislation affecting other EU businesses. This also underlies FINA's decision to rule that costumes are to be considered a swimmer's technical equipment, thus allowing swimmers to choose the best tools for their 'job'. Both of these decisions suggest that sport is to compete on the same basis as other industries – recognition indeed of the extent and strength of the business of sport.

Chapter summary

- Sport is no longer a pastime, run and organised by amateurs: it is a business that competes for scarce resources and uses professional management techniques.
- The commercialisation of sport has been driven by the search for profit and, among state-funded not-for-profit sports organisations, the push towards efficiency, effectiveness and value for money.
- A number of factors make professional sports a distinctive form of business including the irrational passions generated, the tension between making a profit and winning a competition or league, and the existence and general tolerance of cartels.
- Sports sponsorship has grown dramatically in recent years, bringing both additional revenue and greater publicity.
- Sports betting, especially online betting, is one of the fastest-growing sectors of the sports business, but raises significant ethical concerns.

Further reading

Chelladurai (1994) provides an excellent introduction to the field of sports management, while Davis (1994) and Watt (1998) are both comprehensive reviews of the focus of sports management and the techniques employed. Slack and Hinnings (1992) explore the gradual professionalisation of the management of sports organisations such as governing bodies. Wilson (1988) charts the growth and scope of the sports business and Cook (1993) examines the increasingly close relationship between sponsorship and sport.

REFERENCES

Australian Bureau of Statistics (1999) *Sport and Recreation*. Canberra: ABS.

Boucher, R.L. (1991) *Enlightened Management of Sport in the 1990s: a Review of Selected Theories and Trends in Sport for All*. Dordrecht: Elsevier Science Publishers.

Cassey, J. and Finch, J. (2001) 'A message from her sponsor', *Guardian*, 13 February.

CBI (2000) *The CBI Report on Cricket Match Fixing*. www.rediff.com/cricket/

Chelladurai, P. (1994) 'Sport management: defining the field', *The European Journal for Sport Management*, 1 (1): 7–21.

Chelladurai, P. (1997) 'Sport management: past, present, future', *The Sport Manager of the Future*. 5th Sport Management Committee European Seminar Proceedings: University of Northumbria at Newcastle.

Cook, T. (1993) 'Sponsorship and sport', in R. Shaw (ed.), *The Spread of Sponsorship*. Newcastle: Bloodaxe Books.

Craig, S. (1995) *Performance Indicators*. London: Leisure Futures.

Davies, L.E. (2000) 'The economic impact of sport in Sheffield', PhD thesis. Sheffield: Sheffield Hallam University.

Davis, K.A. (1994) *Sport Management: Successful Private Sector Business Strategies*. Madison, WI: Brown & Benchmark.

Farnham, D. and Horton, S. (eds) (1996) *Managing the New Public Services*. 2nd edn. London: Macmillan.

Glendinning, M. (2000) 'Net adding new sponsor options', *SportBusiness*, March.

Gratton, C. and Taylor, P. (2000) *Economics of Sport and Recreation*. London: E. & F. N. Spon.

Independent (2000) 'The integrity of sport has been dealt a heavy blow', *Independent*, 4 November.

Kolah, A. (1999) *Maximising the Value of Sports Sponsorship*. London: Financial Times Media.

Luker, R. (2000) 'US sports sector slips from the summit', *SportBusiness*, March: 48–9.

Major League Baseball (MLB) (2000) 'MLB and tickets.com announce exclusive on-line ticketing agreement', *www.majorleaguebaseball.com/u/baseball/mlbcom/pressrelease/*

Mann, A. (1993) *Sponsorship from the Sponsors' Viewpoint*. London: English Tourist Board.

Meenaghan, T. (1991) 'The role of sponsorship in the marketing communications mix', *International Journal of Advertising*, 10: 35–47.

Mintel (1994) *Leisure Intelligence*. London: Mintel International Group.

Mintel (1999a) *Spectator Sport*. London: Mintel International Group.

Mintel (1999b) *Sports Betting*. London: Mintel International Group.

Monk, K. (2000) 'Who drives Formula One?' MSc thesis, Loughborough: Loughborough University.

Parks, J.B., Zanger, B.R.K. and Quarterman, J. (eds) (1998) *Contemporary Sport Management*. Champaign, IL: Human Kinetics.

Performance Research (1991) 'Economic slump', in B.L. Parkhouse (ed.), *The Management of Sport: its Foundation and Application*. 2nd edn. USA: Mosby.

Robinson, L. (1999) 'Following the quality strategy – the rationale for the use of quality programmes', *Managing Leisure: An International Journal*, 4 (4): 201–17.

Slack, T. and Hinnings, B. (1992) 'Understanding change in national sports organisations: an integration of theoretical perspectives', *Journal of Sport Management*, 6: 114–32.

Smith, A. and Stewart, B. (1999) *Sports Management: A Guide to Professional Practice*. St Leonards: Allen & Unwin.

SportBusiness (2000a) 'Billion dollar net bonanza', *SportBusiness*, March: 1.

SportBusiness (2000b) 'Fans to win in big web battle', *SportBusiness*, March: 50.

Vamplew, W. (1988) *Pay Up and Play the Game*. Cambridge: Cambridge University Press.

Van Puffelen, F., Reijnen, J. and Velthuisjsen, J.W. (1988) *De Macro Economische Betekenis Van Sport*. Amsterdam: Stichting voor Economisch Onderzoek der Universiteint Van Amsterdam, Netherlands.

Watt, D. (1998) *Sports Management and Administration*. London: E. & F. N. Spon.

Wilson, N. (1988) *The Sports Business*. London: Piatkus.

Zimmerman, M. (1997) 'Sport management: past, present, future', *The Sport Manager of the Future*. 5th Sport Management Committee European Seminar Proceedings. University of Northumbria at Newcastle.

10

Sport and the Media

DAVID STEAD

Overview

→ Context and key issues
→ The sport–media partnership
→ The media sport product: characteristics, influences and outcomes
→ The media sport audience
→ Media sport: where to now?

CONTEXT AND KEY ISSUES

In many ways, both today's sport and the media are classic outcomes and, indeed, icons of the far-reaching social, economic and technological change that characterised the twentieth century. Each has developed extensively and rapidly as a major global industry. Each plays a significant part in structuring and informing people's lives. Each has a global as well as more local scope of operation and has the structures and practices to reflect this. Importantly, they are two industries tied together in complex networks of relationships. Their respective histories of development have been fuelled and influenced by the dynamics of this partnership. The evidence of the partnership is all too apparent. The wellbeing of particular sports or, indeed, sport as whole has become linked to income generated directly or indirectly from the media. The way in which sport fills newspaper pages and television and radio schedules bears testimony to the influence it has on the structure and extent of media activity.

However, partnerships are not always equal, stable or constructive for those involved. In this chapter, consideration will be given to a number of themes and issues that characterise the link between sport and the media. Difficulties and tensions exist but ultimately a media sports product emerges whether it is, for example, a live TV broadcast of the Olympic Games or a newspaper report on a local rugby match. This raises a series of issues about the nature of the product. Does the media presentation of sport mirror reality or is it a representation and a construction reflecting the media's objectives and the influences and practices of the professionals working in it? Such questions will also be considered later but they in turn introduce the part played by the audience for media sport. For example, is the viewer knowledgeable about the sports products on offer to them and do they exercise choice about what they view and how they receive the messages and influences inherent in the programmes? The chapter will conclude by addressing this conundrum. Questions about the genesis and content of media products and the influences impacting on them figure prominently in what is a growing sociology of sport literature on media sport (see in particular Kinkema and Harris, 1998; Maguire, 1999; Rowe, 1999; Wenner, 1998; Whannel, 1992).

The mass media entered the twentieth century with the emphasis on the printed word. Today, in the early years of the twenty-first century, it is television and radio that are to the fore. Satellite-based multinational companies like BSkyB TV have appeared on the scene and are now major players in the global sport media marketplace. There are new developments like the Internet which have further extended media activities. Sport has long been an important aspect of media output but more recently there has been a growth in specialist media sports products. Dedicated sports-only TV channels (e.g. SkySport1), radio stations (e.g. TalkSport), and publications (e.g. Sports First) have appeared in ever increasing numbers.

The exposure to and consumption of media products, including those concerned with sport, have increased dramatically. A Henley Centre report has gone as far as to suggest that people in the UK spend nine hours a day consuming media in its various forms, with television viewing occupying the equivalent of a day a week. (*Financial Mail on Sunday*, 31 Jan. 1999: 38). Television

has, indeed, become a principal leisure activity and source of information. Through it we gather our knowledge not only of our immediate world but also of the complex global village in which we now live. It acts as a key socialisation agent and is integral to framing, determining and influencing our picture of reality. Our experience of sport has become increasingly constructed and ordered through television output.

Sport has become 'big business'. It is now a well-established global industry with international organising bodies, like the International Olympic Committee (IOC), eager to promote and structure its further development. Sport, but not necessarily in all its forms, has something to sell. It has its events, leagues, clubs and elite performers. Sport can make money but the costs involved, not least the large rewards paid to the top performers in some sports and the capital and revenue expense of increasingly spectacular sports stadiums, has left it with an insatiable appetite for more and more funding. The world of sport is a competitive one, not just in terms of which team tops the league or who wins the gold medal, but also which sports are able to attract the greatest financial resources. The relationship with the media is central to the political economy of sport. Traditionally, it was the medium through which key information like schedules of events/matches, venues and times was transmitted to the public. Today, the media, primarily television, offer sport-added attractions in terms of finance from broadcasting fees and exposure to advertisers, sponsors and a wider audience. Hence there is the all too apparent readiness of sports organisations to get involved with the media. However, alongside the obvious benefits come some possible costs to sport. To link with the media has meant sport losing a degree of control over its own activities and destiny. The promise of media attention and the wide-ranging spin-offs (in terms of increased profile, status and finance, greater numbers of participants and spectators and enhanced attractiveness to sponsors and advertisers) make such loss of control something sports organisations appear willing to accept (Goldlust, 1987). The ability to appreciate and deal with the full extent of the consequences of its partnership with the media is a major challenge confronting sport in the twenty-first century.

THE SPORT–MEDIA PARTNERSHIP

The media: competition and control

The media sport production process involves the sports organisations, e.g. the Fédération Internationale de Football Association (FIFA), the governing body of world football, working with the media companies. The sports bodies may do this directly or through intermediary marketing and promotional agencies operating on their behalf. They may engage with the media as individual companies or in partnership with others. The media organisation concerned may be a quasi-governmental body, like the British Broadcasting Corporation, or a multinational global commercial one such as BSkyB. A sport has something to sell, such as the TV and radio broadcasting rights to cover its world championships, and it is up to the media companies to submit bids. The competition to become the agreed lead broadcaster can be intense, although the sheer size of the financial undertaking can lead to fierce media rivals working together on a bid. In the example of FIFA selling the rights to its World Cup, the sums involved are considerable and the bidding and decision-making processes are complex and sensitive. Competition for broadcasting rights and the prominence of sport in media schedules have had a dramatic inflationary effect on the fees paid to some sports. An early globally televised Olympics, such as the 1964 Tokyo Games, cost the lead broadcaster around £1m. More recently, it has been reported that the US broadcaster NBC has paid the IOC $3.5bn for the rights to the Winter Olympics of 2002 (Salt Lake City) and 2006 (Turin) and the Summer Olympics of 2004 (Athens) and 2008 (Beijing). These massive sums of money have to be balanced out by the very considerable amount of airtime that can be filled by such events. Indeed, sports broadcasting can be seen as a relatively cheap way to fill schedules. Sports events can also be particularly useful for the all-important audience ratings by attracting large numbers of viewers and listeners. For example, ITV in the UK attracted 23.2 million viewers, some 80 per cent of the available television public, for the England versus Argentina football match at the 1998 World Cup finals. The number of viewers peaked to almost 27 million during the penalty shoot out! (*Sport First*, 3 Jan. 1999: 16).

A successful bidder's production costs for a major global sports event will involve the expense incurred in securing the broadcasting rights plus a heavy investment in people, accommodation, travel and equipment. It is not surprising therefore that a media company will endeavour to exercise considerable control over the event. If the sporting event concerned is not one that is deemed to be particularly attractive, then to get the media on board may involve the sports organisation accepting an especially weak bargaining and control position. Even when the sports organisation involved is powerful, such as the IOC or FIFA, there is still a trade-off in terms of a loss of control.

This can lead to significant changes in sport, for example, to dates, times and venues. The actual structure and presentational style of an event may be strongly reflective of the media's interests. Football's World Cup competition is an example of a particularly large-scale and well-established sport event but it is still not immune from media preferences. Indeed, loss of control needs to be considered whenever a sports organisation, however local and small, gets involved with the media. Many more sports and events are vying for media money and to an extent, the media, notably television with its schedules to fill, are not averse to encouraging sports bodies to approach them.

The rise in the numbers and influence of the private media companies has had a number of important consequences. The private sector is characterised by the existence of some large-scale monopolistic groupings. Global media entrepreneurs like Rupert Murdoch, Alan Bond, Kerry Packer and Silvio Berlusconi have recognised the value of media sport and each has, to a varying degree, made a significant impact on the world of sport. BSkyB in the UK, FoxTV in North America and Channel Seven in Australia form just part of Murdoch's extensive News Corporation media empire. Each has won major sports contracts and invested heavily in sports-related programming. Murdoch's activities cover radio, TV and newspapers and have put him in a powerful position to direct media sport developments. In some cases, these multinational media companies have gone further and strengthened their controlling opportunities by actually moving into sport's ownership through investing in clubs. BSkyB's ambitious, but eventually thwarted, attempt to take a controlling stake in Manchester United is a telling case in point.

Another important control aspect of global media sport is the power exercised by the North American media market. The upward explosion in certain broadcasting fees has been fuelled largely by US media money. Sport on television is particularly popular in the USA and the advertising revenue the media companies can obtain on the back of sports coverage can be enormous. For example, advertising slots around TV coverage of the American Football's Superbowl can cost many thousands of dollars per second.

In the UK, the private satellite-based companies have put themselves in a powerful position with regard to their terrestrial and, sometimes, public sector competitors. BSkyB started buying up the right to cover events and sports as soon as it appeared in the UK. Sport was seen as a particularly useful product through which to sell subscriptions to its service. There had always been competition to broadcast some sports. However, the emergence of BSyB injected new dynamism into the media sport marketplace and highlighted the differential abilities of media organisations to compete financially.

The licence-fee-funded BBC, which for so long had enjoyed a high reputation for its sports programming, has found itself unable to match the sports resources available in the private sector, principally the satellite companies. It has lost out on the rights to cover many major sports or particular events and is now criticised for what appears to be a lack of commitment to sport. Flagship BBC programmes like *Grandstand*, for decades Britain's leading media sports product, has become marginalised as it has sought to fill its time with an increasingly limited diet of available events. From season 2001/02, another symbol of the BBC's long-standing contribution to sport (i.e. its Saturday evening football highlights programme), has been lost to another terrestrial channel (i.e. ITV), albeit working in partnership with BSkyB. Whilst the BBC may be marginalised in the media sport marketplace, other UK media organisations like ITV and Channel 4 have looked to increase their involvement. The latter has wide sporting interests and has invested in motor racing, Italian football, WWF (wrestling) and cricket. To a degree, competition for sports to cover has extended the choice for the television viewer but the question of access is a somewhat more complex question.

Issues of access and equity

As media sport has risen in prominence, so questions have to be asked about whether this represents sport for all or only for some. The extensive involvement of satellite companies and their array of dedicated sports-only channels have clearly led to a major extension of the range and number of sports choices available to viewers. However, this has come at a financial cost to the viewer in terms of the equipment (e.g. satellite discs) and regular subscriptions that are required. These kinds of financial factors, allied to the satellite companies' growing domination of broadcasting rights, highlight the issue of equity in the sense of media sport becoming primarily the preserve of those people who can afford it. Interestingly, the greater involvement, indeed in some ways the re-emergence, of ITV in the media sport marketplace has been through the introduction of a subscription-based channel. The financial implications for the viewer are likely to become even more problematic as the private companies offer more sport on a 'pay-to-view' basis. This involves events (e.g. boxing championships and selected English Premier League football matches), which require the viewer to make a one-off payment on top of their subscription. The introduction of BSkyB's 'pay-to-view' facility (i.e. Sky Box Office), is representative of what may be the greatest challenge to wide access to media sport.

Governments, particularly in the European Union, have been encouraged to respond to this equity concern, particularly when it is access to major national sporting events that is coming under threat. In 1996, ironically one media form (newspapers), led a 'Save our Sport' campaign in the UK which opposed the movement of sports events to the satellite companies. Government intervention was called for. The campaign arose in response to Sky buying up, and attempting to monopolise, the media coverage of top sporting events. An example of Sky's success was the obtaining of the rights to golf's Ryder Cup. The significance and concerns at the time can be summed up in the following quote from a disgruntled BBC producer: 'They've sold it to a station nobody watches. It's like buying *Gone with the Wind* and showing it at the bottom of a coalmine' (*The Mail on Sunday*, 14 Jan. 1996: 86). In the UK, there are a number of 'jewels in the sporting calendar', like the Football Association's Cup Final and the Wimbledon tennis championships, which are on a special government list requiring them to be broadcast on terrestrial TV. This list has protected opportunities for the media sport consumer but it is a safeguard constantly under threat as the satellite media companies see a valuable and popular commodity beyond their grasp and the sports organisations involved see potentially lucrative events being kept out of the broadcasting rights marketplace.

Interestingly, both FIFA and the IOC have resisted approaches from BSkyB on the grounds that a satellite-based broadcaster did not offer access to the highest possible audience. This is not to say that FIFA and the IOC have not gone some way towards appeasing the media. Both these world bodies have extended the number and the scale of their international flagship events. In doing so they have provided even more broadcasting opportunities. The FIFA World Cup finals now involve more teams than previously and the event extends over a longer time period. Such specific changes in sport are now, to a large extent, often part of a deliberate response to the pressures and promises of being part of the media sport partnership.

The media involvement in the changing face of sport

Media's increasing involvement in, and control over, sport and sports organisations has put it in a powerful position to dictate the characteristics of events or, indeed, even to change fundamental aspects of a sport (e.g. its rules). Sport's sovereignty over its own destiny has weakened. In essence, the media have come to play an increasingly influential part in both the construction and destruction of sporting structures and practices. The media have been influential in the genesis and development of new competitions, events and leagues. New sport forms have appeared and old ones have become marginalised. Rules have been changed and playing conditions revised so as to enhance media coverage. Even the clothes athletes wear and the equipment they use have come to reflect media-related interests. The colours and designs can add to the spectacle and the drama. Names on the players' kit help the viewer. Sponsors' logos proliferate. Opportunities to link media, sport and commerce are all too readily available. For example, the increasingly spectacular sports stadiums provide

backdrops 'wallpapered' with advertising hoardings. Sport has become more of a product that is manufactured, bought and sold. The sports organisations have gone along with this and, increasingly, have used agents and marketing companies to get their particular products into the media sport marketplace. Thus further complexity to the web of interdependencies that characterises media sport has been introduced. The media/sport production complex that has emerged today comprises the sports organisations, the media marketing organisations and the media personnel (Wenner, 1998).

Sometimes a sport jumps before it is pushed and, in a quest to make itself attractive as a media product, has been keen to introduce changes itself. Highly traditional aspects of the sporting experience disappear or are diluted. English football was once a Saturday afternoon ritual: today it has become almost a daily event as the television companies endeavour to fill their schedules and, importantly, maximise the return on the considerable sums they have invested in the game. Not only can the sporting day change, but so too can the season. English Rugby League, traditionally a winter sport, has now developed a seemingly made-for-television summer Super League characterised by a quest for entertainment and impact (Falcous, 1998). Clubs have changed their names (e.g. to the Bradford 'Bulls'), so as to enhance the spectacle and to offer potentially more commercial spin-offs. Rugby League in England has come under increasing competition for funding and exposure; the newly professional Rugby Union game has emerged as one notable threat. The media-inspired Super League has offered salvation, even though the trade-off has involved the loss of traditions and even the disappearance or downgrading of long-established and famous clubs. There are numerous examples where sports with a record of limited or reducing attraction to media companies have tried to encourage interest. It is not always easy to establish the extent to which the push originated from the media companies. Night games and coloured clothing and many other changes in cricket, tighter 'figure hugging' clothing in a number of female sports (e.g. netball), and rule changes to speed up play (e.g. hockey), are just a few examples of sports trying to add to the glamour and spectacle and thus make them more marketable.

Specific timetabling changes in sports events have been made that are all too clearly about meeting the needs of the media. Events are sometimes held at times that would not appear to be in the best interests of the athletes involved, but which fit in with the viewing habits of the primarily North American television audience. Olympic or World Championship marathons run at the hottest time of the day and a number of high-profile heavyweight boxing championships in the early hours of the morning are cases in point. In the UK, football and rugby matches are not only played on non-traditional days, but lunchtime or early evening kick-offs have become part of the experience. Sports agree to such conditions so as to secure the best broadcasting fees. However, whether such decisions benefit the spectator or are consistent with the wellbeing of the athletes concerned is questionable. The commercial media gain much of their income from advertising, hence the introduction of more or longer breaks in sports events. North American sport, in so many ways the exemplar of the practical realisation of media influence, is characterised by action frequently and deliberately punctuated by the 'time-outs' or other breaks in proceedings. Association football has a '15-minute' halftime break which apparently ends when the referee receives the signal that the TV advertising has been completed.

Another area of sports development particularly reflective of media involvement has been the growth in the 'big event'. The proliferation of high-profile and spectacular events, notably global championships and competitions (e.g. Rugby Union World Cup), has given the media access to larger and more varied audiences and hence greater potential in terms of recruiting advertisers. The media can also be seen as a central factor in the emergence of new sports (e.g. beach volleyball and beach football). Attention has also been focused on the way in which media companies have attempted to extend the wider global diffusion of sports. The initiatives taken by a partnership of the NFL, its sponsors and media companies to make American football a global game are prime examples (Maguire, 1990). A somewhat less far-reaching but nevertheless revealing initiative has been the coverage of Japanese Sumo wrestling, which has appeared on European television schedules.

Sports, large and small, are vying for media attention, exposure and money but the experience of the media sport partnership is by no means the same for all of them.

Who are the winners and losers?

The greater penetration of the media into the world of sport has had an impact on the relative status of particular sports and also on relationships within sports. Sports that are especially attractive to the media (e.g. football), have gained far greater status, exposure and economic wealth compared with other sports. The more glamorous football clubs in the Premier League, with the wealth of their BSkyB/ITV contracts to support them, have been able to distance themselves from the rest of the clubs in England. The economic and political distance between sports and between clubs and leagues has widened. The media have helped fuel this in a direct sense by their patronage and contracts, but as sponsors and advertisers gravitate to the more glamorous and high-profile sports, events, leagues and clubs, so the differentials further increase. The introduction of media money and influence has also had an impact in pulling elite sport away from its roots. Elite sport, with its media-supported emphasis on spectacle, personalities and financial rewards, can become a somewhat alien activity for the recreational-level participant, who may have difficulty relating to it as the same sport.

The elite performers in a number of sports have become all too aware of their marketability as part of the media sport package and also of the vast amounts of media money that have flowed into sport. Aided by the emergence of agents working on their behalf, an increasing number of elite athletes have sought and obtained very high salaries or substantial prize money. This has further alienated athletes from the people who watch them on television and who read about them in the newspapers. Whilst all this media attention and money may raise the profile and status of elite athletes, this may also contribute to a more restricted life for them. They are now in the public eye and have become part of the media sport spectacle. Their degree of control over their own lives is brought into question. The media creates sporting personalities to help sell their programmes and newspapers and this involves athletes being media commodities in situations that can extend way beyond the direct sporting context.

Media sport is about a production process. As media intrusion into sport continues to grow, it becomes more important to delve more deeply into the actual nature of the media sport product, how it is developed and the objectives behind it. The particular ways in which the media structure, direct and influence the public's experience of sport and with what impact are now key concerns. They are more relevant when one considers the significant degree to which people now gain their sports knowledge and understanding through the media rather than through direct personal involvement in spectating and participation. As implied earlier, the media's objective in engaging with sport is based largely on the profit motive. For the government-supported media bodies there is the responsibility of providing a public service. The production process involves the media professionals using their knowledge and expertise to develop media sports products that reflect their ability and proficiency, and in doing so they are, in part, seeking to enhance their status and reputation, not least amongst their peers. These kinds of objectives impact on what is produced.

THE MEDIA SPORT PRODUCT: CHARACTERISTICS, INFLUENCES AND OUTCOMES

Much of what has been discussed has centred on sport's interrelationship with television and radio. The latter elements of the media are the ones injecting finance into sport and, increasingly, wishing to assume a greater degree of control. However, the media sports products on offer also include the printed word, the traditional mediated way that sports knowledge and understanding have been conveyed to the public at large. This section examines the specific nature of the media sports product and what is influencing this. Therefore much of what is discussed reflects the activities of newspapers and other printed media as well as television and radio.

Meanings and messages

Reference has been made to the higher profile of elite athletes and how the media have been instrumental in bringing this about. However, personality creation is only one of the ways in which the media influence and direct the sporting experience for their customers. This structuring of knowledge, messages and meanings inherent in media sport products has become an increasingly researched and significant area of interest (Lawrence and Rowe, 1986; McKay and Rowe, 1987; Sage, 1990; Whannel, 1992). It is a field of enquiry that encompasses interest in the ideological content of sports coverage and reporting and, in particular, how this reflects the dominant values and ideology prevalent in society. A principal focus is on the ways in which the media transmit the values and support the political and economic objectives of their owners and controllers. At a different level, there is the interest in the roles played by the media professionals and the nature and impact of their particular production codes and techniques on media sports products. In summary, the challenge is to examine the degree to which what the media audience is exposed not to a neutral and objective presentation of reality, but rather to a packaged representation and construction imbued with ideological content and reflective of the practical and professional interests of the production staff involved (Gruneau et al., 1988).

Textual messages and meanings

Research into the textual messages contained in the media sport output of various countries suggests the heavy influence of such ideological factors as capitalism, nationalism, patriarchy and racism (Gruneau, 1989b; Whannel, 1992; Sage, 1990). Each of these factors may reflect the ideological biases evident within the ownership and control of the increasingly dominant multinational media companies and, indeed, the dominant values in a particular society.

Capitalism

Media sport is an area of endeavour where capitalist virtues can come to the fore, not least in the prevalence of the profit motive (Lawrence and Rowe, 1986; McKay and Rowe, 1987). The media, a key cultural industry and so much a symbol and vehicle of capitalist interests, have become, through sports pages and programming, a source of support for ownership values and priorities. Media's implicit and explicit support for the dominance of monopoly capitalism has contributed to the resilience of capitalism in society and for the status quo in the way society is stratified. The inculcation and acceptance of the desired characteristics of the 'workplace' are fostered. The value of hard work and the spirit of free enterprise are characteristics to be found in sport that the media may choose to emphasise and describe in noticeably positive terms. An adherence to the work ethic is deemed worthy of particular praise. Core sporting characteristics such as competitiveness and teamwork are highlighted. An athlete's power, aggression and competitiveness are applauded. The Olympic motto, *Citius, Altius, Fortius*, emphasises the challenge of getting 'Faster, Higher and Stronger'. It is not surprising therefore that sport, particularly as it has become increasingly commercialised, has been seen by the media ownership as a site for promulgating capitalist values and interests.The USA can be portrayed as the leader in promoting the role and importance of capitalism. It is also a world leader in media sport. Bring these factors together and it is clear why the Americanisation tendencies found in media sport production can be highlighted and explained in terms of monopoly capitalist domination. American media sport glorifies organisation and leadership. The qualities and ambitions inherent in the Olympic motto are particularly evident in US media and sport. There is also the fascination with sporting statistics to back up such interests.

Nationalism

Sociological research has highlighted the significance of media sport as a site for nationalistic fervour and national stereotyping (Maguire, 1999; Rowe et al., 1998). Nationalities can be promoted or put down. The home country's athletes and teams are portrayed as heroes and their opposition as the villains of the piece. Sporting events can be used as a vehicle for calling for unity within a nation and for a show of allegiance. Media-led national and local campaigns can be established to encourage the public to rally to the cause. Heightened emotional attachment can sell newspapers and recruit viewers and listeners. Nostalgic memories of past triumphs can be evoked as a way of 'rallying the troops'. Whilst victories of a sporting nature (e.g. the 1966 England football World Cup success), can be revisited by the media; it is not unusual for audiences to be reminded of events of a non-sporting nature. For example, during the Euro '96 Football Championship held in England, the British media drew attention to the Spanish Armada and the Second World War as part of the build-up to the

host countries' matches against Spain and Germany respectively (Maguire and Poulton, 1999). Newspaper coverage of events can involve the use of photographs and headlines to underline the stances being taken. A proliferation of national flags and colours on the sports pages (and even front pages) and emotive banner headlines may serve to direct the reader's interest and enthusiasm. These kinds of media devices can be used extensively in the coverage of events. Story lines strongly reflective of nationalist interests are developed and presented.

Patriarchy

Gender bias and inequality are evident in both sport and media. It is not unexpected therefore that patriarchy is a characteristic of sport media products. It is an area that has come under close and extensive scrutiny (see, for example, Birrell and Cole, 1994; Duncan and Hasbrook, 1988; Eastman and Billings, 2000; Theberge, 1989; Williams et al., 1986). Media sport ownership and production are male dominated; sport and media sport are important aspects of culture which help to underpin male hegemony in society (Birrell and Theberge, 1994). Of particular attention to researchers has been the way in which the media disregard and marginalise women's sport (Daddario, 1994). Female athletes and sports get little coverage in the media relative to their male counterparts. It is rare to find newspaper column inches and photographs allocated to women's sport. Few female sports are to be found in television schedules and those that are tend to be given a low profile.

Not only is the quantity of the media coverage of women's sport highly limited, but its form and quality have also to be questioned. The media are seen to stereotype, trivialise and sexualise female athletes (Duncan, 1990; Duquin, 1989; MacNeil, 1988). Sportswomen are either put down as not fitting male perceptions of appropriate femininity or they are glamorised. Attention has been drawn to photographic approaches that highlight and emphasise the physical characteristics and attractiveness of some female athletes. The narrative that is attached to the media output is of a similar nature, often with sporting prowess disregarded or played down. There are fewer high-profile female athletes, a fact reflective of the low media attention paid to women's sport in general. Those that do exist usually correspond to stereotypical images which frequently view sporting ability as a seemingly secondary consideration. An example is the extensive media coverage afforded to the Russian tennis player, Anna Kournikova: media interest has focused primarily on her physical attributes rather than her prowess on court.

The connection between gender in media sport extends beyond the treatment of female sport and athletes. There is the interest in how the media report male sport. This can encompass a concern with the treatment of violence in sport (Young and Smith, 1989) and the imagery associated with male bodies and masculinity (Trujillo, 1995; Messner et al., 2000).

Racism

The ownership control of the major global media institutions is dominated by white males. National media reflect dominant racial and ethnic interests (Tudor, 1998). The background, values and practices of the professionals working in the media and in sport are usually consistent with such concerns. The consequence of all these factors

is that the sporting achievements of certain groups can either be celebrated or played down in the sports media. In a similar fashion to gender, stereotyping based on racial or ethnic lines may also be evident (Davis and Harris, 1998). For example, black male athletes may well be applauded in the media for their aggression and physicality whilst their hard work and intelligence are disregarded. In contrast, it is the latter attributes that the media assign to the white athletes. On television the performance of black athletes is frequently linked to such stereotypical attributes as natural ability and tactical naïvety (Whannel, 1992: 129). Racism in the media can also be seen to reflect a kind of nationalistic prioritisation. International success by black British athletes can get played down in comparison to similar successes achieved by their white counterparts.

The above kinds of ideological influences are important considerations when examining media sport but so too are the particular professional approaches of the people who actually put together the programmes and newspapers.

The media professionals

The media professionals (e.g. producers, directors, commentators, reporters and cameramen) exist to produce a media sports package that aims to attract, interest and excite their audience. They work in a particularly competitive working environment. The emphasis is on making the product attractive and to this end it is sometimes difficult to establish where the sport starts and the media event ends. Selling a televised sports programme is the paramount concern. Often sport is sold as 'showbiz' with similar characteristics to the Hollywood 'thriller' or the weekly 'soap opera'. It is not surprising that what emerges is a distorted and packaged representation of reality rather than a neutral, objective and natural presentation. Neutrality is clearly a debatable point, as the evidence of the ideological content referred to above illustrates. The various professionals working in television and radio attempt to naturalise events for their audience. They bring to bear the skills and technical developments. They endeavour to provide atmosphere and to encourage a feeling of attachment to what is happening. They present the event as being an experience of reality. The media companies may bill sporting programmes as providing a 'ringside seat', but in many ways nothing could be further from the truth. So much is missed by not being present at the event and so much is added by the media professionals. Not all your senses are brought to bear. The media sports experience is not the same as being there live at the event.

Sociological research has suggested a number of key characteristics of the media sports product (Gruneau, 1989a; McKay and Rowe, 1987; Whannel, 1992). Each of these characteristics reflects the way in which media professionals work to a series of codes, conventions, assumptions and approaches. The outcome is to move the audience away from a sporting and towards a media experience. The media interpret happenings and provide their audience with explanations and meanings. They structure our knowledge and understanding for us. What is offered is not inevitable. Decisions are taken for the audience; you are directed what to see and read and how to make sense of it. The media professionals construct and frame the sport experience for their audience. The pre-event advertising

and build-up, the nature of the presentation and its placement in the programming schedules help to provide the audience with information and points of reference to help explain what is going to happen and why it is significant. There is often harking back to previous events that are deemed to have a bearing on what is about to take place. Statistics and other historical material are presented to contextualise what is about to happen.

Media sport production

The ways in which meanings and messages are organised and influenced are reflected in the narrative, audio-visual and technical and presentational/packaging aspects and objectives of the media sports product. The media personnel involved are the commentators and reporters, photographers, camera operators, sound technicians, producers, editors and directors. These production aspects and individuals are central to what is, in essence, a process of event construction undertaken by the media. Increasingly, media sports programmes are being developed with the following important characteristics to the fore.

There is, first, a growing emphasis on *spectacularisation* (Gruneau, 1989a; Sewart, 1987). Reference has already been made to the growth of the big global sporting occasions. These offer opportunities to add variety, colour and impact, to enhance the entertainment element and to provide a wealth of material for the 'big build-up' to the event. The Olympics have gone far beyond the status of a sports event. The opening ceremonies have become spectaculars tailor-made for the medium of global television.

**Box 10.1   The choreography of the opening of an
Olympics: a made-for-television spectacular**

Spectacular stadiums and locations. A confined and defined space. Colour,
banners and flags. Parades of athletes. Dancers and music. Nationalism and
internationalism. Youthfulness. Oaths and speeches. Nostalgia and vision.
Symbolism: a release of doves (peace), the entrance of the Olympic Torch and
the lighting of the flame.

A second powerful characteristic of media
sport production is that of *dramatisation*.
The media professionals set up story lines
around the sporting event and the individuals involved. They work to script the
event so as to excite. They provide pre-event
discussion and analysis. The audience's
appetite and anticipation are heightened by
the extent and form of the build-up that the
media provides. The media endeavour to
create or home in on tension, emotion and
incidents. Suspense, conflict and confrontation are emphasised so as to add to the
dramatic effect. Event creation has already
been discussed but the media may go further
than just helping in the establishment of a
particular competition or the development
of new sport; they may create happenings
within events. For example, a head-to-head
encounter between the top two track and
field athletes from a particular discipline
can provide the drama and personalisation
on which the media thrive. Television and
radio seek to heighten the dramatic impact
by offering the audience a sense of immedi-
acy. The television sport presentation aims
to provide that ringside seat mentioned earlier. The media claim to get their audience
as close as possible to the action: replays,
camera angles and interviews are employed
to enhance this effect. Stump cameras in
cricket coverage get you close to the action.
You too can see what it is like to face the
bowling! Athletes today face a barrage of
cameras and microphones the moment
their event/ match is over. Cameras are now
even going into changing rooms.

A third aspect of media construction is the
process of *personalisation* that is undertaken.
Individual sportspeople are highlighted,
built up and examined, often in great detail.
Media sport superstars are born. Post-
event/match press conferences are now a
fact of life for many athletes. Both sporting
and non-sporting lives come under the
media microscope. Great deeds or misde-
meanours of the past are resurrected and
inspected. The audience is encouraged to
associate with and warm to an individual.
Alternatively they may be asked to view an
individual in less than favourable terms.
Heroes and villains are created. Interpersonal
rivalries are highlighted, indeed invented by
the media. The media's obsession with the
relationship between Sebastian Coe and
Steve Ovett is a classic example (Whannel,
1992: 140–8). An interesting example from
British media sport is the footballer, Vinnie
Jones, labelled by the media as a 'hard man'
characterised by his uncompromising way
of playing. Reference was frequently made
to his past offences and colourful disciplinary record. Ironically and perhaps reveal-
ingly, Vinnie was later to find stardom as a
stereotypical villain and 'hard man' in
another media form, that of films.

Often criticised but much in evidence in
the construction of media sport production

is the use of expert analysis. The wise head with the penetrating insights to aid the lead commentator and the panel of experts to tell us what is going on and why have now become the norm in so many sports presentations. Love them or hate them, these individuals (usually former players or managers/coaches) are there to take a role in educating the members of the audience, directing them to the salient aspects of what is about to or has happened and, importantly, to structure and influence their opinions.

These various media sport construction characteristics are reinforced and enabled by the actual technical conventions and devices employed in the media world. In newspapers, sports reporting is developed and enhanced through the skills of the editors, headline writers and photo-journalists. Sports reporting lends itself to the emotive and 'catchy' headline and to the dramatic or heart-rending photograph. Often a picture can send a stronger message than words. In television, the programme director is central to making the most of the media opportunities available. They are aided in this task by skilled camera and sound work. A camera angle obtained and then selected by the director can add to the spectacle and drama of the occasion. Event location can help: the coverage of swimming events at the Barcelona Olympics in 1992 will long be remembered for the spectacular backdrop of the city. Similarly sound – imported or at the actual event – can be used to direct the attention and interest of the audience.

THE MEDIA SPORT AUDIENCE

A major question surrounding media sport is the role played by the audience. Are they knowledgeable about the media sport product to which they are exposed? Are they able to make informed choices about what they see, hear and read? One viewpoint maintains that the audience does exercise free choice and is essentially receiving the sports media products that they want. Their wishes are reflected in the output from the media companies and the professionals who work for them. The media are viewed as neutral and pluralist, reflecting the diversity in their audience and respecting the sovereignty of their consumers. A contrary viewpoint sees the media sport audience as one lacking in knowledge and experience.

Despite physical improvements in the many sports venues and the attempts by sports organisations to make the 'live' experience a pleasurable and exciting one, for an increasing number of people, their experience of elite sport is solely through the media. The 'couch spectator' has before them a wealth of media sports products to choose from, together with a growing array of gadgetry to make the involvement more interesting and personal. Interactive television, with the ability to choose highlights, to select camera angles and to have facts and figures at the press of a button, is promoted as superior to being present at the event. It can be argued that one aspect of the changing nature of this engagement with sport is a reduction in first-hand knowledge of what actually goes on at the 'live' event. The sporting knowledge-base of the audience is therefore reduced and thus renders them more susceptible to the interpretations provided by the media.

MEDIA SPORT: WHERE TO NOW?

The media set fashions but are also influenced by wider social change. They are conscious of the importance of keeping their viewers, listeners and readership. Ratings and sales and linked advertising revenues are crucial and are monitored carefully. Sport, by engaging with the media, has increasingly linked itself with what is a volatile industry built powerfully on the profit motive. It is also a highly competitive industry with media sport broadcasting rights a sensitive and significant battleground. Media commitment to sport, and more particularly to certain sports or events, can change, leaving an ever more dependent world of sport vulnerable to instability. How elite commercialised sport continues to operate in such an environment will be of particular interest. Further far-reaching changes in some sports and in some events may result. Will the line between what counts as sport entertainment and what counts as media entertainment become even more blurred? The initial inroads made by media companies into direct ownership of sport may well be extended. This would fundamentally alter the balance of power within the media sport partnership and enhance the likelihood of a growth in 'made-for-television' sport. Is the rise to prominence of WWF wrestling the shape of things to come?

Developments in the forms and technical aspects of media, principally the use of the Internet, may have a profound effect on media sport production. This is yet another unknown factor to take into account. New players in what will become an increasingly global media sport marketplace, perhaps more specialised media sports companies, may further enhance the money flowing into sport, but will the patterning still remain in terms of which sports benefit and which do not? The extension of 'pay-to-view' ways of marketing and receiving media sports products is highly likely and therefore the issues of access and equity are unlikely to disappear in the short term. How the media sport audience reacts to these kinds of developments will be vital. The media live or die on the success or not of their ratings or circulation. Will media sport still retain massive audiences in the years ahead or will the public discover participation and 'live' spectating to be far more satisfying? In doing so, will the audience come to recognise that what they have been receiving as media sport has moved too far away from what sport should be about? Inevitably the answers lie in the capacity of the public to influence their own media usage habits and the ability of the media, in all its forms, to keep its audiences contented with what is offered.

Chapter summary

- Sport and the media have both a global and a local scope of operation and are bound together in a complex network of relationships.
- Since the 1980s the value of sport to media companies and their investment in sport have grown dramatically.
- The power of the small number of major media companies raises important issues of access and equity, especially with the growth of pay-to-view sports events.
- While the media have demonstrated a considerable capacity to influence the character and development of sport, it should be noted that there is little evidence of resistance to commodification from sports bodies or athletes.

(Continued)

(Continued)

- Sports media generally promote and reinforce a distinctive set of values associated with capitalism, nationalism, patriarchy and racism.
- The media production process emphasises spectacle, drama and personalisation.

Further reading

Wenner's edited volume (1998), Gruneau et al. (1988) and Rowe (1999) provide sound general introductions to the field. Birrell and Cole (1994) and Daddario (1994) explore the relationship between media and gender. Davis and Harris (1998) and Tudor (1998) explore the interrelationship between the media and race and ethnicity, and Rowe et al. (1998) examine the impact of the media on sport and nationalism. As regards the role of the media in relation to particular sports, Maguire (1990) offers an analysis of the role of the media in the promotion of American football in Britain and Lawrence and Rowe (1986) provide a similar analysis of cricket. Finally, Young and Smith (1989) and Theberge (1989) explore the treatment of violence in sport by the media.

REFERENCES

Birrell, S. and Cole, L.C. (eds) (1994) *Women, Sport and Culture*. Champaign, IL: Human Kinetics, pp. 245–322.

Birrell, S. and Theberge, N. (1994) 'Ideological control of women in sport', in D.M. Costa and S.R. Guthrie (eds), *Women in Sport: Interdisciplinary Perspectives*. Champaign, IL: Human Kinetics, pp. 341–60.

Daddario, G. (1994) 'Chilly scenes of the 1992 Winter Games: the mass media and the marginalisation of female athletes', *Sociology of Sport Journal*, 11 (3): 275–88.

Davis, L.R. and Harris, O. (1998) 'Race and ethnicity in US sports media', in L.A. Wenner (ed.), *Mediasport*. London: Routledge, pp. 154–69.

Duncan, M.C. (1990) 'Sports photography and sexual difference. Images of women and men in the 1984 and 1988 Olympic Games', *Sociology of Sport Journal*, 7 (1): 22–43.

Duncan, M.C. and Hasbrook, C. (1988) 'Denial of power in televised women's sport', *Sociology of Sport Journal*, 5: 1–21.

Duquin, M. (1989) 'Fashion and fitness images in women's magazine advertisements', *Arena Review*, 13: 97–109.

Eastman, S.T. and Billings, A.C. (2000) 'Sportscasting and sports reporting. The power of gender bias', *Journal of Sport and Social Issues*, 24 (2): 192–213.

Falcous, M. (1998) 'TV made it all a new game: not again! Rugby league and the case of the "Superleague"', *Occasional Papers in Football Studies*: 4–21.

Goldlust, J. (1987) *Playing for Keeps: Sport, the Media and Society*. Melbourne: Longman.

Gruneau, R. (1989a) 'Making a spectacle: a case study in television sports production', in L. Wenner (ed.), *Media, Sports and Society*. London: Sage, pp. 134–56.

Gruneau, R. (1989b) 'Television, the Olympics and the question of ideology', in R. Jackson and T. McPhail (eds), *The Olympic Movement and the Mass Media: Past, Present and Future Issues*. Calgary, AL: Hurford Enterprises 7, pp. 23–34.

Gruneau, R., Whitson, D. and Cantelon, H. (1988) 'Methods and media: studying the sports/television discourse', *Society and Leisure*, 11 (2): 265–81.

Kinkema, K.M. and Harris, J.C. (1998) '*Mediasport* studies: key research and emerging issues', in L.A. Wenner (ed.), *Mediasport*. London: Routledge, pp. 27–54.

Lawrence, G. and Rowe, D. (1986) 'The corporate pitch: televised cricket under capitalism', in G. Lawrence and D. Rowe (eds), *Power Play: the Commercialization of Australian Sport.* Sydney: Hale & Iremonger, pp. 166–78.

MacNeil, M. (1988) 'Active women, media representations and ideology', in J. Harvey and H. Cantelon (eds), *Not Just a Game: Essays in Canadian Sport Sociology.* Ottawa: University of Ottawa Press, pp. 195–211.

McKay, J. and Rowe, D. (1987) 'Ideology, the media and Australian sport', *Sociology of Sport Journal,* 4 (3): 258–73.

Maguire, J. (1990) 'More than a sporting "touchdown". The making of American football in Britain 1982–1989', *Sociology of Sport Journal,* 7: 213–37.

Maguire, J. (1999) *Global Sport. Identities, Societies, Civilizations.* Cambridge: Polity Press, pp. 144–206.

Maguire, J. and Poulton, E. (1999) 'European identity politics in Euro 96: invented traditions and national habitus codes', *International Review for the Sociology of Sport,* 34 (1): 17–29.

Messner, M.A., Dunbar, M. and Hunt, D. (2000) 'The televised sports manhood formula', *Journal of Sport and Social Issues,* 24 (4): 380–94.

Rowe, D. (1999) *Sport, Culture and the Media.* Buckingham: Open University Press.

Rowe, D., McKay, J. and Miller, T. (1998) 'Come together: sport, nationalism and the media image', in L.A. Wenner (ed.), *Mediasport.* London: Routledge, pp. 119–33.

Sage, G. (1990) *Power and Ideology in American Sport.* Champaign, IL: Human Kinetics.

Sewart, J. (1987) 'The commodification of sport', *International Review for the Sociology of Sport,* 22 (3): 171–92.

Theberge, N. (1989) 'A feminist analysis of responses to sports violence: media coverage of the 1987 world junior hockey championship', *Sociology of Sport Journal,* 6: 247–56.

Trujillo, N. (1995) 'Machines, missiles and men: images of the male body on ABC's Monday Night Football', *Sociology of Sport Journal,* 12 (4): 403–23.

Tudor, A. (1998) 'Sports reporting: race, difference and identity', in K. Brants, J. Hermes and L. van Zoonen (eds), *The Media in Question.* London: Sage.

Wenner, L.A. (ed.) (1998) *Mediasport.* London: Routledge.

Whannel, G. (1992) *Fields in Vision: Television Sport and Cultural Transformation.* London: Routledge.

Williams, C., Lawrence, G. and Rowe, D. (1986) 'Patriarchy, media and sport', in G. Lawrence and D. Rowe (eds), *Power Play: the Commercialization of Australian Sport.* Sydney: Hale & Iremonger, pp. 215–29.

Young, K. and Smith, M. (1989) 'Mass media treatment of violence in sports and its effects', *Current Psychology: Research and Reviews,* 1: 298–312.

11

Analysing Sports Organisations: Theory and Practice

JOHN AMIS AND TREVOR SLACK

Overview

→ Organisational structure: complexity, standardisation, centralisation; archetypes and structural configurations
→ External context: factors in the task and general environment
→ Internal context: leadership, power and politics, decision making, organisational culture

Sports organisations come in a variety of different forms and serve a number of functions. There are small, community-based voluntary organisations, such as the local hockey or cricket club that play in regional leagues, and large professionally operated organisations, such as the International Olympic Committee or the Fédération Internationale de Football Association (FIFA), which stage major international events. There are football clubs such as Manchester United and Tottenham Hotspur, which are publicly traded on the Stock Exchange, and village teams that may be sponsored by a local pub. There are local sports shops that are owned and operated by a single individual, and nationwide chains such as JJB Sports. There are multinational apparel and equipment manufacturers such as

Nike and Reebok, and small, independently owned consultancies. There are national governing bodies that are large and wealthy, such as the English Football Association, and others that are smaller with relatively low incomes, such as the English Surfing Federation. Whether they are large or small, rich or poor, run by volunteers or owned by institutional shareholders, the managers of all sports organisations have to face common issues. How is the organisation going to be structured? What external groups does the organisation have to deal with? Who will lead the organisation? How are decisions made? How will the organisation secure key resources? In seeking answers to such questions, organisation theorists try to uncover ways in which managers may be able to design and operate their sports organisations more effectively. Our purpose in this chapter is to highlight some of the issues with which managers in the sports industry have to contend and some of the research that has provided insight into them.

ORGANISATIONAL STRUCTURE

One of the most important questions that organisation theorists address is why organisations are structured in particular ways. This is because structure will directly influence almost every facet of organisational life, from determining how key resources are obtained to how organisation workers are supervised. But what do we mean by the term 'organisational structure'? When we think of how an organisation is structured, a number of things may spring to mind: an organisational chart depicting the various vertical and horizontal relationships; the breakdown and allocation of different tasks to different departments; or the way in which decisions are made. While none of these is incorrect, each provides only a partial view. A useful way to think about structure is that it comprises the formal and informal interactions that make up organisational life. These interactions may include structured meetings between managers from different departments, direct instructions to a subordinate, or a casual work-related conversation in the canteen. Such interactions are seen as useful in bringing order and stability to the organisation so that it may operate effectively; however, they can also produce conflict and uncertainty.

While this is a useful starting point for helping us to understand the concept of organisational structure, it does not really assist us in trying to learn how and why sports organisations are structured differently. To gain insight into this, we need some way to assess the structures of organisations that will in turn allow us to make comparisons. The most common approach in both mainstream organisation theory (Miller and Dröge, 1986; Pugh et al., 1969) and in the study of sport organisations (Amis and Slack, 1996; Amis et al., 2002; Frisby, 1986; Kikulis et al., 1995a; Slack and Hinings, 1994) involves investigation of the structural dimensions of complexity, formalisation and centralisation.

Complexity

The England Rugby Union team has a number of support staff. In addition to head coach Clive Woodward, there is a backs' coach, a forwards' coach, a kicking coach and a conditioning trainer. There are also a number of physiotherapists and doctors; a nutritional expert and sport psychologist are utilised as required. If we look at David Lloyd Leisure, we find an organisation that has 46 leisure clubs spread throughout the United Kingdom co-ordinated from a head office in Hounslow. Although the England rugby team and David Lloyd Leisure are clearly quite different, the breakdown of work, in the first case by task, in the second by geographical location, adds to the complexity of managing each organisation. The complexity of an organisation is determined by the degree to which the work that is carried out is broken down and assigned to different sub-units or individual specialists. This is a process known as differentiation. Differentiation, carried out to improve the efficiency of an organisation, may be horizontal, vertical or spatial.

Horizontal differentiation may occur through either specialisation or departmentalisation. Specialisation refers to the employment of individual specialists to carry out specific tasks, as in the case of the English rugby team, while departmentalisation occurs when necessary tasks within an organisation are assigned to specific units, such as marketing, finance and distribution. The greater the number of specialists or departments, the greater the level of complexity. The degree of vertical differentiation in an organisation is usually indicated by the number of hierarchical levels: the more levels, the more difficult communication, co-ordination and supervision become, and hence the greater the level of complexity. Spatial differentiation occurs when, as with David Lloyd Leisure, different parts of the organisation are located in different geographic areas. Trying to co-ordinate activities among a group of sub-units that may be spread around a country, a continent, or, as is often the case in today's global economy, the world, all adds to the complexity of the manager's task.

Formalisation

The degree of formalisation in an organisation refers to the extent to which policies, procedures, rules and regulations stipulate the way in which the members of an organisation should act. Formalisation is usually directly related to complexity, as the more complex an organisation, the greater the need for formalised co-ordinating mechanisms. Formalisation works as a method of control by reducing the need for direct supervision. As well as varying among different organisations, the level of formalisation will also vary by department and hierarchical position. For example, the Nike Category Product Teams, which move a new athletic shoe from the initial idea through to the marketing of the final product, operate in a much less formalised environment than the production staff that

actually manufacture the shoes in Asian factories. Because of the nature of their tasks, the roles of the latter will be clearly laid out in company and subcontractor regulations, while the former will have little more than broad job descriptions. Similarly, Nike Chief Executive Officer Phil Knight, required to make unusual or even unique decisions on a day-to-day basis, will have very little formalisation of his role. By contrast, a NikeTown shop assistant will have clearly defined procedures outlining every facet of his/her job, from how to greet a customer to the length of time that can be spent on a lunch break. Determining how formalised different roles should be within the organisation is thus another important management role.

Centralisation

Centralisation refers to the locus of decision making within an organisation. An organisation in which senior executives make most decisions is said to be centralised; one in which a decision-making authority is delegated to lower-level staff is thought of as decentralised. Despite the apparent simplicity of this definition, attempts to determine whether or not an organisation is centralised have proved difficult. Consider the case of JJB Sports retail outlets. On the one hand, store managers are given autonomy to run their stores as they see fit; on the other, they must comply with policies and procedures regarding corporate branding and image, store layout and pricing. In other words, despite the appearance of autonomy, the nature and scope of the decisions that a manager can make are quite tightly constrained.

However, this uncertainty should not obscure the basic rationale for operating with a centralised or decentralised decision-making structure. A more centralised operation allows a small group of what are typically the most experienced members of the organisation to make decisions in a way that is co-ordinated and, because it avoids duplication, economically most viable. By contrast, decentralisation allows decisions to be made more rapidly in response to changes at a local level. It also helps motivate employees who feel that they are having an impact on the success of the organisation, and may help them prepare for management careers of their own. Finally, and perhaps most fundamentally for a large organisation, it prevents senior executives from becoming overwhelmed with information that they are unable to process because of cognitive, time and resource limitations.

The structure of sports organisations

Slack and Hinings (1987, 1992, 1994) and Kikulis et al. (1992, 1995a, 1995b, 1995c) have produced a collection of papers that explored the ways in which Canadian national-level sports governing bodies are structured. They discovered that Canadian National Sports Organisations (NSOs) conformed to varying degrees to three basic structural designs, or archetypes: the Kitchen Table, Boardroom and Executive Office. We use this work to illustrate the variations in structure that can be found in similar types of sports organisations.

The *Kitchen Table* archetype has been the traditional design of Canada's NSOs, and many others around the world. Run by a group of dedicated volunteers, these NSOs receive little government funding, relying instead on membership fees and fundraising for their financing. Because they are run by volunteers on an almost ad hoc basis, Kitchen Table-type organisations generally have a low level of complexity and low levels of formalisation. Decision making is highly centralised with the volunteer board of directors, located at the top of the organisational hierarchy, making virtually all strategic and operational decisions.

Organisations that adhere to a *Boardroom* archetype place more emphasis on the performances of elite-level athletes, although catering for the development of lower-level athletes who compete domestically is still a key part of the organisation's role. Although volunteers retain control of this type of organisation, complexity is also influenced by the presence of professional staff who take care of day-to-day operations. With the need to co-ordinate professional staff and a greater number of activities, Boardroom-type organisations are generally more formalised than those with a Kitchen Table design. They are, however, still highly centralised, with decision making continuing to remain almost entirely with the volunteer board of directors assisted by professional staff.

Sports organisations that have an *Executive Office* design focus almost exclusively on the preparation of elite-level athletes for international competition. In order to achieve this, these organisations have to engage the services of many more professional coaching and administrative staff; they set up high-performance centres, and they take part in more international competitions at various age-group levels. As a result, Executive Office-type organisations are much more complex and formalised than either of the other two archetypes. Although a volunteer board of directors is retained, most strategic and operational decisions are devolved to the professional staff in what is a much more decentralised structure.

The work cited above is useful in showing us how and why different sports organisations may have different structures. Whichever design is adopted, it is important for managers of sports organisations to adopt a structure that fits the external and internal contexts within which the organisation has to operate. We explore some of the different contextual features of which sports managers need to be aware after a brief discussion of a different approach that could be used to analyse the structural design of sports organisations.

Mintzberg's structural configurations

Kikulis and her colleagues developed their classification of NSOs based on the dimensions of complexity, formalisation and centralisation. Another approach that can help us understand the way in which sports organisations are designed is based on the work of Henry Mintzberg (1979). Mintzberg developed what he called configurations:

- the simple structure;
- the machine bureaucracy;
- the professional bureaucracy;
- the divisionalised form; and
- the adhocracy.

Each of Mintzberg's configurations consists of up to five component parts. The strategic apex consists of the senior managers who make the key decisions. The operating core is made up of the people who carry out the tasks required to fulfil the basic function of the organisation. The middle line comprises the middle management which connects the operating core to the strategic apex. The technostructure is made up of the technical staff (such as planners and engineers) who help to ensure that the products or services produced are of a similar standard. Finally, the support staff carry out various roles that may range from the cooking of meals to the provision of legal advice to support those carrying out the basic work. In each of the five design types, Mintzberg suggests that one part of

the organisation is most important for successful operation.

The simple structure is the configuration most often found in the sports industry. In this type of organisation, the strategic apex is dominant with usually no technostructure or support staff and often no middle line, but a significant operating core. Most amateur sports clubs correspond to this type of design. For example, a village cricket club may have a club committee consisting of the club chair, treasurer, secretary and team captains. This committee forms the strategic apex of the club, with the rest of the organisation consisting of the players who comprise the operating core and also carry out most of the non-playing roles, such as preparing the ground and cleaning the changing rooms. Co-ordination of activities within the club is carried out through the direct supervision of the players (operating core) by the committee (strategic apex).

The machine bureaucracy is most commonly associated with large-scale, mass-production organisations. Firms that mass-produce sporting equipment tend to make use of this type of design in order to manufacture their products efficiently. This type of organisation usually has a rigid formal hierarchy with roles and responsibilities clearly defined. Dunlop Slazenger International's tennis ball manufacturing plant at Barnsley in Yorkshire provides a good illustration. There are 145 production line workers (operating core) and supervisory staff (middle line) who are overseen by a General Manager (strategic apex). Although major decisions are made by the strategic apex, the middle line also plays an important role in co-ordinating the activities of the production workers. The production process is assisted by several support staff, including secretarial, financial and security personnel. However, the key role within the organisation is played by the engineering staff (technostructure), who ensure that the machinery operates within certain set parameters, so that the 16.8 million tennis balls produced annually conform to a particular standard, whether they are being used on a local park or at the Wimbledon Tennis Championships (pers. comm., Debbie Penfold, HRM manager, 7 August 2001). This emphasis on the techno-structure results in the main co-ordinating mechanism employed by the firm being the standardisation of work processes.

The professional bureaucracy is a design that includes, among others, professional service organisations. Sport physiotherapy clinics, sport marketing firms and sport law practices all readily fit into this design type. According to Mintzberg, the most vital part of this type of organisation is the operating core, made up of the professional staff who provide the service. A good example is Townley's Solicitors, virtually the only dedicated sport law practice in the UK. Stephen Townley himself operates as the strategic apex. The vast majority of the legal work, which is the main operational function within the organ-isation, is carried out by the six partners (middle line) and 24 solicitors (operating core). There are four trainee solicitors, 14 administrative assistants, three accountants and one information technology officer who between them carry out vital support roles that enable the operating core to function effectively. As Mintzberg suggests, organisa-tions like Townley's have no technostruc-ture. Co-ordination is achieved from the standardisation of skills that have been developed during professional training (pers. comm., Stephen Townley, 8 August 2001). This helps to ensure that individuals with similar qualifications and levels of experi-ence provide a broadly similar service.

David Lloyd Leisure, with its centres spread throughout the UK, is an organisation that typifies Mintzberg's *divisionalised form*. The key part of this type of organisation is the middle line, the managers who run each of the individual leisure centres. For exam-ple, at the leisure centre in Milton Keynes, the General Manager and the Assistant General Manager comprise the strategic apex for the Milton Keynes centre and also part of the middle line for David Lloyd Leisure as a whole. The operating core con-sists of the various fitness instructors, life-guards, racquets coaches and bar staff who deliver services to the club members. The centre's middle line are the supervisory staff in each department. The club has a small support staff (cleaners and administrative staff) and two maintenance engineers (tech-nostructure) who deal with any problems with swimming pool or fitness equipment. The majority of support roles, such as accountants, legal staff, equipment buyers and so on reside in corporate headquarters in Hounslow and provide a service for all of the firm's clubs. The main method of co-ordination is in the standardisation of out-puts: in the case of David Lloyd Leisure, management is oriented to provide con-sumers with a broadly similar experience in any of the 46 clubs that they choose to visit.

Adhocracies are designed to respond rapidly to any changes in the external envi-ronment. As such, they tend to be innova-tive organisations that operate in industries characterised by rapid change. With little standardisation of outputs, there is no tech-nostructure; in fact, there is little demarca-tion of roles in terms of operating core, middle line or support staff. Typically, spe-cialist project teams come together to solve specific problems. Although part of a larger organisation, the Nike Category Product Teams, referred to earlier, provide a good example. The need for an innovative envi-ronment requires a flexibility of approach so that the team members, which include designers, developers and marketing specialists, have access to necessary information and can operate in as unconstrained a manner as possible. With no rigid hierarchy, co-ordination is achieved by mutual adjustment whereby individuals in the group try to accommodate each other's needs.

Mintzberg's (1979) configurations and Kikulis et al.'s (1992) archetypes are useful tools for helping us to understand how organisations are structured in different ways. We now move on to explore some of the characteristics of the external and internal contexts that sports managers must consider when deciding how their organisation should be structured and operated.

EXTERNAL CONTEXT

The external environment in which sports organisations operate can be broken down into two parts. On the one hand, there are general issues, such as changes to the political or economic environment, which impact on entire industries. On the other hand, there are factors that can have immediate and direct consequences on an individual organisation, such as the actions of a competitor or supplier. It is these more immediate influences to which we first turn our attention before exploring some general environmental factors.

Task environment

The task, or proximal, environment for a sports organisation comprises those influences that have a direct, day-to-day impact on the way in which it operates. These may include, among other things, an organisation's suppliers, the buyers of its products or services, and its competitors. All of these can have a pronounced effect on the organisation because of the way in which they can add to the uncertainty with which managers have to contend. The greater the uncertainty in a situation, the more difficult it is for managers to make decisions such as how to allocate resources, whether to hire additional personnel, or what hours a facility should be open. Managers therefore try very hard to minimise the uncertainty that they have to face. An example is provided in Box 11.1.

Box 11.1   Task environment

Managers at LA Fitness try to limit uncertainty caused by its various suppliers of equipment and labour in a number of ways. First, the firm controls equipment costs by buying machines in bulk for all of its 35 fitness clubs. Prices are therefore held lower than if each club had to purchase its equipment individually. Second, it enters into various medium- and long-term contracts with its major service providers, ensuring that servicing costs are known well in advance. Third, all staff have contracts that stipulate a period of notice that has to be given before an employee can leave, thus allowing time for management to find an adequate replacement.

The customers of LA Fitness also represent a key variable in the task environment that must be controlled as tightly as possible. For example, during 2001 the club in Bedford wanted to increase its membership from 3,500 to 4,000. This, it

(Continued)

Box 11.1   Continued

was felt, would allow the club to operate most regularly at its optimum carrying capacity of 400 users per day. Various promotional campaigns were conducted so that the centre could attain and retain this number of users (of course, such campaigns were used most intensely in the periods before and shortly after the new club opened). Furthermore, new members had to enter into an initial 12-month contract with the club. These steps were taken so that a predictable, steady income could be assured.

    Industry competitors can also exert a significant effect on an organisation. When LA Fitness opened one club in November 1999, two other major fitness clubs in the town both experienced significant reductions in membership. In order to try and counter this loss and stop further members leaving to join the new club, both organisations engaged in a number of different strategies. These included, at various times, lowering the prices that were charged for particular services, changing the combinations of services bundled together for a particular price, improving the level of customer service, and in one case opening up a new restaurant within the club.

General environment

The general environment, termed 'distal' by some researchers, consists of those factors that, while they may not have a direct effect on an organisation, will influence the industry in which the organisation operates. There are seven such factors that we briefly consider here.

Political factors

The political situation in a country or region will have a direct influence on sports policy. In the UK for example, the last Conservative government introduced Compulsory Competitive Tendering (CCT) and thus created a new market for private leisure service providers. Following the election of a Labour government in 1997, CCT was replaced with the 'Best Value' programme which, among other things, removed the onus on local government to award service contracts to the lowest-cost provider as demanded by CCT, thus affecting the way in which contractors would construct their tender. The impact that different political systems can have on sports organisations is well illustrated by Houlihan's (1997) comparative analyses of sports policy in the UK, Australia, the Republic of Ireland, Canada and the United States.

Economic factors

The general economic framework in which a sports organisation exists will also impact the way in which it operates. Examples of the effect of two general economic factors on a sports organisation can be seen in the 2001 Annual Report of JJB Sports. In the Financial Review, Finance Director J.D. Greenwood noted that two of 'the key financial risks faced by the [firm] ... are fluctuations in interest and exchange rates' (*www.jjb.co.uk*, 27 Nov. 2001). Clearly, an increase in the general interest rate set by the Bank of England will likely increase the amount that the firm has to repay on its bank borrowings. Conversely, a decision made by the government to join the single European currency could do much to reduce any losses incurred by changes in exchange rates. In both cases, changes in the general economic environment will likely have a pronounced effect on the firm.

Legal factors

The legal framework that governs an organisation's activities clearly places constraints on the ways in which it may act. Health and safety legislation plays an important role in providing a safe environment for both customers and employees, particularly in settings that have the potential for serious accidents such as swimming pools. While health and safety legislation applies to all types of organisation, other laws have been introduced to deal specifically with the sporting context. For example, the stadiums that we see hosting Premier League football matches have been radically altered as a consequence of the safety recommendations made in the Taylor Report (1990). One of the most visible changes is that clubs that compete in the Premier League and Division One of the Football League must normally have all-seated stadiums. Other legislative changes have been made to try to protect children from abuse from coaches and officials (Brackenridge and Kirby, 1997) and to reinforce the rights of out-of-contract athletes to work freely across Europe under the so-called Bosman Ruling (McArdle, 2000).

Socio-cultural factors

Socio-cultural factors such as sporting traditions and trends in consumer tastes can be very influential on the success or failure of sports organisations. The attempt in 2001 by the World Wrestling Federation (WWF) and the National Broadcasting Company (NBC) to launch the Xtreme Football League (XFL) in the US is a good example. Despite extensive promotion, the WWF and NBC announced that the XFL had not generated sufficient public interest to warrant a second season. Similar, though less rapid failures have been encountered by organisers of the North American Soccer League in the 1970s and the World League of American Football in the 1990s.

Demographic factors

The demographic profile of a particular area can also have a pronounced effect on the success of an organisation. Ethnicity, wealth, age and gender all impact on the propensity of an individual to participate in certain activities, whether it be joining a rugby club, purchasing a pair of skis or hiring a personal trainer. Such factors need to be considered when deciding where to locate and how to market a particular sports organisation.

Technological factors

Making use of technological advances has always played an important role in the sports industry. Wilson, for example, had to adapt their tennis racquet manufacturing techniques as wood was surpassed initially by various metals and then by graphite and kevlar composites as the materials of choice. Furthermore, as a large-scale manufacturing firm, Wilson had to embrace more automated production line machines that reduced the overall cost of mass production.

Ecological conditions

Ecological factors such as the weather will affect the profitability of many outdoor-based organisations. For example, Scarborough Cricket Club pays a fee to Yorkshire County Cricket Club to play a CricInfo County Championship match and a Norwich Union League one-day game at Scarborough during the club's festival week in August. The club then hopes to make money from its ticket sales, corporate hospitality, and food and beverage sales during the week. Clearly, the weather will be a significant factor in determining how much money is turned over during the week. While it is not possible to change the weather, an organisation may be able to diversify its activities so that one bad period of weather, or one bad season, will not prove fatal. Whistler/ Blackcomb, world famous as a ski resort, is now marketed as one of North America's finest 'four season mountain resorts'. In addition to offering glacier skiing into August, summer visitors can hike, mountain bike or play on one of five golf courses. Ecological factors are also important when expressed through the rising public concern for the environment. As a result, environmental protection has also become a parameter for some sports organisations when planning their activities, be it building a new sports facility on the edge of a town or trying to set up a water-skiing club on a peaceful countryside lake.

INTERNAL CONTEXT

Clearly the external context in which a sports organisation is located will have a pronounced effect on the way in which it is structured and operated. However, equally important is the organisation's internal context. In this section we explore four significant aspects of the internal environment. Although for ease of discussion we consider each aspect individually, they should not be thought of as existing in isolation. Instead they should be considered as interactive dynamic constructs that make the organisation a constantly evolving entity.

Leadership

The study of leadership has long enjoyed great popularity among social scientists. However, leadership research has also been bemoaned as being 'trivial or contradictory' (Bryman, 1999: 26) and overly reductionist (Pettigrew, 1987). Miner (1982) even called for the temporary abandonment of the topic. Despite this, probably because of the standing that we accord organisational leaders, analyses of leadership have continued, both in sport and other domains. Bryman (1999) suggested that leadership research could be classified into four streams: the trait approach, the style approach, the contingency approach and the new leadership approach.

The *trait approach* provides a focus on the personal qualities of leaders, subscribing to the maxim that leaders are born rather than made. Traits that have been identified have tended to fall into three categories:

1 physical, such as height and appearance;
2 the possession of certain abilities, such as intelligence; and
3 personality characteristics, such as conservatism or self-confidence.

Although the validity of trait research has been questioned for many years (see Stogdill, 1948, for an early critique), it has remained a popular approach. Soucie (1994) used the cumulative findings of several studies on trait research to come up with various 'prescriptions' for practising sport administrators. Drawing particularly on Yukl's (1989) review of leadership traits, Soucie (1994: 8) suggested that 'analytical ability, persuasiveness, speaking ability, memory for details, empathy, tact, and charm' were characteristics of effective sport administrators. The major criticism associated with trait research is that it ignores the fact that leaders have to operate in a variety of different settings. As such, it is extremely questionable as to whether it is possible to uncover a definitive set of 'leadership characteristics' that will tell us whether or not an individual will make a good leader.

Proponents of the *style approach* to leadership have held that rather than being born with leadership qualities (as the trait approach suggests), individuals can instead be trained to become good leaders. The best known of these studies featured the development of an instrument known as the Leader Behavior Description Questionnaire (LBDQ) (e.g. Fleishman and Harris, 1962). The LBDQ was used to explore the perception of leaders' behaviour by their subordinates. From this it was suggested that certain preferential leadership styles could be identified and developed, such as a focusing on employee experiences and granting greater individual autonomy to subordinates. While such employee sentiments may appear obvious, and are intuitively appealing as good general management practices, the style approach has been criticised for failing to take account of the different situations in which leaders have to operate (e.g., Bryman, 1999).

The recognition of the need to take into account individual context when determining leadership effectiveness led to the development of the *contingency approach*. The contingency approach is exemplified by the work of Fiedler (1967, 1993), who suggested that different leadership styles should be used in different organisational settings. For example, in situations where work is considered stressful, tedious and low in autonomy, such as on a production assembly line, a leadership style that is supportive and exhibits concern for subordinates is seen as being effective. Where there is little formalisation and tasks are unstructured, such as in a project design team, a more participative leadership style is favoured. While this approach has provided useful insight into how different styles of leadership can be effective in different contexts, in recent years a new approach to the study of leadership has emerged.

The *new leadership approach* is a term that has been used to embrace a variety of research that has coalesced around Burns's (1978) notions of transformational and transactional leadership. Transactional leadership involves an exchange, usually of money or prestige, in return for compliance. While often effective, the parameters of the relationship are set by the contract between leader and follower. By contrast, the transformational leader 'raises the aspirations of his or her followers such that the leader's and the followers' aspirations are fused' (Bryman, 1999: 30). This approach has become popular in the sport management literature, being used to explore leadership in university sport administration in both the US (Kent and Chelladurai, 2001; Quarterman, 1998) and Canada (Doherty, 1997; Doherty and Danylchuk, 1996).

While some of these findings are of interest and worthy of further exploration, there is a need for a more critical approach to leadership behaviour in sports organisations (Slack, 2000). In much of the work cited above, leadership has been seen as a neutral activity with certain behaviours being either exhibited or not. There is a need for work that builds on the current body of research and explores the outcomes of leadership over time in order that more or less effective practices can be identified, and their consequences assessed. In this way, the manner in which leadership interacts with other aspects of organisation, such as culture (e.g. Weese, 1995) or change (e.g. Slack and Hinings, 1992), can be uncovered.

Power and politics

Inextricably linked with leadership is the way in which individuals use power in organisations to achieve certain desired outcomes. While we often think of power being accrued by those in formal leadership positions, individuals may also achieve positions of power outside the formal hierarchy because of the role that they play within the organisation. The functional differentiation of organisational design that was outlined in earlier works to distinguish one group of organisation members from another. Thus, built into any organisation is a structure of advantage and disadvantage (Walsh et al., 1981). In other words, because of their position in the organisation, some groups will have more power than others. Power is therefore seen more as a property of the embedded social relationship resulting from the differentiation

of labour than as a personal characteristic (Hardy and Clegg, 1999).

In addition to having an insight into the bases of power within an organisation, it is also important that sports managers appreciate the ways in which power is utilised. The process of mobilising power has been described by Pettigrew (1973) as the engagement in political behaviour to achieve otherwise unattainable outcomes. There are a number of techniques that can be engaged in to achieve political ends: coalitions can be built with influential individuals; outside experts can be brought in to give a supposedly objective assessment of a situation; and attempts can be made to control who has access to what information.

Decision making

It is clear from the Volvo International Tennis Tournament case that gaining an understanding of how decisions are made is important for any sports manager. In fact, decision making has been described as 'the most crucial part of managerial work'

Box 11.2   Power mobilisation

Sack and Johnson (1996) provide insight as to how bases of power can be mobilised through political behaviour in their analysis of the process of bringing the Volvo International Tennis Tournament to New Haven, Connecticut. They showed how a coalition between various actors in the New Haven region, including Yale University and the New Haven Downtown Council, was formed, subjected to various stresses and strains, and ultimately overcame vocal opposition from local residents to bring the tournament to New Haven.

One of the main outcomes of the study was the way in which the main policy decision to move the tournament to New Haven was made 'by a small group of elites well before the general public became involved'. Thus, through the skilful use of political behaviour, those who favoured bringing the tournament to New Haven were able to manage the decision-making process to such an extent that the outcome was almost assured before any active resistance could be organised.

(Beyer, 1981: 181). The most dominant approach to decision making in the managerial literature, and the most intuitively appealing, is the rational model. Proponents of this approach view decision making as a linear series of steps consisting of a recognition of the need for action, diagnosis of the problem, a search for solutions, evaluation of various alternatives, choice of the optimal solution, and implementation of the selected choice (Miller et al., 1999). The apparent logic behind the process has led to a belief that decisions can be represented quantitatively. For example, Boronico and Newbert (1999) developed a stochastic model to determine various probabilities of the likelihood of certain play sequences leading to the scoring of a touchdown in different American football game scenarios. Using six sets each of 50 simulated plays, Boronico and Newbert's model comprehensively outperformed a college football coach.

Despite the intuitive appeal of the rational linear approach, and its apparent utility in closed situations such as the American football example above, it has been widely criticised. The earliest critique, and one of the most comprehensive, was made by Herbert Simon in his classic *Administrative Behavior* (1945). Though dated, the insights that Simon provides are as pertinent today as they were in the 1940s. Simon argued that decision makers are limited by the complexity of the organisations in which they work, by their own cognitive abilities and emotions, and by the time that they are able to devote to any one decision. Issues are often unclear, outcomes frequently cannot be precisely determined, individuals may disagree about what constitutes a successful outcome, and time and resource constraints will often limit the amount of analysis that can go into a particular decision. Consequently, decision makers have

to operate under what Simon called 'bounded rationality'. Rather than search for the optimal solution, decision makers select the first available solution that meets certain minimum criteria in a process known as 'satisficing'. Simon acknowledged that some decisions that occur frequently and conform to established protocols – programmed decisions – may lend themselves to a more rational approach, as exemplified in the work by Boronico and Newbert (1999). However, non-programmed decisions, those that are rare or unique, are frequently the most important strategic decisions that have to be made in an organisation and have few if any guidelines within which decision-makers can operate. The criticisms of Simon, and analyses of others such as Lindblom (1959) and Quinn (1980), have led to a widespread agreement that key strategic decisions cannot be made using a traditional rational approach.

As a contrast to the rational approach, Miller et al. (1999: 46) suggested that a more accurate view of decision making is as a power struggle 'in which competing interest groups vie with each other for control of scarce resources'. Several studies of Canadian NSOs have endorsed this, with the decision-making process often forming part of a larger struggle for organisational control between professional staff and volunteers (Kikulis et al., 1995a; Thibault et al., 1991). Hill and Kikulis (1999) found that struggle also characterised the way in which decisions were made in western Canadian university athletic departments. In a far cry from the neat rational approach, Hill and Kikulis (1999: 41) observed that decision making was a 'complicated association among the concepts of politicality, complexity, and rules of the game; the actions of interest groups; and the diversity of issues that ... [influence] the direction and pace of the decision process'. In other words, rather than individual decision makers working systematically through a variety of options and selecting the outcome that most benefits the organisation, there are other factors which affect the decision. Perhaps the most important of these are the individual and sub-unit goals that are frequently accorded greater importance than the success of the organisation as a whole (see, for example, Morgan, 1997).

Organisational culture

The culture (or cultures) of an organisation, in much the same way as the culture of a country, region or town, comprises those things that give an organisation its meaning and identity. Culture can encompass a variety of things: beliefs, language, ideology, traditions, myths, rituals and shared understandings – in short, anything that contributes to the way in which people within an organisation come to conceive of the organisation.

The interest in organisational culture can be traced back to the 1970s and, in particular, American managers' and theorists' desire to uncover the characteristics of Japanese firms that were making them more successful than their Western rivals. Much of this success was put down to differences between the organisational cultures of Japanese and Western firms. This has led to various views about how culture affects the ways in which organisations function.

A number of scholars have emphasised the potential integrating role of organisational culture. Proponents of this approach have suggested that effective leaders could create 'strong' cultures that reflected their own values and would ultimately lead to a more harmonious operation. McDonald (1991), in one of the best illustrations of the integrationist approach, found that organisational

commitment was quickly fostered among staff and volunteers working for the Los Angeles Olympic Organising Committee. While McDonald cited evidence of department cultures emerging, these were never really conflictual and always viewed as subservient to the overall culture of the organisation.

Rather than viewing culture as some kind of monolithic all-embracing concept, and trying to determine what constitutes organisational *culture*, other researchers have argued that organisations are in fact made up of multiple *subcultures*. Known as the differentiation perspective (Meyerson and Martin, 1987), proponents have argued for a less ethereal approach that also includes consideration of how more mundane things such as pay, organisational hierarchies, and policies and procedures manuals impact on the culture of the organisation (Martin and Frost, 1999). The differentiation perspective embraces difference and acknowledges conflicts of interest. While there has been very little work that has explored the existence of subcultures within sports organisations, there is evidence that they exist. Amis et al. (1995), for example, highlighted the existence of different groups within Canadian NSOs and the ways in which these groups came into conflict. Although they did not use the term 'subcultures', it is clear that groups formed within NSOs based on technical and administrative responsibilities, commitment to emphasising opportunities for elite-level or mass participation sport, preference for particular events, the use of English or French as a first language, and location in different parts of the country.

While the above approaches have been most popular among cultural scholars, other perspectives have also been suggested. One that appears to have great potential for helping us to understand the development of culture in sports organisations has been termed the *fragmentation perspective* (Martin, 1992). Proponents of this approach have suggested that rather than being permanent features of organisation life, cultures and subcultures are transitory, ephemeral and based around particular issues (Martin and Frost, 1999). This approach has the potential to offer much to our understanding of culture in sports organisations. The mass popularity of sport, its high public profile and the issue-driven nature of its development mean that we frequently see coalitions formed to contest particular issues. The potential location and design of the English National Stadium, the format of the United Kingdom Sports Institute, and who should take responsibility for athlete drug testing, have all been the subject of much contestation over recent years. Understanding how cultures have become manifest in Sport England, UK Sport, the Football Association, and the Ministry for Culture, Media and Sport – organisations that frequently appear fractious – would undoubtedly help in the management of these decision-making processes. As yet, however, such work has not been forthcoming.

Chapter summary

- Deciding on an appropriate organisational structure is one of the more important managerial tasks. Depending on its internal and external context, the organisation will be more or less complex, standardised and centralised. Kikulis et al.'s (1992) archetypes and Mintzberg's (1979) structural configurations can help us to understand how and why organisations have different designs.
- The task environment comprises those external factors that directly affect an organisation. These may include, but are not necessarily limited to, actions of suppliers, consumers and competitors. Managers try to influence the task environment to reduce the amount of uncertainty they face.
- The general environment is composed of those things that influence an industry as a whole rather than one particular organisation. These can include political, economic, legal, socio-cultural, demographic, technological and ecological factors.
- The internal context also has a pronounced effect on the way in which an organisation is designed and operated. Factors that need to be considered include leadership style, the use of power and political behaviour, the way in which decisions are made and the development of cultures.

Further reading

There are several texts that will provide further details on the topics covered in this chapter. Comprehensive insights can be found in the collections edited by Clegg and Hardy (1999) and Clegg et al. (1999). Morgan (1997) provides an alternative and informative way of examining organisations using a variety of different perspectives. Slack (1997) provides a useful analysis of the major concepts and how they can be applied to the sports management setting.

REFERENCES

Amis, J. and Slack, T. (1996) 'The size–structure relationship in voluntary sport organizations', *Journal of Sport Management*, 10: 76–86.

Amis, J., Slack, T. and Berrett, T. (1995) 'The structural antecedents of conflict in voluntary sport organizations', *Leisure Studies*, 14: 1–16.

Amis, J., Slack, T. and Hinings, C.R. (2002) 'Values and organizational change', *Journal of Applied Behavioral Sciences*, 38: 356–85.

Beyer, J.M. (1981) 'Ideologies, values, and decision making in organizations', in P.C. Nystrom and W.H. Starbuck (eds), *Handbook of Organizational Design*. London: Oxford University Press, pp. 166–202.

Boronico, J. and Newbert, S. (1999) 'Play calling strategy in American football: a game-theoretic stochastic dynamic programming approach', *Journal of Sport Management*, 13: 114–38.

Brackenridge, C. and Kirby, S. (1997) 'Playing safe', *International Review for the Sociology of Sport*, 32: 407–20.

Bryman, A. (1999) 'Leadership in organizations', in S.R. Clegg, C. Hardy and W.R. Nord (eds), *Managing Organizations: Current Issues*, Thousand Oaks, CA: Sage, pp. 26–42.

Burns, J.M. (1978) *Leadership*. New York: Harper & Row.

Clegg, S.R. and Hardy, C. (eds) (1999) *Studying Organization: Theory and Method*. Thousand Oaks, CA: Sage.

Clegg, S.R., Hardy, C. and Nord, W.R. (eds) (1999) *Managing Organizations: Current Issues*. Thousand Oaks, CA: Sage, pp. 26–42.

Doherty, A. (1997) 'The effects of leader characteristics on the perceived transformational/transactional leadership and impact of interuniversity athletic administrators', *Journal of Sport Management*, 11: 275–85.

Doherty, A. and Danylchuk, K. (1996) 'Transformational and transactional leadership in interuniversity athletic management', *Journal of Sport Management*, 10: 292–309.

Fiedler, F.E. (1967) *A Theory of Leadership Effectiveness*. New York: McGraw-Hill.

Fiedler, F.E. (1993) 'The leadership situation and the black box in contingency theories', in M.M. Chemers and R. Ayman (eds), *Leadership Theory and Research: Perspectives and Directions*. New York: Academic Press, pp. 1–28.

Fleishman, E.A. and Harris, E.F. (1962) 'Patterns of leader behavior related to employee grievances and turnover', *Personnel Psychology*, 15: 43–56.

Frisby, W. (1986) 'The organizational structure and effectiveness of voluntary organizations: the case of Canadian national sport governing bodies', *Journal of Park and Recreation Administration*, 4: 61–74.

Hardy, C. and Clegg, S.R. (1999) 'Some dare call it power', in S.R. Clegg and C. Hardy (eds), *Studying Organization: Theory and Method*. Thousand Oaks, CA: Sage, pp. 368–87.

Hill, L. and Kikulis, L. (1999) 'Contemplating restructuring: a case study of strategic decision making in interuniversity athletic conferences', *Journal of Sport Management*, 13: 18–44.

Houlihan, B. (1997) *Sport, Policy and Politics: A Comparative Analysis*. London: Routledge.

Kent, A. and Chelladurai, P. (2001) 'Perceived transformational leadership, organizational commitment, and citizenship behaviour: a case study in intercollegiate athletics', *Journal of Sport Management*, 15: 135–59.

Kikulis, L.M., Slack, T. and Hinings, B. (1992) 'Institutionally specific design archetypes: a framework for understanding change in national sport organizations', *International Review for the Sociology of Sport*, 27: 343–70.

Kikulis, L.M., Slack, T. and Hinings, C.R. (1995a) 'Sector-specific patterns of organizational design change', *Journal of Management Studies*, 32: 67–100.

Kikulis, L.M., Slack, T. and Hinings, C.R. (1995b) 'Towards an understanding of the role of agency and choice in the changing structure of Canada's national sport organizations', *Journal of Sport Management*, 9: 135–52.

Kikulis, L.M., Slack, T. and Hinings, C.R. (1995c) 'Does decision making make a difference? An analysis of patterns of change within Canadian national sport organizations', *Journal of Sport Management*, 9: 273–99.

Lindblom, C.E. (1959) 'The science of "muddling through"', *Public Administration Review*, 19 (2): 79–88.

McArdle, D. (2000) *Football, Society and the Law*. London: Cavendish.

McDonald, P. (1991) 'The Los Angeles Olympic Organizing Committee: developing organizational culture in the short run', in P. Frost, L. Moore, M.R. Louis, C. Lundberg and J. Martin (eds), *Reframing Organizational Culture*. Newbury Park, CA: Sage, pp. 26–38.

Martin, J. (1992) *Cultures in Organizations: Three Perspectives.* New York: Oxford University Press.

Martin, J. and Frost, P. (1999) 'The organizational culture war games: a struggle for intellectual dominance', in S.R. Clegg and C. Hardy (eds), *Studying Organization: Theory and Method.* Thousand Oaks, CA: Sage, pp. 345–67.

Meyerson, D. and Martin, J. (1987) 'Cultural change: an integration of three different views', *Journal of Management Studies*, 24: 623–47.

Miller, D. and Dröge, C. (1986) 'Psychological and traditional determinants of structure', *Administrative Science Quarterly*, 31: 539–60.

Miller, S.J., Hickson, D.J. and Wilson, D.C. (1999) 'Decision-making in organizations', in S.R. Clegg, C. Hardy and W.R. Nord (eds), *Managing Organizations: Current Issues.* Thousand Oaks, CA: Sage, pp. 43–62.

Miner, J.B. (1982) 'The uncertain future of the leadership concept: revisions and clarifications', *Journal of Applied Behavioral Science*, 18: 293–307.

Mintzberg, H. (1979) *The Structuring of Organizations.* Englewood Cliffs, NJ: Prentice Hall.

Morgan, G. (1997) *Images of Organisation.* 2nd edn. London: Sage.

Pettigrew, A.M. (1973) *The Politics of Organizational Decision-Making.* London: Tavistock.

Pettigrew, A.M. (1987) 'Context and action in the transformation of the firm', *Journal of Management Studies*, 24: 649–70.

Pugh, D., Hickson, D. and Hinings, C.R. (1969) 'An empirical taxonomy of structures of work organizations', *Administrative Science Quarterly*, 14: 115–26.

Quarterman, J. (1998) 'An assessment of the perceptions of management and leadership skills by intercollegiate athletics conference commissioners', *Journal of Sport Management*, 12: 146–64.

Quinn, J.B. (1980) *Strategies for Change: Logical Incrementalism.* Homewood, IL: Irwin.

Sack, A. and Johnson, A. (1996) 'Politics, economic development and the Volvo International Tennis Tournament', *Journal of Sport Management*, 10: 1–14.

Simon, H.A. (1945) *Administrative Behavior.* New York: Free Press.

Slack, T. (1997) *Understanding Sport Organizations: The Application of Organization Theory.* Champaign, IL: Human Kinetics.

Slack, T. (2000) 'Managing voluntary sport organisations: a critique of popular trends', in R.L. Jones and K.M. Armour (eds), *Sociology of Sport: Theory and Practice.* Harlow: Longman, pp. 44–57.

Slack, T. and Hinings, C.R. (eds) (1987) *The Organization and Administration of Sport.* London, ON: Sport Dynamics.

Slack, T. and Hinings, C.R. (1992) 'Understanding change in national sport organizations: an integration of theoretical perspectives', *Journal of Sport Management*, 6: 114–32.

Slack, T. and Hinings, B. (1994) 'Institutional pressures and isomorphic change: an empirical test', *Organizational Studies*, 15: 803–27.

Soucie, D. (1994) 'Effective managerial leadership in sport organizations', *Journal of Sport Management*, 8: 1–13.

Stogdill, R.M. (1948) 'Personal factors associated with leadership: a survey of the literature', *Journal of Applied Psychology*, 25: 35–71.

Taylor, Rt. Hon. Lord Justice (1990) *The Hillsborough Stadium Disaster: Final Report.* London: HMSO.

Thibault, L., Slack, T. and Hinings, C.R. (1991) 'Professionalism, structures and systems: the impact of professional staff on voluntary sport organizations', *International Review for the Sociology of Sport*, 26: 83–99.

Walsh, K., Hinings, B., Greenwood, R. and Ranson, S. (1981) 'Power and advantage in organizations', *Organization Studies*, 2: 131–52.

Weese, J. (1995) 'Leadership and organizational culture: an investigation of Big Ten and mid-American conference campus recreation administrations', *Journal of Sport Management*, 9: 119–34.

Yukl, G.A. (1989) *Leadership in Organizations.* 2nd edn. Englewood Cliffs, NJ: Prentice Hall.

12

Doping and Sport: More Problems than Solutions?

BARRIE HOULIHAN

Overview

→ Why oppose doping?
→ Satisfying the lawyers – defining doping
→ Progress in establishing an effective anti-doping policy
→ The development of international co-operation
→ The 1998 Tour de France and the establishment of the World Anti-Doping Agency
→ Problems and prospects

Doping in sport is a problem that just will not go away. One scandal has followed another with a steady regularity: in 1998 the Tour de France came to the point of collapse because of the extent of doping uncovered by the French police and customs authorities; in Britain in 1999, 17 positive tests for the anabolic steroid nandrolone were announced involving some of the country's leading athletes including Linford Christie, Dougie Walker and Gary Cadogan; and in 2001 three Dutch footballers, Jaap Stam, Edger Davids and Frank de Boer also tested positive for steroids. Furthermore, there is evidence of the abuse of drugs for which there is currently no reliable test including insulin and human growth hormone. Most worrying of all, there is increasing speculation about the potential of genetic manipulation to build bigger muscles or boost the oxygen-carrying capacity of the blood.

The problems of developing an effective anti-doping policy include:

- establishing a persuasive moral basis for opposing doping;
- devising an acceptable and legally defensible definition of doping (moral justification and actual definition); and
- constructing an effective policy regime (well resourced and politically supported).

Table 12.1   *Major drugs and banned practices based on the IOC list: medical uses,*
             benefits in sport and side-effects

Drugs and banned practices	Illustrative medical uses, if any	Claimed benefits for athletes	Selected side-effects
Stimulants: e.g. amphetamine	Relief of mild depression; eating disorders	Used to increase aggression in sports, e.g. American football; increase energy in endurance sport, e.g. cycling; suppress appetite in weight-related sports, e.g. judo	Addiction; may cause loss of judgement, psychotic behaviour, anorexia and insomnia
Narcotics: e.g. cocaine	Powerful painkiller	Painkillers	Addiction and loss of judgement regarding injury
Anabolic agents: anabolic androgenic steroids	The management of male development at puberty; anaemia, renal failure, treatment of burns	Increased strength and size; help athletes recover from training and train more intensively; increase aggression	In males: shrinkage of the testicles and the development of breast tissue. In females: masculinising effects including deepening of the voice and growth of facial hair. For both males and females: increased aggressiveness and depression
Diuretics	Control the retention of fluids and high blood pressure	Used to flush out other drugs and to achieve weight in weight-related events	Dehydration and possible risks of muscle cramps and a reduction in muscle strength
Peptide and glycoprotein hormones and analogues: e.g. human growth hormone (hGH)	hGH is used to treat growth-deficient children	Aid growth and muscle development. Depress fat accumulation. Strengthen tendons (and thus overcome one of the problems of steroid use)	Over-growth of bones such as the jaw and forehead. Risk of infection from contaminated needles as drug has to be injected

(Continued)

Table 12.1   *Continued*

Drugs and banned practices	Illustrative medical uses, if any	Claimed benefits for athletes	Selected side-effects
EPO	Synthetic erythropoietin (EPO) is used to treat anaemia and renal disease	Increases the red blood cell count which in turn increases the oxygen-carrying capacity of the body	Increased blood pressure and risk of thrombosis and stroke
Prohibited methods: pharmacological, chemical and physical manipulation	This category covers a wide range of activities including the corruption of a urine sample with alcohol for example, the practice of cathetarisation whereby drug-free urine is introduced into the bladder so that a 'clean' sample can be provided, or the inhibition of renal excretion.		

WHY OPPOSE DOPING?

Argument 1: 'Doping is unfair'

Much of the force of this justification rests on the possibility of sustaining a distinction between a fair and an unfair advantage because so much of sport is about seeking an advantage – an 'edge' over one's opponents.[1] That some athletes start with differing physiological and psychological attributes which give them an advantage over others is rarely questioned and is not seen as unfair. Although some sports take account of factors such as weight (judo) and prior success (handicapping in horse-racing and golf), most do not. Perhaps then the important distinction is between a natural and an unnatural advantage. Thus while an advantage gained either at birth (height, balance and reach, etc.) or through rigorous training is acceptable, would an unnatural advantage, such as an ultra-low resistance swimsuit, an ultra-light cycle or an innovative Formula One engine be unacceptable? In all these cases the advantage is, like anabolic steroids, external to the athlete. However, as is clearly the case, technological innovation is an integral and generally accepted part of many sports.

A further possible argument to explore in relation to fairness is not whether the advantage is natural or not, but whether there is an intention to keep the advantage a secret or restricted. Thus innovative design of javelins, poles for pole-vaulting or swimsuits are acceptable if they are made widely available as quickly as possible. However, the implication for doping is that just as there is nothing inherently unacceptable in designing a more aerodynamic javelin, so there is nothing inherently unfair about using drugs, providing all athletes have equal access. While this argument may have some plausibility, many would find its rationalisation of drug use unacceptable. Indeed, it would appear that each avenue that is taken in pursuit of a secure basis for banning drugs on the grounds of fairness leads into a cul-de-sac of ambiguity and inconsistency, or worst of all rebounds on the supporters of drug-free sport and is used to challenge current anti-doping efforts.

It may be that the acceptability of an advantage depends less on whether it is natural or unnatural, or whether it is differentially available but rather on a perception of how the advantage was acquired. Advantages that are the result of location (skiers living in Norway rather than Holland), natural endowments (Michael Owen's speed and balance), or practice and training (Tiger Woods's putting) are all significant but considered to be fair and to be encouraged. The significance of the process by which an advantage is acquired is easily illustrated if we compare the athlete who lives and trains at altitude, and thus acquires naturally a greater oxygen-carrying capacity of his or her blood, with the athlete who achieves the same effect by using EPO. The moral arguments become blurred again if the athlete who trains at altitude is able to do so because of personal wealth or state sponsorship while the EPO user is from a poor country.

Argument 2: 'Doping is bad for an athlete's health'

If arguments based on fairness fail to provide a secure and persuasive basis for opposing doping, then a concern to protect the health of the athlete is an alternative. However, there are a number of difficulties with this rationale, the first of which is lack of scientifically valid evidence regarding the impact on health of drug use. Because of the quantities of drugs, especially steroids, that some drug-abusing athletes take, it is not ethically permissible to replicate their pattern of drug use in clinical trials. Nevertheless there is an accumulation of anecdotal evidence relating to the long-term health effects of some drugs. There has been a high incidence of early death among professional road cyclists, many from liver-related diseases, which might be due to blood-doping. If there is evidence of a link between drug use and damage to health, it is only slowly emerging.

A second difficulty in building an anti-doping argument based on the protection of the athlete's health is that there are many sports (e.g. football, cricket and rugby) where competing with injury is normal. The use by athletes of analgesics and anti-inflammatory preparations is routine, and permissible, in almost all sport. There thus seems little difference between the athlete who risks his/her health by competing when injured and the athlete who risks his/her health by taking drugs to improve their performance. A third difficulty is that there are a number of aspects of elite athlete preparation that are a potential danger to health. Many training regimes are designed to push athletes to their physical limit. More importantly, as Fost argues, 'sport itself carries per se a substantial risk of death and permanent disability' (1991: 481). Boxing, rugby, American football and mountaineering all carry a significant risk of serious injury and on occasion even death.

A fourth difficulty with health arguments is that they can be reversed and used to justify drug use. Black and Pape (1997) argue that the current anti-doping effort puts athletes' health at risk because it results in many obtaining their drugs illegally, when quality and purity cannot be guaranteed; it leads to athletes administering the drugs themselves and thus without professional expertise and possibly without access to clean needles. It is possible to argue that if our primary concern is with athletes' health, we would not drive such potentially dangerous practice underground. The final difficulty concerns the underlying paternalism of arguments based on health. If an athlete wishes to take risks with his/her health, on what basis can society interfere? In Mill's classic statement: 'the only purpose for which power can be rightfully exercised over any member of a civilised community, against his will, is to prevent harm to others. His own good, either physical or moral, is not a sufficient warrant' (1962: 135).

Argument 3: 'Doping undermines the integrity of sport'

This argument is predicated on the belief that sports – collectively and individually – have an essence or set of core values that are undermined by drug use. The rules of each sport attempt to encapsulate the mix of skills and challenges which make for a 'good competition'. One basis for determining whether doping should be prohibited is whether it undermines or invalidates the essential challenge of the sport. Thus, just as adding a motor to a cycle would not be acceptable in the Tour de France, nor should blood doping by cyclists as both undermine the essence of the competition. From a broadly similar starting point, Simon provides an argument that may be applied to most, if not all sports. He suggests that 'competition in athletics is best thought of as a mutual quest for excellence'. An opponent is not an obstacle to winning, to be overcome by whatever means, but a co-worker in a joint undertaking: 'athletic competition, rather than being incompatible with respect for our opponents as persons, actually presupposes it' (Simon, 1984: 10). Though persuasive, Simon's position does have problems, the most significant of which is the vagueness of some of the underlying concepts.

Given the difficulty of establishing an unassailable foundation for opposing doping in sport, it is not surprising that supporters of current anti-doping policy rely on a combination of the above arguments or simply argue that avoiding the use of certain drugs is one of the rules of a sport and should therefore be respected. Many of the rules in sport are arbitrary (playing 18 holes in golf or not picking the ball up in football) and that anti-doping rules should be treated as simply an addition to the rules of play. If a footballer wants to be able to pick the ball up during a match and run with it, he or she will be penalised; or if he or she wants to use amphetamines to increase their energy levels, he or she should also be disqualified because they are not playing the sport of football as described in the rule book.

Unfortunately, relying solely on the rule book is not a strong basis for opposing doping and, in practice, anti-doping policy is justified on a mix of grounds selected from those discussed and on the continuing public perception of doping as anathema to sport. As with so many other ambiguous moral issues (divorce, abortion, euthanasia, etc.), policy-makers rely on a combination of principle and public support to sustain policy efforts. However, once the hurdle of devising a plausible justification for an anti-doping strategy is overcome, there still remain many other problems not the least of which is the apparently simple matter of defining what doping is.

SATISFYING THE LAWYERS: DEFINING DOPING

If a successful anti-doping strategy is to be developed, it is important to formulate a clear statement of the nature of the problem. Yet providing a clear, succinct and, most importantly of all in these litigious times, legally secure definition of doping has proved extremely difficult and is one of the tasks facing the recently formed World Anti-Doping Agency. Charles Dubin, who chaired the Commission of Inquiry following the positive test result on Ben Johnson at the 1988 Seoul Olympic Games, argued that a definition was 'impossible to achieve' (Dubin, 1990: 77). While many would sympathise with the difficulty facing Dubin, a workable definition of doping is essential, given the frequency of legal challenge to the decisions of domestic and international federations on doping infractions. Many definitions adopted by international federations referred variously to the 'intention to seek an unfair advantage', 'the use of substances damaging to the athlete's health' or 'substances that confer an unfair advantage'. All these phrases are laudable in their desire to clarify the basis for objecting to doping but, as should be clear from the discussion in the previous section, they are all fraught with problems. How might intent rather than accident, chance, ignorance or sabotage be proved? Proving that the drugs taken damage the athlete's health is all but impossible given that many of the drugs are available from any pharmacist and most have well-recognised therapeutic applications. The problems with the concept of an unfair advantage were made clear earlier in this chapter.

One response by some international federations (e.g. the IAAF) has been to adopt a strict liability definition, according to which a doping offence is deemed to have been committed if a prohibited substance is present in an athlete's urine sample, irrespective of whether the drug was taken knowingly or whether the drug was capable of enhancing performance. According to Wise, the strict liability definition means that an athlete can be found guilty of a doping infraction 'without the sports governing body proving culpable intent, knowledge or fault; or without the athlete being allowed to prove he or she was faultless' (Wise, 1996).

Support for the IAAF definition and for a clearly worded definition came from the British judge who heard the case brought by Sandra Gasser against the IAAF in which she challenged their strict liability definition. The judge referred approvingly to the IAAF representative's concern that 'if a defence of moral innocence were open, the floodgates

would be opened and the IAAF's attempts to prevent drug taking by athletes would be rendered futile' (quoted in Gay, n.d.). Writing in 1995 and using the IAAF strict liability definition as the benchmark, Vrijman reviewed the definitions of 33 other international federations and found, first, that all of them had definitions that were potentially vulnerable to legal challenge and, second, that there was very little uniformity between sports. Many sports, such as squash and badminton, did not provide a definition of doping at all, while others included a sentence in their rules that associated them with the IOC rules on doping. Of those that did provide a definition, many were unclear and confused and, as mentioned earlier, vulnerable to legal challenge. By 1999 there had been some progress in amending anti-doping rules to make them less vulnerable to legal challenge. Seven federations, including those for gymnastics and ice hockey, had adopted definitions similar to that used by the IAAF, but the vast majority had left their definitions unrevised.

Despite the strong support provided by Gay and other lawyers, there is some doubt regarding the value of a strict liability definition, particularly in the United States. In 1995 the swimmer, Jessica Foschi, tested positive for the anabolic steroid mesterolone and was penalised under the rules of the international federation (FINA). She appealed against the penalty to the American Arbitration Association (AAA), the body prescribed under the terms of the United States Amateur Sports Act 1978. The AAA was emphatic in its rejection of the FINA decision and the application of the concept of strict liability. The arbitrators argued that:

Having concluded that the claimant and all those connected with her are innocent and without fault, we unanimously conclude that the imposition of any sanction on the claimant so offends our deeply rooted and historical concepts of fundamental fairness as to be arbitrary and capricious. (Quoted in Wise, 1996: 1161)

Similar rejections of the concept of strict liability have been provided by the Swiss courts and the Legal Committee of the German track and field federation, with the latter arguing that 'the maxim *"nulla poena sine culpa"* (no penalty without fault) has the status of a constitutional principle since the principle of the State Rechtsstaatlichkeit is infringed, the corresponding provision in that case is grossly unfair and thus unenforceable' (quoted in Wise, 1996: 1162). Strict liability may well be the preferred definition in terms of relative security from legal challenge, but it is clearly not without problems.

ESTABLISHING AN EFFECTIVE ANTI-DOPING POLICY

While the debates about the moral basis for opposing doping and the most informative and legally secure definition of doping have been taking place, there have been continuing attempts to establish an effective anti-doping policy in practice. The current doping problem dates from the middle of the last century and especially the period of the Second World War. The substantial advances made in the synthesis of drugs at that time coincided with the widespread experimentation by the military with amphetamines and steroids, thereby indicating the potential value of these drugs outside a therapeutic context. Soon after the end of the war, evidence began to accumulate of the increasingly widespread use of synthetic drugs in sport. Dramatic evidence appeared during the 1960s, when a

series of high-profile fatalities occurred, including that of a Danish cyclist at the 1960 Rome Olympic Games who had taken amphetamines. Amphetamines were also found to be present in the body of Tom Simpson, who died during the climb of Mont Ventoux in 1967 during the Tour de France. Just when the international federations were beginning to address the issue of the use of narcotics and amphetamines, they were reminded of the dynamic nature of the problem as rumours began to surface of the increasing use of anabolic steroids. The initial reports of their use coincided with the return of the Soviet Union to Olympic competition in 1952, and were followed by a period of intense experimentation with steroids in both the Soviet Union and the United States, frequently justified by the assumed imperatives of the Cold War.

The initial reaction of many federations to evidence of doping by athletes involved in their sports was to ignore the problem in the hope that it would disappear. Most federations in the late 1960s and 1970s variously perceived incidents of doping as exceptions in their sport or as a set of largely unsubstantiated allegations that it was convenient to ignore. For both the Olympic movement and the major federations, there were strong incentives not to investigate the allegations of doping too closely, first, because of the likely cost and complexity of any action and second, because of the potential damage to the image of sport that might result.

Up until the mid-1980s, doping policy was being formulated within a number of largely self-contained forums based on a perception of the problem as one that could be confined to particular sports, competitions or countries. Thus the IOC sought to protect the integrity of the Olympic Games through the use of in-competition testing;

Table 12.2   *Milestones in the development of anti-doping policy*

Year(s)	Event
1960	• Death of Knud Jensen at the Rome Olympics
1961	• IOC establishes a Medical Commission
1962	• IOC passes a resolution condemning doping
1963	• Convention of international federations led to the formulation of a definition of doping
mid-1960s	• Union Cycliste International introduce drug testing
1964	• IOC adopts a definition of doping
1965	• France and Belgium are among the first countries to introduce legislation concerning doping in sport
1966	• Five elite cyclists in the world road race championships refuse to provide a urine sample
	• FIFA conducts tests at the World Cup in England
1968	• IOC conducts tests at the summer and winter Olympic Games
1970	• Testing introduced at the Commonwealth Games
1971	• IOC produces the first list of banned substances and practices
1972	• IOC conducts over 2,000 tests at the Munich Olympic Games
	• Test for anabolic steroids piloted
	• IAAF establishes a Medical Committee
1974	• Testing conducted at the European Athletics Championships
1976	• First use of test for the detection of anabolic steroids at the Montreal Olympic Games
	• Accreditation of laboratories by the IOC introduced
1977	• First use of out-of-competition tests
1978	• Some harmonisation on penalties between federations
	• Council of Europe formulates a recommendation to member states on doping
late 1970s and 1980s	• Series of international conferences to exchange information and discuss common problems
1981	• 11th Olympic Congress at Baden-Baden passed a resolution from athletes endorsing the IOC anti-doping policy
early 1980s	• Development of more sensitive testing methods based on gas chromatography/mass spectrometry (GC/MS)
1983	• A large number of athletes withdraw from the Pan-American Games when the use of GC/MS is announced
1988	• Canadian Ben Johnson, winner of the 100 m Olympic final, tests positive for steroids
1989	• IAAF establish 'flying squads' of doping control officers to conduct unannounced out-of-competition testing especially for steroids
	• Council of Europe publishes the Anti-Doping Convention
late 1980s	• Series of trials begin in Germany which expose the extent of state-organised doping in former East Germany
1998	• Near collapse of the Tour de France because of the seizure of drugs by customs officials and the subsequent police enquiries
1999	• Lausanne Anti-Doping Conference proposes a global anti-doping agency
	• World Anti-Doping Agency (WADA) formed
2000	• 2,500 tests conducted by WADA in the run-up to the Sydney Olympic Games

the major federations also considered that in-competition testing would ensure the continued probity of their elite events; and governments established legal frameworks and instituted domestic testing regimes on the assumption that the practice of sport within their borders could be isolated from cross-border contamination. As a result there was only minimal contact between sports organisations, governments and international bodies such as the Council of Europe. However, by the mid to late 1980s, such a view of the nature of the problem was no longer sustainable owing, in very large part, to the rapid globalisation of sport. Not only did the 1980s witness the expansion in the number of world championships and grand prix events but, following the widespread abandonment of amateurism, athletes increasingly moved outside their home country to train. International competition circuits and athlete mobility meant that many athletes spent little time in their home country. This highlights the importance of consistency of regulations between domestic federations and the importance of mutual recognition of jurisdiction across national boundaries. In addition, the weakness of an anti-doping regime based on in-competition testing was increasingly apparent in view of the growing use of anabolic steroids as training aids. However, the introduction of out-of-competition testing involved a level of transnational co-operation and an expenditure of resources that few federations or governments had anticipated.

The end of amateurism brought about one further significant change. As more athletes, particularly in track and field, saw sport not only as their primary source of income, but also as a source of substantial wealth, they were consequently much more willing to use the courts to protect their income if it were threatened by a ban for a doping offence. Well-documented cases involving elite athletes such as the German Katrin Krabbe and the Australian Martin Vinnicombe drew the attention of the domestic federations to the potential cost of defending their decisions in court and also made them aware of just how vulnerable many of their decisions were, due to the poor drafting of regulations and the failure to ensure compatibility of domestic regulations with those of the international federation and with the domestic federations in other countries.

THE DEVELOPMENT OF INTERNATIONAL CO-OPERATION

By the end of the 1980s it was clear that the attempts to tackle doping as a series of discrete problems were proving ineffective. If doping were to be successfully challenged, there was a need for a high level of co-operation between the international federations and the IOC and also between sports organisations and governments. The impetus for closer co-operation came from the recognition of the increasing complexity of the problem arising from the greater wealth and mobility of athletes, and also from an awareness that a successful anti-doping programme would be expensive and well beyond the resources of individual federations or the IOC. Co-operation at the political level was therefore a primary requirement.

During the 1970s and 1980s the federations had been highly suspicious of the motives of many governments in the area of doping and were generally sceptical of their commitment. Apart from the small number of governments who were prepared to commit resources to the problem, the majority were inactive and a very small, but highly significant number were subversive.

The inactive included those who simply did not possess the necessary resources to support an anti-doping programme but also included a group of governments whose public condemnation of doping was matched by a determination to ignore the signs of doping among their own athletes. The Dubin Inquiry in Canada following the Ben Johnson incident in 1988 and the Senate Committee's investigation of allegations of doping at the Australian Institute of Sport provided ample evidence of inaction by both governments and sporting authorities (Dubin, 1990; Australian Government, 1989). Most damaging to the claims from governments to policy leadership were the revelations from the series of trials in Germany regarding the extent to which the former government of the GDR had constructed a state-co-ordinated and funded doping programme for its Olympic athletes (Franke and Berendonk, 1997).

The state enquiries in Canada and Australia prompted a radical change in attitude and led both countries to establish state-supported anti-doping agencies which are currently among the most respected. However, it was not just the cathartic effect of scandal and public scrutiny that led to an improved climate of co-operation between governments and sports organisations. Of equal significance was the ending of the Cold War and the consequent removal of international sport as a surrogate for the ideological confrontation between communism and capitalism. The capitalist democracies could no longer implicitly rationalise their relative inaction on doping. Furthermore the countries of the former communist bloc were keen to rebuild democracy and its civil institutions, of which sports organisations were an important part, and also distance themselves from the tainted reputation of their previous leaders.

In addition to the much more positive political environment of the early 1990s, there was also an emerging global infrastructure of international organisations and forums concerned with the issue of doping. The Council of Europe enhanced the status of the Recommendation on doping, first to a Charter and then to that of a Convention in 1989 which sought to establish a set of standards and objectives that would reach beyond the Council's European membership by inviting non-member states to express their support. The Council's profile on anti-doping policy was further strengthened due to its many new members from the former communist countries of central and eastern Europe. The work of the Council was complemented by the series of Permanent World Conferences on doping, which sought to create a global forum for policy discussion largely at a governmental level. There was also considerable activity at the regional level with a number of bilateral and multilateral agreements between governments relating to the exchange of information and agreement on mutual testing arrangements (Houlihan, 1999).

Sports organisations had also sought to establish forums, such as the International Athletic Foundation's symposia, where common problems associated with doping could be discussed and information exchanged. However, action by sports organisations was far from dynamic. Although the IOC remained a key organisation, its role was confined to little more than updating the list of banned substances and practices, advising the Council of Europe on the anti-doping Charter, and the overseeing of testing at its own events. The leading federations, with a small number of exceptions, such as those for swimming (FINA) and track and field events (IAAF), adopted a passive and reactive stance with regard to the issue. Such was the growing disparity between the level of policy activity between governments and sports organisations that the IOC was prompted into action in 1994, when it initiated discussions among the Olympic federations that culminated in the publication of the Lausanne Agreement. While the Agreement was important in bringing together all the key sports bodies, and despite the establishment of a working group on harmonisation which contained representatives from governments and governmental bodies, the Agreement was perceived by many governments as further evidence of a lack of urgency and a failure of policy leadership within sport.

By the mid-1990s policy towards doping was at a watershed and the prospects for further progress were mixed. Optimistically one could point to the vastly improved international political climate. Among the major Olympic nations there was only one, the People's Republic of China, where strong suspicions of state inaction towards doping still remained. Second, there were an increasing number of countries that had established anti-doping agencies which could command widespread respect. Third, more countries were involved in multilateral agreements, such as the International Anti-Doping Arrangement between a small group of countries, including Australia, Canada, The Netherlands and Sweden, which enabled the diffusion of good practice in testing and education and also acted as a lobby within the wider global political and sports community. Fourth, the number of forums available for the exchange of information among sports organisations and between sports and governmental organisations had increased significantly.

A more pessimistic assessment of the state of anti-doping policy in the mid-1990s balanced the evidence of progress against the acknowledged limitations of the current testing regime. Ben Johnson, for example,

had been tested over 15 times while using steroids before he tested positive at Seoul. Second, the commitment of some domestic and international federations was being weakened by the increasing frequency of legal challenge. It was not just the fear of bankruptcy should a federation lose a case, as the cost of successfully defending decisions was equally crippling. The overall effect was to fuel the suspicion among governments that federations were being overly cautious in deciding when to determine that a doping positive constituted a doping infraction. Third, there was the growing evidence of the use of drugs that could not be detected with current testing methods. Erythropoietin (EPO) and human growth hormone (hGH) were two of the drugs that were causing greatest concern and the IOC and the federations were acutely aware of the cost of devising a valid and reliable test.

THE 1998 TOUR DE FRANCE AND THE ESTABLISHMENT OF WADA

As is so often the case in policy making, it was a crisis – in this case one that occurred during the 1998 Tour de France – that prompted a renewed round of policy activity. A number of factors combined to force a renewed effort to increase the momentum behind anti-doping policy:

1 the extent of doping discovered during the Tour and the number of riders and team officials implicated;
2 the global prestige of the Tour;
3 the claims by the international federation for cycling, the UCI, to be a leader in the anti-doping campaign; and
4 the strength and intensity of intervention by the French government.

That one of the world's major sports events should be brought near to collapse by doping was serious enough to warrant a review of policy, but it was the intervention by the French government which caused the greatest concern among international federations and the IOC. The decision to treat the doping allegations as a public matter of law and order rather than a matter best left to the disciplinary processes of the UCI and its French affiliate left sports organisations on the margins, as they were effectively barred from investigating the allegations of doping until the various court cases had reached a conclusion. Sports organisations clearly perceived a need to regain the initiative on policy formation or, at the very least, ensure that their voice was heard in the governmental forums that were discussing the matter. The decision by the IOC to convene a conference on doping in February 1999 was a direct consequence of the events surrounding the Tour.

The aim set for the conference was to 'discuss and adopt measures allowing the fight against doping to be intensified'. Most of the first day of the conference was given over to a series of position statements by sports ministers and representatives of government anti-doping agencies which, with only a few exceptions, were fiercely critical of the IOC in general and the leadership provided by its President Samaranch in particular. The IOC was criticised for its complacency towards doping, with a number of speakers questioning its moral authority to lead the global fight against doping. The intensity of criticism was not due solely to the perceived lack of commitment to anti-doping by the IOC, but was overlain with indignation at the unfolding story of corruption among IOC members concerning the selection of Salt Lake City to host the 2002 Winter Olympics.

The intensity of criticism eased on the second day, when consideration was given to the remit, financing, location and accountability of the proposed new agency. The initial suggestion was that the Agency be established

as a foundation under Swiss law ... be head-quartered in Lausanne, governed by a Council presided over by the IOC President, consisting of three representatives each of the IOC, the International Federations, the National Olympic Committees, athletes designated by the IOC Athletes Commission, international governmental organisations and three persons representing sponsors, the pharmaceutical industry and the sporting goods industry. (IOC, 1998)

The Council would direct the work of the Agency and be responsible, *inter alia*, for funding, revising the list of banned substances and practices, validating the accreditation of IOC-approved laboratories and appointing the director of the Agency. As regards funding, the working group proposed the designation of an initial sum of at least US$25m to cover running costs and to commission research to develop reliable tests for the detection of natural steroids, EPO and hGH.

While there was general support for an international agency, there was a broad insistence that it should be completely independent of the IOC. Consequently, the Declaration agreed at the conclusion of the Lausanne Conference was ambiguous about the relationship between the proposed agency and the IOC. It was agreed that an 'independent ... Agency shall be established so as to be fully operational in time for the XXVII Olympiad in Sydney in 2000', but the brief of the body was less clear as this would now be determined by a new working group convened by the IOC and with membership drawn from among athletes, governments and the Olympic movement.

The central issue was not whether there should be an international anti-doping body, but who would control it. The focus and remit of the new agency, the World Anti-Doping Agency, did not differ greatly from the initial IOC proposals.

The Agency's principal task will be to co-ordinate a comprehensive anti-doping program at international level, developing common, effective, minimum standards for doping control ... Among its duties, the new Agency is expected to commission unannounced out-of-competition controls in full agreement with [the] public and private bodies concerned.

The Agency is expected to work with existing authorities to promote the harmonisation of anti-doping policies and procedures, identify a reference laboratory to advise the accredited testing laboratories, and co-ordinate the numerous educational efforts now underway. It also is expected to publish an annual list of prohibited substances. (IOC press release, 9 Sept. 1999)

It was acknowledged that the Agency would not seek responsibility for the determination of doping infractions nor for the imposition of sanctions: both these responsibilities would remain with the international federations. The most significant recommendation, strongly supported by the Council of Europe, the European Union and the United States, was that the Agency would now be far more independent of the IOC. Thus membership of the Agency's board would have equal representation from sports bodies and governments (or international governmental bodies). Responsibility for funding would also be shared equally between governments and sports bodies with the IOC agreeing to fund the Agency for its first two years at US$4m per year until the governments could finalise their funding formula. As regards location, it was agreed that WADA would be located initially in Lausanne, but that a competition be held to find a permanent home for the Agency. It was also agreed that

Richard Pound, IOC Vice-President, would be the first President. However some, including General McCaffrey, considered that Pound had a conflict of interests by virtue of the fact that he was an IOC Vice-President and, more importantly, was responsible for the marketing of the Olympic Games – a product that can only be damaged by revelations of doping.

Although the timescale was tight, WADA made a significant and favourable impression at the Sydney Olympic Games. Not only did the Agency fund some 2,500 additional tests prior to the Games, but it also acted as an independent observer evaluating the doping control procedures during the Games. Following the conclusion of the Sydney Games, WADA concentrated on formalising its internal procedures and finances, and also agreeing its permanent location. By late 2001 the Agency had agreed the basis on which the various regions of the world would be represented and by whom. Agreement had also been reached on the formula for apportioning the 50 per cent financial contribution of the public authorities to WADA and it had been agreed that Montreal would be the Agency's permanent location. In addition to finalising its organisation and finance, WADA has acted quickly to establish an agenda and work programme for the next two to three years. At its meeting in January 2000 it was agreed that there were three priorities:

1 reaching agreement with the international federations on protocols for out-of-competition testing and embarking on the first round of testing;
2 the development of an accreditation mechanism for laboratories; and
3 the design of a test results management system.

That WADA has clearly developed considerable momentum since its establishment is in part a tribute to the commitment of its members and the support of the Australian government during its early activities at the Sydney Olympic Games. However, the promising start by the Agency is also partially due to significant changes in the policy environment. There have been three changes of particular note: the increasing interest of the European Union; the active involvement of the United States; and the formation of the International Intergovernmental Consultative Group on Anti-Doping (IICGAD).

While it is possible to trace EU interest back to the early 1990s when two declarations against doping in sport were made, it was not until the late 1990s that the EU became more directly involved. In December 1998 the European Council expressed its concern 'at the extent and seriousness of doping in sport, which undermines the sporting ethic and endangers public health' and it encouraged the involvement of the Commission in working with international sports bodies to 'fight against this danger' (European Commission, 1999: 1). The views of the European Council were endorsed by the European Parliament later in 1999 and by a series of informal meetings of EU ministers for sport. With its deepening interest in sport in general and doping in particular, it is not surprising that the EU was closely involved in negotiating the statutes that would define the remit and govern the operation of WADA. From the perspective of the IOC, the EU has a range of existing programmes that could support the work of WADA, particularly in relation to the funding of scientific research, furthering the harmonisation of laws among member states, and the funding and co-ordination of public health campaigns aimed at doping in sport.[2] But while the IOC was doubtless aware of the value of harnessing EU resources to the anti-doping campaign, they were probably more acutely aware of the EU's interventionist and regulatory culture and the threat that posed to the independence of sports organisations.

Of comparable significance to the increasing involvement of the European Union was the new-found enthusiasm for action on doping within the United States. This was stimulated partly by accumulated pressure from other countries for the United States to adopt a more proactive and positive policy towards doping and partly due to the central position of America in the bribery scandal concerning the selection of host cities for the Olympic Games. In December 1999 the USOC called for the creation of an independent body to enhance the credibility and effectiveness of US efforts to tackle doping. The US Anti-Doping Agency was duly established in late 2000 with responsibility for sample collection, testing, adjudication, sanctions and research. USADA will receive enhanced funding, part of which will come from the federal government and part from the USOC, enabling the Agency to increase the number of tests to approximately 7,000 per year as well as fund research. By putting its own house in order, the United States has substantially enhanced its credibility in relation to global anti-doping policy and enabled one of the major world 'sports powers' to be fully involved in the establishment of WADA.

The final development in the context of global anti-doping policy was the formation of the International Intergovernmental Consultative Group on Anti-Doping (IICGAD). IICGAD was established because of the need for a collective voice for the public authorities in relation to the IOC proposal for a new global anti-doping agency and also because of the need for a constituency from which representatives of public authorities could be selected. The governments of Canada and Australia were instrumental in convening the International Summit on Drugs in Sport in November 1999 in Sydney, which led to the formation of IICGAD. This organisation was given a brief to co-ordinate worldwide government participation in WADA and to facilitate the process of harmonisation of policies, especially in areas of exclusive government jurisdiction or responsibility such as customs regulations and the labelling of medicines and supplements. For the first time there now existed a permanent global forum for governments to exchange views on doping issues and to co-ordinate their contribution to WADA.

PROBLEMS AND PROSPECTS

Identifying the ingredients of an effective policy response to a problem as complex and multifaceted as doping is difficult, but there do appear to be five factors that are necessary for progress:

- a global organisational infrastructure;
- adequate financial resources;
- scientific research capacity;
- political support; and
- public support.

There is no doubt that the establishment of WADA marked a major development in establishing an organisational infrastructure to tackle doping. It is generally accepted that the various resources of the IOC (e.g. global leadership and network of accredited laboratories), the international federations (IFs) (links with domestic federations and thus with athletes), and governments (legal, financial and administrative capacity) need to be combined if an effective global response to doping is to be achieved. However, while the period since 1999 has been one of remarkable harmony between the Olympic movement, the major federations and governments, the long-standing tensions between these bodies is

never far from the surface. The IFs remain concerned that they might lose control over 'their' athletes and there is still considerable uncertainty regarding the respective roles of WADA, the IOC Medical Commission and the Medical Committees of the major IFs, especially over the management of the testing regime.

The second problem facing WADA is securing a sufficient resource base. The scale of the funding problem is easily illustrated. According to Dr Don Catlin, one of the most respected authorities on doping in sport, 'the labs' ability to respond to [doping] is restricted by funding because doping has never been a serious priority for sport' (*Salt Lake Tribune*, 20 Oct. 1999). He added that although the USOC had paid US$500,000 for a high-resolution mass spectrometer, his laboratory did not have the funds to employ staff with the necessary qualifications to make the machine fully operational. John Hoberman went further and talked of a strategy of 'calculated underinvestment' by the IOC and the major federations. WADA's budget for 2002 is US$18.27m rising to just under US$25m by 2006 and will cover not only the cost of out-of-competition tests, but also its administrative costs and a contribution to scientific research. The sum is substantial, particularly when added to the amounts already being spent by the IFs and by state anti-doping agencies, but the challenge is to maintain the financial commitment of partner organisations once the initial enthusiasm for the work of WADA has passed.

The third problem is closely related to financial resources and concerns the capacity to meet the scientific challenges that lie ahead as a result of the continuing experimentation by athletes with new drugs. Although scientists have recently successfully developed a dual urine/blood test to detect rEPO, a new drug, perfluorocarbon (PFC) with 'enormous oxygen-carrying capacity', is allegedly being used by some speed-skaters and cross-country skiers (Wadler, 1999: 5). Another new drug is IGF-1, a polypeptide that is responsible for the growth-promoting effects of hGH and is currently undetectable. There are also rumours of genetically engineered blood substitutes that will allow IGF-1 to be used without there being any adverse effects on the rest of the body. Each new generation of drugs requires more sophisticated and consequently more expensive laboratories, research teams and clinical trials. Despite the income to WADA, it will rely heavily on research programmes funded directly by sympathetic governments or bodies such as the European Union.

The fourth problem concerns the maintenance of political support for anti-doping efforts. It is only just over ten years ago that the main impediments to tackling doping in sport were a series of subversive governments, most notably East Germany and the Soviet Union, and a further group of apathetic governments which included Canada, Australia and the USA. Although much has changed, there remains an intense scepticism among many sports organisations regarding the depth of commitment of

governments. However, there are a number of positive developments which augur well for the future. Most notable is the number of examples of co-operation on anti-doping issues between governmental and sports organisations. At the scientific level, the GH2000 project aimed at developing a test to identify the presence of growth hormones relies on joint funding of £1.8m by the IOC and the European Union. The European Union was also involved in the joint production of *The Clean Sport Guide* along with the Council of Europe (Council of Europe, 1998).

Finally, perhaps the greatest threat to the anti-doping campaign is the loss of public commitment to an anti-doping policy. The foundation of existing policy is the sustained disapproval of doping by the majority of those involved in sport and the continuing vocal public support for current anti-doping efforts. Possibly the greatest danger at the present time is that the debate on the future direction of policy becomes too esoteric for the public, too much the province of experts, and too dissociated from the sports that the mass of the public play and events that the public enjoy watching.

Chapter summary

- There are a number of justifications for opposing doping in sport, none of which is, on its own, convincing.
- The fundamental question of how to define doping in a way that is not unduly vulnerable to legal challenge remains unanswered.
- Over the last 35 years there has been slow and often erratic progress towards a more coherent and effective response to the problem of doping.
- Scandal (e.g. doping by Ben Johnson at the Seoul Olympics in 1988 or doping at the 1998 Tour de France), has often been the catalyst for renewed efforts to strengthen anti-doping policy.
- The establishment of the World Anti-Doping Agency in 1999 is a major landmark in policy development, although substantial problems remain, including the steady stream of new drugs available to athletes and the high cost of doping control and the associated research.

Further reading

Houlihan (2002) and Waddington (2000) both provide reviews of the topic of doping in sport. Black and Pape (1997), Simon (1984) and Fost (1991) explore the philosophical bases for opposing doping in sport, while Wise (1996) discusses the difficulties in producing a legally sound definition of doping. Franke and Berendonk (1997) provide an important insight into doping in the former East Germany. Houlihan (1999) evaluates the progress in establishing a global anti-doping policy and achieving closer harmonisation.

NOTES

1 See Houlihan (2002) for a fuller discussion of the basis on which doping might be opposed.

2 See The Helsinki Report on Sport (Commission of the European Communities (1999) Report from the Commission to the European Council) for an indication of the scope of EU interest in sport, its general priorities and its specific objectives in relation to doping. The EU's acknowledgement of the importance of sport and its potentially central role is in part due to the pre-eminent role of Europe as the focus for elite-level sport. In 1999 Europe hosted 77 world championships and over 100 European championships.

REFERENCES

Australian Government (1989) *Drugs in Sport.* Interim report of the Senate Standing Committee on the Environment, Recreation and the Arts. Canberra: Australian Government Publishing Service.

Black, T. and Pape, A. (1997) 'The ban on drugs in sport, the solution or the problem?', *Journal of Sport and Social Issues,* 21 (1): 83–92.

Council of Europe (1998) *The Clean Sport Guide.* Strasbourg: Council of Europe.

Dubin, C.L. (1990) *Commission of Inquiry into the Use of Drugs and Banned Practices Intended to Increase Athletic Performance.* Ottawa: Canadian Government Publishing Centre.

European Commission (1999) *Doping in Sport: the Fight against Doping at Community Level – State of Play.* Brussels: European Commission.

Fost, N.C. (1991) 'Ethical and social issues in anti-doping strategies in sport', in F. Landry, M. Landry and M. Yerles (eds), *Sport ... The Third Millennium.* Sainte-Foy: Les Presses de l'Université de Laval.

Franke, W.W. and Berendonk, B. (1997) 'Hormonal doping and androgenization of athletes: a secret program of the German Democratic Republic', *Clinical Chemistry,* 43 (7): 1262–79.

Gay, M. (n.d.) 'Constitutional aspects of testing for prohibited substance'. London: n.p.

Houlihan, B. (1999) 'Policy harmonization: the example of global anti-doping policy', *Journal of Sport Management,* 13 (3): 197–215.

Houlihan, B. (2002) *Dying to Win: Doping in Sport and the Development of Anti-doping Policy.* 2nd edn. Strasbourg: Council of Europe Publishing.

International Olympic Committee (IOC) (1998) *Summary of Conclusion from the Meeting of the Working Group 'Financial Considerations'.* Lausanne: IOC.

Mill, J.S. (1962) 'On liberty', in M. Warnock (ed.), *Utilitarianism: Essays of John Stuart Mill.* London: Fontana.

Simon, R.L. (1984) 'Good competition and drug-enhanced performance', *Journal of the Philosophy of Sport,* XI: 6–13.

Waddington, I. (2000) *Sport, Health and Drugs: a Critical Sociological Perspective.* London: E. & F. N. Spon.

Wadler, G. (1999) *Evidence to Senate Commerce, Science and Transportation Committee,* 20 October.

Wise, A.N. (1996) '"Strict liability" drug rules of sports governing bodies', *New Law Journal,* 2 August, p. 1161.

13

The Sport–Tourism Interrelationship

GUY JACKSON AND MIKE WEED

Overview

→ Sports tourism demand
→ Sports tourism supply
→ Sports tourism impacts
→ Conclusions and future direction

In this chapter, we look at the growth and significance of sports-related tourism. While sport and tourism, as two distinct elements of the leisure industry, clearly have great significance in their own right, so-called 'sports tourism' has developed significantly over the last two decades and the interrelationship continues to evolve in both the demand and supply structures of contemporary leisure.

Until relatively recently, this growing interrelationship and its significance to the leisure sector were not matched with substantive research or literature specifically examining the links. Work by Glyptis (1982, 1991) and subsequently the report commissioned by the Sports Council on the interrelationship between sport and tourism (Jackson and Glyptis, 1992) were some of the earliest substantive works in the area. Other valuable reviews of the field were carried out by De Knop (1990) and Standeven and Tomlinson (1994). The joint work by Standeven and De Knop (1999) was one of the first dedicated books to provide an introduction to the sports tourism phenomenon. Different facets of the interrelationship between sport and tourism have also been researched (e.g. Redmond, 1991; Jackson and Reeves, 1996; Collins and Jackson, 1999; Weed, 1999; Vrondou, 1999; Reeves, 2000). A number of commercial leisure analysts have reviewed the volume and value of this emerging sector of the leisure industry (Leisure Consultants, 1992; Mintel, 1999).

The potential of the linkage between sport and tourism clearly has economic, social and environmental impacts, both positive and negative. These have now increasingly been recognised, particularly by the commercial leisure industry, which very quickly saw the market potential and economic benefits of utilising sport within the development of tourism, and subsequently in its diversification and niche marketing strategies.

Initially slow to develop, but increasingly evident, has been a recognition of the importance of a collaborative approach to sport and tourism among the government agencies charged with development planning, policy administration and resource allocation in these fields. For example, Weed and Bull (1997a) described the lack of integration among regional agencies responsible for sport and tourism in England, suggesting in other work (Weed and Bull, 1997b) that government policy for sport and for tourism in the 1990s unwittingly worked against greater integration of these areas. Weed (2003) also suggests that the historically separate development of these functions, along with their very different cultures, is a substantial obstacle to collaborative policy initiatives. Consequently, both in the UK and in Europe, conscious integration between the bodies responsible for the separate sectors of sport and tourism is still rare, except perhaps where major events are concerned. Thus, there remains scope for further integration of sports policy and tourism policy in many places in order to produce joint investment strategies, more effective facility development, and greater economic and social benefit.

Only the commercial tourism sector has really embraced and benefited economically from a recognition of the contribution of sport to tourism product development, whether this be in widening the appeal of products, or inflating the tariff of tourism facilities, or in producing new and broader types of holiday package to include sports participation and/or spectating tourism. There is, however, far more to the sport–tourism relationship than these basic types suggest, as will be demonstrated below via an exploration of sports tourism's demand and supply structures and an examination of its impacts.

SPORTS TOURISM DEMAND

Several typologies of sports tourism *demand* have been attempted (e.g. Glyptis, 1982; Hall, 1992; Standeven and De Knop, 1999), invariably but inconsistently linked to specific types of activity, motivation or forms of supply. One of the most robust typologies, which amply illustrates the breadth of the sports tourism phenomenon, is that by Jackson and Reeves (1996), which was substantiated with empirical work from across the range of types (Jackson and Reeves, 1998; Reeves, 2000). They identify a '*sports tourism continuum*' which encompasses the complete range of sports tourism participation types, from 'incidental' participation (where sport is carried out as an occasional or very sporadic result of being away from the home environment usually during vacation time), through 'sporadic' and 'occasional' sports activity whilst away from the home area, to 'regular' and 'committed' activity, to 'driven' sports tourism (where the act or level of travel is dictated by, and dedicated to, the conduct of sport on a very regular basis – typically the professional or elite sports performer). Figure 13.1 outlines the findings with a number of significant subtypes of sports tourist, and summarises some of their main behavioural characteristics.

The proposed continuum and the associated cross-sectional study identify the complexity of sports tourism demand. The work is recognised to be far from all-encompassing. For example, the research to date does

SPORTS–TOURISM DEMAND CONTINUUM

	INCIDENTAL	SPORADIC	OCCASIONAL	REGULAR	COMMITTED	DRIVEN
Summary characteristics						
DECISION-MAKING FACTORS	Impromptu	Unimportant	Can be determining factor	Important	Very important	Essential
PARTICIPATION FACTORS	Fun or duty to others	If convenient	Welcome addition to tourism experience	Significant part of experience	Central to experience	Often sole reason for travel
NON-PARTICIPATION FACTORS	Prefer relaxation non-activity	Easily constrained or put off. Not essential to life profile	Many commitment preferences	Money or time constraints	Only unforeseen or significant constraints	Injury, illness or fear of illness
TYPICAL GROUP PROFILE	Family groups	Family and friendship groups	Often friendship or business groups	Group or individuals	Invariably groups of like-minded people	Elite groups or individuals with support
LIFESTYLE	Sport is insignificant	Sport is non-essential. Liked but not a priority	Sport is not essential but significant	Sport is important	Sport is a defining part of life	Sport is professionally significant
SPORTS EXPENDITURE	Minimal	Minimal except sporadic interest	High on occasions	Considerable	Extremely high and consistent	Extremely significant. Funding support from others

Figure 13.1   Sports–tourism demand continuum

Sources: Derived from Jackson and Reeves (1996)

not clarify the influence of aspects such as the extent to which sports tourism participation changes or develops over time or over the life history, or through other social variables. More work is required and clearly explanations of sports tourism behaviour are multidimensional. However, the work does allow us to fit most types of sports tourism (whether sports-interested individuals on holiday, or regular spectator travel, or the travel patterns of professional or otherwise dedicated sports performers) on to a 'scale' that helps us to untangle the complex demand profile of the overall sports tourism market. It also provides empirically identified key types within which researchers may focus future attention and the industry may target.

These and other studies are beginning to provide a demand profile of sports tourists that differs from that of more 'traditional' tourism subsectors. Sports tourists are (unsurprisingly) more activity oriented than most tourists. Sports tourism is more commonly undertaken during 'short' holidays or weekend breaks/trips than much tourism, but is also increasingly significant within longer holidays. Sports tourism tends to be more evenly spread throughout the year, is less focused on coastal destinations, and is more likely to be taken by childless (often young adult) age groups and those with above-average incomes.

What emerges from such an analysis is that sport is significant to, for example, the generation of day-visit tourism. Whilst some analysts do not consider that this should be included within tourism, because no overnight stay is involved, the industry makes no such distinction and day-visit tourism is now a hugely significant element of overall tourism volume (and to a lesser extent its value); and one that continues to grow. Few studies have systematically isolated the sporting component of day-trip

tourism, but it can reasonably be estimated as responsible for, or involved in, between 10 and 15 per cent of day trips in the UK (Baty and Richards, 1991; Collins and Jackson, 1999). Accurate and consistent volume estimates are problematic and hinge largely around different definitions of what represents sport in such trips (e.g. whether the large number of the more rigorous walking/hiking trips are included) and at what point such recreational travel becomes a day trip. Also, there is a paucity of reliable data on the overall volume of spectator travel across the full range of sports.

As the deliberate development of sports facilities in tourism contexts has emerged, sport has also become increasingly significant in the generation of holiday tourism. Hotels and tourism packages increasingly specifically target the growing number of holiday-makers wanting 'activity' as part of their vacation. Again, whilst estimates vary, it appears that around 10 to 15 per cent of holidays involve sport as a significant component (Smith and Jenner, 1990; BTA/ETB, 1992; Jackson and Reeves, 1998; Mintel, 1999, 2000). Some estimates are significantly higher, but tend to include substantial levels of recreational (non-sport) holiday activity, particularly 'swimming' within the data. Beyond the former broad, but informed, estimates of the volume of the sector, assessing both the volume and the value of sports tourism remains a frustratingly imprecise science. As Collins and Jackson (1999: 171) note,

there are very few reliable sources of data which are sufficiently precise to allow an accurate overall view of the volume and economic significance of sports tourism. This is a further indication of the inability of tourism statistics to accurately profile the behaviour of tourists, which has long been noted.

Major sports events can also be seen to generate significant tourism volumes, and the more identifiable tourism impacts of major events have generated interest amongst researchers and potential hosts. Jackson and Reeves (1996), for example, describe the significant growth in sports event tourism, as both demand and commercial suppliers have developed. Such growth provides opportunities for the many tourists for whom, both domestically and internationally, sports spectating has become a primary reason for holiday trips. Major 'hallmark' events (Olympic, Commonwealth and Pan-American Games, and World and European Championships in individual sports etc.) provide opportunities for tourists to take a holiday based solely around high-class sports spectating, or to incorporate sports spectating into their holiday. Travel to a vast array of sports events is now possible, enabled by both traditional and new specialist tour and travel companies, and sports events have become major tourism generators. Examples abound, but the 1992 Barcelona Olympics attracted nearly half a million visitors to the region (Truno, 1994; Collins and Jackson, 1999). In the UK, whilst largely starved of major international competition, the Euro '96 European Football Championships attracted 280,000 visiting spectators and media to the UK, spending £120m in the eight host cities and surrounding regions (Dobson et al., 1997).

However, sports spectating is not limited to major events. Much spectator tourism involves travel to watch a family member or friend compete. The spectator following of events such as the London or New York Marathons and, indeed, many smaller mass participation events illustrate this point, as do the large numbers (mainly parents and family) who turn up to watch junior sports tournaments and events. In addition, the weekly leagues in a range of sports, although mostly football, in a range of countries around the world provide for regular domestic sports spectating day trips. However, as football becomes more popular and competitions such as the European Champions League develop, such trips become international and in the vast majority of cases involve at least one overnight stay, with resulting economic benefits to the destination.

The term 'activity holiday' has entered our vocabulary and in the UK this is now a multi-billion-pound subsector of the tourism market (Mintel, 1999). The majority of activity holidays are sports-related and this has boosted the sector, and particularly the rural communities where much of this tourism activity takes place. A whole new 'genre' of tourism activity has emerged which is identifiably different from the exclusively relaxation-oriented, sun-seeking tourism of the 1970s and early 1980s. The activity holiday consumer profile is diverse, including independent adults, parents and families, school parties, or groups of children at summer camps. Activity holiday markets in the UK are predominantly domestic, with 85 per cent of British consumers taking their activity holidays within Britain. Many see activity holidays as an extra break, taken outside the traditional holiday period (KPMG/Tourism Company, 1994).

Found more outside the UK is the German concept of *Volkssports*, which translates as 'people's sports' or 'life sports'. Volkssports are family-oriented active recreations which originated in Germany, Austria and Switzerland in the early 1960s. The American Volkssports Association, which co-ordinates over 500 clubs in the USA, promotes the activities – walking, cycling, swimming and cross-country skiing – as sports in which anyone can participate with friends and family throughout his or her life. The concept is now found in over 20 countries around the world under the auspices of Der Internationale Volkssportverband (IVV) (The International Federation of Popular Sports). However, as Agne-Traub (1989) described, their increasing international popularity means that they can easily be incorporated into business or pleasure travel and are often scheduled to attract day-tripping tourists. More recent equivalents would be the range of events established and calendared by local and municipal authorities to attract visitors and their spending, as well as providing a recreational, sometimes elite performance event, for the benefit of the local population, and sometimes to promote the city or area. British examples would be events such as the London (and others) Marathon, the Great North Run, the Scarborough Cricket Festival and the Worthing Bowls Festival.

There is great potential for such initiatives to stimulate sporting activity in a range of areas. Moreover, because many such activities lend themselves to universal participation, they can be linked to health promotion and active living programmes – something that has been largely neglected by sports development and health promotion professionals. The potential for sports tourism to play a role in the 'sports development process' was outlined in the early work by Jackson and Glyptis (1992), and more recently by Weed (2001a). Both studies noted that there are a vast number of people who only pick up a racquet or a ball while on holiday. If the playful and health-related benefits of sport are stressed by those organising sports activities on holidays, then this can have a great impact on developing active and healthy lifestyles when the tourist returns home. In this way, holidays can be used to entice individuals to take up a sport; activity holidays by

schools and youth groups often generate interests for life. In addition, 'performance camps' away from home are increasingly common for some of the nation's best young sportspeople. Such examples show the potential for sport within the sport–tourism relationship.

SPORTS TOURISM SUPPLY

Turning to the *supply profile* of sports tourism, there has been a 'quiet revolution' in tourism supply development. This started with the provision of better hotel facilities (initially the inclusion of swimming pools in the product portfolio) and continued through the addition of health club facilities and access to tennis and golf provision, until the highest tariff/quality accommodation (outside city centres) now sees hotels set alongside their own golf and multi-sport complexes. Sport has became an integral part of the established tourism product, with conference and business tourists in particular now having high-class, prestigious facilities made available to them as competition increases for their custom. Manchester, for example, used its Olympic bids to spearhead its push for the conference market and its successful bid to host the 2002 Commonwealth Games is being used in a similar way. Sports facilities are now seen as almost essential in attracting the highly lucrative conference market. However, in addition to providing for the conference market, many 'country-house'-type hotels cater for the 'up-market' sports tourist. It is often the range and quality of the facilities as well as the luxurious nature of the accommodation that define this product as 'up-market' (Weed, 2001b). In fact, in a number of cases this market has been provided for by the addition of five-star accommodation to long-established and renowned sports facilities. For enthusiasts who cannot afford such hotels, many smaller hotel operators have agreements with local sports providers to attract visitors for mutual benefit. Furthermore a substantial number of farms have diversified into tourism and provide sport and recreation activities for those on a tighter budget.

Both major travel operators (e.g. Thomson) and smaller 'independents' have diversified their product offers into sports tourism holidays, particularly over recent years. Within the latter group, the number of specialists and products available in activities of all types has grown significantly. Larger operators typically now offer multi-activity holidays, as well as sun/sea packages, and most of the latter include sports activity options. The UK now boasts over a hundred accredited independent tour operators (often specialising exclusively in activity tourism niches) offering sport and activity tourism ranging from golf holidays to high mountain range trekking. Several other independent operators directly market their multi-activity facilities and packages, such as walking, biking, pony trekking, canoeing adventure holidays; or aquatic-oriented pursuits such as sailing, surfing, wind-surfing, diving, etc. These commercial operators are supplemented by education-sector centres and other commercial professional training/team-building centres. The diversity of sport/adventure tourism opportunities, as illustrated by these few examples, is substantial and still growing.

Sports holidays, particularly those in rural areas, have provided a whole range of tourism development opportunities ranging from those operated from enterprising small hotels, to the farm diversification projects mentioned earlier. As such, there is a range of examples of the effective use of countryside resources for sport and recreation

from all around the world. Jackson (1999) notes the environmentally friendly nature of cycling as an activity in National Parks in America, whilst in Crete and Thrace 'soft' forms of sports tourism, such as hiking, orienteering and cycling, have been promoted in rural areas (Vrondou, 1999). In this Greek case, these 'soft' forms of sports tourism have been seen as having the potential to diversify tourism beyond the traditional 'mass' product for which Greece is known, and to have substantial potential for the future of the Greek tourism industry. Vrondou (1999) provides an example of a characteristic of sports tourism that is found elsewhere. Here, sports tourism is seen as a sustainable form of tourism that might 'minimise negative effects and maximise social, environmental and economic benefits' (Regional Programme for Crete, 1994–99) whilst also having the potential to promote local cultures, as the activities result in greater access to alternative routes and localities, with distinct natural and cultural characteristics. This is something which the World Tourism Organisation (1988) also recognised and promoted, commenting that the sport and recreation dimension can enrich the tourism experience by allowing greater interaction with destinations and a fuller appreciation of the social and cultural life of local communities.

Beneficially, there is also much evidence (see Jackson and Glyptis, 1992) that tourism can play a role, particularly in coastal or rural areas where the population may be dispersed, in supporting standards of sports facilities that would otherwise be unavailable to local residents. There is a range of examples of tourist support for the upkeep of recreational parkland and sports facilities in rural communities in France, North America, Australia and even Thailand. This concept was also supported, albeit briefly, by the British government in its planning policy guidance on sport and recreation (DoE/Welsh Office, 1991: 4). The guidance calls for: 'local plan policies to take into account the recreational needs of tourists and where appropriate encourage the development of facilities that benefit both visitors and residents'.

In many cases, as well as catering for the local market, facility developers find it essential to account for the recreational needs of tourists. In fact, in order to realise financial targets, leisure pool developments must often attract a high proportion of visitors from outside the immediate area. It is also important to ensure that these visitors spend money both inside and outside the facility, because without this visitor support many significant leisure developments would simply not be viable. Thus, tourism is sometimes essential in supporting local-level sports provision, as well as the local economy.

SPORTS TOURISM IMPACTS

As the above discussion intimates, there are clear *impacts* from sports tourism development. The economic impact is perhaps the most obvious and has already been evidenced in terms of adding value to individual facilities and sometimes to whole destinations. Broadly, sports tourism is a dynamic and expanding sector of the tourism economy, and by definition this is attractive economically. Sports-related facilities and events are clearly capable of generating visitors from outside the local area, and of attracting more and/or higher-spending visitors to existing tourist locations. There is economic benefit locally from sales of accommodation, food, beverages, gifts, admission fees, other spending at facilities, hire fees, use of transport, etc. Thus, there are clear benefits from attracting

visitors, using sport or sports facilities as a key part of the tourism product offer. Sport and its events may also generate sponsorship income, inward investment, media exposure, ongoing tourist appeal and secondary multiplier effects. There are potentially significant economic benefits to be accrued from the additional revenue, employment, infrastructure, etc. to local and national economies which sports-oriented tourism provides.

The estimate (Jackson and Reeves, 1996) that 10–15 per cent of domestic holidays in Northern Europe have a sports orientation is not unreasonable. However, the authors called for a more specific and consistent focus on this information gap in future tourism statistics collection. Three years later, Collins and Jackson attempted to synthesise a range of previous economic impact studies in disparate disciplines to present an overview of the economic impacts of the sport–tourism link, focusing on the UK. In doing so they commented that their work could only be considered 'indicative of the overall economic impact because of the inconsistent and invariably incompatible nature of the available data' (Collins and Jackson, 1999). Their 'conservative' estimates for the value of sports tourism in the UK are illustrated in Table 13.1, which suggests an overall value of over £2.5bn annually. A more 'bullish' estimate is provided by market analysts Mintel (1999), who value UK sports tourism at £3.4bn annually, but have a more 'inclusive' view of the sport component.

It has tended to be in the area of sports events that most economic impact research has been conducted, and it is therefore useful to review some of this research here. The obvious direct benefits of major sporting events (new facilities and visitor spending) are supplemented in most cases by a post-event tourism boost. Resulting publicity

Table 13.1   *The economic impact of sports tourism in the UK*

Types of sports tourism	Value £m
Sports as a prime activity on domestic holidays	1,640
Sports as a prime activity by overseas visitors	142
Sport as a prime activity on day trips	831
Total	2,611

Source: After Collins and Jackson (1999)

and the positive influence on local tourism are clear advantages of staging such events.

Although earlier Olympics made losses for the host cities (Munich and Montreal), since the commercial success of the Los Angeles Games in 1984 (which realised a surplus of £215m), there has been considerable competition for the privilege of being the host city for the Olympic Games. There is now far greater understanding of the broad and indirect benefits to cities, regions and governments of hosting major events, even where there is an initial cost to a city (see Mules and Faulkner, 1996). The additional economic activity as a result of the event is invariably massive.

The act of winning the Olympic Games is a catalyst for bringing forward general infrastructure investments that may have been on the drawing board for a number of years. As a result of the 1992 Games, Barcelona gained a ring-road, a new airport and the redevelopment of an area of derelict waterfront for the Olympic Village, as well as the associated spending in the wider region of 422,000 visitors and other event-related income. The worldwide publicity and infrastructure investment that the Games bring should enable a host city to attract further general investment, future events and more tourists. Even a failed Olympic bid can attract a large amount of public and private sector investment to provide some facilities and infrastructure. Manchester gained a world-class Velodrome and several local

infrastructure projects from its Olympic bid. The level of public investment is usually justified along these lines, with many cities attaching importance to establishing an identity as a 'world-class city' in the circuits of international business, culture and tourism. At the city level, a major motivator for attracting sports tourism events may be the significant level of central government funding that is often attached to such projects. In fact, the group responsible for initiating Victoria's successful bid for the 1994 Commonwealth Games cite the infusion of federal funds into the city as one of the most important reasons for putting in a bid for the Games (D'Abaco, 1991). Rarely are major events viable without significant public sector investment. Invariably there is a cost to the host authority, but significant benefits to the wider economy (see Mules and Faulkner, 1996).

Having staged a major games, it is important that cities seek to attract a string of future events. Subsequent events can be staged at a fraction of the cost of the original event as the infrastructure is already in place. However, the promotional, image and economic effects still persist. In this vein, Bramwell (1997) discusses the use of the 1991 World Student Games in Sheffield as part of a sustainable development strategy that promoted, and continues to promote, economic efficiency, social equity and environmental integrity in the city of Sheffield. Although initially unpopular and generating much local and external criticism, the continued legacy of these games is reflected in Sheffield's ongoing major sports events strategy that has attracted events such as Euro '96 and the World Masters Swimming Championships to the city with significant economic benefit (Dobson and Gratton, 1997). However, it is not only large-scale events that can generate economic benefits for local communities. Dobson and Gratton (1997) identify this point for Sheffield, whilst an early analysis from America of the Peterborough Church League Atom Hockey Tournament in the early 1980s showed that even junior tournaments can generate considerable visitor spending (Marsh, 1984).

In order for major sports facilities built for mega-events to be sustainable in the long term, they need to be adaptable for local community use. One of the legacies of the World Student Games in Sheffield is the Ponds Forge International Sports Centre, which comprises a 50 m swimming pool, a pool with full diving facilities, a leisure pool and an indoor sports centre. This facility is perhaps the most flexible in the world, the pools having movable floors and bulkheads which make them adaptable for a large range of community uses. In fact, Bramwell (1997) describes the provision of new sport and recreation facilities for the long-term use of Sheffield residents as a key objective for the hosting of the World Student Games. However, it is important to note that many facilities built for major games may not be best suited to ongoing community use, either for participation or spectating.

It is also important to include factors other than economic impacts in the cost/benefit assessment of tourist-attracting sports events. For example, many such events, particularly those where regeneration is a major objective, often require the demolition of at least some existing provision or housing to make way

for facilities, infrastructure or development. At worst, this can result in the traumatic break-up of entire communities. A displacement of indigenous communities occurred in the development of Barcelona's waterfront for the 1992 Olympic Games and in Beijing's preparation for the 2008 Games. Whilst many would see such redevelopment as a positive benefit that enhances the environment and image of the city, for those communities that are displaced the experience can be traumatic, and such socio-economic 'engineering' now receives very negative exposure, which denudes the positive impact which such developments and events are designed to secure.

Overall, however, sports tourism is viewed as having primarily positive impacts in comparison to many commercial development forms. Sports tourism has played a significant part in a number of countries in the generation of community identity and pride and in the economic and social regeneration of decaying urban areas. In addition, its economic potential has been harnessed in many rural areas to support the local economy and services. In the immediate aftermath of apartheid in South Africa, Nelson Mandela spoke of the role of the 1995 Rugby World Cup, hosted and won by South Africa, in 'nation building' after the years of internal turmoil and international isolation the country had suffered.

Both in Britain and the USA, sports-related tourism initiatives have been at the forefront of urban regeneration programmes (see Bianchini and Schwengel, 1991; Roche, 1994; Collins and Jackson, 1996). In many urban areas, the use of sport within the tourism strategies of local government for regenerative purposes is also well documented (Buckley and Witt, 1985; Law, 1992; SCLG, 1994). In Scotland, for example, Glasgow developed the Scottish Exhibition and Conference Centre in 1985, which provided a major venue in the city. This was followed by the conversion of the Kelvin Hall into an indoor sports arena, which became Britain's premier indoor athletics venue. It was estimated by Friel (1990) that Glasgow spent £90m on events and infrastructure, but that this investment generated £300m in income for the city.

North American research by Chapin (1996) and more recently Rosentraub (2000) discusses the substantial surge, since the early 1990s, in the number of new sports and entertainment facilities – largely aimed at staging sports events, concerts, conventions, conferences, exhibitions and any other events requiring a facility with a capacity of around 20,000 people. The prime objective identified in almost all of these cases has been economic development and revitalisation. Chapin (1996) specifically reviews the varying strategies of three facilities: Key Arena in Seattle, The Rose Garden in Portland, and GM Palace in Vancouver. The construction of the Key Arena in Seattle was part of a plan to revitalise an ageing, but culturally highly significant, civic centre. Here the former Seattle Coliseum arena was reconstructed and re-named as the Key Arena, as an integral part of the Seattle Centre Entertainment District, resulting in a revamped city centre that retained much of its original heritage. In contrast, Portland chose to locate a new facility alongside an older, much smaller arena, and relatively new convention centre in an out-of-town development that is now specifically marketed as a Sports Entertainment District. Finally, Vancouver, like Seattle, located the GM Palace within its city centre, but focused on a newly built sports arena with the aim of enhancing the city centre as a 'metropolitan core'. These cases illustrate three widely popular strategies for urban regeneration utilising sports and entertainment facilities likely to attract visitors, namely: reinvestment in existing facilities, development of new sports entertainment districts, and investment in inner-city revitalisation and redevelopment. However, a key factor in each of these cases, and one relevant to any town seeking to use sport in urban regeneration, is that it be developed alongside other leisure, entertainment and tourism facilities.

In rural areas too, sports tourism has made a number of significant impacts, particularly over recent years. Despite the evident sensitivity of rural environments and the fact that there will be some negative impacts of sports tourism development (see Standeven and De Knop, 1999), sports tourism has for the most part maintained a reputation as 'soft' tourism (discussed earlier in the Greek example), capable of contributing to the rural economy in a range of contexts across the world. Countryside pursuits, such as hiking, climbing, orienteering, fell-running and cycling all increasingly contribute to the rural economy, but perhaps the latter has received the most recent attention in the literature. For example, research in the USA by Schuett and Holmes (1996) demonstrates that the construction of an entire regional marketing plan for the Adirondack North Country Region of New York State has been based on the opportunities it offers for cycle tourism. Such a plan brings together local businesses, tourism organisations and bicycle-related firms and organisations in seeking to use such tourism to develop local economies. Increasingly, similar findings are emerging in the UK, particularly as the National Cycle Network develops and rural districts and small local businesses invest in cycle tourism as a key element in rural economic development strategies (see Jackson and Morpeth, 1999). The authors note that the National Cycle Network is seen as having the potential to generate £150m in tourism receipts annually across the UK and over 3,000 jobs nationally, particularly focused in rural areas. The 'C2C Cycle Route' across the rural north of England, for example, is estimated to already generate £1.5m annually for the communities along its route.

A cautionary note, however, should be sounded about an overreliance on the leisure economy. For example, Keith et al. (1996) describe how those counties in Utah that are dependent on tourism and recreation to maintain economic viability have a much greater annual employment variability than those counties that have a wider portfolio of economic activities. In fact, in the literature focusing on tourism's potential to generate employment, much similar concern has been expressed about the part-time, seasonal and casual nature of the jobs that are created (see Shaw and Williams, 1994). Such dependency on recreation and tourism can also result in a neglect of ecological and environmental concerns. For example, Weiss et al. (1998) studied reactions to ski tourism among ski tourists and ski resort residents in Austria and Belgium. They found that ski tourists and locals who were not financially dependent on tourism had a much higher ecological awareness than tourism-dependent locals. This was clearly a result of the latter group's vested economic interest in the industry and was further highlighted by the fact that differences between these groups on general environmental issues were minimal. Environmental concerns in relation to ski tourism were found to vary according to the extent of the personal sacrifice involved in addressing such issues.

CONCLUSIONS AND FUTURE DIRECTIONS

This chapter has provided a broad overview of the significance and impacts of sports-related tourism from both a demand (participation) and supply (opportunity and facility provision) standpoint. It has also provided summary indications of the types of impact, both positive and negative, that sports tourism is now known to have. While conclusions *per se* are perhaps inappropriate in such a review chapter, there are some key points in this analysis that are worthy of emphasis. Most significant of these is that, despite its relative lack of recognition within leisure research and economic analysis, which often treat the sectors of sport and tourism separately, sports-related tourism is highly significant and continues its growth trend.

Notwithstanding the growth of security fears, further development of tourism seems assured worldwide, particularly as the Asia-Pacific region opens itself to visitation and trip generation. The Beijing Olympics is indicative of this process, and indicative too of sport's globalisation, as international competition and sport-associated travel filters from the traditional national representative matches and well-spaced world championships to embrace far more regular international competition and global 'tour' events almost weekly (fuelled by the emergence of a global television audience and attendant commercial opportunity). Even club and individual sports participation has developed an international element.

Clear corollaries are that international sports travel and spectator sports tourism will also grow and will have an increasing and significant economic impact. Whilst estimates of value in this area are notoriously difficult to extrapolate, if a conservative figure of 'around' 10 per cent of tourists have sport as a main or significant activity within their travel (Collins and Jackson, 1999; Standeven and De Knop, 1999; Mintel, 1999), then sports tourism is a multi-billion-pound sector worldwide, and significant too within individual national economies. In addition, in terms of pure participation, it is clear that within holiday activity (i.e. a subset of overall tourism activity), the significance of sporting activity within the decision of whether and where to travel/stay is even more significant. In terms of participation, sports tourism is a significant element of the leisure and tourism market, and continues to grow.

We have shown through the concept of a 'sports tourism continuum' that within these macro-level figures there is a complete range of sports tourist types. These range from individuals who are 'driven' sports tourists (typically the professional or elite sports performer) through a continuum of interest types from those whose travel behaviour is regularly and significantly influenced by sport spectating or participation considerations in one or a number of sports, to those whose vacation time provides an occasional or irregular opportunity to experience sporting activity that everyday life largely precludes. In between lies a whole range of sports tourist types whose behaviour patterns vary in the level and type of activity.

Needless to say, our analysis shows that facility and other opportunity provision for sports tourism also continues to broaden and develop. An increasing proportion of accommodation, tour operating and other commercial companies, destination authorities and some national governments have identified and embraced the notion that sports tourism generates an important subset of the tourism market. This is particularly attractive as the tourism it generates is often supplementary to, rather than replacing, current demand. Consequently, sports events, large-scale sports facility developments and sports tourism have been seen, and continue to be viewed, as beneficial activity and/or facilities capable of maintaining the attractiveness, visitworthiness,

and the economic viability of destination settings as diverse as major industrial cities, ailing (or developing) coastal resorts and declining (or evolving) rural economies, looking for means to attract visitors and spending into peripheral regions, and limited and often tenuous local economic systems. The natural resources and space on which sports tourism often thrives are sometimes the only asset of such locations, other than an underemployed workforce.

Notwithstanding the fact that evidence can be found of events and facility developments where the proposed economic gains have not materialised, or have been overstated, or where there has been unwise investment, inadequate and over-ambitious planning and poorly managed activity, the overall conclusion has to be that the great majority of sports tourism developments have resulted in positive economic impacts. In fact, economic considerations continue to serve as the primary motivation for most sports tourism developments. Consequently, better-measured and more considered impact statements are now emerging for major events and facility developments of all scales, where previously these were underanalysed and sometimes fanciful.

We have also noted that in analysing the interrelationship between sport and tourism, it would be folly to focus solely on the economic impacts. Clearly there are socio-cultural and environmental externalities that must also be considered. In these two broad areas of analysis it is commonplace and understandable that negative impacts are highlighted and often emphasised. However, it is equally clear that while negative externalities exist – as with most forms of development and growth markets – a host of positive non-economic benefits may well result from sports-related tourism growth. This is particularly the case when the scale and pace of development are controlled, and if integrated and sustainable development and management approaches are implemented.

Although sports tourism's relatively 'clean', 'inexpensive' operation makes it acceptable to most locations, and certainly more suitable than many tourism forms, a cost–benefit approach juxtaposing economic gains and environmental impacts is fraught with danger, and unlikely to lead to an agreed 'bottom line' between those with very different perspectives of 'value', who are invariably drawn into such debates. However positive we might want to be about sports tourism and its benefits, we have to pay attention to the fact that sports or active visitors (walkers, trekkers, runners, bikers, climbers and others) do intrude into sensitive, sometimes unspoilt locations. Furthermore, sports tourists do occasionally compete for scarce resources with local communities, who may not always share the profit from such economic developments – golf is often highlighted in this context. There are undeniable impacts on the physical and social environment from many sports tourism activities and to ignore these is myopic.

Again, the answer has to lie in considered and sensitive approaches, and sustainable development and management of sports tourism – as has been identified for other, often more intrusive types of tourism. Despite its reputation for having 'soft' impacts, sports tourism must embrace these considerations. In fact, as Standeven and De Knop (1999) also identify, this may be one of the linchpins around which sports tourism can continue to develop, whilst also maintaining its reputation for primarily positive impacts. The future of sports tourism operations, particularly in some of the more sensitive coastal and rural locations, has to include those management policies and elements of self-regulation that have become the essence of sustainable tourism management (see Bramwell et al., 1996). Bramwell has also shown (e.g. in his analysis of sports tourism developments in Sheffield [1997]), that this is the case not solely in sensitive environments.

A secure future for sports tourism developments includes, for example, a sensitive level and pace of development, limiting environmental damage, inclusion of local residents in the decision-making processes, use of local products and services, etc. While self-regulation and responsible management within the tourism industry have been identified as ultimately far more valuable and beneficial, such responsible action will almost certainly have to be backed up by an appropriate level of state and local-level regulation and/or legislation, to ensure that sports tourism development and activity continue to grow, but in a sustainable way that does not damage the very resources on which it depends and flourishes.

From this analysis then, it should be clear that sport and tourism interrelate in a multiplicity of ways, and this interrelationship is likely to continue to grow as participation and opportunity continue to increase. This has clear implications for both analysts and providers of sport and tourism activity, for policy-makers, investors, developers and managers involved in these fields. Whilst long unrecognised or underemphasised, the extent of the overlap and interrelationship between sport and tourism, as two traditionally separately treated elements of the leisure market and industry, is now increasingly recognised as highly significant.

The sports tourism interrelationship is manifest in a number of substantial characteristics of contemporary leisure activity and supply. These, in turn, have significance for the future leisure industry. These characteristics can be summarised as:

1 the now substantial volume and continuing growth of sports-related tourism demand activity (both spectating and participatory);
2 the extent, nature and continued growth of joint provision and infrastructure (sports facilities and events designed to attract both tourists and the resident market; and the increasing level of tourism programmes focusing on, or marketed to, sports-oriented individuals or groups);
3 particularly the economic impacts, but also the social and environmental considerations, that result from this now significant and increasing integration of sport and tourism activity; and
4 the implications for future integrated management and policy making for sport and for tourism, particularly where the boundaries between them are blurred.

Chapter summary

- Sports tourism has developed significantly over the last two decades and the interrelationship continues to evolve in both the demand and the supply structure of contemporary leisure.
- Sports tourism demand can be conceptualised in terms of a continuum from, at one end, incidental participation in sport as part of a vacation, through to the other end where travel away from home is dictated by sports activity.
- Sports tourism supply has expanded rapidly and sport is now an important and integral part of the tourism product.
- The impact of sports tourism can be evaluated in terms of costs and benefits to the economy, to urban regeneration efforts, and to the local environment.

Further reading

Weed and Bull (2003) and Standeven and De Knop (1999) provide overviews of the field of sport tourism. Bianchini and Schwengel (1991) examine the impact of sports tourism on urban regeneration. Weiss et al. (1998) discuss environmental issues associated with winter sports tourism, and Collins and Jackson (1999) explore the economic impact of sports tourism. Bramwell (1997) and Roche (1994) both examine the wide-ranging impact of mega-events. Finally, Weed (2003) examines the policy context of sports tourism.

REFERENCES

Agne-Traub, L. (1989) 'Volkssporting and tourism: something for the working class', *Leisure Information Quarterly*, 15 (4): 6–8.

Baty, B. and Richards, S. (1991) 'The leisure day visit survey', *Employment Gazette*, May: 257–68.

Bianchini, F. and Schwengel, H. (1991) 'Re-imaging the city', in J. Corner and S. Harvey (eds), *Enterprise and Heritage: Crosscurrents of National Culture*. London and New York: Routledge, pp. 214–34.

Bramwell, B. (1997) 'A sport mega-event as a sustainable tourism development strategy', *Tourism Recreation Research*, 22 (2): 13–19.

Bramwell, B., Henry, I.P. and Jackson, G.A.M. (1996) 'A framework for understanding sustainable tourism management', in B. Bramwell et al. (eds), *Sustainable Tourism*

Management: Principles and Practice. Tilburg: Tilburg University Press.

British Tourist Authority/English Tourist Board (BTA/ETB) (1992) *Activities by the British on Holiday in Britain*. London: BTA/ETB/NOP Market Research Ltd.

Buckley, P. and Witt, S. (1985) 'Tourism in difficult areas: case studies of Bradford, Bristol, Glasgow and Hamm', *Tourism Management*, 6 (3): 205–13.

Chapin, T.S. (1996) 'A new era of professional sports in the Northwest: facility location as an economic development strategy in Seattle, Portland and Vancouver'. Paper presented to the 'Sport in the City' Conference, Sheffield, UK.

Collins, M.F. and Jackson, G.A.M. (1996) 'The economic impact of a growing symbiosis: sport and tourism'. Paper presented at the 4th European Congress on Sports Management. Montpelier, France.

Collins, M.F. and Jackson, G.A.M. (1999) 'The economic impact of sport and tourism', in J. Standeven and P. De Knop, *Sport Tourism*. Champaign, IL: Human Kinetics.

Countryside Commission (1998) *UK Leisure Day Visits: Summary of the 1996 Survey Findings*.

D'Abaco, G. (1991) 'Marketing parks and recreational facilities as tourism attractions – experiences from the Victoria Tourism Commission's "Melbourne Now" campaign', in *Who Dares Wins – Parks, Recreation and Tourism*, Conference Proceedings, Volume 2. Canberra: Royal Institute of Parks and Recreation.

De Knop, P. (1990) 'Sport for all and active tourism', *Journal of the World Leisure and Recreation Association*, Fall: 30–6.

Department of the Environment/Welsh Office (1991) *Planning Policy Guidance 17, Sport and Recreation*. London: HMSO.

Dobson, N. and Gratton, C. (1997) *The Economic Impact of Sports Events: Euro '96 and VI Fina World Masters Swimming Championships in Sheffield*. Sheffield: Leisure Industries Research Centre.

Dobson, N., Holliday, S. and Gratton, C. (1997) *Football Came Home: The Economic Impact of Euro '96*. Sheffield: Leisure Industries Research Centre.

Friel, E. (1990) 'Tourism as an aid to improving the economy of Glasgow'. Paper presented at the 'Tourism and Job Creation' Conference. Edinburgh: Centre for Leisure Research.

Glyptis, S.A. (1982) *Sport and Tourism in Western Europe*. London: British Travel Education Trust.

Glyptis, S.A. (1991) 'Sport and tourism', in C.P. Cooper (ed.), *Progress in Tourism, Recreation and Hospitality Management* (Vol. 3). London: Belhaven Press.

Hall, C.M. (1992) 'Adventure, sport and health', in C.M. Hall and B. Weiler (eds), *Special Interest Tourism*. London: Belhaven Press.

Jackson, C. (1999) 'Pedalling in the parks', *National Parks*, March/April: 34–6.

Jackson, G.A.M. and Glyptis, S.A. (1992) *Sport and Tourism: A Review of the Literature*. Report to the Sports Council, Recreation Management Group, Loughborough University.

Jackson, G.A.M. and Morpeth, N. (1999) 'Local Agenda 21 and community participation in tourism policy and planning: future or fallacy?', *Current Issues in Tourism*, 2 (1): 1–38.

Jackson, G.A.M. and Reeves, M.R. (1996) 'Conceptualising the sport–tourism interrelationship: a case study approach'. Paper to the LSA/VVA Conference, Wageningen, The Netherlands, September.

Jackson, G.A.M. and Reeves, M.R. (1998) 'Evidencing the sport tourism interrelationship: a case study of elite British athletes', in M.F. Collins and I.S. Cooper (eds), *Leisure Management: Issues and Applications*. Wallingford: CABI Publications.

Keith, J., Fawson, C. and Chang, T. (1996) 'Recreation as an economic development strategy: some evidence from Utah', *Journal of Leisure Research*, 28 (2): 96–107.

KPMG/Tourism Company (1994) *Activity Holidays in Scotland*. Edinburgh: STB.

Law, C. (1992) 'Urban tourism and its contribution to economic regeneration', *Urban Studies*, 29 (3–4): 599–618.

Leisure Consultants (1992) *Activity Holidays: a Growth Market in Tourism*. Sudbury: Leisure Consultants.

Marsh, J. (1984) 'The economic impact of a small city annual sporting event: an initial case study of the Peterborough Church League Atoms Hockey Tournament', *Recreation Research Review*, 11: 48–55.

Mintel (1999) 'Activity holidays', *Leisure Intelligence*, London: Mintel.

Mintel (2000) 'Special interest holidays', *Leisure Intelligence*, London: Mintel.

Mules, T. and Faulkner, B. (1996) 'An economic perspective on special events', *Tourism Economics*, 2 (2): 107–17.

Redmond, G. (1991) 'Changing styles of sports tourism: industry/consumer interactions in Canada, the USA and Europe', in M.J. Sinclair and M.J. Stabler (eds), *The Tourist Industry: an International Analysis*. Wallingford: CABI Publications.

Reeves, M.R. (2000) 'Evidencing the sport–tourism interrelationship'. Unpublished PhD thesis, Loughborough University.

Roche, M. (1994) 'Mega events and urban policy', *Annals of Tourism Research*, 21: 1–19.

Rosentraub, M.S. (2000) 'Sports facilities, redevelopment and the centrality of downtown areas: observations and lessons from experiences in the Rustbelt and Sunbelt City', *Marquette Sports Law Journal*, 10 (2): 219–35.

Schuett, M.A. and Holmes, T.P. (1996) 'Using a collaborative approach to developing a regional bicycle tourism plan', *Journal of Hospitality and Leisure Marketing*, 4 (1): 83–95.

Shaw, G. and Williams, A.M. (1994) *Critical Issues in Tourism: A Geographical Perspective*. Oxford: Blackwell.

Sheffield City Council Sports Development and Event Unit (SCCSDEU) (1995) *Major Sports Events Strategy*. Sheffield: SCCSDEU.

Sheffield City Liaison Group (SCLG) (1994) *The Way Ahead – Plans for the Economic Regeneration of Sheffield*. Sheffield: SCLG.

Smith, C. and Jenner, P. (1990) 'Activity holidays in Europe', *Travel and Tourism Analyst*, 5: 58–78.

Standeven, J. and De Knop, P. (1999) *Sport Tourism*. Champaign, IL: Human Kinetics.

Standeven, J. and Tomlinson, A. (1994) *Sport and Tourism in South East England*. London: South East Council for Sport and Recreation.

Truno, E. (1994) 'Sport for All and the Barcelona Olympic Games'. Paper presented at the 2nd European Congress on Sport for All in Cities, Barcelona, Spain, October.

Vrondou, O. (1999) 'Sports related tourism and the product repositioning of traditional mass tourism destinations: a case study of Greece'. Unpublished PhD thesis, Loughborough University.

Weed, M.E. (1999) 'Consensual policies for sport and tourism in the UK: an analysis of organisational behaviour and attitudes'. Unpublished PhD thesis, Canterbury Christ Church University College/University of Kent at Canterbury.

Weed, M.E. (2001a) 'Tourism and sports development: providing the foundation for healthy lifestyles'. Paper presented at the International Conference, 'Sport and Quality of Life', Vila Real, December.

Weed, M.E. (2001b) 'Developing a sports tourism product'. Paper presented at the First International Conference of the Pan Hellenic Association of Sports Economists and Managers, 'The Economic Impact of Sport', Athens, February.

Weed, M.E. (2003) 'Why the two won't tango: explaining the lack of consensual policies for sport and tourism in the UK', *Journal of Sports Management*. Special Edition on Sports Tourism (forthcoming).

Weed, M.E. and Bull, C.J. (1997a) 'Integrating sport and tourism: a review of regional policies in England', *Progress in Tourism and Hospitality Research*, 3 (2): 129–48.

Weed, M.E. and Bull, C.J. (1997b) 'Influences on sport–tourism relations in England: the effects of government policy', *Tourism Recreation Research*, 22 (2): 5–12.

Weed, M.E. and Bull, C.J. (2003) *Sports Tourism: Participants, Policy and Providers*. Oxford: Butterworth Heinemann.

Weiss, O., Norden, G., Hilschers, P. and Vanreusel, B. (1998) 'Ski tourism and environmental problems', *International Review for the Sociology of Sport*, 33 (4): 367–79.

World Tourism Organisation (1988) *Special Interest Tourism*. Madrid: WTO.

14

The Economics of the Olympic Games: Winners and Losers

HOLGER PREUSS

'The best Games ever', is the remark IOC President J.A. Samaranch made at the conclusion of 'successful' Games. But how can he measure the success of the Olympic Games? Does he mean the financial, social, organisational or sportive success? And from what point of view does he measure the success: from that of politicians, the construction industry, medal winners, prosperous citizens or the IOC – in other words from the point of view of the 'winners'? Even if it were possible to answer these questions, a central problem remains, namely that of comparing the recently completed Games with previous Games.

A comparative judgement of the Games is impossible because the aim of each Olympic host city is different. In Los Angeles, for example, the primary aim was to avoid a deficit and the organisers therefore used existing infrastructure whenever possible (Ueberroth et al., 1985), whereas in Barcelona the priority was urban regeneration (Millet, 1995). The purpose of this chapter is not to identify the 'best Games ever', but to provide an economic analysis of the Games from Munich in 1972 and to identify the various interested parties and determine the 'winners' and 'losers' in an Olympic host city.

AN ECONOMIC HISTORY OF THE OLYMPIC GAMES

Economic considerations have been associated with the Olympic Games throughout the entire history of the modern Olympics, although the nature of the association has varied greatly. Dividing the history of the modern Olympic Games into four periods illustrates the developing relationship and the shifting pattern of winners and losers.

The first period, 1896–1968, is characterised by the financial problems experienced by many Organising Committees of the Olympic Games (OCOG). The first Games in Athens 1896 took place at a time when the Greek state had just been declared bankrupt with the Games only taking place due to the generosity of wealthy Greeks living abroad (Georgiadis, 2000: 208–17). After staging five Games, each of which had substantial financial problems, de Coubertin drew the conclusion that 'the question is not whether they will be held, but how they will be held, and at whose expense' (1913: 183). During this period it is notable how many governments developed new financing sources in an attempt to limit their financial obligations. Some financial sources were used only once, while others became established elements in the financing of the Games (see Landry and Yerlès, 1996: 183–7).

In the second period, 1969–80, the urgency to develop new sources of finance increased in parallel with the scale of the Olympics. However, although the sale of broadcasting rights and sponsorship emerged as an additional source of finance, they were still of minor importance by comparison to public finance. Munich 1972 is a good example of publicly financed Games and especially the use of 'special financing means', which refers to those OCOG revenue sources that require government approval, such as the sale of Olympic coins or the organising of an Olympic lottery. Apart from the revenues generated by the OCOG itself, for example from ticket sales (approx. 19 per cent), the 1972 Games were financed by special financing means (approx. 50 per cent) and by federal government, state and city subsidies (approx. 31 per cent). The public deficit of US$743m[1] was covered by the federal government (50 per cent), by the states (25 per cent) and by the cities Munich and Kiel (25 per cent) (OC Munich, 1974: 53–4).

The Montreal Olympics of 1976 also relied heavily on public subsidy, but differed from

---

Box 14.2   The economic history of the Olympic Games

Period 1 (1896–1968): recurring financial problems, identification of new sources
   of income
Period 2 (1969–80): publicly financed Olympic Games
Period 3 (1981–96): increasing importance of private finance
Period 4 (1997–2008): mixed financing, long-term relationships between sponsors,
   TV networks and IOC

---

the 1972 Games in that the Canadian federal government did not give the City of Montreal a financial guarantee. Because of a 'written guarantee that the federal government would not be called upon to absorb the deficit nor to assume interim financing for organization' (OC Montreal, 1976: 55), the OCOG had to stage the Games relying solely on financial support from the city. At the conclusion of the Games the private revenues generated by the OCOG amounted to a mere 5 per cent of the funds required. The remaining 95 per cent was provided by special financing means and by the public sector (1976: 59). The deficit of US$2bn had to be covered exclusively by the City of Montreal, which had provided the official guarantee to the IOC. Montreal's taxpayers will have to pay off the debt until 2005/06 from a special local tobacco tax. It should be noted that the deficit was not the result of low revenues, instead it was caused by large investment in infrastructure, mismanagement, strikes by construction workers and imbalance in the market (Commission of Inquiry, n.d.: 314). After the experience of Montreal, cities were reluctant to bid for the 1984 Games because the cost was no longer considered tenable (Figure 14.1). There is a lack of financial information concerning the Moscow Games, although it is safe to assume that they were financed overwhelmingly by state subsidy owing to the

political aim to demonstrate the superiority of the communist system (see Ueberroth et al., 1985: 55–9). What Lord Killanin, IOC President during this period, said about the amateur issue in sport is also applicable to the financing of the Games: 'The word amateur unfortunately no longer refers to a lover of sports but, possibly, a lack of proficiency' (Killanin, 1982: 43).

The third period, 1981–96, paralleled much of the presidency of J.A. Samaranch. It was during this period that the removal of the word 'amateur' from the Olympic Charter during Lord Killanin's presidency was followed by the opening up of the Games to professional athletes in almost all sports. This contributed to the dramatic increase in sponsorship and television revenues for the Olympic Movement. The development of a worldwide Olympic network of sponsors and the pressure for Ueberroth to finance the Los Angeles Games without public money characterised the true beginning of commercialisation. In the previous period sponsorship constituted a few well-placed logos with the simple aim of brand recall, but during this period some sponsorships turned into close partnerships which opened up many new promotional opportunities for the Olympic Movement and host cities. The prospect of high revenues from both sponsorship and television attracted the interest of many cities to host the Olympics. This fundamental

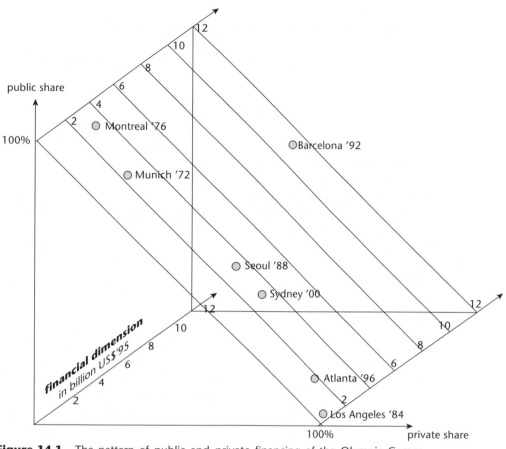

Figure 14.1   The pattern of public and private financing of the Olympic Games, 1972–2000

Source: Preuss, 2000a: 34

change secured the financial independence of the Olympic Movement and contributed to the ending of the political and financial crises of the 1970s and 1980s described in detail by Hoberman (1986).

The first Games of this period were those in Los Angeles, 1984. At the election on 1 July 1978, there were no candidates except for Los Angeles, which had failed in its bid for the Games of 1980 and 1976. The deficit of Montreal's Games encouraged the citizens of Los Angeles to vote against public financial support of the Olympics (Agreement, 1978). The OCOG promised to

meet the city's costs for security, transportation and other services which were not covered by the 0.5 per cent hotel tax and 6 per cent surcharge on the entrance tickets (Ueberroth et al., 1985: 121–2). The absence of other bidders and the lack of public financial support enabled, and indeed forced, the OCOG to impose conditions that the IOC would not otherwise have agreed to (Hill, 1992: 159; Reich, 1986: 24; Ueberroth et al., 1985: 53). After long negotiations, stipulations in the Olympic Charter were eventually declared void, thereby allowing the City of Los Angeles to

Box 14.3   The history of financing sources

1896   Stamps, private donations, tickets, commemorative medals, advertisements in the official programme
1912   Olympic lottery
1924   Advertising inside the venue (once only)
1928   Copyright of Olympic emblems – first form of merchandising
1932   First Olympic pin (merchandising) and sponsoring
1948   Identification of television rights – which started in 1960
1951   First commemorative coin
1952   Concept of international marketing
1964   Surcharge to 'Olympic cigarettes' (merchandising)
1968   First mascot 'Schuss' (merchandising)
1972   Concept of licensees
1985   TOP-Program (worldwide sponsoring)
1996   International pin trading society

decline a number of financial obligations associated with the Games (see Olympic Charter 1978 in comparison to that of 1979). These Games were the first in history without organisational links to the host city and the first to be financed from purely private sources; not surprisingly, little was invested in the transport infrastructure and in sports facilities. The overall cost of the Games amounted to a mere US$602m, which was covered by the OCOG revenues. There was even an official surplus of US$335m that was distributed between the United States Olympic Committee, the Amateur Athletic Foundation and the support of national institutions of Olympic sports (Taylor and Gratton, 1988: 34). The Games of Los Angeles marked the transition from Games that relied overwhelmingly on public money to Games that were now increasingly dependent on private finance.

However, public finance was still important, especially when the state had clear objectives to achieve, as illustrated by the Seoul Games. The Korean state was keen to

use the Games, *inter alia*, to demonstrate the country's economic growth, to improve its status in international sport, and to establish diplomatic relations with both communist and non-aligned nations (Park, 1991: 2–5). Additionally, the state wanted to promote the country for tourism and to market Korean products in order to stimulate foreign trade. Consequently, 53 per cent of the costs were covered by public finance (Kim et al., 1989: 42) and the alleged surplus of almost US$148m must be qualified in view of this large public contribution (Hill, 1992: 93).

The Barcelona public authorities also used the Games for the achievement of public policy objectives, in this case the redevelopment of the city and its promotion as a rival to Madrid, as an international site for industry and tourism. These reasons were used to justify the substantial public investment during the Olympiad and to create within the city and the province of Catalonia the desired impetus to make good the long-term under-investment in leisure, culture, sport and transportation during previous decades (Millet, 1995: 191). Despite public investment amounting to US$6.2bn, the share of privately financed, Games-related expenditures at 38 per cent, was still substantial. The official profit of only US$3m must also be treated with some scepticism (Brunet, 1993: 113).

Soon after the award of the Games to Atlanta, which appeared to be the most commercialised Games of the modern era, Samaranch commented:

Marketing has become an increasing important issue ... The revenues derived from television, sponsorship and general fundraising help to provide the Movement with its financial independence. However, in developing these programs, we must always remember that it is sport that must control its destiny, not commercial interests. (Samaranch, 1992: 2)

Similar to Los Angeles 1984, the city of Atlanta refused to accept any significant financial obligations. The OCOG had to use mainly private sources which promoted commercialisation. Compared to Seoul and Barcelona, the Games of 1996 had a very small budget with the overall Games-related expenditure amounting to US$2bn (OC Atlanta, 1998: 222; French and Disher, 1997: 384). The city infrastructure hardly changed, although a few new sports facilities were erected. After the Games many facilities were reconstructed, seat capacity was reduced and temporarily erected facilities disappeared. With the exception of the publicly funded rowing facility, all sports sites were financed by the OCOG. As a result, the Games did not produce a surplus, much to the irritation of the IOC. The hoped-for surplus was supposed to support the Olympic Movement but instead was used to pay for the Olympic Stadium which would subsequently serve as a baseball stadium for the Atlanta Braves.

The final period, 1997–2008, started with the Olympiad of Sydney 2000. This time the OCOG was only responsible for staging the Games, while the Olympic Co-ordination Authority (OCA), established in 1995, was responsible for delivering the infrastructure for the Games. The investment in infrastructure was almost US$1bn (NSW Government, 2001: 6.5). Sydney staged the XXVII Olympic Games with a budget of US$3bn (Audit Office, 1999: 59, 161, 156, 157). Learning from negative effects of OCOG's independence from the city of Atlanta, this period is marked by mixed financing of the Games.

For over 20 years commercialisation has had a decisive influence on the Olympic Movement. The extent of dependency on commerce has forced a reassessment of the relationships by the IOC in order to avoid over-commercialisation and to strengthen the Olympic ideals. Consequently, the IOC puts increasing effort into raising the sponsors' understanding of how to use the Olympic ideals for their commercial purposes without corrupting them. Today the IOC tends to favour developing long-term contracts with sponsors and TV networks in order to develop a more mutually beneficial relationship. As a result, the IOC took direct control of the negotiations with both TOP sponsors and the television companies. On the one hand the power of the IOC increased; on the other hand the financial risk of bidding cities decreased owing to the fact that the IOC now provides 40 per cent of the OCOG revenues before the selection of the next host is complete.

INTERESTS AND THE STAGING OF THE OLYMPIC GAMES

The range of interests involved in the staging of the Olympic Games is wide and

> **Box 14.4   Major objectives of host cities and countries**
>
> - *Promotion of a new image*: e.g. Munich 1972, Korea 1988, Sydney 2000
> - *City redevelopment*: e.g. Munich 1972, Montreal 1976, Seoul 1988, Barcelona 1992, Torino 2006
> - *Demonstration/promotion of a political system*: e.g. Moscow 1980, Los Angeles 1984
> - *Increase in tourism*: e.g. Barcelona 1992, Sydney 2000
> - *Enhance city status*: e.g. Barcelona 1992, Atlanta 1996, Nagano 1998
> - *Increasing inward investment*: e.g. Lillehammer 1994, Barcelona 1992, Atlanta 1996, Nagano 1998

differs from host to host. To identify the interested parties, and especially to identify 'winners', we have to look at the pattern of financial and ideological support at the bidding stage of the process of host selection. All interests that are mentioned here are drawn from specific Games and while some common patterns emerge, caution is required regarding generalisation because of the distinctive socio-cultural, political, historical and economic circumstances of each country.

The first interest is the *regional groupings of IOC members* whose cultural identity is, according to Huntington (1996: 315–16), an important factor in determining how their vote is cast (see also Persson, 2000: 157–61; Preuss, 2000b). The second interest is that of the *host governments* who recognise the value of the Games in three particular areas, namely international relations, national morale and public relations. As regards international relations, the Seoul Games, for example, were an opportunity for the government to attempt to improve relations with North Korea and other socialist countries as well as to raise international awareness of Korean manufactured products (Kim et al., 1989: 48–66; Kramar, 1994: 141–84). The extra resources that are usually

invested in developing the country's high-performance athletes prior to the Games provide a useful diplomatic resource, as the athletes give the country a higher profile at international sports events (Bernard and Busse, 2000). In addition, the host nation stages more international sports events before and after the Olympic Games; this provides further opportunities for strengthening links with foreign nations. Prior to the Sydney Games almost every member of the Olympic squad competed internationally between September 1999 and March 2000, which included participation in seven World Cups (OC Sydney, 2000: 75).

As regards improvements to national morale, the Seoul Olympics created 'a national perspective, a feeling of vitality, taking part, being recognised, modern and technologically up-to-date' (Denis et al., 1988: 229). However, in addition to feelings of enhanced national pride, hosting the Games can also lead to a deeper understanding of disability through hosting of the Paralympic Games or a greater motivation to participate in sport as a result of watching the Games. Finally, the Games also provide important public relations opportunities. In earlier times one motivation to stage the Games was to demonstrate

> **Box 14.5   Interest groups and the Olympic Games**
>
> - *IOC members*: cultural and geographical interests
> - *State*: interests in improvement of international relations, positive psychological aspects for inhabitants and chance to demonstrate changes, such as modernisation
>
> - *Politicians of the host city*: interest in
>   - increased tourism;
>   - becoming a 'global city';
>   - getting recognised by the capital city;
>   - a huge one-time economic boost;
>   - rapid city development;
>   - career enhancement.
>
> - *Local construction industry*: additional local demand for construction and international contracts
> - *National sponsors*: interest in using the Games to improve relations to customers, contractors, partners and employees
> - *TV networks*: interest in broadcasting the Games live during 'Prime Time'.

the superiority of a political system. The communist regimes of the 1970s and 1980s as well as the German Reich in 1936 saw the Games as a chance to prove the superiority of their systems. More recently, the motivation has been to announce or demonstrate to the world major changes in the host country. For example, Munich wanted to show that West Germany had rid itself of its Nazi past (Hattig, 2001). South Korea wanted to showcase its modern, high-technology national industries and replace its image as a developing country. Australia used the Games to enhance the tourist image of Australia as a whole and not just of Sydney (Morse, 2001) and was keen to raise its international profile as being more than merely 'a good source for raw material' (Parker, 2001: 9). Finally, Beijing, which is to host the 2008 Games, is keen to demonstrate the growing importance of China to the world economy.

In general, the Olympic Games is the biggest advertising opportunity that a city and a country can hope for. Years before the Games, companies will promote their association with the Games. In the months before the opening ceremony, reporters will write stories about the country. And in the weeks prior to the Games, the torch relay generates further media attention. The Opening Ceremony, which showcases the culture of the host, is watched by at least 3 billion people while the Games themselves are watched by 92.5 per cent of all adults who have access to a television. The number of hours of Games coverage and the number of countries that broadcast the Games have increased at every Olympics (IOC, 2000: 5). The type and intensity of the promotion depend on the hosts and the media. In Sydney the Australian Tourist Commission (ATC) developed a strategy with well over 1,000 individual projects and provided not only good working conditions for the media, but also much additional information about Australia and Sydney (ATC, 2001: 3).

The third interest is the *politicians of the host city*, one of whose aims is to achieve a lasting increase in general tourist arrivals and in congress and convention business in particular (Dunn and McGuirk, 1999: 20; Hall, 1992: 17; Persson, 2001). This was a clear aim for both Barcelona and Sydney, and is often also the case for cities hosting the Olympic Winter Games. A second common objective of local politicians is to promote a city as a *'global city'* with the ambition to generate international investment (Weirick, 1999: 70). At present there is evidence of the development of a network of 'global cities' based on combined global and transnational-regional links through which the international economic relations of industry are co-ordinated. Olympic hosts develop the factors that are important to become a 'global city', such as new office accommodation, improvements in telecommunications, gentrification of parts of the city, first-class tourist facilities, and an international airport (Sassen, 1996: 123). In Seoul the increased awareness of the host city and its improved infrastructure stimulated the location of foreign industry and increased the sales of national products on foreign markets (Roulac, 1993: 18). A third, and related, objective of local politicians is to help host cities that are not the capital to become recognised nationally. Scott (1997) admitted that one objective of the Manchester bid was to project a sharper profile by comparison to other second-rank cities in the UK. Other examples include Barcelona establishing itself as a second centre of economic growth after Madrid, or Munich improving its status prior to the Games of 1972.

Local politicians are also concerned to stimulate the local economy by attracting funding that does not come from the city itself or which would otherwise have left the city. In this way they hope to create an economic impact, defined as a concentrated boost to the local economy. External or 'autonomous' money stems from the financial support of the state government and the OCOG. Most revenues of the OCOG are autonomous because they are from sponsors and television networks that are not located in the host city. Therefore, the argument of Olympic opponents that public funds used for the Olympic Games could be better spent on other projects has to be qualified (Preuss, 1998: 201). Politicians of Lillehammer aimed to improve the long-term employment situation by creating an autonomous economic impact through the Games in 1994 (Spilling, 2001). However, the assumption of a positive economic impact must be qualified. For a city the impact may be large because most money is external/ autonomous, but for a nation the impact will be much smaller. In addition the economic situation at the time of investment has to be considered as Olympic-related investment can lead to 'crowding out' of other possible investment. Therefore, it should not be assumed that hosting the Games is always the best way to stimulate the local or national economy (Baade, 2001).

The Games are often used as an instrument to help solve urban problems. When a city is elected host city, the time pressures that it experiences frequently lead to the breaking of deadlocks in urban planning. The Games offer the chance of achieving an acceleration of development and so may serve as a further motive for local politicians. Furthermore, association with the Games can positively affect the image of politicians. In the media the names of politicians involved in the Games are often mentioned, allowing them to 'bask in the reflected glory' (Snyder et al., 1986), as was clearly evident during Sydney 2000.

A fourth set of interests is the *local/regional construction industry* which benefits most obviously from the building of infrastructure and sport facilities. During an economic boom, the price paid for building work increases, which means that they earn more money for the same work. During a recession, companies receive additional orders which they would not otherwise have obtained. Moreover, the companies also gain publicity. Multiplex, for example, which constructed Stadium Australia, has used its Olympic credentials to win large contracts overseas, such as the contract to build Britain's new National Stadium (Parker, 2001: 9). Other local businesses may be Olympic 'partners' and also see the Games as an important, though unique, opportunity to initiate business, develop contacts, and promote their image internally and externally.

The final interest group is the *television networks*. Not only is broadcasting the Games a source of prestige, but the networks can generate profit from the sale of advertising, provided the Games can be broadcast during network 'prime time'. NBC bought the American rights to the Games between 2000 and 2008 for US$3.53bn, but due to the time difference, the viewing figures during the Sydney Games were much lower than anticipated (no author, 2000). The 2004 Games will take place in Athens and again the events will not be staged during American prime time. Consequently, there was a strong preference among American broadcasters to have the 2008 Games in Toronto or, since the Games were awarded to Beijing, to have the 2012 Games in New York, which is currently planning to bid, or at least another city located in either North or South America.

One indicator of the significance of the interests identified above is the steady increase in the number of cities bidding to host the Games since the mid-1970s (see Figure 14.2). Figure 14.2 shows that the number of bids for the Winter Games roughly equals that for the Olympic Games and that the number of bid cities for both the Winter and the Olympic Games increased after the financial success of the Games in 1984. A further rise in the number of bids was evident after 1992 owing to the success of Seoul and especially Barcelona in demonstrating the significant regenerative benefits that could be achieved through hosting the Olympics. The successful exploitation of the Games for country marketing by Australia added a further incentive to bid.

MACROECONOMIC ASPECTS OF OLYMPIC GAMES

The foregoing review of interests suggests a number of potential winners of the Olympic Games. The losers, however, only become visible through an examination of the macroeconomic aspects. The frequently claimed benefits to employment are dependent upon the size of the economic impulse. Staging the Games increases demand, which produces employment and income, with the additional income inducing further income and so on: in other words a multiplier effect. However, imports and savings reduce the impact of the unique economic impulse and within a few years the economic effect has vanished completely. Only in the period directly associated with the Games is the economic impact significant in creating new employment or securing existing jobs. Referring to this phenomenon, Preuss (2000a: 64–72) calculated that the Games in Munich

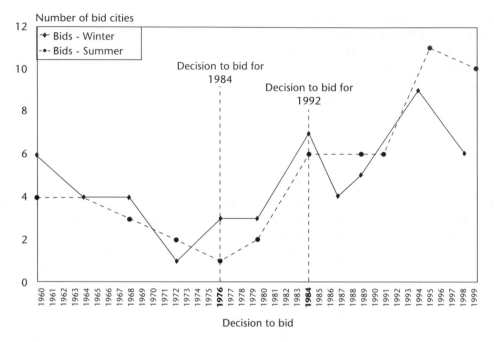

Figure 14.2   Number of bid cities two years before the election
Sources: IOC, 1997; (no author), 1993; Schollmeier, 2001: 27

created, from direct spending, employment equivalent to 23,199 person-years; 37,924 in Montreal; 28,634 in Los Angeles; 191,341 in Seoul and 281,213 in Barcelona. Through the impact of the multiplier, the effect will become greater. It is more difficult to calculate Olympic-related employment after the immediate impact has dissipated. The increased attractiveness of the city as a location for tourism, business, conventions and other high-performance sports events may induce new economic and stimulate additional economic activity.

The initial economic response to increased demand due to Olympic-related investment is to increase production, while the second reaction is to regulate demand through price adjustments. New investment will only be made if there is a strong expectation that demand will be sustained. While an increase in production or capital investment could satisfy the increased demand without the need to regulate through price, the limited capacity within business often results in price increases, thus leading to 'crowding out'. Crowding out can occur in sectors of high Olympic demand, such as construction, services and tourism. Many tourists, for example, avoid the Olympic region and some citizens of the host city will leave in order to escape the traffic congestion, noise and Olympic crowd. Consequently they spend their money outside the Olympic city (Preuss, 2002). Some potential tourists may be lost for subsequent years if they thereby discover a new tourist destination. Non-Olympic tourist attractions in the host city might be adversely affected by reallocation of consumption expenditure by local residents (Development Action Group, 1996: 16). Local politicians might also reallocate public expenditure to Olympic priorities and away from established public services, thus creating the possibility of socially unjust distribution.

Price increases, which have the potential to affect all who live in the host city, have three causes: first, the Olympics cause demand to exceed supply; second, property speculation; and third, general inflation. Leaving aside property speculation, which is often a temporary phenomenon, it is important to consider whether, and to what extent, the Games have an independent effect on the cost of living within the city. From an examination of the Olympic Games over the last 30 years it is clear that, apart from Munich and Barcelona, there was no evidence of a link between the Games and price indexes for either the cost or living or rents (Preuss, 1998: 210). The sustained rise in both indexes in Munich and Barcelona is possibly explained by the increasing economic importance of both cities within their national economies to which hosting the Games might have contributed (see Preuss, 2000a: 74–6).

However, hosting the Games increases overall demand, which leads to temporary price increases in specific sectors often due to the simple fact that shortages of some goods and services inevitably occur. Nevertheless, even temporary price rises may result in socially unjust reallocation as the poor may now be priced out of some markets (Development Action Group, 1996: 31).

The ecological effects of hosting the Games also need to be considered as most host cities commit themselves to the construction of new sports venues, parks and new transport infrastructure. Because of the increasing emphasis within the IOC and at national level on environmental issues, one could assume that the overall ecological effect is beneficial for citizens. While there might be doubts about the beneficial effect

on hosts of the Winter Games (because they are often staged in smaller cities where many sports facilities are constructed in the open country), the analysis of summer host cities is more positive, as Table 14.1 shows. An examination of the locations of Olympic sports facilities since 1972 shows clearly that brown sites were chosen that were disused or had to be decontaminated. This pattern should not be surprising, since the construction of new sports facilities requires land relatively close to the city centre and only former industrial land is likely to be affordable.

The redevelopment of these areas is often expensive but the ecological benefit from the upgrading of the area may compensate for the costs in the long term. It is clear that the Olympics help to solve some urban problems and that the improved environment benefits all classes. However, time pressure may, as Hall (1992: 131) suggests, result in a relaxation in environmental guidelines or may 'crowd out' other ecologically superior projects.

There is often considerable time pressure on cities to complete structural changes required of the host city. From the moment a city is chosen as an Olympic host city, it suffers from great time constraints as the Games cannot be postponed. If a city did not succeed in changing its infrastructure in time for the Games, it would be subject to worldwide criticism and the image of the city would be severely damaged. The time constraints and the fear of 'disgrace' provide such momentum for development activities that the period of 'normal' development is skipped (Cox et al., 1994: 35; Daume, 1976: 155; Garcia, 1993: 263; Geipel et al., 1993: 296). With the exceptions of the privately financed Olympics in Los Angeles and Atlanta, all other host cities used the period before the Games to carry out 'accelerated urban development' and

Table 14.1   *Changed land utilisation caused by the Olympic Games*

Year and location	Previous use of selected areas: ecological view	Post-Games use of selected areas: benefit for the population
1972 Munich	Disused estate, rubble, brickworks	Olympic park, traffic connection and recreational area
1988 Seoul	Contaminated site (Chamsil, Han River)	Olympic park, leisure venues (sports facilities), water purification and recreational area
1992 Barcelona	Decaying industrial site, old railway lines, run-down port	Housing, port atmosphere, parks, services complex, recreational area
1996 Atlanta	Light industrial property rife with environmental problems	Office buildings, recreational area
2000 Sydney	Contaminated site, waste dump (Homebush Bay)	Residential area, recreational area
2004 Athens	Airport, decaying industrial site next to the sea	Port atmosphere, integration of old airport as sports and recreational area

Sources: Garcia, 1993: 251–70; Geipel et al., 1993: 287–9; Lee, 1988: 60–1; OCA, 1998

realised long-term plans in a short time-span. Frequently, the external pressures help to resolve internal urban conflicts and break logjams between planners, politicians and citizens regarding important projects. Internal compromises are often a response to the pressure for unity in the face of potential external critics. For example, Seoul was driven by its rivalry with Japan. Barcelona's momentum came in part from its ambition for local autonomy in Spain, while Atlanta was concerned to demonstrate Southern capability to the Northern states. Host cities were therefore concerned to demonstrate their efficiency and capacity not only to the world as a whole, but also to certain particular rivals.

While the 'acceleration effect' of the Games on planning decisions may be welcome, there is always the danger of irreversible planning errors due to time pressure, the 'crowding out' of other more worthwhile projects due to the shortage of public investment, or the infringements of social justice. The last point is especially important as there is considerable evidence that the deadline of the Games is used as an excuse for ignoring the interests of socially weaker groups. Evidence suggests that socially deprived groups are especially affected by airport expansion, road building or decisions on the location of the Olympic village. The Olympic Games have given urban planners a justification to evacuate whole suburbs and relocate the residents (Development Action Group, 1996: 9), as occurred in Atlanta (Gladitz and Günther, 1995), Barcelona, Seoul (Denis et al., 1988: 230) and Munich.

Moreover the impact of urban land use planning for the Games often alters the balance between public and private space and the capacity of certain groups to access remaining public space (Siebel, 1994: 18).

Not only is public space privatised, but remaining public space is redeveloped for use by the adult customer with purchasing power and not for children, the elderly or the poor. Thus, the city loses a major element of its urbanity, namely its openness to the public as a whole. Host cities appear to enhance the quality of public space by installing pedestrian precincts or public parks, but the precincts contain shops for the affluent and the parks host fee-paying events. Poorer social groups gain little benefit if they are excluded by cost from the attractive post-Games leisure events or are priced out of the market for the housing that replaced their previous dwellings. The gentrification of residential areas produces socially exclusive housing near the city centre in an attractive and vibrant city atmosphere (Development Action Group, 1996: 9).

THE WINNERS AND LOSERS

The foregoing macroeconomic analysis indicates that it is possible to identify those social groups or interests who receive a net increase in benefits from the hosting of the Olympic Games (i.e. the winners) and that these can be distinguished from those with a decrease in net benefits level (i.e. the losers). However, due to the complexity of the interrelationships the effects can only be described on a relatively abstract level.

It is assumed in Figure 14.3 that the Olympics have had a positive effect on the city image and that there was a financial

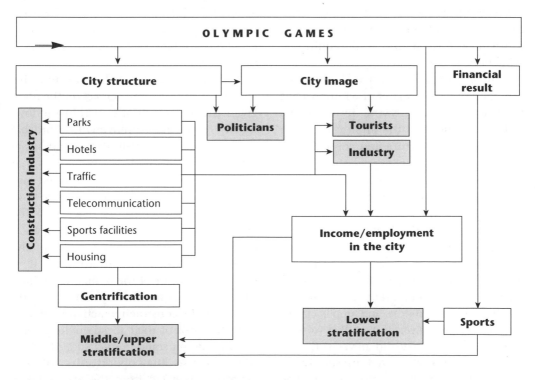

Key: direction of positive effect

Figure 14.3   'Winners' of the overall economic effects of the Olympic Games

surplus. The first group of 'winners' is the local politicians who have been able to use the external resources flowing into the city, such government subsidies, plus the reallocations within the city budget to change the structure of the city according to their political priorities. Frequently, their arguments for implementing certain projects are justified by claims that the Olympic Games 'demand' a certain structure or certain facilities within the city. The second group of 'winners' is the construction industry, which can confidently expect to receive contracts for extensive construction projects including parks, hotels, roads, sports facilities, housing, and sometimes convention and trade fair centres. Many of these projects contribute to the gentrification of areas of the city, a process that benefits higher-income groups which constitute the third set of 'winners'. The fourth group is tourists who benefit from an improved tourism infrastructure and additional attractions in the host city.

A further group of 'winners' is the city's general population, many of whom benefit from the general upswing in economic activity produced by the improvements to the urban infrastructure and consequently to the image of the city. Although the extent of Games-related economic activity differs greatly between the host cities reviewed here, the improved structure, the better image and the higher expenditures produced higher income and additional employment in all host cities. The frequently made criticism that additional income and employment only benefit members of the middle and upper classes must be rejected. Even if unskilled workers were underpaid, they did have work and their income was improved, irrespective of the duration of their employment. The capacity of the Games to create jobs and protect existing jobs is frequently overlooked.

The generality of the city's population may also benefit if the Games produces a surplus. Normally, any surplus is distributed between the IOC, the NOC of the host country and various institutions that promote sport in the city. The last-mentioned recipients have the potential to use the income to the benefit of citizens irrespective of their social status. The city can maximise its financial benefit if it can persuade the OCOG to invest an anticipated surplus before the final balance is compiled, thus avoiding the risk of money being siphoned out of the city to the host country NOC or, via the IOC, to the NOCs of other countries and the international federations.

Turning attention to the 'losers', Figure 14.4 identifies the groups that were negatively affected by Olympic Games. In this scenario it is assumed that the Games negatively affected the image of the city and that they were run at a financial deficit. The fact that even this scenario will produce winners is not ignored.

It is not surprising that many negative effects have the greatest impact on the poor, given the obvious priority within the low-income group for employment, affordable housing, adequate medical care and social integration. Hosting the Games means that other projects in the city are crowded out, as indicated by (1) in Figure 14.4. Prior to the Games, the sites of newly erected Olympic facilities were often housing areas of the poor (former workers' areas in the vicinity of industrial enterprises). It is exactly this sector of the population which suffers from expropriation and relocation caused by the construction activities, which leads to a loss of their social environment. Without doubt some municipal authorities tried to use the opportunity of the Olympics to expel from the area socially marginal groups, such as the homeless, street traders and prostitutes who, in their

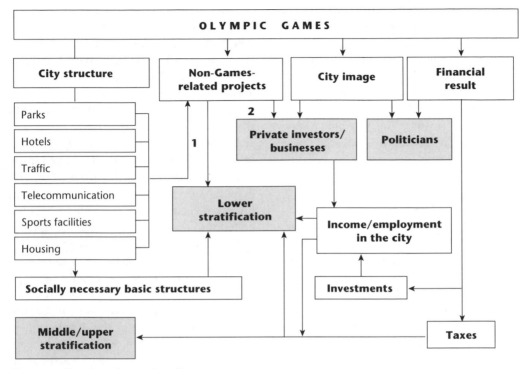

Key ⟶ direction of negative effect

Figure 14.4 'Losers' of the overall economic effects of the Olympic Games

opinion, conflict with the image of a modern city open to tourism which they are attempting to manufacture. (For Los Angeles and Seoul, see no author, 1996; for Barcelona see Garcia, 1993: 260–1); for Atlanta, see Gladitz and Günther, 1995; in general see Lenskyj, 1996: 395). It must also be noted that the poor are forced out of their residential areas not just by major construction projects but also by the subsequent gentrification of areas (Cox et al., 1994: 75).

If the Olympics worsens the image of the host city or prevents investments in non-Games-related projects because of a strong reallocation of resources, the general economic activity in the host city (2) is negatively affected. Local enterprises in the city will not expand, nor will businesses be encouraged to relocate to the city. The reduced economic activity has a negative effect on income and employment with consequences for all citizens. Should the Olympics produce a deficit that has to be covered by the city, then there are consequences for future public investment and the level of municipal taxes which may well have to rise, again producing negative effects for all citizens. The Development Action Group (1996: 31) suggest that the lessons from previous Games are clear in so far as they stress that those who pay for the Games do not necessarily profit from the Games, and that the poor are more affected by capacity constraints and therefore are far more vulnerable to eviction and displacement than middle-income groups.

When bidding for the Olympics, the risk of possible negative effects and whether they can be borne from an economic point of view must be measured. This review has shown that hosting the Olympic Games runs the risk of deepening the social polarisation in the city.

CONCLUSION

Evidence from recent Olympic Games suggests that host cities benefit in three ways: improved infrastructure; increased income/ employment; and an improved city image. Autonomous investments and consumption expenditures raise the general prosperity of the local population, but it is the upper-income groups that benefit disproportionately and, as has been suggested, there are some poorer income groups who suffer substantial dislocation of housing and community.

Even if one accepts the argument that the Olympic Games result in net benefits for the host city, the question remains whether an alternative project would have led to a higher net benefit for the city and/or a socially more just allocation. However, such a calculation is fraught with difficulty as it is so difficult to determine that the increase in benefits of one group is less valuable than that of another. Based on the Pareto optimum, it can be assumed that, economically, the Olympic Games produce greater benefits than costs to the citizens and that after taking all impacts and legacies into account, the Olympics are positive for a host city. The challenge for the future is to ensure that the general host city benefits are more evenly distributed. In future, the city could and should be integrated into the financing of the Olympics in order to enable the positive macroeconomic potential of the Olympic Games to be used for the greater benefit of socially deprived classes. However, the structure of city-based and national interest groups is such that prioritising social justice in the distribution of economic benefits over the profits of construction and redevelopment businesses is unlikely. It is possible that the IOC could link the awarding of Olympics to the publication of an acceptable plan for the distribution of economic benefits. However, given the close links between the IOC and international business and its general reluctance to interfere in the internal political decisions of the bid cities, such an expanded role for the Committee might be welcome but is unlikely.

Chapter summary

- Since the 1980s OCOGs can be confident that they will be able to host the Games and produce a surplus of revenues over operating costs.
- The Games now require a huge infrastructure for athletes, tourists and the media, which often involves substantial urban restructuring in most host cities affecting a wide range of interests and dividing them into winners and losers.
- Improvement to a city's image from media coverage can lead to increased tourism and conference business and also to business relocation and a consequent increase in jobs and tax income to the city.

(Continued)

(Continued)

- While some consequences of hosting the Olympic Games will benefit all social groups, in general upper-income groups derive greater advantages than the poor, who are less likely to benefit from gentrification, a new airport, less public space, expensive entertainment or a new fibre-optic network.

Further reading

A more detailed analysis of the economic consequences of hosting the Olympic Games is provided in Preuss (2000a). Studies of individual Games include Atlanta (French and Disher, 1997), Seoul (Kim et al., 1989; Park, 1991) and Barcelona (Millet, 1995). Lenskyj (2000) provides an extended critical review of the Sydney Olympic Games.

NOTE

1 All financial sums are expressed in 1995 dollars.

REFERENCES

Agreement (1978) between IOC and the City of Los Angeles (27 Oct.), typescript.

ATC (Australia Tourist Commission) (2001) 'Olympic Games tourism strategy. Overview', Sydney, typescript.

Audit Office (1999) 'Performance audit report. The Sydney 2000 Olympic and Paralympic Games. Review of estimates'. Sydney, typescript.

Baade, Robert (2001) 'Assessing the economic impact of the Summer Olympic Games: the experience of Los Angeles and Atlanta'. Paper presented at the International Conference of the Panhellenic Association of Sports Economists & Managers, Athens.

Bernard, Andrew B. and Busse, Meghan R. (2000) 'Who wins the Olympic Games? Economic development and medals totals'. Working paper no. 7998. National Bureau of Economic Research, Cambridge, MA.

Brunet, Ferrán (1993) *Economy of the 1992 Barcelona Olympic Games*. Lausanne: IOC Publications.

Commission of Inquiry (n.d.) 'Report of the Commission of Inquiry into the cost of the 21st Olympiad' Montreal, Vol. 1, typescript.

Coubertin, Pierre de (1913) 'La question d'argent', *Revue Olympique*, 13 (12): 183–5.

Cox, G., Darcy, M. and Bounds, M. (1994) 'The Olympics and housing. A study of six international events and analysis of potential impacts of the Sydney 2000 Olympics'. Paper prepared for the Shelter NSW and Housing and Urban Studies Research Group University of Western Sydney, Macarthur.

Daume, W. (1976) 'Organising the Games', in Lord Killanin and J. Rodda (eds), *The Olympic Games. 80 Years of People, Events and Records*. London: Barrie & Jenkins, pp. 153–6.

Denis, M., Dischereit, E., Song, D.-Y. and Werning, R. (1988) *Südkorea. Kein Land für friedliche Spiele*. Reinbeck: rororo.

Development Action Group (1996) *The Olympics and Development. Lessons and Suggestions*. Observatory, South Africa.

Dunn, K.M. and McGuirk, P.M. (1999) 'Hallmark events', in R. Cashman and A. Hughes (eds), *Staging the Olympics. The Event and Its Impact*. Sydney: Griffin Press, pp. 18–34.

French, Steven P. and Disher, Mike E. (1997) 'Atlanta and the Olympics. A one-year retrospective', *Journal of the American Planning Association*, 63 (3): 379–92.

Garcia, S. (1993) 'Barcelona und die Olympischen Spiele', in H. Häusermann and W. Siebel (eds), *Festivalisierung der Stadtpolitik. Stadtentwicklung durch große Projekte* in Leviathan. Zeitschrift für Sozialwissenschaft. Special vol. 13. Opladen, pp. 251–77.

Geipel, R., Helbrecht, I. and Pohl, J. (1993) 'Die Münchener Olympischen Spiele von 1972 als Instrument der Stadtentwicklungspolitik', in H. Häusermann and W. Siebel (eds), *Festivalisierung der Stadtpolitik. Stadtentwicklung durch große Projekte* in Leviathan. Zeitschrift für Sozialwissenschaft. Special vol. 13. Opladen, pp. 278–304.

Georgiadis, Konstantinos (2000) 'Die ideengeschichtliche Grundlage der Erneuerung der Olympischen Spiele im 19. Jahrhundert in Griechenland und ihre Umsetzung 1896 in Athen'. PhD dissertation, Johannes Gutenberg-Universität, Mainz.

Gladitz, R. and Günther, W. (1995) 'Das Spiel mit den Spielen. Ein Themenabend: Atlanta und die Olympiade'. Broadcast by the TV station *Arte* (18 Jan. 1996, 23:05 hrs).

Hall, C.M. (1992) *Hallmark Tourist Events. Impacts, Management & Planning.* London: Belhaven.

Hattig, Fritz (2001) Member of the Bid Committee for Munich 1972. Interview in Mainz.

Hill, Christopher R. (1992) *Olympic Politics.* Manchester: Manchester University Press.

Hoberman, John (1986) *The Olympic Crisis. Sport, Politics and the Moral Order.* New Rochelle, NY: Aristide D. Caratzas.

Huntington, Samuel P. (1996) *Kampf der Kulturen. Die Neugestaltung der Weltpolitik im 21. Jahrhundert.* Munich and Vienna: Europaverlag.

International Olympic Committee (IOC) (1978) *Olympic Charter.* Lausanne: IOC Publications.

International Olympic Committee (1979) *Olympic Charter.* Lausanne: IOC Publications.

International Olympic Committee (1993) 'Les villes candidates à l'organisation des Jeux de la XXVIIe Olympiade en 2000', *Message Olympique*, 36: 1–68.

International Olympic Committee (1997) *Report of the IOC Evaluation Commission for the Games of the XXVIII Olympiad 2004*, Lausanne: IOC Publications.

International Olympic Committee (2000) 'Marketing Matters', No. 17.

Killanin, Lord (1982) 'The Olympic Movement since Varna', in IOC (ed.), *Report of the XIth Olympic Congress in Baden-Baden.* Vol. 1. Lausanne: IOC Publications.

Kim, J.-G., Rhee, S.-W., Yu, J.-Ch., Koo, K.-M. and Hong, J.-Ch. (1989) *Impact of the Seoul Olympic Games on National Development.* Korea Development Institute. Seoul: KDI Press.

Kramar, M.A. (1994) 'Development of East European and Soviet direct trade relations with South Korea, 1970–1991'. PhD dissertation, Florida State University, Tallahassee.

Landry, Fernand and Yerlès, Magdeleine (1996) *The International Olympic Committee: One Hundred Years. The Idea – the Presidents – the Achievements.* Vol. 3. Lausanne: IOC Publications.

Lee, Charles (1988) 'From wartime rubble to Olympic host', *Far Eastern Economic Review*, 140 (36): 60–5.

Lenskyj, Helen J. (1996) 'When winners are losers. Toronto and Sydney bids for the Summer Olympics', *Journal of Sport & Social Issues*, 20 (4): 392–410.

Lenskyj, Helen J. (2000) *Inside the Olympic Industry: Power, Politics and Activism.* New York: State University of New York.

Millet, Lluís (1995) 'The Games of the city', in Miguel de Moragas and Miguel Botella (eds), *The Keys to Success.* Barcelona: Centre d'Estudis Olímpics i de l'Esport.

Morse, John (2001) 'The Olympic Games and Australian tourism'. Paper presented at the world conference on Sport & Tourism, Barcelona.

(no author) (1993) 'Olympiasonderdienst des sid', news of the AGSPORT agency, 23 August.

(no author) (1996) 'Olympics 2004', *Argus* (South Africa), 14 February.

(no author) (2000) 'Sydney gives NBC their lowest ratings since Tokyo in '64', *The Sydney Morning Herald.* Internet, 1 October.

NSW Government (2001) *Budget Statement 2001–2002, Sydney 2000 Olympic and Paralympic Games.* Sydney, pp. 6.1–6.10.

OC Atlanta (1998) *Official Report of the XXVI Olympic Games.* Vol. 1. Atlanta.

OC Montreal (1976) *Games of the XXI. Olympiad, Montreal 1976, Official Report.* Vol. 1. Montreal.

OC Munich (1974) *Die Spiele – Die Organisation.* Vol. 1. Munich.

OC Sydney (2000) *The Games of the XXVII Olympiad. Sports Commission Report 1996–2000.* Sydney.

OCA (Olympic Co-ordination Authority) (1998) 'Environment fact sheet: clean up'. Sydney.

Park, Seh-Jik (1991) *The Seoul Olympics. The Inside Story*. London: Bellew Publishing.

Parker, Lesley (2001) 'Business lands', *Clayton UTZ Magazine*, pp. 7–9.

Persson, Christer (2000) 'The Olympic host selection process'. PhD dissertation, University of Technology, Lulea.

Persson, Christer (2001) President of the Bidding Committee Östersund 2002. Letter of 11 March.

Preuss, Holger (1998) 'Problematizing arguments of the opponents of Olympic Games', in R.K. Barney, K.G. Wamsley, S.G. Martyn and G.H. MacDonald (eds), *Global and Cultural Critique: Problematizing the Olympic Games. Fourth International Symposium for Olympic Research*. London, ON: University of Western Ontario, pp. 197–218.

Preuss, Holger (2000a) *Economics of the Olympic Games. Hosting the Games from 1972 to 2000*. Sydney: Walla Walla Press.

Preuss, Holger (2000b) 'Electing an Olympic host city: a multidimensional decision', in K.G. Wamsley, G.H. MacDonald, S.G. Martyn and R.K. Barney (eds), *Bridging Three Centuries: Intellectual Crossroads and the Modern Olympic Movement. Fifth International Symposium for Olympic Research*. London, ON: University of Western Ontario, pp. 89–104.

Preuss, Holger (2002) 'Le implicazioni economiche delle Olimpiadi', in L. Bobbio and Ch. Guala (eds), Olimpiadi e grandi eventi. Rome: Verso Torino 2006, pp. 37–55.

Reich, K. (1986) *Making It Happen: Peter Ueberroth and the 1984 Olympics*. Santa Barbara, CA: Capra Press.

Roulac, S.E. (1993) 'Place wars and the Olympic Games', *Futurist*, 6: 18–19.

Samaranch, Juan Antonio (1992) 'Message from the IOC President', in *Olympic Solidarity Itinerant School*, Marketing Manual. Lausanne: IOC Publications, p. 2.

Sassen, Saskia (1996) *Metropolen des Weltmarktes. Die neue Rolle der Global Cities*. Frankfurt and New York: Campus.

Schollmeier, Peter (2001) *Bewerbungen um Olympische Spiele. Von Athen 1896 bis Athen 2004*. Germany: Books on Demand GmbH.

Scott, Robert (1997) President of the Manchester 2000 Bid Committee. Interview in Olympia.

Siebel, W. (1994) 'Was macht eine Stadt urban?', in F.W. Busch and H. Haverost (eds), *Oldenburger Universitätsreden – Ausprachen, Auspräcke, Verträge*, 61, Oldenburg.

Snyder, C.R., Lassegard, M.A. and Ford, C.E. (1986) 'Distancing after group success and failure: basking in reflected glory and cutting off reflected failure', *Journal of Personality and Social Psychology*, 51 (2): 382–8.

Spilling, Olav (2001) Unpublished letter to author, 23 May.

Taylor, P. and Gratton, Chris (1988) 'The Olympic Games: an economic analysis', *Leisure Management*, 8 (3): 32–4.

Ueberroth, P., Levin, R. and Quinn, A. (1985) *Made in America. His Own Story*. New York: William Morrow & Co.

Weirick, James (1999) 'Urban design', in R. Cashman and A. Hughes (eds), *Staging the Olympics. The Event and Its Impact*. Sydney: Griffin Press, pp. 70–82.

15

Sport and Recreation and the Environment

MICHAEL F. COLLINS

Overview

→ Growing professional/academic interest in sport and the environment
→ Sport in the built environment
→ Sport in the natural environment – can the countryside take it?
→ Mega-events and facilities – case study of the Albertville and Lillehammer Olympics
→ Conclusions

GROWING PROFESSIONAL AND ACADEMIC INTEREST IN SPORT AND THE ENVIRONMENT

Awareness of the need to protect the natural environment has been growing since the 1960s, but was focused by the World Commission on Environment and Development's report *Our Common Future* in 1986 and subsequent international conferences (Da Costa, 2001). Six years later it was highlighted by the Rio (de Janeiro) Earth Summit Conference and the obvious adverse impacts of the Albertville Winter Olympic Games. Rio led to a popularisation of the concept of sustainability, which can be defined as: ways to meet 'the needs of the present without compromising the ability of future generations to meet their own needs' (see Box 15.1).

As Lenskyj (1998: 341) has pointed out, except for golf and downhill skiing, sport has received relatively little criticism for its environmental impact until recently. By the same token there has been only limited research. Chernushenko (1994: 15–17) described how the great majority of sport is now undertaken in either modified natural settings like skiing pistes, grass pitches and courts, rowing courses, or in purpose-built facilities rather than natural environments. Vuolle (1991: 602) pointed out that this has a generational effect whereby younger people are socialised or acclimatised to taking part in these artificial settings, and 'distanced from nature'. Incidentally, it allows more of sport, both participant and spectator to be packaged and 'commodified'.

Oittinen and Tiezzi (1998) argued for sustainable sport on three levels:

Box 15.1   Sustainable and unsustainable actions according to Nickerson (1990)

Sustainable actions

1 Use materials in continuous cycles
2 Use continuously reliable energy sources
3 Spring from human qualities (of creativity, communication, co-ordination, appreciation)

Unsustainable actions

1 Require continual input of non-renewable resources
2 Use renewable resources faster than their renewal
3 Cause cumulative degradation of the environment

1 *The global*: being responsible to the planet and future generations and protecting the quality of sites where sport is played.
2 *The institutional*: taking into account international obligations, the carrying capacity of sites, combining ecology with economy, and making environmental protection a criterion for marketing, financial and sponsorship decisions.
3 *The individual*: where every citizen has equal opportunity for sport as close to home as possible (to minimise transport costs), all year round, and wherever possible through multiple use (to reduce land and energy use).

Oittinen and Tiezzi went on to provide perhaps the broadest view of sport's impacts, concentrating on those on the natural environment, referring in particular to golf, skiing, shooting, orienteering, motor sports, water sports and big events like the Olympics. UK Sports Council (1998) in its *An Agenda for Sport and the Environment* drew up a more slender 'checklist' for commissioning new facilities involving prior assessment of biotic impact, energy-efficient construction, minimising transport and waste disposal, and requiring bidders and

managers of events to adhere to environmentally green operating conditions.

In the UK greater attention has been paid to the impact of countryside sport rather than urban sport, particularly to walking on turf and disturbance of bird life (Sidaway, 1990, 1994). It could be argued that the impacts on townscapes are more neglected, and it is on those impacts that this chapter now focuses.

SPORT IN THE BUILT ENVIRONMENT

Much of the work has focused around high-profile events, mainly held in or near cities generally called hallmark (Whitson and Mcintosh, 1993) or mega-events (Rooney, 1976; Roche, 1994). The emphasis of such research has tended to be on economic impacts (see Collins and Jackson, 1999). Table 15.1 outlines the sorts of impacts mega-events can have. For all the furious competition to host mega-events like the Olympics or to attract franchises in the four main American stadium sports, some say that the economic effects are short-lived, and that either they have no long-term effect on a city's economy, or even a depressing one, through employing many

Box 15.2   UK Sport's typology of events

		No. in UK 1997
A:	irregular, one-off events generating significant economic activity and media interest, e.g. World Cup, Olympics, Euro '96	none
B:	also major events, part of an annual cycle, e.g. FA Cup Final, Wimbledon	43
C:	irregular, one-off major events generating limited economic activity, e.g. European Junior boxing/swimming etc. championships, World badminton, IAAF Grand Prix	248 (for both C and D)
D:	Major events generating limited economic activity, part of an annual cycle, often not generating economic benefits commensurate to costs, e.g. national championships in most sports	

unskilled, low-income workers. Indeed, it can also be argued that little account is generally taken of the opportunity cost of investing in the stadiums or arenas (Baade, 1995). UK Sport (UK Sports Council, 1998, 1999a, 1999b) measured the economic impacts of six world and European events, distinguished between spectator- and competitor-driven events, and constructed a typology (Box 15.2).

Apart from these debates on the economic costs and benefits of major events, there are other significant impacts that have been neglected.

Visual impact

Exciting as major stadiums and arenas can look when full of spectators, light and fireworks, their stands and halls are large and more often than not ugly concrete or brick constructions. Many stadiums, especially for soccer, date from the late nineteenth and early twentieth centuries, and are in inner cities, physically and psychologically overshadowing the housing, often of the poorer groups (Bale, 1990; Churchman, 1995). Many modern stands are huge, unattractive and dominate their surroundings, even if it is possible occasionally to lessen the impact by burying them partly in holes or slopes.

Nevertheless not all stadium designs are poor or intrusive, and good design can lead to 'landmark' buildings that are a credit to their architects, clubs and communities. Examples include the Reebok Stadium on the edge of Bolton and Pride Park on industrial wasteland near Derby rail station. To pay their large costs (£40–60m) they become multifunctional places for rallies and pop concerts, and have a multitude of

Table 15.1   *Impacts of major facilities and events*

Impact	Positive	Negative
Economic	• Increased expenditure and jobs (Euro '96, Sydney Olympics) • Base for winning subsequent events (Barcelona/Calgary Olympics, Sheffield World Student Games [WSG])	• Price 'hikes' during event (Atlanta OG) • Exaggerated benefits/legacy of debts (Montreal OG, Sheffield WSG) • Real estate speculation (Sydney OG, US stadiums) • Under-used facilities after event (Calgary ice rink)
Tourism/ Commerce	• Increased awareness of region for tourism/jobs (Lillehammer/Seoul/Olympics, Fremantle America's Cup)	• Poor reputation as a result of failures/shortcomings (Atlanta Olympics traffic/prices/information) • Failure to attract/retain long-haul tourists (Fremantle Admiral's Cup) • Crowding out of regular/expected visitors (almost any mega-event)
Physical	• New/improved facilities/regenerated environments (Barcelona/Sydney Olympics, Sheffield WSG) • Improved local facilities (Sheffield WSG)	• Environmental damage (Albertville Olympics) • Litter/noise/traffic accidents (Adelaide Grand Prix) • Overcrowding (almost any mega-event) • Reduction of local facilities (Sheffield WSG swimming)
Socio-cultural	• Permanent increase in interest/participation in sport after event • Strengthening regional traditions/values	• Commercialisation of personal/private activities (ice hockey in UK, Rugby Union World Cup) • Excessive drinking/thefts/muggings/hooliganism (some England soccer matches overseas) • Modify event for tourism (Edinburgh Festival)
Psychological	• Increased National/regional pride (England 1966 World Cup, Seoul Olympics) • Greater awareness of outsiders' perceptions (Moscow Olympics)	• Defensive local attitudes • Misunderstandings/visitor hostility (Atlanta Olympics)
Political	• Enhanced reputation of host for investors (Barcelona OG, Adelaide GP) • Unify a nation (Montreal OG) • Distinguish region/nation (Seoul/Barcelona OG) • Propagation of political values (Berlin/Moscow OG)	• Exploitation of local people – displaced poor (Moscow/Mexico OG) • Distortion of event to reflect political values (Berlin/Moscow OG)

Sources: adapted from Ritchie, 1988; Whitson and Macintosh, 1993; Collins and Jackson, 1999; Taylor, 2001

meeting/conference/catering and indoor sport spaces under the stands, all increasing the range and weight of their environmental 'footprints', in terms of noise, litter, traffic and hours of operation.

Traffic and noise

Stadiums provide theatres for spectacle for some of the largest frequent gatherings of humankind, especially young men. Consequently they generate large volumes of traffic and loud crowd noises. Moreover, whether drunk or sober, some spectators create problems around the grounds, in rail and bus stations, on the streets parking their cars, often having to be shepherded by police to and from bus and rail stations. Humphries et al. (1983) termed and mapped these impacts as 'nuisance fields'. These issues, combined with the requirement for all-seater stadiums in the wake of tragic multiple deaths at Hillsborough in 1989, led to many clubs considering relocation, often on the outskirts of a city at a site adjacent to ring roads and inter-city motorways (Churchman, 1995). These may be at a distance from the homes of many fans; the news that both Liverpool and Everton were contemplating moving led a local MP to comment: 'It is essential that at least one club stays, otherwise the community is socially excluded' (Peter Kilfoyle, *Guardian Society*, 24 Oct. 2001).

Many relocation attempts fail, however, as a result of planning authorities' demands, objections to impacts on protected landscapes, or local amenity groups' opposition. Thus many clubs opt instead for refurbishing or more expensive *in situ* redevelopment. For example, by late 2000, Southampton FC had obtained planning permission to move, after more than a dozen abortive attempts and having borne the costs of feasibility studies on 19 alternative sites, environmental impact assessments and public inquiries. Likewise, with the restrictions inherent in a historic city and a fiercely protected Green Belt, Oxford United FC have been unable to devise a move from the Manor Ground despite 45 years of trying.

Sports buildings and energy use

In the total energy budget, sport is not a major user, but in temperate climates buildings like sports halls, ice rinks and swimming pools can consume large amounts of electricity or fossil fuels. Table 15.2 gives some idea of the range of annual energy consumption and cost, and carbon dioxide emissions. Pools use 3,000–4,300 kWh per sq m of actual pool surface. Buildings

Table 15.2 *Typical annual energy consumption, cost and CO_2 emissions in sports buildings (total area)*

Type	Source	Use (kWh/m²) Good to poor		Cost 1996 (£/m²) Good to poor		CO_2 (kg/m²) Good to poor	
No pool	Fossil	215	325	2.6	4.0	41	62
	Electricity	75	85	4.7	5.3	47	54
With pool	Fossil	360	540	4.4	6.6	68	100
	Electricity	150	205	9.4	12.8	95	130
Pool only	Fossil	775	1,120	9.5	13.8	150	210
	Electricity	165	235	10.3	14.7	100	150

Table 15.3   *Saving energy in sports facilities*

Area	Aim	Measures
Fabric	Reduce air intake Better insulation	Door closers/draught lobbies/insulate walls/roof/double glazing/reflective glass
Space heating	Reduce cost	Thermostats/time controls/recover exhaust heat/modern boilers/combined heat and power plant
Water heating	Reduce costs	Insulate/small point-of-use devices
Swimming pool	Reduce heat loss	Fit pool cover/heat pump/clean filters
Ventilation	Reduce cost	Variable fans/clean filters/recover waste heat
Lighting	Reduce cost	Fluorescent instead of tungsten/time controls

Sources: DETR, 1994a, 1994b, 1996, 1997

pre-dating 1980 were rarely designed with much thought paid to energy conservation, and although the Building Research Establishment has estimated that 20 per cent of cost could be saved, worth close to £200m a year in the late 1990s, many operators have not been convinced to invest in the necessary technology, despite often short pay-back periods.

There are numerous ways to save energy, as shown in Table 15.3, ranging from better staff training to closing doors, turning off dripping taps, and switching off lights in unused spaces, to installing computerised whole-building energy control systems. At the design stage, major savings can be made, for example, if an ice rink shares a site with a sports hall, or better a pool where the waste heat from the rink cooling plant can be used to warm the water in the pool and the air in either building.

While visual intrusion, noise, traffic congestion and energy consumption are important and generally under-researched issues for urban sport, it is the impact of sport on the countryside that causes the greatest friction between interest groups, and which poses the most awkward problems for policy-makers.

SPORT IN THE COUNTRYSIDE: CAN THE COUNTRYSIDE TAKE IT?

Recreational pressures on the countryside

Most Britons and overseas visitors carry an image of an idyllic countryside with small tree-lined fields, peaceful rippling streams, and picturesque villages. It is not that such places do not exist in abundance, but that they co-exist with:

- noisy arms testing, tree felling and quarrying;
- the huge fields of mechanised intensive agriculture;
- the spread of bracken on the hills;
- a shortage of jobs and affordable housing for agricultural workers;
- as high a level of rural as urban deprivation; and
- 19.6 million tourist and 18.2 million day trips annually, bringing motor cars into narrow valleys and bays, and into 'honeypot' villages and attractions in numbers never conceived or planned for (Countryside Agency, 2001).

Table 15.4   *Potential impacts of recreation*

Biological effects	Environmental effects	Physical impacts
Damaging vegetation/soils	Wear and tear, vegetation loss, fires	Wear and tear on buildings, landscapes (cumulative in popular areas)
Incremental effects		
Disturbing fauna	Disturbing fauna, local communities	Damage/disturbance/intrusion, e.g. from motor sports, mountain biking
Removal of wildlife	Inappropriate development	Inappropriate infrastructure developments, e.g. golf courses, holiday villages
Habitat loss from development	Overcrowding	
Habitat creation and improvement		
Recreational traffic		
Pollution, noise	Noise, emissions, nuisance to local communities	Traffic growth/parking
Wave erosion/turbidity from power boats		

Sources: Sidaway, 1994; DoE et al., 1995; CPRE, 1995

This has turned the countryside from a mainly productive area (crops, animals, wood, water, minerals) to a mixed economy where production co-exists with consumption (nature study, sightseeing, sport and recreation). Vigorous debate about whether the countryside can 'take it' is no new thing, having ranged from the workers' mass trespasses in the Pennines in the 1930s to the recent debate over 'the right to roam' over 4 million acres (1.8 million ha) of mountain, moor, heath, down and common land before the passage of the Countryside and Rights of Way Act 2000.

By far the most thoroughly studied impacts are those of walkers' wear and tear on vegetation, and the disturbance of birds, especially nesting or migrating waterfowl (Sidaway, 1995; see also Sidaway, 1991, 1994; Elson and Sidaway, 1995). These and other rural impacts of sport and recreation are spelled out in Table 15.4.

Despite the research of Sidaway and others, there is no consensus on the significance of the impacts. Arguments to suggest that fears of lasting and widespread environmental damage have been exaggerated include the following:

- The numbers of visits grew rapidly in the 1970s, but, whether because of a slowing down in acquiring cars, or greater commuting from home- or town-based leisure activities, the level has plateaued in recent years.
- Peak visiting has been spreading into the spring and autumn.
- While the number of people seeking active and adventurous recreations has grown, the average size of countryside sporting clubs and groups is small, mostly under 50 people, except where larger numbers are needed to finance buying land or access rights, e.g. to fishing water, gliding and flying fields or water ski sites.
- Even when there are negative impacts, they are small compared with the impact of land use changes, for housing and industry, or the removal of thousands of kilometres of hedgerows, and the heavy use of herbicides and pesticides which

have reduced biodiversity, food and cover for insects and birds throughout Britain and Europe (English Nature, 1995).

Focusing more closely on countryside sports, growth has slowed in recent years, with women's participation actually falling, possibly because more of them are in paid work and have less time for such activities. For children, outdoor activities have been downgraded in priority owing to changes in the National Curriculum. Moreover numerous local authority outdoor centres have been closed, and there are far fewer Sport Development Officers to help promote outdoor than urban sports (Glyptis et al., 1995).

A very different view was taken in the *Leisure Landscapes* study (CPRE/Lancaster, 1994), whose authors felt that golf, holiday villages and other developments were so numerous that they were changing the ethos of the countryside in a radical way. They claimed that this was being misrepresented and misunderstood in its scale and seriousness by the main agencies (Sports Council, English Tourist Board and Countryside Commission).

A parliamentary Select Committee (HC, 1995: xiv) disagreed, expressing the view that

compared to other activities, leisure and tourism do not cause significant widespread ecological damage to the countryside. However ... there are important issues to address, involving transport, rural culture, and leisure management, as well as local conflicts in specific areas.

One of the guardians of birdlife, the Royal Society for the Protection of Birds, is of the same opinion: 'Is there a problem? Yes, there is, but only in some places, and for some habitats', instancing heathland in Southern England near towns (Hounsden, 1999).

Thus experienced researchers (Sidaway, 1991; Elson and Sidaway, 1995; Curry, 1994) and the main agencies (Sports

Council, Countryside Commission, English Tourist Board) believed that the pressures were seasonal or sporadic, localised and amenable to management solutions.

There is no space here to spell out in detail the planning and management techniques for dealing with impacts and conflicts (Sidaway, 1991; Elson and Sidaway, 1995), but they depend on two principles: that of separation in space and time and that of restriction on activity. The strengths and weaknesses of the principles, with examples of their use, are set out in Table 15.5. The techniques are difficult to apply, however, in the following situations:

• where activities and impacts grow incrementally, and it is problematic to distinguish cumulative wear and tear from vandalism;
• where habitats are not resilient, e.g. mountain vegetation and sand dunes;
• where new activities are trying to obtain space to function amongst established activities, for instance, mountain biking competing with ramblers and horse riders (Berridge, 2000) and jet skiing with anglers and sailors.

Light pollution

The volume of lights from roads, advertisements and buildings in urbanised zones is such as to make whole regions seem alight when viewed from space, especially in Western Europe and North-eastern USA. The Council for the Protection of Rural England (CPRE, 2000) noted that many Britons cannot easily experience dark, and suggested that some rural areas should be designated to remain dark. With regard to sport, one of the most common local issues concerns light spilling into houses from the floodlights on playing fields; this often leads planning officers and inspectors to refuse planning permission, even when demand exists for more evening sports

Table 15.5   *Managing recreation impacts*

Strengths	Weaknesses	Examples
SEPARATION		
Zoning in space		
• Minimises impact	• Restricts freedom • May be difficult to change	• Density of use in Peak NP • Different activities • Sefton coast, large reservoirs like Rutland Water
Seasonal or daily restrictions		
• Avoids disturbance at critical times • Easier to modify	• Restricts freedom	• Water skiing on River Crouch • Fishing seasons
RESTRICTION		
Voluntary		
• Works in clubs/peer groups • Works when clear target, justified and understood message • Works where pressure is not extreme	• Does not work where mainly unaffiliated/casual • Users, or high turnover • Does not work where messages vague, no clear responsibility on clubs, individuals	• Mountain bike routes on Snowdon • Climbing on sea cliffs where birds nest • Hierarchy of green lane routes in Lake District
Management control		
• Works where need is accepted • Signposted, evident	• Restricts freedom • May be temporary and difficult to police, e.g. chasing off motor cyclists • May be regarded as arbitrary	• Walking/cycling in the Goyt Valley • Separating cycling/riding on bridleways • Water ski 10 mph limit on Lake Windermere

Sources: Glyptis et al., 1995; Elson and Sidaway, 1995; Sidaway, 1991, 1995

activity in the winter. Although lanterns and lamps have been redesigned and placed on lower poles to reduce lateral spillage, and although restrictions have been placed on hours of use, light still remains a sensitive issue for neighbours of sports grounds.

Noisy sports in 'quiet' landscapes

The 1995 Select Committee drew attention to different cultural perceptions of the countryside and nowhere is this more marked than in the matter of noisy sports.

Under the 1949 National Parks and Access to the Countryside Act, National Parks were established for two original purposes, namely preserving and enhancing rural natural beauty, and promoting its enjoyment by the public. But while John Dower, a National Park architect, spoke of town dwellers 'enjoying the peace [of the countryside], and spiritual refreshment'; another, Minister Lewis Silkin, spoke of the Act as a charter for hikers and ramblers.

From its inception in 1968, the Countryside Commission added riding, climbing, camping and cycling to walking as the main recreational beneficiaries. Quietness was first mentioned in policy documents concerned with common land in 1986, and in relation to designated areas in 1994 (Pearlman et al., 1999). In 1991 the Edwards Committee (NPRP, 1991), reviewing the purposes and management of the Parks after 40 years, supported the emphasis on 'quiet enjoyment'. Commenting on this, Adrian Phillips, a former Director of the Countryside Commission, said: 'greater public awareness of environmental concerns means there is a growing impatience with forms of recreation which do violence to the qualities of national parks, noisy sports for example and those which disturb wildlife' (Phillips, 1994: 231). The Council for National Parks (1994: 2) reinforced this view strongly: 'Quiet enjoyment should only include those activities which stem from the appreciation of natural beauty. They should be activities which require human muscle power for their pursuit, rather than rely on motorisation.'

Attempts to insert the term 'quiet enjoyment' into a private member's Bill and into the 1995 Environment Act failed. The main reason given was that a legal definition of quiet behaviour existed for a very different purpose in landlord and tenant legislation which lawyers did not wish to compromise (Pearlman et al., 1999). In addition, the subjectivity of noise and disputes over how to measure it (UKCEED, 1993) would have made it very difficult to produce a legally robust definition. The outcome was that the 1995 Act referred to 'enjoyment of the special qualities of the National Parks', and soon thereafter DoE Circular 12/96 indicated that particular activities should not be excluded from the Parks as a matter of principle, though they might not be appropriate everywhere.

It is undoubtedly true that the noise of modern society – roads, railways, airports,

industry – is spreading. The CPRE produced Tranquil Area maps for England in the 1960s and again in the 1990s, and its analysis showed a reduction of the tranquil area by 21 per cent (from 70 per cent of the country to 56 per cent), and, perhaps more important in the long term, the fragmentation and hence reduction in the size of such areas by 73 per cent (CPRE, 1995). I have asserted elsewhere (Collins, 1999) that noise in the countryside is a new target for environmental interest groups.

CASE STUDY 1: MOTORISED SPORTS IN THE LAKE DISTRICT

Water skiing – shut out of the local policy community

Water skiing at 40–70 mph requires large areas of water which are scarce inland in Britain. Boats are powerful and attractive to some onlookers, but a painful noise nuisance to others. They are also expensive, and so nearly 90 per cent of skiers take part through clubs, which can regulate usage effectively (Elson et al., 1989). Only four of the 15 larger lakes in the National Park have a public right of navigation, which, it should be noted, is indivisible and applies to all classes of boats. As activity grew and after a public inquiry, a 10 mph speed limit was imposed by byelaw in 1973 on Coniston, Derwent and Ullswater. It was informally agreed with the Sports Council that Lake Windermere should remain for sports requiring powered boats that had used the lake since the 1920s.

But the number of boats registered had trebled by the early 1990s, and 1,500 craft of all types could be found together on a busy summer's day. Two attempts to agree a management plan failed. Concerned about safety of other lake users, and the peaceful enjoyment of the valley by tourists and residents, the National Park Authority applied for another 10 mph byelaw, not challenging the legal right of navigation, but in effect regulating water skiing and power boating out of existence. The Park's policy community was divided. Supporting the idea were the two District Councils, the Countryside Commission, the Council for National Parks, the Ramblers' Association, the Youth Hostels Association, the influential Friends of the Lake District, and local amenity and sailing and canoeing groups. Opposing it were the British Water Ski Federation (BWSF), the Sports Council (with a further management plan proposal), the Cumbrian Tourist Board and local lakeside businesses, concerned about job losses.

A long and costly 48-day public inquiry was held in 1994–95; the proponents on both sides had noise experts who argued about different measurements and their meanings. Many witnesses gave evidence about the growth of boat traffic, safety, conflicts and other amenity issues. The inspector, in a massive report published in February 1996, rejected the Sports Council's proposals as not addressing the conflict issue, and recommended the byelaw to John Gummer, then Secretary of State (Alesbury, 1996). After deliberation, however, John Gummer rejected the proposal in a brief letter, and asked the parties to work on a management plan. Incensed, the Park Authority considered a High Court appeal on the grounds of inadequate consideration. However, with the coming to power of the Blair Labour government with a manifesto pledge to protect the environment, the Minister, Chris Mullin, invited new submissions.

The Sports Council and BWSF were happy to discuss a management agreement, including registering boats and licensing drivers, but the Park Authority saw no

change in circumstances and no need to re-enter debate (Collins and Ellison, 2001). In February 2000 the Minister confirmed the byelaws, to come into force in 2005, so as to give the Lakeside businesses time to adjust, saying: 'there was a fundamental problem of incompatibility in the confined area of the Lake … there is no reason why the Lake District should be expected to accommodate every recreational activity for which there is a demand'.

Now the howls of pain and cries of victory were reversed. The problem is that having searched diligently at scores of sites, no adequate alternative for water skiing could be found within 100 km, and no one was planning a new or reclaimed suitable water site.

Motor sports: getting into the local policy community

Off-road motor cycling has been a real and widespread problem for 75 per cent of English councils, dealt with more by the short-term response of using police or wardens to move trespassers on rather than attempting to produce a sustainable long-term solution by providing alternative sites. In the 1980s the search for satisfactory outcomes was hampered by the divided nature of motor sports and their poor image (Elson et al., 1986), even though major events like road rallies were well organised and caused only localised noise and negligible environmental impacts (e.g. the 1,000 Lakes Rally in Finland (Salo et al., n.d.)).

The Land Access and Rights Association (LARA) was formed and started to negotiate with local planning and highway authorities, including National Parks. Often, the use of green lanes by motor cycles or four-wheel-drive cars is challenged by landowners and environmental groups, and LARA would sooner advise its members to avoid disputes rather than have use by motor vehicles selectively barred, which can be done by a Traffic Regulation Order (TRO) (LARA, 1996).

There are 250 such 'green lanes' in the National Park, and little had been achieved over 20 years of claim and counter-claim by motorists, landowners and walkers. The NP Authority sought in the late 1990s to fulfil an objective of eliminating unsustainable use (*Park Management Plan*, 1998), but recognised the legal claims of motorists and the need for a co-operative, user-led, non-statutory management approach. With LARA, therefore, it developed the idea of a Hierarchy of Trail Routes (LARA, 1997), identifying three categories of route:

1 those that can be used by the general public with little regulation;
2 those that should be publicised only to LARA members, in compliance with a strict code of conduct; and
3 those that should not be used at all, because of erosion, or disturbance to farming or wildlife.

LARA had four principles which had to be observed if the scheme was to work (Box 15.3).

A Trail Management Advisory Group (TMAG) was set up (the Chairman was from LARA, the Vice-chair from the NPA) involving also representatives of riders, ramblers, cyclists, Forest Enterprise, National Trust and landowners. A Trail Officer was appointed, and in 2000, 115 signs were erected on 250 miles of routes. The annual cost for the three-year experiment is estimated to be £145,000. Initially there were problems with two companies bringing in large groups of 4WD vehicles, but this seems to have been resolved. LARA accepts that the NPA may have to impose TROs where damage is sustained, but that the existence of Category 3 will minimise this. The problem, of course, was whether non-LARA riders would honour the system, but in the first year, contraventions and vandalism of signs reported to the Advisory Group were few. Obviously, LARA has been able to persuade the other members of the local policy community to accept its legitimacy and consider its case. The Friends of the Lake District are against the scheme, waiting sceptically to see how far non-LARA members comply, and fearing an increase

---

Box 15.3   LARA's four principles for the Hierarchy of Trail Routes

1 Recreational motor use of minor highways is a lawful pursuit requiring proper management like any other countryside recreation or use.
2 The use of 'hard position' reactive management generally fails to deliver sustainable use in terms of fairness, adherence and an improved situation.
3 Motor users must understand and acknowledge that there is a constantly changing hierarchy of sustainability inherent in trail routes.
4 Free of the threat of claim and counter-claim by other user groups, vehicular users will be given the opportunity to apply reasonable self-regulation of their own use of these Ways.

of traffic once riders discover rights of way they did not know they had.

Why were there such different outcomes to the two noisy sport issues? Collins and Ellison (2001) suggested that for water skiing the BWSF, Sports Council and Tourist Board were isolated against a local and national coalition of environmental amenity and recreation organisations behind which the Blair administration finally threw its weight; that the lack of flexibility in navigation law and of workable alternative waters made defence of water-skiing on Windermere necessary if a lost cause. Also the situations for which the byelaw could be precedential were fewer. In the case of green lane driving, a dispersed and difficult problem held many more potential precedents, and despite overt opposition from Friends of the Lake District, the rest of the policy community wished a resolution, and LARA had worked skilfully and developed more alliances than BWSF.

It is too soon to tell whether the Hierarchy experiment will work. If it fails, land-based motor sports could find their choices in and beyond National Parks curtailed as much as water skiing. Sport England's current planning guidance (1999) is seeking to get national governing bodies of sport to identify Significant Areas for Sport (SASPs) where it will oppose developments that threaten such sites, and will try to encourage planning authorities to acknowledge them. However, SASPs are most unlikely to gain statutory support because each serves only a small number of people compared to the community-wide benefits of national designations for landscape, nature or heritage conservation.

The real problem is that rural sports need to be planned at a regional level. Since the government abolished the advisory Regional Councils for Sport and Recreation in 1995, there has been no obvious mechanism for this. Meanwhile local authorities are heavily influenced by the NIMBY (Not In My Backyard) attitudes of local interest groups, or by co-ordinated pressure from well-organised regional or national environmental groups rather than sports governing bodies which have a poor record of mutual support. If recreation as a whole is a 'Cinderella' in the planning system in National Parks (Simkins, cited in Ravenscroft and Reeves, 1998), this is truer still of motor sports.

MEGA EVENTS AND FACILITIES: THE OLYMPICS

Sport has found a potent partner in television: the global reach of major networks has not only brought major fees to the governing bodies and organisations that own the events, but has brought in third partners in the form of sponsors of goods and services which find exposure to new markets (Maguire, 2000: 144–75; Andreff, 2000). These income streams have become major financial lifelines for the sports organisations, and have totally transformed the finances of the Olympic Games. The Games have continued to grow in terms of participating nations and, in the Summer Games, in terms of number of events, athletes and media workers attending (Preuss, 2000; Toohey and Veal, 2000). TV revenues grew astonishingly from US$83.7m in 1976 to US$1.124bn in 2000, at 1995 prices (Preuss, 2000: 108). This rapid growth in scale has increased the impacts on the host cities and their countrysides.

Referring specifically to environmental impacts, Essex and Chalkley (1998) distinguished three types of Summer Games:

1   *Low impact*: involving mainly refurbished and few new facilities, e.g. Athens 1896, London 1948 and Mexico

City 1968. After a period where state-of-the-art new buildings had prevailed, Los Angeles in 1984 showed how, using mainly existing 1932 and other sites, costs could be cut, leading to a surplus of US$215m, and rekindling the interest of cities in bidding, which had waned after major debts in Munich and Montreal.

2 *New facility-based*: major stadiums, pools, and general and specialist arenas (for cycling, canoeing, rowing, riding, shooting, etc.) and new housing for the athletes, e.g. Stockholm 1912, Los Angeles 1932, Berlin 1936 and Atlanta 1996.

3 *Stimulating*: environmental transformation of a wide range and large scale, e.g. Rome 1960, Montreal 1976, Moscow 1980, Barcelona 1992, Sydney 2000 (see Table 15.7). The soaring costs of Munich and Montreal with little after-use (e.g. the structural and locational unsuitability of the latter's Olympic village for housing) led to a crisis, for which Los Angeles gave a solution, but one where there was much more private entrepreneurial involvement.

The third type used the Summer Games as a trigger for a major transformation of the image and fabric of the host city, involving major public infrastructure and cultural investment, often compressing public investment into eight or ten years that might otherwise have taken 20 to generate, if indeed it would have come at all without such a 'flagship' event (see Table 15.6).

Developing Games facilities anywhere near the central city with its cultural, entertainment, hotel and shopping services involves using 'brown land' sites, usually of two main types. The first includes areas of low-cost housing occupied by lower-skilled, lower-paid workers who are needed in Games- and tourist-related services, but who are often displaced by the sports and related new facilities, as happened in Mexico City, Moscow and Barcelona. It is doubtful whether there are any environmental benefits to offset these social and economic costs. The second type includes industrial, often contaminated land where reclamation and redevelopment nominally present clear environmental gains but which requires generating high values to pay the costs, as in Homebush Bay, Sydney. There are concerns that the tight timescale for preparing the Games and their high political and media profile result in the overriding of normal environmental checks and procedures (Lenskyj, 1996). The stirring of environmental awareness in the Games movement led the Munich OCOG to invite all participating NOCs to plant a shrub in the Olympic Park and to support the sentiments of its slogan '*Certatio sana in natura sana*' ('Healthy competition in an intact environment').

More recently the Rio Conference also committed the Olympic movement to be a part of Agenda 21, and the IOC (1997) has developed a manual of environmental requirements of bidders. Essex and Chalkley's (1998: 203) comment still holds, that 'what began as a festival of sport has grown into an unusually conspicuous element in urban global competition'.

CASE STUDY 2: THE ALBERTVILLE AND LILLEHAMMER GAMES

Although the debt for the 1968 Grenoble Winter Games was still being paid off, Albertville bid and won the rights to host the 1992 Games. Concerns had built up about the impact of clearing forest and flora for skiing pistes, extending facilities and hotels to higher altitudes, and the trampling of much larger numbers of summer

Table 15.6 *Urban transformation through the Olympic Games*

Host city/year	Urban developments
Rome 1960	New facilities, new Olympic Way, new water supply, airport
Tokyo 1964	New facilities, 2 new metro lines; new road link plus 22 other road schemes
Munich 1972	Reclaim 280 ha disused housing area for new sports facilities; pedestrianise historic quarter, improve expressways, shops, hotels, public transport and underground car parking
Montreal 1976	New Olympic park and village; 20 km of metro; new roads, hotels and airport
Moscow 1980	12 new sports facilities; hotels; airport terminal; TV and communications centres
Seoul 1988	New sports facilities and village; 3 metro lines, 47 bus routes, new arts centre, classical music institute, Chongju museum, refurbishing shrines; renewed rubbish collection and water supply systems, de-polluting the River Han and Chamsil site
Barcelona 1992	15 new sports venues; new airport link, ring road and rail station; new beaches and marina, offices, conference centre; Olympic village to become housing as part of revitalised historic quarter; energy saving
Sydney 2000	New sports facilities

Source: after Essex and Chalkley, 1998

Table 15.7 *Impacts of the Albertville Games*

Positive	Negative
• Reuse of derelict sites (e.g. aluminium plant) • Designs to minimise impact • Improved water quality in Isere and waste • re-use (up from 36 per cent to 90 per cent) • Reduction of eutrophy in lakes downstream	• Destruction of forest, highland peat, upland and valley wetlands, nature reserve • Disruption of animal migration routes by roads and pistes • Motorway construction works

Sources: May, 1995; Klausen, 1999

visitors. Other worries were the pollution from increased car traffic, and the hydrological impact of snow-making equipment (see Table 15.7). To make 1 hectare of ski surface takes 200,000 litres of water – the equivalent of daily use of 1,000 people. Only 0.28 per cent of the construction budget was allocated to planting around buildings and pistes, though electricity and telephone cables were buried in 'sensitive' landscapes by the utility companies.

Seven Alpine countries and DGXI of the European Commission committed themselves to an Alpine Convention for sustainable activity, promoted by the Commission Internationale de la Protection des Alpes (see Van't Zelfde et al., 1996). Already a French law of 1985 had required Environmental Impact Assessments in mountain areas, but May (1995) pointed out that such site-specific measures cannot cover the post-event and wider regional impacts, such as:

• the growth of 4WD and mountain bike use, scarring the landscape of Les Saisies;
• continuing debts of FF200m on the event and FF120m on the TV centre;

- increased demand for snow-making;
- the arrival of more summer visitors as a consequence of improved accessibility and new accommodation capacity, with extra pressures on other communal services; and
- reduced biological diversity and productivity in rivers.

Meantime Lillehammer, a small town of 20,000 people in Norway whose region had won the honour of coping with the 1994 Games, determined to do better. It sought to place Lillehammer on the same skiing map as the established and heavily invested resorts of the Alps and Rockies. The OCOG had budgeted for an estimated expenditure of $1.17bn, 46 per cent above income, on the grounds that 'the Games are expected to yield general spin-offs for the Olympic region and the country as a whole' (Lillehammer '94 Guide: 132–3).

The measures that Lillehammer took included:

- having regular meetings with citizens;
- educating volunteers including army personnel;
- employing energy-saving devices like using heat from the rink to heat the Hamar arenas (saving about US$100,000 a year); and
- requiring all suppliers to use recycled paper and non-carcinogenic or ozone-depleting agents (Chernushenko, 1994; Klausen, 1999).

These and many similar measures led the Norwegian Society for the Conservation of Nature to accept that serious attempts had been made to reduce the Games' impact. However, as Chernushenko argued (1994: 51–2), there had to be compromises, such as realigning a ski jump to optimise light for TV, and building a third ice rink to bring

spectator seating to 20,000, even though after the Games only 1,000 seats would be needed for ice hockey matches.

Even after these efforts, and a very successful event, the following criticisms were made:

- In embodying the latest technical standards, the jumps and buildings made the White Mountain just like the developed slopes they were trying to compete with, rather than preserving vernacular styles of structures and landscape.
- Too few local place names had been preserved and too many misapplied.
- Special places like the mating sites of capercaillies and lynx had been disturbed.
- A wetland area had been lost.
- The area had been commodified to attract and satisfy tourists, for instance through creating Troll Park, with a consequential increased use of cars.

Ironically, one of Lillehammer's best legacies was not sporting: the expensive media centre was converted to a higher education centre for audio-visual arts and technology training for all of Scandinavia, making a year-round source of income it would have been most unlikely to achieve in the absence of the Games.

In 1995 there was a first World Conference on Sport and the Environment, at which President Samaranch said that the IOC would consider environmental aspects as the third pillar of its future work, alongside sport and culture (Kidane, 1997). In 1997 it produced its *Manual on Sport and the Environment* (IOC, 1997), asking host cities to include an environmental action plan in their bids, to undertake EIAs, and to establish an awareness programme for partners, citizens and guests. The *Manual* covers not only impact on nature but issues of design, energy saving, water, air and waste treatment, and issues of transport, ticketing, catering and noise.

For the most recent summer event in 2000 in Sydney, the OCOG wanted the event to be known both as the 'Athletes' Games' and the 'Green Games'. The main site and the Bay had been very heavily polluted, and despite an acclaimed success in sporting and tourism terms, it became clear that the reclamation costs of A\$667m had been underestimated (Toohey and Veal, 2000: 195–207).

CONCLUSIONS

Ideally one would want to see approaches to countryside sport and recreation promoted that maximise its potential for positive environmental effects. While it is possible to compile a long list of environmental impacts associated with sport and recreation (including noise, traffic congestion, visual blight, high energy demands), one should not lose sight of the fact that these activities and events can also produce environmental benefits. Mention has been made of the reclamation of brownfield sites in preparing the facilities for major events like the Olympics. Sport does not always damage environments, it can create or restore them, by, for example:

- reclaiming dry mineral workings/quarries for motor sports, climbing and shooting;
- reclaiming wet pits for water sports, e.g. in Pugneys (Wakefield) and Rother Valley Country Parks (Glyptis et al., 1995);
- replacing monocultural fields with greater biodiversity in the rough of new golf courses and with newly planted trees 98 golf courses in England and Scotland contain Sites of Special Scientific Interest (see Wheat, 1995); and

- providing access, recreation and culture, timber and other products through new National and Community Forests around cities (Countryside Agency, 1999).

In addition, one can point to modest help in supporting rural public transport. There are also a large number of specialised recreational public transport services in areas popular for landscape beauty and recreation, from Beeline Community Cars in Atherstone, Warwickshire, and the Hadrian's Wall bus to Tandridge taxi vouchers (Countryside Agency, 2001). Many bus services, however, run only on summer weekends, and their patchy passenger loadings mean that most need substantial subsidies, although there are exceptions such as the normally scheduled services of West Yorks Traction, running from Huddersfield and Halifax to tourist and recreation attractions (Glyptis et al., 1995). There are also a few train services to day-trip and holiday areas, like the Hope Valley line in Derbyshire. Against all their shareholders' expectations, restored steam railways are now making money as tourist attractions, e.g. the Severn Valley, the Great Central in Leicestershire and the Settle–Carlisle railway, which is of real benefit to residents (Salveson, 1993).

As Chernushenko (1994) wrote, 'any harm done by the sports industry to the planet is thus a strike against the future of the sport itself'. Sport can bring great joy, boundless enjoyment and the creation of income and 'symbolic capital' for individuals, teams and clubs, and nations (Bourdieu, 1984). I have sought to show that sport can be a minor threat to the earth and/or a modest force for improving the environment. Therefore it needs to tread lightly on the earth, and sports planners and administrators still have much to learn in order to do that consistently and successfully. We are still a long way from Oittinen and Tiezzi's (1998) 'sustainable sport'.

Chapter summary

- The concept of sustainable sport can be operationalised at three levels: global; institutionals; and of individual citizens.
- Visual intrusion, traffic, noise and energy use are important elements of the environmental impact of sport within the built environment.
- While sporting use of the countryside grew in the 1970s, it has stabilised in recent years. However, environmental issues such as erosion of grass by informal recreation and light pollution and noise from active sports remain prominent sources of tension in rural areas.
- Negotiating management agreements to cover the use of popular sites for outdoor sports has been widespread, but can prove difficult, as in the case of water sports on Lake Windermere. However, it is not impossible, as shown by the agreement covering motor sports in the same area.
- The IOC requires cities bidding to host the Olympic Games to undertake an environmental impact analysis. While some hosts, such as Sydney and Lillehammer have sought to minimise the environmental impact, it is often achieved only at significant financial cost.

Further reading

Curry (1994), Chernushenko (1994) and Da Costa (2001) provide overviews of the complex interrelationship between sport and the environment. Works that provide a more detailed focus on particular issues include Collins's (1999) study of noisy sports in the English countryside, and analyses of the Olympic Games by Essex and Chalkley (1998), Lenskyj (1998) and May (1995).

REFERENCES

Alesbury, A. (1996) *Report of the Inspector upon the Public Inquiry into Byelaws made by the Lake District Special Planning Board*. London: Dept of the Environment.

Andreff, W. (2000) 'Financing modern sport in the face of a sporting ethic', *European Journal of Sport Management*, 7 (1): 5–30.

Baade, R.A. (1995) 'Stadiums, professional sports and city economics: an analysis of the US experience', in J. Bale and O. Moen (eds), *The Stadium and the City*. Keele: Keele University Press, pp. 277–94.

Bale, J. (1990) 'In the shadow of the stadium: football grounds as urban nuisances', *Geography*, 75: 325–34.

Berridge, G. (2000) 'Mountain biking and access in the countryside', in M.F. Collins (ed.), *Leisure Planning in Transitory Societies*. Publication no. 58. Eastbourne: Leisure Studies Association, pp. 51–67.

Bourdieu, P. (1984) *Distinction: a Social Critique of the Judgement of Taste*. London: Routledge.

Chernushenko, D. (1994) *Greening Our Games: Running Sports Events and Facilities that Won't Cost the Earth*. Ottawa: Centurion Publishing and Marketing.

Churchman, C. (1995) 'Sports stadia and the landscape', *Built Environment*, 21 (1), 6–24.

Collins, M.F. (1999) 'Quiet, please! Sport in the British countryside', in M. Foley et al. (eds), *Leisure, Tourism and the Environment: Sustainability and Environmental Policies*.

Publication 50.1. Eastbourne: Leisure Studies Association, pp. 77–101.

Collins, M.F. and Ellison, M. (2001) 'Insiders and outsiders to local policy networks: motorised recreations in National Parks'. Unpublished paper.

Collins, M.F. and Jackson, G.A.M. (1999) 'The economic impact of sport tourism', in P. de Knop and J. Standeven (eds), *Sport Tourism*. Champaign, IL: Human Kinetics, pp. 169–202.

Council for the Protection of Rural England/Lancaster University (1994) *Leisure Landscapes: Leisure, Culture and the English Countryside*. Lancaster: Lancaster University.

Council for the Protection of Rural England (CPRE) (1995) *Tranquil Area Maps*. London: CPRE.

Council for the Protection of Rural England (1999) *Traffic Trauma or Tranquillity?* London: CPRE.

Council for the Protection of Rural England (2000) *Starry, Starry Night*. London: CPRE.

Countryside Agency (CA) (1999) *Regeneration around Cities: the Role of England's Community Forests*. CAX33. Cheltenham: CA.

Countryside Agency (2001) *Great Ways to Go: Good Practice in Rural Transport*. CA62. Cheltenham: CA.

Curry, N.C. (1994) *Countryside Recreation, Access and Land Use Planning*. London: E. & F.N. Spon.

Da Costa, L. (2001) *International Trends in Sport and the Environment – a 2001 Overview*. Paper to ECSS Congress, Cologne, 24–28 July.

Departments of the Environment/of Agriculture, Fisheries and Food/of Transport (1995) *Written Evidence to the House of Commons Committee into the Environmental Impact of Leisure Activities*. London: Doe/ MAFF/DoT.

Department of the Environment, Transport and the Regions (DETR) (1994a) *Good Housekeeping in Dry Sports Centres*. Good Practice Guide no. 129. London: DETR. [Obtainable from BRECSU Enquiries Bureau.]

Department of the Environment, Transport and the Regions (1994b) *Good Housekeeping in Swimming Pools*. Good Practice Guide no. 130. London: DETR.

Department of the Environment, Transport and the Regions (1996) *Energy Efficiency in Sports and Recreation Buildings*. Good Practice Guide no. 51. London: DETR.

Department of the Environment, Transport and the Regions (1997) *Energy Efficiency in Swimming Pools*. Good Practice Guide no. 219. London: DETR.

Elson, M. and Sidaway, R. (1995) *Good Practice in the Planning and Management of Sport and Active Recreation in the Countryside*. Cheltenham: Countryside Commission/ London: Sports Council.

Elson, M., Buller, H. and Stanley, D. (1986) *Providing for Motorsports: from Image to Reality*. Study no. 28. London: Sports Council.

Elson, M., Lloyd, J. and Thorpe, I. (1989) *Providing for Motorised Water Sports*. Study no. 36. London: Sports Council.

English Nature (EN) (1995) *Written Evidence to the House of Commons Committee into the Environmental Impact of Leisure Activities*. London: English Nature.

Essex, S. and Chalkley, B. (1998) 'Olympic Games: catalyst of urban change', *Leisure Studies*, 17: 187–206.

Glyptis, S.A., Collins, M.F. and Randolph, L. (1995) *The Sporting Claim: a Countryside and Water Recreation Strategy for Yorkshire and Humberside*. Vol. 3: *Good Practice Case Studies*. Leeds: Y&H Council for Sport & Recreation.

Hounsden, S. (1999) 'The overflowing honeypot: is there a problem, or is there not?', in J. Hughes (ed.), *Is the Honeypot Overflowing? How Much Recreation Can We Have?* CRN 1998 conference proceedings. Cardiff: Countryside Recreation Network, pp. 5–10.

House of Commons Select Committee on the Environment (HC) (1995) *The Environmental Impact of Leisure Activities*. London: HMSO.

Humphries, D.C., Mason, C.M. and Pinch, S.P. (1983) 'The externality fields of football: a case study of the Dell, Southampton', *Geoforum*, 14 (4): 401–11.

International Olympic Committee (IOC) (1997) *Manual on Sport and the Environment*. Lausanne: IOC.

Kidane, F. (1997) 'The Olympic movement and the environment', in L. Da Costa (ed.), *Environment and Sport: an International Overview*. Porto: University of Porto, pp. 246–54.

Klausen, A.M. (ed.) (1999) *Olympic Games as Performance and Public Event: the Case of the*

XVII Winter Olympic Games in Norway.
New York: Berghahn Books.

Land Access and Rights Association (LARA)
(1996) *Access Guide: for Motorised Recreation and
Motor Sport in the Countryside.* Rugby: LARA.

Land Access and Rights Association (1997)
Hierarchy of Trial Routes: First Report 1997.
Rugby: LARA.

Lenskyj, H.J. (1996) 'When losers are winners:
Toronto and Sydney bids for the summer
Olympics', *Journal of Sport and Social Issues,*
24: 392–410.

Lenskyj, H.J. (1998) 'Sport and corporate envi-
ronmentalism: the case of the Sydney 2000
Olympics', *International Review for the
Sociology of Sport,* 33 (4): 341–54.

Maguire, J. (2000) *Global Sport: Identities,
Societies, Civilizations.* Cambridge: Polity Press.

May, V. (1995) 'Environmental implications of
the 1992 winter Olympic Games', *Tourism
Management,* 16 (4): 260–75.

National Parks Review Panel (NPRP) (the
Edwards Committee) (1991) *Fit for the
Future? Report of the NPR Panel,* CCP334.
Cheltenham: Countryside Commission.

Nickerson, M. (1990) *Planning for Seven
Generations: Guideposts for a Sustainable
Future.* Bakavi: School of Permaculture.

Oittinen, A. and Tiezzi, E. (1998) *'Mens sane in
corpore sano': a scientific review of the information available on the links between the environment and sport.* CDDS (98)45. Strasbourg:
Council of Europe, Committee for the
Development of Sport.

Pearlman, D.J. et al. (1999) 'The Environment Act
1995 and quiet enjoyment: implications for
countryside recreation in the National Parks of
England and Wales, UK', *Area,* 31 (1): 59–66.

Phillips, A. (1994) 'Access, recreation and
tourism in the National Parks of England and
Wales: "a third look at the second purpose"',
in S.A. Glyptis (ed.), *Leisure and the Environment.*
London: Belhaven Press, pp. 225–35.

Preuss, H. (2000) *Economics of the Olympic
Games: Hosting the Games 1972–2000.*
Petersham, NSW: Walla Walla Press.

Ravenscroft, N. and Reeves, J. (1998) 'Planning
for recreation in rural England', *Leisure
Studies Association Newsletter,* 50: 24–30.

Roche, M. (1994) 'Mega-events and urban
policy', *Annals of Tourism Research,* 21: 1–19.

Rooney, J.F. (1976) 'Mega-sports events as
tourist attractions: a geographical analysis'.

Travel and Tourism Research Association
conference, *Proceedings,* Montreal, pp. 93–9.

Salo, H. et al. (n.d.) *The Neste 1000 Lakes Rally,
Finland: Environmental, Economic and Social
Impacts.* Jyvaskula: Institute for Environmental
Research, University of Jyvaskula.

Salveson, P. (1993) *New Future for Rural Trains:
the Full Report.* London: Transnet.

Sidaway, R. (1990) *Birds and Walkers: a Review
of Research.* London: Ramblers' Association.

Sidaway, R. (1991) *Good Conservation Practice
for Sport and Recreation.* London: Sports
Council, Countryside Commission, Nature
Conservancy Council and WWF.

Sidaway, R. (1994) *Recreation and the Natural
Heritage: a Research Review.* Edinburgh:
Scottish National Heritage.

Sidaway, R. (1995) 'Sport in the countryside: current trends, studies and practice', in C. Etchell
(ed.), *Sport in the Countryside.* Cardiff: Countryside Recreation Network, pp. 3–8.

Sport England (1999) *Motorsports.* Planning
Bulletin 6. London: Sport England.

Toohey, K. and Veal, A.J. (2000) *The Olympic
Games: a Social Science Perspective.*
Wallingford: CABI Publishing.

UK Centre for Economic and Environmental
Development (UKCEED) (1993) *Water Skiing
and the Environment: a Literature Review.*
London: Sports Council.

UK Sports Council (1998) *An Agenda for Sport and
the Environment.* London: UK Sports Council.

UK Sports Council (1999a) *Major Events – the
Economics.* London: UK Sports Council.

UK Sports Council (1999b) *Major Events – the
Economics: Measuring Success.* London: UK
Sports Council.

Van't Zelfde, J., Richards, G. and van der
Straaten, J. (1996) 'Developing sustainability
in the Alps', in B. Bramwell et al. (eds),
*Sustainable Tourism Management: Principles and
Practice.* Tilburg: Tilburg University Press,
pp. 73–86.

Vuolle, P. (1991) 'Nature and environments for
physical activity', in P. Oja and R. Telama (eds),
Sport for All. Amsterdam: Elsevier, pp. 597–606.

Wheat, S. (1995) 'Green golf', *Leisure Management,* 13 (11): 38–40.

Whitson, D. and Macintosh, D. (1993)
'Becoming a world class city: hallmark
events and sports franchises in the growth
strategies of western Canadian cities',
Sociology of Sport Journal, 10: 221–40.

Part Four   *International Comparison and Context*

16

Sport in the United States and Canada

TREVOR SLACK

Overview

→ Youth sport – community-level sport, high school sport
→ Intercollegiate sport
→ Professional team sport

Sport is an integral and pervasive part of social life in North America and for many people North America, and in particular the United States, is the centre of the sporting world. North American athletes such as Michael Jordan, Tiger Woods, Venus and Serena Williams, Wayne Gretzky and Marion Jones are global icons who exemplify the pinnacle of excellence in their respective sports. North American-based sporting goods companies such as Nike, Spalding and TaylorMade are global brands that lead the sporting goods field. Teams such as the Chicago Bulls, the New York Yankees and the Montreal Canadiens are widely recognised in all corners of the world. North American athletes, particularly from the US, dominate the Olympic Games and the events themselves are invariably scheduled so as to coincide with prime-time television slots in the East Coast

of the United States. The Super Bowl, the World Series, and the National Basketball Association finals are some of the most watched sporting events, not just in North America but throughout the world. Nowhere is sport more visible and more widely consumed.

In this chapter we look at the way sport is structured and organised in North America. We focus specifically on three levels. First we look at the way youth sport is delivered through community organisations and schools. We then look at intercollegiate sport and the way this is organised. Finally we look at the highly commercialised professional sports leagues. We look critically at some of the problems and issues confronting these three levels of the sport system. As a result of its size and sporting prowess, the United States tends to dominate when one thinks of North American sport. Notwithstanding, we also look at Canada which, while geographically linked to the US, shows some marked differences in the way in which it organises and operates sport.

YOUTH SPORT

In both the United States and Canada sporting opportunities for the country's youth are delivered in one of two ways, either through community-based programmes or through schools. Ewing and Seefeldt (1996) suggest that in the US community-based programmes serve twice as many participants as school programmes. They argue that diminishing resources in public schools (government-funded schools) have led to fewer school teams and fewer qualified staff to coach. In contrast, community programmes, which rely primarily on volunteers, have not been subjected to the same resource pressures. In Canada a 1992 World Health Organisation study (King and Coles, 1992) found a similar but not as marked trend with 62 per cent of 11-year-old boys and 49 per cent of 11-year-old girls being involved in community sport programmes and 45 per cent of both boys and girls being involved in school programmes. Hall et al. (1991: 196) suggest that school sport, like other programmes within the public education system, has experienced 'pressures to cut back or at least do the same job with fewer resources'. They also note that as teachers' workloads have increased, many have withdrawn their voluntary services, making it necessary to cut programmes; as a result fewer children are able to participate.

Weiss and Hayashi (1996) suggest that there are four types of community sport programmes and although they are writing about the United States, these are for the most part also applicable to Canada. Agency-based programmes operate sport teams and leagues within the local community. They are primarily self-supporting with money being raised through membership fees and fundraising ventures. However, some may receive support or even be sponsored by service clubs such as Kinsmen or Rotary and they also obtain help from their local municipalities who provide, increasingly at a cost, the facilities where games are played. In the United States these agency-based programmes are often 'an affiliate of a larger national sponsor of a specific sport (e.g. Little League Baseball, American Youth Soccer Organization) that governs regulations for these sports' (Weiss and Hayashi, 1996: 44). In Canada the teams and leagues are frequently affiliated with a regional or provincial sport governing body which, in turn, is a part of a national organisation such as the Canadian Soccer Association or the Canadian Hockey Association. In addition to being responsible for the staging of sports events in their community, many of these organisations also run coaching and officiating programmes which, while developed at the national level, are delivered locally through these community-based organisations.

As well as agency-based programmes, which in both the US and Canada have the largest number of participants, sporting opportunities are also delivered through national youth organisations (e.g. YMCA/ YWCA, Scouts and Guides, and Boys and Girls Clubs of America), privately operated sports clubs, and municipal recreation programmes. National Youth organisations such as the YMCA and YWCA have a long history of involvement in sport but this has been used primarily as an avenue for developing social skills and 'building character' rather than as an end in itself. Today such organisations, while still involved in providing sporting opportunities, offer relatively few programmes in comparison with agency-based programmes.

Private sports clubs are a growing phenomenon in both the US and Canada but they are most prevalent in sports like gymnastics, figure skating and swimming. Here parents often pay significant fees and are involved in fundraising to hire high-performance coaches and to help operate the club. While many of these clubs provide supportive and realistic programmes, Ryan (1995) has documented many examples of the abuse that some young athletes, specifically gymnasts and figure skaters, are subjected to in the pursuit of athletic excellence. In recent years the US has also seen a rise in the number of club teams in basketball. Many of these are sponsored by the three major athletic footwear companies Nike, Reebok and Adidas, which financially endorse teams, leagues and camps.

Kevin Gaines, a freshman at Michigan who attended the 1998 Nike camp prior to his senior year at Clark High School in Las Vegas [suggested that] it's for the guys who are going to college and hopefully the NBA. Then (once you are in the NBA) they'll get you down for a shoe contract. (Wetzel and Yaeger, 2000: 48)

Such is the pressure to secure the next Michael Jordan or Chamique Holdsclaw that athletic footwear companies can no longer wait until a player is in his or her junior year at college – they must now start identifying such talented youngsters at the junior high school level. Financially supporting non-school basketball clubs, leagues and camps is one way of doing this. As Weiss and Hayashi (1996: 44) also note, such clubs 'serve either as a farm system to high school or college sports or as a legal outlet for year-round participation'.

The final form of community-based sports delivery involves city and town recreation departments. In addition to the provision of facilities for agency-based programmes, these departments, in both the US and Canada, also usually offer a range of introductory sports programmes as well as supporting less competitive activities such as camping, climbing, etc.

School sport in Canada and the US incorporates both intramural and interscholastic competition, although intramural programmes are very much the poor cousins of the interschool programmes. High school sport in the United States is governed by the National Federation of State High School Associations (NFHS). The mission of the NFHS is 'to serve its members and its related professional groups by providing leadership and national coordination for the administration of interscholastic activities which will enhance the educational experiences of high school students and reduce risks of their participation' (*www.nfhs.org*). It is based in Indianapolis, has approximately 40 staff, and operates through 50 member state high school athletic associations plus the District of Columbia. The number of participants in high school sport in the US is nearly 7 million, just under 4 million boys and just under 3 million girls. The most popular sports in 2000 in terms of participation were football[1] (1,012,420) and basketball (539,749) for boys, and basketball (452,728) and outdoor track and field (415,666) for girls (NFHS[*], 2001 Athletics Participation[2]). Many schools and certainly most of the larger ones will employ athletic directors to co-ordinate interschool athletic teams, while many of the bigger sports have paid coaches.

State high school athletic associations such as the California Interscholastic Federation, the New Hampshire Interscholastic Athletic Association, and the Georgia High School Association are segmented into a number of regions and offer state championships in selected sports. The sports offered vary from state to state but most include the major sports such as football, basketball, track and field, soccer, cross-country running, and swimming and diving. Schools compete against similar size schools and there may be up to five different size classifications within some of the larger, more populous states. There are no formal national championships; most competition culminates at the state championship. However, in a number of sports there are All-Star games such as the McDonald's All-American High School Basketball Game and the Roundball Classic, where the top players compete on representative teams. In many ways these events serve as showcases for college scouts looking to recruit players. There are also numerous 'All-American' polls and ranking lists for the top high school teams produced by publications such as *USAToday** and *Sporting News,** Wire Service agencies (see Associated Press*), Coaches Associations (NSCAA*) and sporting good manufacturers (see Rivals High*). Various bodies also produce lists of regional or state All-Stars and Academic All-Americans; these are athletes who have done well in their sport while maintaining a high level of academic work.

In Canada education is the role of the provincial not the federal government and high school sport is operated under the auspices of the various provincial organisations such as the Alberta Schools Athletic Association and the Ontario Federation of School Athletic Associations. Unlike in the US, Canadian schools are unlikely to employ athletic directors and coaches will be drawn primarily from the ranks of teachers or interested volunteers. There is a Canadian School Sport Federation (CSSF) but it plays a very minor role in the operation of high school sport. The various provinces hold championship tournaments

in a number of sports such as volleyball, soccer, basketball, and track and field. Interestingly, competitive ice hockey (in many ways Canada's primary sport) is not played competitively a great deal within the school system. In large part this is because of the existence in many provinces of a strong agency-based league system. As in the US, provincial championships are held but there is no national schools championship. Inter-provincial tournaments do take place but these are generally on a far less grandiose scale than their equivalent in the US.

While organisations such as the NFHS, the CSSF and the various state and provincial governing bodies extol the virtues of high school competition, its emphasis on sportsmanship, and its links to educational goals, there have been and continue to be problems for high school sport. While in many ways a number of these problems are more pronounced in the US than in Canada, there are commonalities. First, there is a concern in both countries that coaches and athletic directors model their programmes on professional or high-level elite sport. As a result there is an over-emphasis on winning and on the higher-profile sports, which often cater to male participants. As Coakley (1998: 461) points out, 'in the process of trying to build high-profile sports programs they often overlook the educational needs of all students in their schools. Their goal is to be "ranked" rather than to respond to the needs of students.' Many US schools encourage students to focus on a single sport, whereas in Canada seasons are generally shorter and students are encouraged to play several sports (Hall et al., 1991). Because coaches in the US are hired primarily as coaches rather than as teachers, their win/lose record is often more important than the educational values they impart to players. In Canada where the majority of coaches are primarily hired as teachers, win/lose records are not a factor in continuing employment.

Linked to the increased emphasis on winning in youth sport, there has also been a growing involvement from corporate sponsors. While most prevalent at the collegiate and professional levels of competition, both high school and community sports programmes in the US and Canada have been appropriated by corporations anxious to capitalise on the qualities that are often associated with such activities. For example, many community-level teams carry the name of a local, regional or national business on their sweaters. High school sports organisations such as the Alberta Schools Athletic Association (McDonald's, Adidas & Yonex) and the California Interscholastic Federation (Spalding, Marriott & Teamsports) are supported by corporate sponsors. Likewise many major tournaments and events are endorsed by corporations. While the financial support that is given certainly helps youth sport, sponsorship means that corporate interests may take priority over the educational interests of students. Wetzel and Yaeger in their aptly named book *Sole Influence: Basketball, Corporate Greed and the Corruption of America's Youth* (2000) provide numerous examples of the way major athletic footwear companies have prioritised their requirements over the educational or social needs of athletes.

High school sports have also been criticised for the fact that they focus mainly on participation opportunities for males. As noted above, in the US the figures for boys and girls show that males represent 59 per cent of the total participants in high school sport. In Ontario, Canada's most populous province, the situation is better with 55 per cent of participants being male. Prior to the early 1970s, some US states actually had legislation which prohibited interscholastic sports for girls (Sage, 1998). However, since

this time the number of girls involved in high school sports in the US has increased dramatically as a result of the passage of Title IX of the Educational Amendment Act. This called for abolition of sex discrimination in all educational programmes, including sports activities. However, while the participation of girls in high school sport has gone up, this has not been accompanied by a concomitant increase in the number of female coaches and administrators. As Coakley (1998: 226) notes, 'In North America ... there has been a significant decline in the number and proportion of women coaches and administrators in many sports organizations, especially the athletic departments of high schools and colleges.' While there are a number of reasons for this decline, one of the main ones relates to the fact that as women's and girls' sports have become increasingly popular and more visible, they have offered sources of power and prestige and as such have been appropriated by men.

A final criticism of high school sports is that it may foster and perpetuate violence. There is some evidence to suggest that violence in sport is less common today than it was in the past (cf. Scheinin, 1994). Nevertheless, there is still a concern about the incidence of physical violence in youth sport and that participation in high school sport may be linked to violence off the field. Evidence suggests that male athletes in contact sports, such as ice hockey, basketball and football, accept a certain level of violence in sport and as the amount of contact in the sport increases, so too does the acceptance of violence (Weinstein et al., 1995). Certainly there have been a number incidents of violence in these sports at youth level (see Olson*; Lapchick*); some of these have resulted in criminal prosecution but most are dismissed as part of the game. As Malina* notes, athletes involved in violence are often given a second, third, or fourth chance in sport essentially because of their skills. These athletes are also often preferentially treated by coaches and sport systems (and occasionally by the legal system) for the simple reason that they are central to winning and to the success of a coach or team.

Reports of violent behaviour by adults at youth sport events are also on the rise. The most vivid recent example involves a man in Boston accused of beating another father to death after their sons' hockey practice (*Washington Post**).

Box 16.1   High school sport and violence

While no one can condone the violence that occurs during and after games, a far more disturbing link between high school sport and violence is evidenced in the events that took place at Columbine High School on 20 April 1999 and those graphically detailed in Bernard Lefkowitz's (1997) book *Our Guys: the Glen Ridge Rape and the Secret Life of the Perfect Suburb*. The Columbine situation involved two teenagers – allegedly youth sport dropouts – in a murderous rampage that left 13 dead and 21 wounded. Much of the aggression by the two teenagers was directed at high school athletes. When the killing began, the two gunmen apparently began their rampage with the words 'All jocks stand up' and 'Anybody with a white hat [a trademark of the school's athletes] or a shirt with a sports emblem is dead.' Columbine was apparently a school that favoured athletes.

Various incidents were reported in the run-up to the killings: the state wrestling champion was regularly allowed to park his $100,000 Hummer (an all-terrain type vehicle) all day in a 15 minute slot; a football player teased a girl about her breasts but was not reprimanded by the teacher who was also his coach; and the homecoming king, a football player, was on probation for burglary. Initiation rituals involved senior wrestlers twisting the nipples of freshmen wrestlers until they turned purple and tennis players volleying balls at younger players' backsides. It was suggested that 'some parents and students believe a schoolwide indulgence of certain jocks – their criminal convictions, physical abuse, sexual and racial bullying – intensified the killers' feelings of powerlessness and galvanized their fantasies of revenge' (Adams and Russakoff*).

While thankfully a rare occurrence, the Columbine situation is not the only one where killings may have been linked to the favouritism shown to high school athletes. After a March 2001 shooting at Santana High School in Santee, California, Borger* notes that an angry reader wrote to the *Los Angeles Times* stating

> For school personnel to be at a loss as to the motives of the shootings at Santana High School is hypocritical. Anyone who has attended high school knows there is the 'in crowd' made up of sports heroes, class officers and their entourage. To this group the teachers and administrators pander allowing them to do pretty much as they please. Those not in the 'in group' become the subjects of bullying, taunting and ridicule.

(Continued)

Box 16.1   Continued

The situation described by Lefkowitz involved a group of high school athletes who lured a retarded girl to a basement with a promise that if she joined them she would get a date with one of their friends. They then raped her with a broomstick, a baseball bat and a stick. Lefkowitz* documents how

> the gang-rape – which town residents euphemistically called the boys' 'alleged misconduct' – provoked no community introspection in Glen Ridge. Instead adults and fellow students rallied around the accused athletes ... and dismissed the victim, who had the mental age of an 8 year old, as a slut.

Such issues certainly raise debate about the status that is attached to outstanding high school athletes and teams in North America, particularly in the US. While the United States is often held up as the epitome of athletic excellence, the excesses of such a system, as has been shown, often lead to broader social problems.

INTERCOLLEGIATE SPORT

Unlike many countries of the world, intercollegiate sport in North America, particularly the US, is a highly structured and commercialised activity. Student input is minimal and programmes are operated by paid professional staff. The governing body of intercollegiate sport in the US is the National Collegiate Athletic Association (NCAA); in Canada it is Canadian Interuniversity Sport (CIS) which prior to September 2001 was known as the Canadian Interuniversity Athletic Union (CIAU). The 2001–02 NCAA Manual describes its members' competitive athletic programmes as 'a vital part of the educational system' and 'the athlete is an integral part of the student body'. This, it is suggested, helps 'retain a clear line of demarcation between intercollegiate athletics and

professional sports'. As Zimbalist (1999: 4) cynically states, 'Whom do they think they are kidding?' At its highest levels, interuniversity sport in the United States is very much the same type of entertainment spectacle as professional sport. In Canada the situation is less severe and it is generally accepted that university sport has stronger links to the educational ambitions of the university than it does in the US.

The NCAA is a large complex organisation which in the 2001–02 year had budgeted revenues of just under US$346m. Of this amount US$271.5m (79 per cent) came from television revenues and a further US$26.7m (8 per cent) came from Licensing and Royalties, thus showing the entertainment orientation of US collegiate sport. The NCAA's national offices are in Indianapolis, Indiana, and there is a staff of more than 320. The member institutions of the NCAA are divided into Divisions I, II and III. There are 321 Division I institutions, 260 Division II institutions, and 396 at Division III level. To be classified as a Division I school (the American term used to denote a college or university), an institution must meet a number of criteria. These include but are not limited to: sponsoring at least seven sports for men and seven for women (or six for men and eight for women) with at least two team sports for each gender; playing a minimum percentage of games against Division I opponents (this is slightly different for football and basketball); and meeting minimum financial aid award (scholarship) levels. Division I schools that offer football programmes are divided into Division I-A or Division I-AA (those Division I schools that do not offer football are I-AAA). Division I-A schools have to meet minimum attendance requirements for football –

17,000 people in attendance per home game, or 20,000 average of all football games in the last four years, or 30,000 permanent seats in their stadium and average 17,000 per home game, or 20,000 average of all football games in the last four years, or be in a member conference in which at least six conference members sponsor football or more than half of football schools meet attendance criterion. (NCAA (c)*)

Division I-AA schools do not need to meet attendance requirements.

Division II institutions must sponsor at least four sports for men and four for women with at least two team sports for each. Like Division I, there are scheduling requirements as regards which member institutions teams can play against (other than for football and basketball). There are no attendance requirements but there is a maximum for financial aid awards that Division II schools can offer. Division II schools are in many ways more regionally focused than Division I schools which compete nationally. Division III schools must sponsor at least five sports for each sex, again with a minimum of two team sports. There are minimum contest and participation requirements, but Division III student athletes receive no financial aid. The NCAA description of the three divisions suggests that 'Division III athletics departments place special importance on the impact of

athletics on the participants rather than on the spectators', perhaps further emphasising the entertainment focus of the higher Divisions' sport programmes (NCAA (c)*). Universities such as Ohio State and University of Southern California are examples of Division I schools, North Dakota and New Haven Division II, and Colby-Sawyer and Frostberg State Division III. The average operating expenses for Division I athletic programmes in 1999–2000 were just under US$6.5m (with approximately 28 per cent going to women's programmes). The figures for Division II and III schools were respectively just under US$2m (approx. 37 per cent on women's sport) and just under US$700,000 with approximately 39 per cent on women's sport (NCAA (a)*).

The vast majority of universities compete in one of the nearly 90 member collegiate athletic conferences. These function in the same way as leagues, with position in the conference determining eligibility for post-conference tournaments (or Bowls in Football). The NCAA sponsors 87 national championships, ten of which all divisions are eligible for and the rest being evenly spread between Divisions I, II and III. The biggest events are the men's basketball championship, colloquially know as 'March Madness', the women's basketball championship and the various football bowl games, of which there are currently 24 certified by the NCAA. The best known of these is the Rose Bowl. National championships in most sports are decided through tournament play. In football, participation in the national championship game is decided by a poll of various stakeholders. The NCAA itself does not conduct polls for most Division I sports but these are carried out by agencies such as USAToday/ESPN, Associated Press, etc. Because of the number of polls, it is possible that some will produce different 'national champions'.

University sport is far less grandiose in Canada than in the US. It is also fair to say that in Canada its links to educational objectives are closer than those found in many US programmes. This notwithstanding Canadian university sport is still more commercially oriented than student sport in countries like England and Australia and it is mainly operated by paid staff hired by their respective universities primarily for this purpose. The CIS operates with a staff of 11 and in 2000–01 had a revenue budget of C$1,153,451 (approx. US$725,000) (Danylchuk and MacLean, 2001), figures which pale in comparison to those of the NCAA. It serves over 10,000 students through four conferences: the Canada West Universities Athletic Association (12 universities); Ontario University Athletics (18 universities); the Quebec Student Sport Federation (8 universities); and the Atlantic University Sport Conference (11 universities). Member universities compete within their respective units for conference and ultimately national titles in 19 national championships (9 for men and 10 for women) in 11 different sports. The CIS is involved in the selection of 'All-Canadians' and in conjunction with the Royal Bank selects 'Academic All-Canadians', athletes who apart from performing at a high level also maintain a high grade point average. Some of the national championships and semi-final games in major sports (football, ice hockey and basketball) are shown on TSN (Canada's Sport Network), however there is nowhere near the type of TV exposure to collegiate sport that is found in the US. Likewise it is fair to say that with the possible exception of Eastern Canada, where university sport is very popular (probably due to the absence of any professional sport franchises), intercollegiate competitions do not engender the type of passion and community interest that characterise US campuses.

In addition to their primary roles in interuniversity sport, the NCAA and CIS also perform other functions. These involve co-operating with national sports organisations in the preparation of athletes for national teams, running drug awareness

---

Box 16.2   Sports scholarships

One issue that has long plagued Canadian interuniversity sport is the awarding of athletic scholarships. Unlike the US where scholarships are an integral part of university sport, Canadian universities have for a long time resisted the awarding of scholarships, a fact that perhaps underscores the different priorities attached to university sport in the two countries. While there were 'unofficial' scholarships given to athletes (mainly in Atlantic province universities), these were disguised as part-time jobs and were technically against CIAU rules. Over the years athletic awards have become more prevalent and in June 2000 CIS members agreed to report all athletic awards. The results of a study released in December showed that C$2,396,500 were awarded to CIS student athletes, with the average amount of an award being C$1,160 (again a figure which pales in comparison to US awards). The sports that received the largest amount of awards were football, ice hockey and basketball for men, and basketball, volleyball and soccer for women.

programmes, working towards gender equity, and enhancing leadership skills. Individual universities will also often have community-based programmes and will run summer sport camps for local athletes.

As with high school sport, interuniversity sport in both the US and Canada generates a number of issues and concerns. Again many of these are more pronounced in the US system than they are in Canada. Here I look briefly at three issues: gender equity, increasing commercialisation and lack of student involvement.

While both the CIS and the NCAA have a stated commitment to gender equity, the figures of each of these organisations show they have a way to go before equity is achieved. Statistics released by the NCAA in December 2001 show that approximately 41 per cent of participating athletes in NCAA competition are female. The numbers have however improved considerably since 1971, the year before the passage of Title IX, when only 7.4 per cent of total participants were female (Zimbalist, 1999). Current scholarship and expenditure figures showed more pronounced inequalities, with the average number of scholarship equivalents per Division I university being 91.8 for men and 61.3 (40 per cent of total) for women. Total average operating expenses for Division I men's programmes are US$4,649,667 and for women US$1,776,160 (27.6 per cent of the total). A major argument for these inequities has been that men play football, often seen as a revenue-generating sport at Division IA level, and there is no equivalent for women. However, Messner et al. (1996) have argued that women's sport could be revenue generating if it were to be marketed properly, and that the inequities that exist are because athletic administrators are not interested in promoting women's programmes. The majority of these administrators are men. In fact,

Zimbalist (1999) reports that since 1972, when over 90 per cent of women's athletic programmes were directed by women, the figures have declined and in 1996 only 18.5 per cent were in this category. A similar situation exists in coaching, where the 1972 and 1996 figures were 90 per cent and 47.7 per cent respectively.

Figures for CIS athletes are not as readily available, but a December 2001 press release (CIS*) notes that 66 per cent of athletic awards in Canadian university sport went to male athletes. In addition, Danylchuk and MacLean (2001: 368) report that within Canadian university sport, 'there are still slightly more male participants overall, primarily due to the large roster size of football and a larger roster size for men's wrestling than women's due to three additional weight classes'. In addition they add that of the 49 CIS member universities, only 11 (22 per cent) have female athletic directors and only 30.2 per cent of coaches of women's teams are female. While the percentage of athletic directors has increased from 13 per cent five years ago, the situation of coaches has worsened with a drop of just over 10 per cent from 40.6 per cent. Marketing efforts, it is claimed are similarly directed primarily at the major men's sports of football, basketball and ice hockey. Clearly, while progress has been made in both countries, total gender equity is some way off.

The high-profile nature of college sport means that it is of decided interest to commercial sponsors. In 1995 the average NCAA Division IA school earned US$459,000 in sponsorship and signage income, US$96,000 in programme advertising and sales, and US$833,000 in miscellaneous income, which included licensing (Zimbalist, 1999). Sponsorship comes from companies such as those involved in the production of athletic footwear, soft drinks and beer. A single sponsorship for a high-profile Division I university can be in the millions of dollars. Television contracts also bring in considerable revenue for individual universities and conferences, which negotiate for transmission of regular season games. In addition, in November 1999 the NCAA announced that it had reached a deal with CBS Sports which gave it exclusive television rights to the NCAA men's Division I basketball Championship event and associated marketing. The deal, which begins in the 2002–03 academic year, runs for 11 years and is worth a minimum of US$6bn (NCAA (b)*). The various football bowl games are sponsored by such corporate bodies as FedEx, Jeep, Nokia and Toyota. Commercial connections also exist through the sale of designated seats and boxes at games (primarily football and basketball) to corporate bodies who use them for entertainment purposes.

As we have seen in other areas, although Canada in some ways mirrors the US, it is on a much smaller scale. For example, the 2000–01 CIS revenue budget shows C$281,900 (approx. US$177,000) coming from sponsorship. The majority of the budget for CIS comes from public funds with Sport Canada, the federal government agency responsible for sport giving nearly C$350,000. Danylchuk and MacLean (2001: 374) predict that the funds available from Sport Canada are likely to decline in the future and this will 'force an increase in reliance on marketing initiatives'. But they note that this will be difficult, as the CIS has no critical mass of corporate support and in fact in 1999 the Board of Directors (of the then CIAU) overturned a consultant's suggestion to open a second office in Toronto, the heart of corporate Canada.

The Canadian problems notwithstanding, in the US increased commercialisation has meant that intercollegiate sport has become an 'entertainment conglomerate,

with operating methods and objectives totally separate from and mainly opposed to, the educational aims of the schools that house its franchises' (Sperber, 1990: 56). The involvement of commercial bodies and media organisations in intercollegiate sport has meant that in many cases it has lost its educational objectives and become a business. In this situation the academic progress of players becomes less important than the win/loss record of the team and the television ratings that are generated. The big sports of football and basketball, which are the main revenue generators, become all important and other sports such as field hockey and cross-country running are marginalised because they have little spectator appeal. Sack and Staurowsky (1998) suggest that the commercialisation of college sport has led to the professionalisation of college athletes. These athletes as a group tend to have a markedly different demographic profile from the rest of the student body. 'Teams tend to have a higher proportion of blacks than can be found on their campuses as a whole. Also the overall gap between athletes and nonathletes in academic preparedness tends to be rather large' (Sack and Staurowsky, 1998: 5).

In Canada this situation is not as grave as it is in the US, a fact which reflects the relative lack of importance of intercollegiate sport on Canadian campuses. However, this is not to say that Canadian university sport is immune from the pressures and problems of commercialism (cf. Hall et al., 1991). Football and ice hockey, two sports predominantly played by men, are the major recipients of commercial support, and men's basketball teams are often given scheduling priority over women because of their 'commercial' appeal. There are instances where staff who are primarily hired to coach have sacrificed students' educational objectives for their involvement in sport. It is important to note, however, that the problems that do exist in Canada as a result of commercial pressures are minuscule compared to those that exist in the US.

As noted earlier, student sport in the US and Canada is different from many countries in that it is primarily run by paid staff. As a result there are often concerns about the lack of student input into an activity which is ostensibly for the benefit of students. (See Sage (1998: 230–1) for a brief history of the decline of student control of sport in the US.) Eitzen (1999: 115) notes that 'students, who typically help the athletic department through their fees (which total more than $1 million annually at most big-time programs) have no influence over how their money is spent'. Yet, as he goes on to note, donors who give large but significantly smaller sums often have considerable input into the operation of programmes. In the US, where the demand for seats at the major sporting events is relatively high, students are given a relatively small allocation, most seats going to alumni and donors. Eitzen (1999) gives the example first of the University of Louisville, which only allocates 10 per cent of its seats to students, and second the University of Arizona, which holds a lottery to choose which students can attend basketball games. In Canada student input into university athletic programmes is, like the US, relatively limited. However, students are usually able to obtain seats at university sporting events as the popularity of these events is limited in comparison to the US. Sack and Staurowsky (1998) suggest that one of the solutions to many of the problems of intercollegiate sport in the US would be to return control to the students. However, neither they nor any other observer of intercollegiate sport seriously expects this to happen.

PROFESSIONAL SPORT

The major professional team sports leagues in North America are the National Football League (NFL), the National Hockey League (NHL), the National Basketball Association (NBA), Major League Baseball (MLB), and the Women's National Basketball Association (WNBA). Although the NBA (1), NHL (6), and MLB (2) have teams in Canada, the majority of franchises of these leagues are located in the US. The NFL is entirely US based. The Canadian equivalent is the Canadian Football League (CFL)[3] which has teams in eight cities in Canada. In addition to these team sports, North Americans are of course extensively involved in professional sports such as golf, tennis, boxing and auto racing. Here we focus on the professional team sports. The NFL has 31 teams (a 32nd will be added in Houston for the 2002–03 season) which compete in two conferences: the American Football Conference (AFC) and the National Football Conference (NFC). Each conference is divided into three divisions. The winners of each division plus selected 'wild cards' enter the playoffs with the AFC and NFC Champions competing in the Super Bowl. The NHL has 30 teams, which compete in an Eastern and a Western Conference, each of which is split into three divisions. As with football divisions, winners as well as the five best teams (based on regular season points total) in each conference enters the playoffs. The winners of the two conferences meet for the Stanley Cup. All playoff games and the Stanley Cup final are seven-game series.

Major League Baseball has 30 teams which compete in two leagues: the American League (AL) and the National League (NL). Each league has three divisions. The division winner and the team with the next best record compete in the semi-finals of the league championships with the ultimate winner of the AL meeting the winner of the NL in a seven-game 'World Series'. The WNBA is the only major professional team sport league for women. The NBA Board of Governors announced the formation of the league in April 1996 and play began in June 1997. The WNBA has been extremely successful and has grown from an initial eight teams to 16 teams which play in an Eastern and a Western Conference.

Professional sport franchises are extremely valuable. A 1998 report by *Forbes* magazine estimated the most valuable franchises in each of the men's leagues as follows: NFL, Dallas Cowboys US$413m; MLB, New York Yankees US$362m; NBA, Chicago Bulls US$303m; NHL, New York Rangers US$195m. In the 1997–98 season the average player salary in the NBA was over US$4m; in MLB over US$2.5m; the NFL just over US$1m; and NHL US$1.75m (Quirk and Fort, 1999). Money comes to teams from television revenues, merchandising and licensing, ticket sales (particularly corporate hospitality suites), parking revenues and concessions. Unlike professional sport franchises in many other countries, franchises in North America are portable, that is to say they can be moved from one city to the next. One of the most recent moves involved the struggling Vancouver Grizzlies of the NBA moving to Memphis.

Like all professional sport, the major North American Leagues face a number of problems. These include, but are not limited to, escalating player salaries, increasing violence, drug abuse, labour relations between players and owners, and free agency issues. Here we focus on two current and controversial issues that are somewhat unique to North America; the problems of 'small market' teams and public subsidies of stadiums.

The problem of small market teams is particularly, but not exclusively, related to Canadian teams that play in the major professional sport leagues. The basic issues are that several of the cities in which Canadian teams play are significantly smaller than their US counterparts. This means that the fan base for the team is smaller, as is the local and regional television market. In addition, the Canadian dollar is worth significantly less than the US dollar. Furthermore the tax situation in relation to the municipal bonds that are often used to fund sport facilities, and the rate of taxation for high-paid earners such as professional athletes are both more advantageous in the US. Also because of the portable nature of sport franchises in North America, a number of US cities have built teams modern stadiums which they are allowed to use for little or no charge. This situation has meant that since 1995 the Quebec Nordiques and the Winnipeg Jets of the NHL and the Vancouver Grizzlies of the NBA have all moved to US cities. In addition, the owners of the Montreal Expos have indicated that unless a new stadium is built for them in downtown Montreal, half of it financed by public funds, they will look to move to a US city (Whitson et al., 2000). Similar threats have been made by several of the other NHL teams and Canadian cities have also not been the beneficiaries of the expansion programmes in which the leagues have been involved. What this means, particularly for ice hockey, is that Canada, traditionally the sport's home and the site of its most dedicated fans, is losing teams to US cities with no tradition or interest in the sport. In order to counteract this trend, the Canadian government formed a subcommittee under the chairmanship of Liberal MP Dennis Mills. The committee held hearings in winter–spring of 1997–98. In late 1998 the Mills subcommittee made a number of recommendations to Parliament which involved a series of tax measures that would benefit the professional sports industry. The recommendations were rejected by Parliament. However, the NHL continued to lobby and in January 2000 John Manley, the Minister of Industry, announced an aid package of public support for professional sport. Such was the public outcry that after only three days the offer was withdrawn (see Whitson et al., 2000, for more details). As such, the problems for small market teams in Canada persist.

Related to the concerns of small market teams is the issue of public subsidies for the stadiums and arenas in which professional sport is played. Rosentraub (1997) suggests that a welfare system exists in professional sport where hundreds of millions of dollars are transferred from taxpayers to wealthy investors, who own professional sport teams, and their extraordinarily paid employees (the athletes). This system exists, Rosentraub (1997: 3) claims, because 'state [province] and local government leaders, dazzled by promises of economic growth from sports, mesmerized by visions of enhanced images for their community, and captivated by the mythology of the importance of professional sports, have failed to do their homework'. Bast* for example, argues that 'subsidies to professional sports facilities cost taxpayers some $500m a year [and] more than $7bn will be spent on new facilities by the year 2006 with most of it coming from public sources'. Cagan and DeMause (1998) suggest that even arenas, which are more likely to be privately funded than stadiums (as a result of their smaller size and greater potential for income generation), are actually heavily publicly subsidised. They note the example of the 'privately built' Fleet Center in Boston which is located on a US$100m city-funded parking garage and Philadelphia's

US$217m CoreStates Center, which included US$32m in state funds. The arguments presented by public officials who support such subsidies are that professional sport teams generate jobs and make a city an attractive venue for corporate investment – claims that academics such as Rosentraub (1997) and Danielson (1997) suggest are at best difficult to prove and at worst totally incorrect. Those who argue against public subsidies for sport facilities suggest that such money is better spent on other more essential services such as education and health, that such subsidies are unfair to the taxpayers who are essentially supporting private enterprises, and to other businesses who do not receive such concessions.

CONCLUDING COMMENTS

What should be evident from the preceding account is that the structure and operation of sport in North America are characterised by three key features: commercialisation, professionalisation and media involvement. The impact of each of these forces is more pronounced in the US than in Canada and as one moves from the high school to the professional levels. However, there can be little doubt that much sport in North America is driven by a concern with developing a commercially viable, elite-focused and professionally oriented entertainment spectacle. As noted at the start of this chapter, this system has produced some of the world's best-known athletes but, one might ask, at what price? Unlike many other parts of the Western world, there is little emphasis on 'sport for all' in North America. The United States government has had no substantial involvement in promoting participation in sport or fitness programmes (see Houlihan, 1997). The Canadian government has in the past directed some funds towards promoting participation in sport and domestic sports development (Thibault et al., 1993) but these have paled in comparison to the money it has put into its elite sports programmes. This system, which is driven by the forces of commercialisation, professionalisation and media involvement, has, as has been shown, also produced a number of broader social issues. This has caused many people to question whether or not such an approach serves to enhance sport or merely reduces it to a crass form of entertainment which exemplifies little of what many of us would regard as the intrinsic values of sport.

Chapter summary

- Youth sport in North America is delivered through a variety of community organisations and through schools. There are more participants in community programmes than school programmes. In sports like basketball and football, particularly in the US, both community and youth sport are highly structured and commercialised.
- Intercollegiate sport in North America is big business. Many universities in the US operate athletics programmes with multi-million-dollar budgets. The situation in Canada is less grandiose. College sports are in many ways a training ground for professional or high-performance sport. The commercial orientation of college sport has led to a number of problems.
- There are five major professional team sport leagues in North America; all but one of these cater to male athletes. The teams that make up these leagues generate large sums of money for their owners yet often receive public financial support. Canadian teams are often disadvantaged in terms of their ability to compete with the more populous cities of the US.
- The sport system in North America is often the envy of many other countries. However, as has been shown, the success of this system does not come without significant social and economic costs.

Further reading

Hall et al.'s (1991) text provides the only comprehensive in-depth look at the way sport is structured and organised in Canada and the problems and issues that confront Canadian sport. Sack and Staurowsky (1998) and Zimbalist (1999) both provide critical evaluations of US intercollegiate sport. Sack and Staurowsky show how college athletes on scholarship essentially function as employees of the university. Zimbalist continues this theme and suggests that college sport is a large commercialised industry, which is harmful to the education of students. Quirk and Fort's (1999) book focuses on the economic aspects of professional sport in North America. The various web sites for organisations like the NCAA, the NBA, NFL, etc. also provide useful information.

NOTES

1 In this chapter the term 'football' refers to American or Canadian football. What Europeans generally refer to as football is termed soccer.

2 Sources for asterisked cross-references can be found in the 'Web sources' section at the end of the References that follow.

3 Canadian football is slightly different from American football, primarily in the number of players and the number of 'downs' allowed.

REFERENCES

Cagan, J. and DeMause, N. (1998) *Field of Schemes*. Monroe, ME: Common Courage Press.

Coakley, J.J. (1998) *Sport in Society: Issues and Controversies*. 6th edn. Boston, MA: Irwin McGraw-Hill.

Danielson, M. (1997) *Home Team: Sport and the American Metropolis*. Princeton, NJ: Princeton University Press.

Danylchuk, K. and MacLean, J. (2001) 'Intercollegiate athletics in Canadian universities: perspectives on the future', *Journal of Sports Management*, 15: 364–79.

Eitzen, D.S. (1999) *Fair and Foul*. Boulder, CO: Rowman & Littlefield Publishers, Inc.

Ewing, M.E. and Seefeldt, V. (1996) 'Patterns of participation and attrition in American agency-sponsored youth sports', in F.L. Smoll and R.E. Smith (eds), *Children in Sport: a Biopsychological Perspective*. Indianapolis, IN: Brown & Benchmark, pp. 31–45.

Hall, A., Slack, T., Smith, G. and Whitson, D. (1991) *Sport in Canadian Society*. Oxford: Oxford University Press.

Houlihan, B. (1987) *Sport, Policy and Politics: a Comparative Analysis*. London: Routledge.

King, A.J.C. and Coles, B. (1992) *The Health of Canada's Youth: Views and Behaviours of 11-, 13-, and 15-Year Olds from 11 Countries*. Ottawa, ON: Ministry of Supply and Services, Canada.

Lefkowitz, B. (1997) *Our Guys: the Glen Ridge Rape and the Secret Life of the Perfect Suburb*. New York, NY: Vintage Books.

Messner, M., Duncan, M. and Wachs, F. (1996)

'The gender of audience building', *Sociological Inquiry*, 66: 422–39.

Quirk, J. and Fort, R. (1999) *Pay Dirt: the Business of Professional Team Sports*. Princeton, NJ: Princeton University Press.

Rosentraub, M. (1997) *Major League Losers*. New York, NY: Basic Books.

Ryan, J. (1995) *Little Girls in Pretty Boxes: the Making and Breaking of Elite Gymnasts and Figure Skaters*. New York, NY: Doubleday.

Sack, A.L. and Staurowsky, E.J. (1998) *College Athletes for Hire: the Evolution and Legacy of the NCAA's Amateur Myth*. Westport, CT: Praeger.

Sage, G. (1998) *Power and Ideology in American Sport*. 2nd edn. Champaign, IL: Human Kinetics.

Scheinin, R. (1994) *Field of Screams: the Dark Underside of America's National Pastime*. New York, NY: Norton.

Sperber, M. (1990) *College Sport Inc*. New York, NY: Holt.

Thibault, L., Slack, T. and Hining, C.R. (1993) 'A framework for the analysis of strategy in voluntary sport organisations'. *Journal of Sport Management*, 7: 25–43.

Weinstein, M.D., Smith, M.D. and Wiesenthal, D.L. (1995) 'Masculinity and hockey violence', *Sex Roles*, 33: 831–47.

Weiss, M.R. and Hayashi, C.T. (1996) 'The United States', in P. de Knop, L.-M. Engström, B. Skirstad and M.R. Weiss (eds), *Worldwide Trends in Youth Sport*. Champaign, IL: Human Kinetics, pp. 43–57.

Wetzel, D. and Yaeger, D. (2000) *Sole Influence: Basketball, Corporate Greed and the Corruption of America's Youth*. New York, NY: Warner Books.

Whitson, D., Harvey, J. and Lavoie, M. (2000) 'The Mills Report, the Manley Subsidy proposals and the business of professional sport', *Canadian Public Administration*, 43.

Zimbalist, A. (1999) *Unpaid Professionals: Commercialism and Conflict in Big-time College Sports*. Princeton, NJ: Princeton University Press.

Web sources

Note: All the sources below were extracted in January 2002.

Adams, L. and Russakoff, D. 'Dissecting Columbine's cult of the athlete' *www.washington-post.com/wp-srv/national/daily/june99/columbine 12.htm*

Associated Press national ranking
www.latimes.com/sports/highschool/la-preps-bbb-aprank.story

Bast, J. 'Sport stadium madness: why it started. How to stop it'
www.heartland.org/studies/sports/madness-sum.htm

Borger, J. 'School sports culture leads to violence'
www.guardian.co.uk/elsewhere/journalis/story/0,7792,463895,00.html

CIS, 'Canadian Interuniversity Sport announces results of data collection on athletic awards'
www.cisport.ca/awards/200_data

Lapchick, R. 'When sports violence is a criminal act'
www.csmonitor.com/durable/2000/02/28/text/pls5.html

Lefkowitz, B. 'Did Glen Ridge raise its sons to be rapists?'
www.salon.com/aug97/mothers/guys970813.html

Malina, R.M. 'Sport, violence and Littleton – a perspective'
http://ed-web3.educ.msu.edu/ysi/Spring%201999%20Bob.htm

National Federation of State High School Associations (NFHS)
www.nfhs.org

National Federation of State High School Associations (NFHS), 2001 Athletics Participation Totals
www.nfhs.og/Participation/SportsPart01.htm

National Soccer Coaches Association of America (NSCAA), High School All-Americans
www.nscaa.com/scripts/runisa.dll?m2.131502:gp:586637:14028+awards/2001/HSAll

NCAA (a)
www1.ncaa.org/membership/governance/division

NCAA (b), 'NCAA reaches rights agreement with CBS Sports'
www.ncaa.org/releases/makepage.cgi/champother/1999111801co

NCAA (c), 'What's the difference between Divisions I, II and III?'
www.ncaa.org/about/div_criteria.html

Olson, D. 'Body checking in high school hockey'
http://news.mpr.org/features/199803/04_olsond_hockey/

Rivals High: The inside source for High School sports
http://rivalshigh.rivals.com/default.asp?SID=950&FP=2301

Sporting News, 'Student sport fab 50 national football rankings'
www.sportingnews.com/hsfootball/fab50.html

USAToday, 'Super 25 softball rankings'
www.usatoday.com/sports/preps/softball/sbhssb.htm

Washington Post: 'Trial begins in beating death stemming from sports fight'
www.washingtonpost.com/wp-dyn/articles/a54541-2002jan2.html

17

Sport in Australia

MURRAY PHILLIPS AND TARA MAGDALINSKI

The success of the recent Sydney 2000 Olympics confirmed for many that Australia is a nation 'obsessed' with sport. Sport pervades the national media, and news bulletins dedicate around a third of their broadcasts to reporting Australia's latest sporting achievements. Icons and sporting heroes are commemorated and revered by politicians, the media and the general public. Throughout the 16 days of Olympic competition, the national obsession with sport was displayed on a global stage, and the world reaffirmed what Australians believed they had known all along: that Australia celebrates sport like nowhere else on earth.

The validity of these claims is, however, part of an ongoing debate about the nature of sport and physical activity in Australia. Whilst large-scale sporting events suggest an expertise in event management, what do they really reveal about sport in Australia? Are Australians more likely to participate in sport and enjoy greater levels of physical fitness than other nations? Do all Australians enjoy similar levels of access to sporting experiences? Do citizens purchase larger amounts of merchandise than citizens of other developed nations? What is it that makes Australia stand out as a 'sporty nation'?

The claims about Australia's 'obsession' with sport derive from several sources. First, those who promulgate this mythology turn to attendance figures at sporting events to prove that Australians are 'sports mad'. Others claim that international sporting success, given the nation's relatively small population, reveals a national dedication to physical activity. Finally, the ability and willingness to host global sporting events such as the Olympics suggest that the nation is geared to produce memorable sporting experiences. Such arguments invariably conclude that there is something 'special' about Australia's infatuation with sport.

Throughout the 1990s, several academic texts have sought to expose the Australian sporting psyche, and a brief look at the titles is useful. From Brian Stoddart's *Saturday Afternoon Fever* (1986) and Richard Cashman's *Paradise of Sport* (1995) through to Jim McKay's *No Pain, No Gain?* (1991) and Douglas Booth and Colin Tatz's *One-Eyed* (2000), the academic debate has gradually adopted a more critical edge, initially supporting, then qualifying, questioning and gradually rejecting this notion of a national 'obsession'. Challenging these myths has certainly been difficult, yet through the careful analysis of sport participation, attendance, coverage and rituals, a series of authors have carefully deconstructed these widely held beliefs.

Whilst this debate is interesting, it is time to move on and focus on what actually constitutes the national sporting cultures. We discuss sport in terms of 'cultures' to highlight that sport may be interpreted in contrasting ways by different sections of Australian society. In this chapter, we pose the following questions: What has contributed to the creation of sporting cultures in Australia, and what makes them distinct from or similar to other countries' sporting practices? And what, if any, are the defining features of Australia's sporting cultures? Of course, these are simple questions requiring complex answers for which we simply do not have the space. Instead, we focus here on the intersection between Australian sport and government, business, gender, ethnicity and race.

SPORTING HERITAGE

Whilst Australia was settled prior to the codification of modern sport in Europe, its primary sporting cultures remain highly derivative, a result of Australia's establishment as an outpost of the British Empire. Throughout the nineteenth century, colonisers brought British cultural practices with them to Australia, just as British social structures were disseminated to other parts of the Empire (Cashman, 1995). This 'cultural baggage' of the Anglo-Celts included sports such as boxing, cricket, horse racing, hunting, rowing, Rugby Union, soccer, and track and field; gambling too was firmly entrenched in early colonial sport.

Despite the dominance of British physical culture in Australia, local games and sports emerged, though without the might of an Empire to facilitate their diffusion to the rest of the world, they remained parochial practices. The nation's most popular, unique and locally created sport is Australian Rules football. 'Aussie Rules' was identifiable by 1859 and codified some seven years later, around the same time that other games, such as soccer and rugby, were undergoing similar processes in Britain (Hess and Stewart, 1998). The development of such a sport was a rebellion against the 'overriding dominance of the British Empire', which assisted in stressing 'national independence and cultural difference' (Cronin, 1998: 170).

On the whole, it can be said that Australians have contributed little to sporting forms in other nations, whilst domestic conditions have created a distinctly local tenor to British and American sporting forms. City life has been crucial to organised sport, as leagues were established in Adelaide, Brisbane, Darwin, Hobart, Melbourne, Perth and Sydney. Suburban-based teams in a range of sports engaged in city-wide competitions, yet it took some time before national leagues developed. Communication and transport restrictions in a large continent as well as the parochial nature of colonial life ensured that sport remained largely local for most of the late nineteenth and early twentieth centuries (Cashman, 1995). The historical exceptions to localised, city-based competitions were cricket, some individual sports, and to a lesser degree the rugby codes.

As in other parts of the British Empire, social class and status have played a central role in defining the contours of Australian sport. For instance, Rugby League was closely linked to working-class culture whereas Rugby Union was fostered in the fee-paying, exclusive schools and by university graduates in New South Wales and Queensland. In other sports, including Australian Rules football, class affiliations have been structured differently. Australian Rules football has traditionally been played and watched by a cross-section of people; however, individual clubs established initially in Melbourne, Adelaide, Perth and Hobart suburbs have been aligned to the socio-economic status of their communities (Stoddart, 1986). The class affiliations in the football codes support the large-scale empirical studies of participation patterns which indicate that sport and physical activities are inextricably linked to income, education and occupation (McKay, 1990, 1991). The evidence clearly indicates that 'economic class and social status determine what sports Australians play and how, when and where they play' (Booth and Tatz, 2000: 8). In addition to the class affiliations, gender, ethnic and racial issues have influenced Australian sport.

GOVERNMENT INVOLVEMENT IN SPORT

Many of the structural changes to Australian sport throughout the twentieth century were closely aligned to government involvement. For over 70 years, federal governments, whether Liberal/National or Labor, had only an ad hoc involvement with the organisation, administration and/or provision of sport, and developed no formal national policies or strategies. Athletes and sporting organisations were, for the most part, expected to fund their activities largely independently of the public purse. This is not to say that there was no governmental support at all. Indeed, the considerable growth of sport through the second half of the nineteenth century and beyond was only possible by the 'in-kind' support by local and state governments (Cashman, 1995). Facilities were built and subsidised by ratepayers, and local politicians allocated resources to the development of sporting communities and talents. Gradually, the federal government became more involved, first placing restrictions on sport during the First World War, passing the National Fitness Act during the Second World War, and making irregular financial contributions to Olympic Games, Commonwealth Games and other teams competing in the Asian region, as well as providing federal assistance to the Life Saving Movement (Armstrong, 1988). When Gough Whitlam came to power in 1972, these attitudes changed and the Labor Party's period of office until 1975 is recognised as a 'watershed in government involvement in sport, recreation and other forms of culture' (Armstrong, 1994: 189). The Whitlam government established the first federal Ministry for Tourism and Recreation, aimed at 'catering for the masses', whilst state governments followed suit and founded their own respective departments of sport (Cashman, 1995: 124).

Growing recognition of the political and electoral mileage of international sporting success and two critical reports about the state of Australian sport paved the way for the creation of the Australian Institute of Sport in 1981 (Daly, 1991). The following Hawke/Keating Labor governments (1983–96) further increased financial and political support for sport and initiated the formation in 1985 of the largest sporting bureaucracy, the Australian Sports Commission. Four years later, the Australian Sports Commission became a statutory authority and subsumed the Australian Institute of Sport (AIS) (Shilbury and Deane, 1998). There is little doubt that sporting administrators argued for and welcomed the financial assistance from governments, yet at the same time this jeopardised their autonomy.

As international sport has grown in importance, and government involvement has increased in many countries, a host of domestic and foreign policy issues have emerged. In Australia, two issues, namely apartheid in sport and Olympic boycotts, were highly contested political terrain. While the 1971 Springbok Rugby tour and the 1980 Moscow Olympic Games caused heated public debate and divided the Australian sporting public, more recently domestic concerns have dominated. Some critics have questioned government funding of Olympic and Commonwealth Games bids, the staging of the major sporting festivals, and the financing of elite sport on the basis that expenditure is redirected from more needy areas of education, health and welfare (Booth and Tatz, 1994; Lenskyj, 2000). The support of elite sport and events is justified on the grounds that sporting success promotes Australia internationally, inculcates national identity, provides economic benefits and stimulates activity levels of the population (Houlihan, 1997, 2000).

The promotion of elite sport, however, has come at a cost, as there have been continual reductions in funding of participation-based activities. Even though the Whitlam government championed participation over sporting success, this trend was reversed from the late 1970s (McKay, 1991), typified by the establishment of the AIS, and this has continued through successive governments. In the years 1999–2000, for example, elite sport consumed 78 per cent of the total sports budget (Hogan and Norton, 2000: 210), justified on the assumption that sporting success encourages the public to be physically active. Yet, politicians do not recognise that 'gender, age, ethnicity, race and income and wealth are far more significant than elite role models' (Booth and Tatz, 2000: 175). Questions have also been raised about the inequities of funding models which privilege Olympic over non-Olympic sports, Olympic over Paralympic sports, and Olympic medal-winning sports over less successful sports (Cashman and Hughes, 1998).

COMMODIFICATION OF AUSTRALIAN SPORT

Interwoven with government involvement has been the process of commodification. In reality, sport in Australia has always been a commodity. Until the 1960s, spectator-orientated sports in Australia were similar to those in the United Kingdom and in North America, where gate receipts raised financial capital to be spent according to the dictates of the administrators or owners (Holt, 1989; Horne et al., 1999). Gradually, many spectator-orientated sports created markets for commercial companies who invested in order to sell goods and services (Sage, 1990). The key dimensions in the commercial trajectory of sport in Australia were the businesses that have sponsored sporting events, the television companies that have broadcast mainly male sports, and the sport organisations themselves. Following David Rowe's (1999) work, we refer to this tripartite alliance as the media sports cultural complex.

The media sports cultural complex was a post-1960s phenomenon. Commercial sponsors have been involved in sport from the late nineteenth century, but only in an irregular, transient and peripheral way. Similarly, the symbiotic relationship between sport and television in Australia was not widely recognised before the middle of the 1970s. Following the introduction of television in 1956, sport administrators were happy to have their events televised as long as they could regulate the coverage (partial and often delayed) to ensure that gate receipts were not affected. Television networks covered football, cricket and some international sport, but were reluctant to invest heavily because they were unsure of the ability of televised sports to attract regular, long-term audiences (Stoddart, 1986). Television stations, commercial companies and sport had yet to realise their mutual strengths and benefits.

The nascent relationship between the constituents of the sports media cultural complex changed with the introduction of colour television in 1975. This medium presented sport to viewers in a far more appealing visual package, as colour images were enhanced by innovations in camera positions and presentation techniques principally derived from American televised sport. Ratings boomed. The increased audience prompted greater interest from commercial sponsors, particularly those selling cigarettes and alcohol, who became close partners with televised spectator sports. Today there is a visual saturation of corporate logos and insignia to the point where some athletes represent little more than mobile corporate billboards (Phillips, 1998). In this respect, Australian sport differs from American professional sports where television has traditionally required 'clean screens' free from commercial clutter (Barnett, 1990). The visual display of corporate capitalism in Australian sport reminds us that the media sports cultural complex, while a useful analytical tool, needs to be both culturally and historically contextualised (Rowe et al., 1994).

Box 17.1   Pyjama cricket

Kerry Packer's cricket revolution is an example of the importance of spectator-orientated sports for television and also the power of media organisations in the emerging media sports cultural complex. Packer, the owner of Channel Nine in Australia, sought to purchase cricket for his station, but was thwarted by the Australian Cricket Board when the traditional broadcasters, the Australian Broadcasting Commission (the equivalent of the British Broadcasting Corporation), retained the rights. In retaliation, Packer established a rebel competition with disgruntled local and international players and eventually forced the Australian Cricket Board to compromise. Channel Nine was delivered the broadcast rights to cricket that it has since retained.

World Series Cricket, as it was known, provided a fillip to one-day cricket on the international scene, and introduced the game under lights, coloured clothing for players and new technological advances. While televised sport in Australia before

(Continued)

Box 17.1   Continued

colour television mimicked an 'imported BBC house style' with a small number of fixed cameras widely sweeping as much of the action as possible in a simulation of a single spectator getting the 'best seat in the house' (Rowe, 2000: 135), after World Series Cricket, sport on television increasingly resembled American versions of broadcasting which emphasise action, drama and entertainment.

The introduction of colour television was followed by three key events: the Kerry Packer-inspired one-day cricket revolution (1977), victory by Australia in the America's Cup yachting (1983) and, as we have already discussed, government involvement in sport, each of which have been regarded as catalysts accelerating the commodification of Australian sport and leisure. While World Series Cricket indicated a paradigm shift in the presentation style of televised sport, Packer's involvement highlighted the increasing importance placed on sport in television profiling, marketing and scheduling. Sport had become a valuable television commodity. The most prized asset is 'live' sport, but in recent years a host of hybrid shows have adopted current affairs format or merged sport into comedy, quiz shows or discussion formats (Rowe, 2000). 'Live' coverage of a select group of sports, such as Australian football, cricket, Rugby League, Rugby Union and soccer, as well as the Commonwealth and Olympic Games, command large fees for exclusive broadcast rights. These rights vary according to the competition between stations and the state of the television industry, and have raised issues about the role of media companies in shaping Australian sport.

The most recent example of media dominance over sport in Australia is Rupert Murdoch's News Corp's foray into Rugby League. Murdoch's Australian corporate arm, News Limited, acquired a large stake in one of the licences available during the introduction of pay television in 1995. Rugby League, as a consequence, became a bloody battleground for pay television (Rowe, 1997). Thwarted by the rival pay television station holding the exclusive Rugby League rights, News Limited bought half of the competition in Australia as well as leagues in New Zealand, England and elsewhere. After two court cases, divided competitions and a massive decline in public support, a compromise was reached. A united, smaller competition was formed which resulted in the loss or merger of several foundation clubs and large-scale resistance from supporters of vanquished clubs. Through this turmoil and at an unprecedented cost, News Limited secured broadcast rights to Rugby League. The Rugby League case points to a number of crucial issues in Australian sport: the changing power relationship in the media sports cultural complex; the increasing global forces, including powerful transnational media companies; and the growing difficulty separating the ideologies, structures and practices of media and sporting organisations.

GENDER

As with most countries, sport in Australia has been a gendered activity and a site for the reproduction of perceived differences between appropriate female and male physicality. In the nineteenth century, sport was deemed a natural activity for men, while women were actively discouraged from playing sports. For men, sport became a central part of an emerging masculine nationalist ethos, particularly in international competition within the British Empire. Courage, aggression, strength, endurance and physical prowess were the qualities built through sport and instilled in the young male participants. Early women's physical activity was conducted within the grounds and behind the walls of private schools and the competitive model of male sport was initially rejected. At the same time, men had a wide range of sporting opportunities, whilst the only sports initially available to women were those that complemented traditional notions of femininity, fitted within the ideology of biological determinism, did not threaten the procreative functions of women and were recognised as having health benefits (King, 1979). As a consequence, women played only a limited range of 'feminine' sports, such as croquet, golf and tennis, and their incursions into 'masculine' sports were resented, resisted and prevented by conservative women and men alike.

Despite these social, structural and ideological barriers, women developed separate competitions in some Olympic sports as well as in cricket, netball, softball, hockey and waterpolo. In these sports, Australian women have a very impressive record, winning world championships and/or Olympic medals (Phillips, 1992). A new dimension for sporting women since the 1980s has been their increasing participation in former male-only contact sports – Australian football, boxing, Rugby Union, Rugby League, soccer – and physical activities centring on muscularity, strength and power

such as powerlifting and bodybuilding. The involvement of women in these activities has extended the debate about the appropriateness of specific sports for female athletes, a debate rarely entertained in regard to male sporting participation. Women in violent or strength-based activities continually have to reconfirm their femininity by reproducing acceptable gendered practices. The consequences of not reproducing traditional femininity has meant that women are 'marginalized and criticized for being too masculine, [have] their sexuality called into question and [are] labeled as not being "real" women' (Burroughs and Nauright, 2000: 189).

The discrimination faced by women with respect to participation also extends to the labour and power dimensions of sport (McKay et al., 2000). Women perform a disproportionate amount of ancillary work in the sport setting (cooking, cleaning and fundraising) and provide the labour for sporting children and partners (Thompson, 1999). In terms of power, women have struggled to gain access and develop careers in coaching and administration (McKay, 1997). In coaching, female aspirants have many barriers not faced by their male counterparts, including limited career opportunities and few female role models, as well as the growing trend of male coaches being employed in women's sport (Phillips, 2000).

Another common feature shared by sporting women in the Western world is minimal media coverage. A succession of reports (Gordon, 1989; Menzies, 1989; Phillips, 1997; Stoddart, 1994) have detailed the quantitative differences in media coverage in Australia accorded to male and female athletes in Australia. As Table 17.1 indicates, women's sports receive minimal attention compared to their male counterparts in newspapers, and on television and radio (Phillips, 1997). In many cases,

Table 17.1   *Media coverage of women's, mixed and men's sports, 1996*

	Newspaper (%)	Television (%)	Radio (%)
Women	10.7	2.0	1.4
Mixed	10.2	41.8	3.5
Men	79.1	56.2	95.1

Source: Phillips, 1997

international sport, including American basketball and European soccer, and animal sports such as horse and greyhound racing, receive more coverage than female athletes. The effect of this marginalisation is debilitating. As two prominent feminist researchers contend:

This underrepresentation by the mass media does more than simply create an impression that women are absent from the sporting arena. Rather, it creates a false impression of women's athleticism by denying the reality of the modern feminine athlete. (Kane and Greendorfer, 1994: 36)

Compounding this underrepresentation are the messages contained in the portrayals of female athletes. What has appeared in the printed and electronic press has tended to sexualise or trivialise the female athlete, consigning them to the roles of wives and mothers, sex objects, and in the case of contact sports, freaks. Achieving appropriate recognition for their athletic performances has been difficult, and Jim McKay (1994) argues that women are forced to market their sports according to voyeuristic potential, confirming their appeal and availability

to men, in short, their 'heterosexiness'. Where female athletes transgress such boundaries, the media have treated them harshly, such as in the coverage of lesbian athletes (McKay et al., 1999), of women who have used steroids (Magdalinski, 2001) or of women who play violent sports such as Rugby Union (Carle and Nauright, 1999).

Male athletes, on the other hand, have not been subject to the same levels of sexploitation. Whilst there have been a proliferation of 'beefcake' calendars in Australian men's sport, organised primarily to attract a larger female demographic, none of these has included full-frontal nudity. Indeed, when the genitals of Rugby League player Andrew Ettingshausen were exposed in a women's magazine, he successfully sued for defamation (Burroughs and Nauright, 2000). Thus, whilst there have been moves to use sexiness to sell both men's and women's sports, the coverage of men's sports still focuses primarily on the active physical moving body as subject, while women sporting stars are still framed most often as objects for the male voyeuristic gaze.

Box 17.2   'Sex sells'

In the majority of cases, the sexualisation of elite female athletes has been the dominant form of coverage and is used by sports organisations to try to attract sponsorship and greater media coverage. Magazines such as *Inside Sport* promote an 'emphasized femininity' by exclusively depicting semi-naked 'sports models' on their covers and in centrefold sections (Lenskyj, 1998).

(Continued)

Box 17.2   Continued

But it has not only been male editors and publishers who have relied on the 'Sex Sells' concept. Women too have been willing contributors to the reproduction of a masculine hegemony within sport. For example, former Australian hept-athlete Jane Fleming organised the production of the 1995 Golden Girls Calendar, which portrayed a range of Australian female track and field athletes, naked and bodypainted, in highly suggestive poses (Mikosza and Phillips, 1999; Lenskyj, 1995). More recently, the Australian women's soccer team, the Matildas, posed nude for a calendar shoot, designed to 'raise the profile' of women's soccer. The publisher's rationale for producing such a display was that: 'It is not appetising to watch women in baggy shorts and tops and socks up to their knees. There are feminine, athletic bodies underneath' (*Sunday Herald Sun*, 1999).

Women's exterior appearance rather than their playing skill is thus suggested as sufficient for interest in the sport. Female athletes themselves have been complicit in their sexual exploitation, choosing to strip for promotional purposes or adopting explicit sportswear that displays advertisers' logos in suggestive places. Throughout the 1990s, a plethora of women's sports leagues and teams, such as basketball and hockey, have adopted skintight bodysuits as uniforms, and some netball teams even took to wearing sponsors' logos on their athletic briefs worn under their skirts (Burroughs and Nauright, 2000).

ETHNICITY

The discrimination faced by female athletes has also been experienced in different ways by sporting immigrants in Australia. As the British settled in Australia, it is not surprising that their traditional sports were transported as part of the cultural baggage. Traditional British sports served to introduce those born in the colonies to the ways of the 'home country' and became an important mechanism for the sustenance of English cultural values and norms, in short, of 'civilisation'. Besides the English, notable immigrant minorities in the colonies who added to the sporting tapestry were the Irish, the Scottish and, from the late 1830s, the Germans. Irish sports such as hurling and the Scottish Caledonian Games were enjoyed by those from their homelands, while the Germans who settled in South

Australia established shooting and rifle clubs, and were responsible for the introduction of *kegel* and gymnastics through the Turner Movement (Mosely et al., 1997).

Ethnic diversity in Australia increased with the migration waves that resulted from the discovery of gold in the 1850s. Men from Western Europe, China and the Americas joined British and Irish settlers. Amongst these immigrants, the Irish played an early version of Gaelic football, the Scots were crucial in the establishment and growth of golf, bowls and soccer, Germans spread the Turner Movement beyond South Australia, Norwegians introduced the locals of the Snowy Mountains to skiing, the Chinese played the gambling games of *fan-tan* and *pak-a-pu*, and the Americans built bowling alleys. All of these activities created distinct sporting cultures inextricably linked to ethnic groups and served an important role in maintaining migrant cultural traditions (Mosely et al., 1997). In the social milieu of colonial Australia, these sporting activities raised questions, which persisted throughout the twentieth century, about whether immigrants should assimilate by abandoning their own customs and traditions, or whether cultural pluralism should be adopted by embracing non-British ethnic cultures as part of the nation's identity.

The tension over assimilation and cultural pluralism grew in intensity as a consequence of the mass migration following the Second World War. Under the Federal Government policy of 'populate or perish', 1.5 million Europeans, mostly from Italy, Greece, Yugoslavia, Holland, Germany and Poland, came to Australia between 1945 and 1965 (Mosely et al., 1997). Many of these immigrants found affordable accommodation in the inner suburbs of Australian cities and, as a result, distinctive 'ethnic enclaves' were created (Booth and Tatz, 2000). These 'new Australians', like the colonisers before them, brought their regional and national sporting practices, and associations were quickly established to service these groups. As Mosely et al. (1997: xv) argue: 'It was in leisure activities or church organisations, rather than at work, that most immigrants of the 1950s and 1960s found the social, educational and support networks so necessary for newcomers in a strange land.' Sport served the important function of connecting pre-existing ethnic groups. Immigrants expressed their cultural heritage through new activities like *bocce* (Italian bowls), through existing sports like soccer, and through specific styles of participation and spectatorship. These endeavours, however, proved problematic in the context of the Federal Government social policy of assimilation which mandated the submission of imported customs and traditions to the dominant Anglo-Australian way of life (Booth and Tatz, 2000).

The pressure to assimilate ethnic cultures into Australian society was no more evident than in the sport of soccer. Although Australia was one of the first places in the world to form a soccer association (1882), prior to the Second World War, soccer was largely underdeveloped and did not enjoy the popularity it did throughout the rest of the world. It was regarded as a working-class game, flourishing in the New South Wales mining districts, and as a 'pommie' game, organised by English and Scottish migrants, at a time when Australian sports, run by locals, were gaining popularity during a period of emerging nationalism. This was compounded by the fact that Australian sports teams were organised around regions and districts, whilst the British-inspired soccer teams more often represent ethnic groupings, such as the Caledonians or the Rangers (Mosely and Murray, 1994).

With the influx of southern European migrants, soccer soon became associated almost exclusively with 'new Australians'. By 1949, teams that represented Italian, Maltese, Dutch, Yugoslav, Greek and Macedonian communities were founded, quickly followed by Jewish, Hungarian, Czechoslovakian, Polish, Serbian, Croatian and Ukrainian teams, amongst others. The British influence on soccer slowly dissipated as clubs came to represent much more than simply an avenue for physical expression. As Mosely and Murray (1994: 223) contend, there was simply less of a need for British migrants to 'seek shelter in a club of their own language and culture'.

But the greatest challenge to migrant clubs was the Australian postwar policy of assimilation, and 'those groups which more easily fitted into the "Australian way of life" were more easily accepted' (Mosely and

Murray, 1994: 224). Assimilation was based on assurances that the Australian 'way of life' would not change despite the influx of immigrants unfamiliar with the culture (Murphy, 2000). As a result, challenges to that 'way of life' were viewed with suspicion, and soccer clubs were considered to be exclusive ethnic enclaves which deliberately resisted assimilation (Hughson, 1997). Such attitudes are ironic, given that these clubs became a 'haven' for migrants suffering from racism, discrimination and a lack of familiarity with local customs.

Since this era, soccer has undergone a process of mainstreaming, whereby traditional 'ethnic' clubs have been forbidden from identifying with an ethnic community. In 1997, David Hill, then President of Soccer Australia, argued that:

If you take some of the old Sydney and Melbourne clubs, we are saying, look we really don't want you to play any more, decked out with the colours and insignia of a European country. We don't want you presenting yourselves as exclusively a team for Australian Croatians or exclusively for Australian Greeks. You should be appealing to all people in Australia. (Cited in Brabazon, 1998: 54)

The stance by soccer officials contradicts the contemporary appreciation of the multicultural dimensions of Australian society. Multiculturalism encourages and endorses members of ethnic groups 'to flaunt their ethnicity, [but] soccer clubs are expected to hide it' (Mosely and Murray, 1994: 229–30). The problem is not 'ethnicity' *per se*, but the kinds of ethnicities that are deemed undesirable. For example, Perth Glory, a soccer team that actively and loudly celebrates its Englishness, is not asked to ban the Union Jack flag from its games, nor is it asked to forbid the singing of English anthems. The rationale is that Englishness is a 'safe or

invisible ethnicity, whereas Greekness or Croatianness is [regarded as] dangerous to the sport' (Brabazon, 1998: 55). Soccer, as perhaps the only truly national game, is expected to appeal to 'all Australians', rather than minority segments. Overall, soccer indicates the historical and contemporary tensions in Australia, during periods of the contrasting social policies of assimilation and multiculturalism, that have shaped ethnic involvement in a predominantly Anglo-Australian sporting culture.

RACE

Like ethnicity, the concept of race, as well as racism, has permeated Australia's sporting cultures since the arrival of white colonisers in the late eighteenth century. To celebrate the centenary of the federation of Australia and as part of the ongoing process of reconciliation, in early 2001 Prime Minister John Howard announced that a cricket match would take place between black and white Australians. Howard revealed that the forthcoming match was 'a very important event symbolically because it recognises the importance of sport and particularly cricket to all Australians, indigenous and other Australians' and thus was 'an aid to reconciliation' (Howard, 2001). That an adversarial event would be used as a vehicle for reconciliation reveals much about racial tensions in Australian sport.

Whilst cricket may be depicted as a national pastime, one that is important to 'all Australians', the reality is that for most of Australia's history, sport has been enmeshed in racial politics. Academics have taken two contrasting approaches to Aboriginal history. One side of the debate, that of the 'oppositionists', stresses 'racial discrimination and the structures of colonial dominance' while their antagonists, the 'revisionists' emphasise 'Aboriginal agency in resisting or accommodating colonial power' (Broome, 2000: 130). Our stance in this debate supports the oppositionists' view of history. Sport remained the preserve of the white Anglo-Celtic man, and a means of maintaining racial exclusivity. Whilst some Aborigines have excelled in elite, competitive sport, the history of indigenous involvement in sport is a tale of prejudice, racism, discrimination, intolerance, active exclusion and denial of access to funding, selection and facilities (Tatz, 1995). This is not to say that Aborigines have not enjoyed a robust sporting culture (Tatz and Tatz, 2000), however, their inclusion in formal organised sporting structures has been sporadic at best, and only since the 1970s has there been any real effort to address the inequalities faced by Aboriginal athletes (Tatz, 1995).

Regarded by scientists as a 'doomed race', Aborigines were placed at the bottom of the human evolutionary chain. Many scientists in the nineteenth century thought that 'primitive' races either had to adapt to modern civilisation or face extinction. Whilst some early settlers treated Aborigines no better than wild animals, others believed that Aborigines should be taught the virtues of British and Christian civilisation. In this process, sport, particularly cricket, played a key role (Whimpress, 1999). Many believed that in order to 'become civilised', British cultural values had to be inculcated into indigenous Australians. As a result, cricket and other British cultural activities were established on Aboriginal mission stations and were used to teach indigenous peoples the values of 'sportsmanship' and 'fair play' (Tatz, 1995).

During the 1850s and 1860s, Aborigines were able to pursue a range of sporting activities and succeeded in cricket, pedestrianism (running) and boxing. Cricket remained popular and 'Aborigines played talented and enthusiastic cricket in an era which, while free legally, saw geographic isolation, rigid missionary control, settler animosity, poor diet, rampant illness and, of course, killing' (Tatz, 1994: 3). This limited access to sports ended by the late nineteenth century with greater legal and physical separation from white Australian society, an institutionalised racism that heralded the era of forced relocations and removals of mixed race children. As Booth

---

Box 17.3   Racial vilification and Australian Rules Football

Athletes still face racial slurs on and off the field, and the problem of racial vilification is best highlighted in a 1993 incident where fans of Collingwood Football Club taunted St Kilda player, Nicky Winmar, who responded by lifting his shirt and pointing to his skin. Collingwood President Allan McCalister's retort revealed the levels of racism inherent in Australian sport. McCalister suggested: 'as long as they [indigenous players] conduct themselves like white people ... everyone would admire and respect them' (cited in Nadel, 1998: 243). Following a public and media outcry, the Australian Football League Commission was forced to react, eventually implementing a code of conduct in 1995 to rid the game of racism and ethnic taunts (Nadel, 1998).

and Tatz (2000: 88) note, the exclusion of Aborigines from mainstream sport was 'virtually complete' by 1911. Settlements and reserves often had few or no facilities, many without even a patch of grass upon which to play, and many of these conditions remain today. Most Aborigines, particularly those living in remote communities, continue to have little if any access to adequate health and educational facilities, let alone formal organised sport.

Aboriginal athletes have endured active isolation and exclusion as well as overt racism within sport that has served to inhibit, if not destroy, the careers of some. Whilst many are still subjected to racist attacks within sport, increasingly, sports federations and leagues are being required to implement policies that will ensure protection from verbal assault, as well as greater access to facilities, funding and programmes. Critical commentators acknowledge these positive initiatives, but realise that racial ideologies are deeply embedded and change requires continuing reform from players, spectators, the media, sports organisations and governments.

CONCLUSION

The 2000 Games illustrate the increasing involvement of government in Australian sport. For the initial Olympic bid to be successful, state and federal governments had to underwrite the Games and commit large amounts of capital to finance the infrastructure. Few people criticised this expenditure at the same time that budgets for education, welfare and other social programmes were stripped (Booth and Tatz, 1994, 2000; Lenskyj, 2000). Equally importantly, state and federal governments poured more money than ever before into

producing international sporting stars. In 1994, a year after the Games were awarded to Sydney, the Australian Sports Commission began a six-year elite development programme aimed at winning 60 medals. One of the programmes implemented, the Olympic Athlete Programme (OAP), received over A$400m through a combination of state and federal government funding, including A$72m from the Australian Olympic Committee (Magdalinski, 2000). When Australia won a record number of medals, the links between governments, government-funded sporting agencies and elite sport were further enhanced.

The Games also illustrate the continuing commodification of Australian sport. The rights to broadcast the Sydney 2000 Games were hotly contested between the two leading networks, Channel Seven and Channel Nine. Seven won the rights to televise the Games at a cost of A$100m and for this received exclusive broadcasting throughout Australia. The Games rated very well, rarely slipping below 65 per cent of the total viewing audience and producing some of the highest rating shows in television history. Channel Seven sold advertising according to expected ratings, and used their broadcasts to satisfy other commercial needs, including station profiling, personality exposure and programming identification. The Olympic strategy was extremely effective. As a result of the Games, Channel Seven beat Channel Nine in the annual ratings for the first time in 44 years (*The Australian*, 2001) and earned a surplus revenue estimated at A$170–180m (*The Australian*, 2000).

Similarly, commercial companies tendered for the rights to be 'official' Olympic sponsors. These rights were sold to international sponsors, National Olympic Committee sponsors and Sydney 2000 sponsors who could advertise their association, in exclusive product categories, with the Games. These companies sought to take commercial advantage of this alliance while other competing businesses devised methods to circumvent their lack of Olympic association. The most obvious corporate battle was fought between the airline companies, Ansett, the 'official' Olympic airline, and Qantas. Qantas implemented a number of corporate ploys including running advertisements on Channel Seven during major Olympic events to create the impression they were associated with the Games. Their corporate battle was mimicked by telecommunications companies Optus and Telstra, sport equipment multinationals Nike and Adidas, car manufacturers Holden and Mitsubishi, and computer giants IBM and Microsoft. As the television networks and the commercial companies illustrate, the Olympic Games, like much of Australian sport, has become enmeshed in local, national and transnational corporate strategies.

Whilst the Games were a playground for corporate battles, they worked at a different level to interact with the racial, ethnic and gendered nature of Australian sport. Racial issues were always going to be central to the Games, with Aboriginal sprinter Cathy Freeman lighting the flame during the opening ceremony and winning Australia's only gold medal on the track. Her athletic successes were achieved against a backdrop of the Federal Government's refusal to apologise to Australia's indigenous people about past injustices, and massive street marches urging reconciliation. In this context, Freeman is regarded as a 'success' story. Her life is the kind of rags-to-riches drama that elides greater structural inequalities facing most Aboriginal athletes. She represents the struggle of a 'poor black kid from the bush' who, through hard work and determination, has 'made it' in sport and is held up as an exemplar for other Aboriginal Australians. Like cricket in the nineteenth century, Freeman is, in a sense, a modern-day 'civilising tool' that espouses individual effort over structural constraints. Her role is well summed up in her earlier athletic career by a newspaper comic, where an overweight white Australian male, with a beer in one hand, speaks to a group of Aboriginal women, who sit in front of ramshackle accommodation, cooking their meals over an open fire. He asks 'Why can't you all be like Cathy Freeman?' (*The Australian*, 1996). If Cathy Freeman's profile does little to address white Australia's treatment of its indigenous people and promote reconciliation issues, her success will remain just one more gold medal to add to the list.

As much as Cathy Freeman's medal victory, her role in lighting the Olympic flame and the centrality of Aboriginal culture in the opening and closing Olympic ceremonies belie the historical and contemporary plight of Aborigines in Australia, the same argument can be put forward for Australian sporting women. In some ways, the Olympic Games showcase women's sport. It was one of the few opportunities for female athletes to gain the recognition that is commonplace for their male counterparts. Previous research during the Olympic Games indicates that unlike any other time, women's sport is accorded larger amounts of media coverage (Mikosza, 1997). For two weeks successful female athletes like Freeman, Susie O'Neill and others are afforded the attention their athleticism deserves. From a quantitative perspective, women's sport is recognised, but much of this attention focuses on traditional aspects of femininity (Phillips, 1997), thereby reinforcing rather than confronting stereotypes. Of course, some female athletes use this media attention and profile to attract large endorsements and to establish careers built around their prowess, similar to male athletes. The reality for many is that there are still fewer activities available for female athletes, as well as fewer coaching and administration positions.

The Sydney 2000 Olympics highlighted other tensions. Prior to the opening match in the soccer event, questions were raised over whether Melbourne's sizeable Italian community would be more likely to barrack for Australia or Italy. Streetside interviews were held by major television stations and many third- and fourth-generation Italian-Australians were broadcast professing their allegiance to Italy. Anglo-Australians responded with incredulity that 'Aussies' were thinking of supporting a rival nation. On the other hand, recent immigrants such as Russian-born polevaulter Tatiana Grigorieva and her husband Viktor Tchistiakov were hailed as successful members of the Australian team, and coaches and athletes from former European communist countries were accepted as part of the Australian sporting landscape. For the most part, however, the ethnic origins of Australian Olympic athletes were ignored and the team members were incorporated into a generic 'Aussieness' that neglected the tensions and struggles faced by athletes from immigrant communities.

The Sydney 2000 Games are an outstanding example of nationalism overriding the gendered, racial and ethnic dimensions of Australian sport. For a fleeting nationalistic moment, successful women, Aborigines and non-Anglo-Saxons, and in the case of the Paralympics, people with disabilities, are embraced by the wider Australian community. Unfortunately, when the flame was extinguished, so too was the equal sporting citizenship temporarily accorded to these athletes. In stark contrast, the Games reinforced the increasing role for governments as well as the inextricable link with local, national and transnational companies and corporations, as political and economic incentives increased with the global exposure provided by the most watched sporting event in the world.

Chapter summary

- The development of Australian sport is a mixture of local, British and American sport.
- Government involvement in Australian sport has existed at local, state and national levels.
- Australian sport has always been a commodity but the level of commodification has increased with the development of the media sports cultural complex.
- Opportunities for men and women have been important in creating gendered identities through sport.
- The social policies of assimilation and multiculturalism have shaped ethnic involvement in a predominantly Anglo-Australian sporting culture.
- Racial ideologies have limited indigenous participation to a small number of sports and have been a dominant feature of the sporting landscape.

Further reading

There have been four relatively recent books which have looked at Australian sport from contemporary and historical perspectives. McKay (1991) is an excellent analysis of contemporary Australian sport, while Adair and Vamplew (1997), Booth and Tatz (2000) and Cashman (1995) analyse contemporary sport in Australia from a historical basis.

REFERENCES

Adair, D. and Vamplew, W. (1997) *Sport in Australian History*. Melbourne: Oxford University Press.

Armstrong, T. (1988) 'Goldlust: federal sports policy since 1975'. Unpublished PhD thesis. Macquarie University, Sydney.

Armstrong, T. (1994) 'Government policy', in W. Vamplew, K. Moore, J. O'Hara, R. Cashman and I. Jobling (eds), *The Oxford Companion to Australian Sport*. 2nd edn. Melbourne: Oxford University Press, pp. 188–200.

The Australian (1996) 3–4 August: 20.

The Australian (2000) 7–8 October: 12.

The Australian (2001) 12 February: 3.

Barnett, S. (1990) *Games and Sets: the Changing Face of Sport on Television*. London: BFI Publishing.

Booth, D. and Tatz, C. (1994) '"Swimming with the big boys"? The politics of Sydney's 2000 Olympic bid', *Sporting Traditions*, 11 (1): 3–23.

Booth, D. and Tatz, C. (2000) *One-Eyed: a View of Australian Sport*. St Leonards, NSW: Allen & Unwin.

Brabazon, T. (1998) 'What's the story Morning Glory? Perth Glory and the imagining of Englishness', *Sporting Traditions*, 14 (2): 53–66.

Broome, R. (2000) Review of: Bernard Whimpress, *Passport to Nowhere: Aborigines in Australian Cricket 1850–1939*. *Sporting Traditions*, 16 (2): 129–31.

Burroughs, A. and Nauright, J. (2000) 'Women's sport and embodiment in Australia and New Zealand', *International Journal of the History of Sport*, 17 (2/3): 188–205.

Carle, A. and Nauright, J. (1999) 'Women playing a "man's game": a case study of women playing Rugby Union in Australia', *Football Studies*, 2 (1): 55–74.

Cashman, R. (1995) *Paradise of Sport: the Rise of Organised Sport in Australia*. South Melbourne, Vic.: Oxford University Press.

Cashman, R. and Hughes, A. (1998) 'Sydney 2000: cargo cult of Australian sport?', in D. Rowe and G. Lawrence (eds), *Tourism, Leisure, Sport: Critical Perspectives*. Sydney: Hodder Headline, pp. 216–25.

Cronin, M. (1998) '"When the World Soccer Cup is played on roller skates": the attempt to make Gaelic Games international: the Meath-Australia matches of 1967–68', in M. Cronin and D. Mayall (eds), *Sporting Nationalisms: Identity, Ethnicity, Immigration, and Assimilation*. London: Cass, pp. 170–88.

Daly, J.A. (1991) *Quest for Excellence: the Australian Institute of Sport*. Canberra: Australian Government Publishing Service.

Gordon, S. (1989) *Drop-out Phenomenon in Organised Sport*. Perth: Department of Human Movement and Recreation Studies, University of Western Australia.

Hallinan, C. (1991) 'Aborigines and positional segregation in Australian Rugby League', *International Review for Sociology of Sport*, 26 (2): 69–79.

Hallinan, C.J., Bruce, T. and Coram, S. (1999) 'Up front and beyond the centre line: Australian Aborigines in elite Australian Rules Football', *International Review for Sociology of Sport*, 34 (4): 369–83.

Hess, R. and Stewart, B. (1998) *More Than A Game: an Unauthorised History of Australian Rules Football*. Melbourne: Melbourne University Press.

Hogan, K. and Norton, K. (2000) 'The "price" of Olympic gold', *Journal of Science and Medicine in Sport*, 3 (2): 203–18.

Holt, R. (1989) *Sport and the British: a Modern History*. Oxford: Clarendon Press.

Horne, J., Tomlinson, A. and Whannel, G. (1999) *Understanding Sport: an Introduction to* the Sociological and Cultural Analysis of Sport. London: E. & F. N. Spon.

Houlihan, B. (1997) Sport, Policy, and Politics: a Comparative Analysis. London and New York: Routledge.

Houlihan, B. (2000) 'Politics and sport', in J. Coakley and E. Dunning (eds), Handbook of Sport Studies. London: Sage, pp. 213–27.

Howard, J. (2001) Transcript of the Prime Minister the Hon. John Howard MP. Joint Press Conference with Mr Geoff Clark, Chairman of ATSIC–SCG, Sydney, 3 January 2001. Retrieved 17 January 2001, http://www.pm.gov.au/news/interviews/2001/interview636.htm

Hughson, J. (1997) 'The Croatian community', in P.A. Mosely, R. Cashman, J. O'Hara and H. Weatherburn (eds), Sporting Immigrants: Sport and Ethnicity in Australia. Sydney: Walla Walla Press, pp. 50–62.

Hutchins, B. and Phillips, M.G. (1999) 'The global union: globalization and the Rugby World Cup', in T.J.L. Chandler and J. Nauright (eds), Making the Rugby World: Race, Gender, Commerce. London: Frank Cass, pp. 149–64.

Kane, M. and Greendorfer, S. (1994) 'The media's role in accommodating and resisting stereotyped images of women in sport', in P. Creedon (ed.), Women, Media and Sport: Challenging Gender Values. California: Sage, pp. 28–44.

King, H. (1979) 'The sexual politics of sport: an Australian perspective', in M. McKernan and R. Cashman (eds), Sport in History: the Making of Modern Sporting History. St Lucia, Brisbane: University of Queensland Press.

Lenskyj, H. (1995) 'Sport and the threat to gender boundaries', Sporting Traditions, 12 (1): 47–60.

Lenskyj, H. (1998) '"Inside sport" or "On the margins"?', International Review for Sociology of Sport, 33 (1): 19–32.

Lenskyj, H. (2000) Inside the Olympic Industry: Power, Politics and Activism. Albany, NY: State University of New York Press.

McKay, J. (1990) 'Sport, leisure and social inequality in Australia', in D. Rowe and G. Lawrence (eds), Sport and Leisure: Trends in Australian Popular Culture. Sydney: Harcourt Brace Jovanovich, pp. 125–60.

McKay, J. (1991) No Pain, No Gain? Sport and Australian Culture. New York: Prentice Hall.

McKay, J. (1994) 'Embodying the "new" sporting woman', Hecate, 20 (1): 68–83.

McKay, J. (1997) Managing Gender: Affirmative Action and Organizational Power in Australian, Canadian and New Zealand Sport. Albany, NY: State University of New York Press.

McKay, J., Martin, R. and Miller, T. (1999) 'Mauresmo, the media and homophobia'. Paper presented at the Teams and Fans Conference, Mudjimba Beach, Queensland, 15–18 July.

McKay, J., Hughson, J., Lawrence, G. and Rowe, D. (2000) 'Sport and Australian society', in J.M. Najman and J.S. Western (eds), A Sociology of Australian Society. 3rd edn. Melbourne: Macmillan, pp. 275–300.

Magdalinski, T. (2000) 'The reinvention of Australia for the Sydney 2000 Olympic Games', International Journal of the History of Sport, 17 (2/3): 305–22.

Magdalinski, T. (2001) 'Drugs Inside Sport: the rehabilitation of Samantha Riley', Sporting Traditions, 17 (2): 17–32.

Menzies, H. (1989) 'Women's sport: treatment by the media', in K. Dwyer (ed.), Sportswomen towards 2000: a Celebration. Adelaide: University of Adelaide, pp. 220–31.

Mikosza, J. (1997) Inching Forward: Newspaper Coverage and Portrayal of Women's Sport in Australia: a Quantitative and Qualitative Analysis. Canberra: Womensport Australia.

Mikosza, J. and Phillips, M. (1999) 'Gender, sport and the body politic: framing femininity in the Golden Girls of Sport Calendar and The Atlanta Dream', International Review for Sociology of Sport, 34 (1): 5–16.

Mosely, P. and Murray, B. (1994) 'Soccer', in W. Vamplew and B. Stoddart (eds), Sport in Australia: a Social History. Melbourne: Cambridge University Press, pp. 213–30.

Mosely, P.A., Cashman, R., O'Hara, J. and Weatherburn, H. (eds) (1997) Sporting Immigrants: Sport and Ethnicity in Australia. Sydney: Walla Walla Press.

Murphy, J. (2000) Imagining the Fifties: Private Sentiment and Political Culture in Menzies' Australia. Sydney: University of New South Wales Press.

Nadel, D. (1998) 'The League goes national, 1986–1997', in R. Hess and B. Stewart (eds), More Than A Game: an Unauthorised History of Australian Rules Football. Melbourne: Melbourne University Press, pp. 243–55.

Phillips, D. (1992) Australian Women at the Olympic Games 1912–92. Kenthurst, NSW: Kangaroo Press.

Phillips, M.G. (1997) *An Illusory Image: a Report on the Media Coverage and Portrayal of Women's Sport in Australia 1996*. Canberra: Australian Sports Commission.

Phillips, M.G. (1998) 'From suburban football to international spectacle: the commodification of Rugby League in Australia, 1907–1995', *Australian Historical Studies*, 29 (110): 27–48.

Phillips, M.G. (2000) *From Sidelines to Centre Field: a History of Sports Coaching in Australia*. Sydney: University of New South Wales Press.

Rowe, D. (1997) 'Rugby League in Australia: the Super League saga', *Journal of Sport and Social Issues*, 21 (2): 221–6.

Rowe, D. (1999) *Sport, Culture and the Media: the Unruly Trinity*. Buckingham: Open University Press.

Rowe, D. (2000) 'Sport: the genre that runs and runs', in G. Turner and S. Cunningham (eds), *The Australian TV Book*. Sydney: Allen & Unwin, pp. 130–41.

Rowe, D., Lawrence, G., Miller, T. and McKay, J. (1994) 'Global sport? Core concern and peripheral vision', *Media, Culture & Society*, 16 (4): 661–75.

Sage, G.H. (1990) *Power and Ideology in American Sport: a Critical Perspective*. Champaign, IL: Human Kinetics.

Shilbury, D. and Deane, J. (1998) *Sport Management in Australia: An Organisational Overview*. Burwood, Vic.: Bowater School of Management and Marketing Deakin University.

Stoddart, B. (1986) *Saturday Afternoon Fever: Sport in Australian Culture*. North Ryde, Sydney: Angus & Robertson.

Stoddart, B. (1994) *Invisible Games: a Report on the Media Coverage of Women's Sport*. Canberra: Australian Sports Commission.

Sunday Herald Sun (1999) 28 November.

Tatz, C. (1994) 'Aborigines in sport', in W. Vamplew, K. Moore, J. O'Hara, R. Cashman and I. Jobling (eds), *The Oxford Companion to Australian Sport*. Melbourne: Oxford University Press, pp. 3–7.

Tatz, C. (1995) *Obstacle Race: Aborigines in Sport*. Sydney: University of New South Wales Press.

Tatz, C. and Tatz, P. (2000) *Black Gold: the Aboriginal and Islander Sports Hall of Fame*. Canberra: Aboriginal Studies Press.

Thompson, S. (1999) *Mother's Taxi: Sport and Women's Labour*. Albany, NY: State University of New York Press.

Whimpress, B. (1999) *Passport to Nowhere: Aborigines in Australian Cricket 1850–1939*. Sydney: Walla Walla Press.

18

Sport, the Role of the European Union and the Decline of the Nation State?

IAN P. HENRY

Overview

→ The evolution of the European project
→ The nature of national sovereignty and its erosion in the later twentieth century
→ Evolving competences for the EU in respect of leisure policy
→ Five rationales for EU intervention in sport
→ The future of the EU and the nation state in sport policy – some conclusions

The rapid intensification and expanding scope of interactions between societies and polities in the contemporary world has led some authors to project a significant weakening of nation states and occasionally even to question whether we are likely to see the demise of the nation state as an institution (Mann, 1997; Morris, 1997; Schachter, 1997; van Deth, 1995). The decline of the nation state is, for many commentators, most strongly evidenced in the construction of the European Union. Core functions of the nation state, such as the production of a national currency, and the macroeconomic policy associated with this, have already been ceded to a European institution. However, such predictions of the nation state's demise are keenly contested (Hirst and Thompson, 1995; Shaw, 1997). The emergence of political, economic or cultural transnational bodies, it is pointed out, are controlled, regulated and legitimated at local level by local institutions, often by the nation state itself. Within this context, this chapter seeks to evaluate the impact of the European project on the relationship between the European Union and the nation state, focusing in particular on its implications for sports policy.

The aim of this chapter is to evaluate not simply the nature, but also the significance of, and rationales for, policy shifts in sport in relation to the European Union. The chapter is divided into five sections: the first considers the stages in the development of the unfolding European project; the second deals with the changing nature of national sovereignty in contemporary Europe; the third highlights the shifting of competences[1] in sport from the national to the European level; the fourth provides a typology of the rationales behind policy intervention in the leisure field at the European level; and the final section considers the implications of this for the relationship between the European Union and member states, arguing that claims for the demise of the state are exaggerated, and that a new set of tensions and balances is being negotiated between the European Union, the nation state and civil institutions.

The first two of these sections relate to the generic context of the European project, while the remainder focus more specifically on sports policy issues.

THE EVOLUTION OF THE EUROPEANISATION PROJECT: INTERGOVERNMENTAL VERSUS SUPRAGOVERNMENTAL APPROACHES

The development of sports policy in the European Union is inevitably a reflection of the nature of the Union itself, and in particular the tension between those who would wish to see it operate as an *intergovernmental* body rather than a *supranational* entity. The distinction here is between a body which has power by virtue of agreements between governments – thus intergovernmental – and one that can require governments to act in particular ways whether or not they so wish to act – supranational. The changing nature of the Union and its conception are evident in the evolving nomenclature

which is used to refer to it, which reflects three principal stages in the development: from 'Common Market', which indicated a primary concern with elimination of tariff barriers; through 'European Community', which implied a wider communal set of interests; to 'European Union', with a clearer emphasis on political integration, and, some might argue, federalism. The significance of these name changes is that each implies a different stage in the development of the project, and a different relationship between the EU and the nation state with further implications for policy.

The development of the 'Common Market'

The European Economic Community, or the Common Market as it was initially popularly titled, was established in 1957 with the Treaty of Rome. It set itself the principal goal of eliminating tariff barriers within approximately 15 years. While it is clear that for many of those involved in the inception of the EU, the Treaty of Rome was intended as a road that would lead to political union, this was not reflected in the wording of the Treaty itself.

However, although the Treaty dealt almost exclusively with the requirements to establish a common market area of free trade, there was a declared intention to move forward on matters relating to European Union. Discussions at the time of the drawing up the Treaty had clearly signalled the intention to introduce majority voting for certain policy issues, which would have removed the possibility of any given state vetoing action in those areas and thus reduced the power of the governments of the member states.

This was a matter of real contention. General de Gaulle, promoting the notion of *l'Europe des Patries*, tipped the balance in favour of those who opposed stronger integration by simply refusing to have France represented at European Community meetings – the 'empty chair' policy – thereby frustrating any advance on this and other issues such as Britain's membership. The 'Luxembourg compromise', which was agreed as a way out of this impasse, de facto set back the introduction of majority voting, offering member states a virtual veto by allowing them to appeal against the use of majority votes on matters that they deemed to be of 'national interest'.

With de Gaulle's political demise, there was progress towards a more centralised and interventionist stance for the EC, with the resourcing of the Common Agricultural Policy from European sources rather than from national funds, and the introduction of a targeted regional funding system. However, the global economic and oil crises of the early 1970s turned governments back to more national goals. Progress at the beginning of the 1970s had seemed possible. The term 'European Union' was, for example, actually introduced at the Paris Summit of 1971 but it was vague and undefined and met with little opposition because it signified very little. European Monetary Union originally envisaged to be achieved by 1980 was also deferred in the aftermath of crises of global economies.

The European Community

Despite these delays and frustrations, the establishment of a European Community, as opposed to a common market of European nations, was to be effected in the 1980s following the enhancement of the power of the Commission, the increased legitimacy of the European Parliament which was directly elected from 1979; and the institu-tionalisation of the Council of Ministers from 1974. Enlargement, with the accession of the southern European states in the 1980s, also implied an extension to the majority voting procedure if political paralysis were to be avoided and this itself also implied some weakening of the sovereignty of states.

The move to European Union was to be promoted at the Fontainebleau summit of 1983 which established two groups, the Dooge Committee which was to assess the options for political change, and a *Committee for a People's Europe*, which was charged with evaluating how the EC might promote the growth of a European identity across the populations of the member states. In terms of the significance of sport in the process of Europeanisation, the Adonino Report of the Committee for a Peoples' Europe is of key importance.

However it was the Single European Act (SEA), ratified in the late 1980s to take effect in 1992, which represented the springboard to the next stage of development. On the face of it, this establishment of a frontierless internal market via the Single European Act was the core of the minimalist view of the Common Market. However, allowing the free flow of capital, people, goods and services across frontiers is more than a simple matter of economics. Put crudely, the move to a single market would mean increasing pressure to move to one business culture (southern European business hours and practices differ from those of northern Europe) and perhaps one language of business – which was likely to be English.

The European Union

The SEA thus opened the back door to the deepening of co-operation between member states in more than just economic matters, and, though being concerned with market reform, it made explicit reference to areas such as regional disparity, improvement in living and working conditions, and the quality of life. The next major move was also in effect in the economic domain, with the establishing of a Single European Currency. However, the Treaty on European Union negotiated at Maastricht and its successor Treaty of Amsterdam in 1997, incorporated not only the mechanism and timetable for organising monetary union, but also included for the first time an article on culture and, in the Amsterdam Treaty, a declaration on sport, reflecting the twin deepening of the cultural and the economic dimensions of the Union. This set of concerns in relation to sport was also to be developed further in the fuller statement on sport in Appendix IV of the Nice Treaty in 2001.

What is provided above is a thumbnail sketch of the history of the development of the European Union. Nevertheless it serves to illustrate how the construction of simply a common market requires a degree of political integration to enforce common rules. This in turn implies a requirement for greater cultural integration to ensure public acceptance and legitimacy for this political project. Each of these elements is bound up with questions of national sovereignty and thus before going on to discuss European Union intervention in sport, some clarification of the nature of sovereignty is required.

THE NATURE OF NATIONAL SOVEREIGNTY AND ITS EROSION IN THE LATER TWENTIETH CENTURY

It is perhaps ironic that while we are discussing the purported erosion of the significance of the nation state by the European project, the notion of the nation state itself is generally attributed to its roots in Europe.

The flexibility of the European state system has been apparent in its ability to adapt to changing circumstances with, for example, the absolute monarchies of the eighteenth century transforming into the industrial and national states of the nineteenth century, and into the welfare states of the twentieth century (Laffan et al., 2000). The question that faces the state at the beginning of the twenty-first century is whether, in the context of a globalised political economy, it has exhausted its capacity for transformation and adaptation, or whether new forms of governance are likely to supplant it. It is in this context that we are evaluating the emerging division of labour and responsibility in sports policy between the European Union and the nation state.

If we wish to evaluate the nature of the erosion of sovereignty for European states, it will be important to distinguish different types of sovereignty – legal, political and popular, since, as Laffan et al. (2000) point out, there are different trajectories in respect of each of these three forms. The loss of sovereignty of member states to the European Union is most clearly evident in respect of *legal sovereignty*, since the EU has, through the European Court of Justice, established a legal order such that 'each member state now has two interlocking constitutions' (Temple-Lang, 1996: 126). The ways in which the EU imposes legal obligation on its member states generally takes one of two forms: a directive, which requires that national legislation be adapted to achieve specified ends; or a regulation, which in effect specifies a legal requirement directly. Since EU legislation can be made without reference to domestic parliaments, it is argued by some commentators that this fosters a democratic deficit.

In terms of *legal* sovereignty then, there are clearly grounds to make the claim that aspects of sovereignty have been eroded and this, as we shall see, can have specific implications, for example, in a nation's laws in respect of sport or leisure. *Political* sovereignty, the right to make political decisions in respect of one's own territory and people, might also be said to have been undermined by the introduction of majority voting. As we have already noted, there is a considerable amount of disagreement as to whether one should regard the EU as an intergovernmental body, or a supragovernmental body. The matter is complicated by the fact that EU arrangements are framed by intergovernmental agreements, the founding treaties, for example, and when certain aspects such as the removal of passport controls under the Schengen Agreement, the social chapter in the Maastricht Treaty, or the establishment of European Monetary Union, have not been to a government's liking, it has been possible for that state to opt out. Nevertheless the process of centralisation of power in the institutions of the Community has proceeded apace. With the likelihood of further extension of majority voting, decisions affecting the internal affairs of member states will, in principle at least, be subject to decisions made externally, but only where intergovernmental agreement exists. It seems, therefore, that the most one can claim about political sovereignty is that it has been compromised or 'pooled', through processes of voluntary collaboration in intergovernmental agreements, rather than diluted (Laffan et al., 2000).

Popular sovereignty stands in contrast to the other two forms of sovereignty in that democracy in the form of voting arrangements and political representation is organised solely along national lines. Nationally defined popular sovereignty remains in place, even for elections to the European Parliament, though there has been recent debate about direct election of a European President, counting votes across national boundaries which would breach the principle of national, popular sovereignty.

One of the reasons why nationalism is so deeply entrenched is that it is a key element of the cultural identity of individuals. It is partly imbued through what Anthony Smith (1983) calls myths of shared 'primordial' national origins, and is promoted through the construction of 'imagined communities', to coin Anderson's term (Anderson, 1983). Thus, if the nation state were to be weakened as an organising unit, then alternative sources of identity would be required. Leisure, culture and sport are of course important elements in the development of national identities and thus leisure, cultural and sports policy are likely to be key to discussions about the diminution of the nation state.

EVOLVING COMPETENCES FOR THE EUROPEAN UNION IN RESPECT OF LEISURE POLICY AND THE GOVERNANCE OF RELATED POLICY DOMAINS

Intrinsically bound up with the development of the European project and with the erosion, pooling or loss of sovereignty, are issues of subsidiarity. Subsidiarity is a concept related to governance which is central to the philosophy of the European Community. Vertical subsidiarity is the principle by which decisions are taken at the lowest level of government possible. Decisions about, for example, whether to teach in minority languages, such as Basque, are a matter for local decision-makers, while policy relating, for example, to the monitoring and control of pollution can only really be effective if agreed at the transnational level, since pollution produced in one country may potentially affect many others. Horizontal subsidiarity is the principle by which matters of policy are only decided by government if they cannot be effectively displaced on to the voluntary or commercial sector.

Which policy domains then lend themselves to 'governmental' intervention at the European or supranational level? There are some obvious candidates, such as environmental policy or trade policy, and some contested areas such as defence and foreign policy. But what of cultural and leisure policy – at what levels are decisions best taken for this policy domain? There are some aspects, such as broadcasting policy, which clearly require supranational regulation because broadcasts cannot be restricted by national boundaries. Nevertheless other areas of cultural policy, such as sport, at first glance seem likely to lend themselves to the application of the principles of vertical and horizontal subsidiarity. Such a suggestion is, however, at odds with the fact that the Maastricht Treaty defined a new competence for the EU in respect of culture, and its revision at Amsterdam in 1997 incorporated a declaration on sport, effectively laying down a marker for future definition of the EU's legitimate interest in sport, which was partially articulated in an appendix on sport to the Nice Treaty in 2001. Nevertheless, there is a problem for those who advocate European intervention in sport or culture of defending the basis or the rationale for such intervention.

FIVE RATIONALES FOR EU INTERVENTION IN SPORT

1 Sport as trade

While the European Union may have no clear and unambiguous competence in matters of sport, it certainly does in respect of trade. Policy in respect of trade provides one of the *raisons d'être* of the European Community, and sport is an increasingly significant area of trading activity representing an estimated 3 per cent of gross domestic product for all Council of Europe member states. Intervention in the sports field in the early years of the European Community was restricted solely to that justified by policy relating to trade, as the 1973 decision of the European Court of Justice (ECJ) in the Walrave and Koch case illustrates, when the Court declared that: 'the practice of sport is subject to Community law so far as it constitutes an economic activity in the meaning of Article 2 of the Treaty'.

The economic rationale for intervention in sport also underpins the Heylens decision of the ECJ in 1986. Heylens was a Belgian football coach employed in France who was taken to the French courts for practising his trade without obtaining a French football coaching qualification. He did, however, hold a Belgian qualification which the ECJ accepted was of equivalent standing. In this case the ECJ overruled the French court's decision that a specific French qualification could be required. This decision, although made on the grounds of restraint of trade, had clear implications for vertical subsidiarity in sport. National legislation could be subordinate to European rulings in the field of sport.

While the Heylens case illustrates the erosion of vertical subsidiarity, the Bosman case of 1995 illustrates the clear erosion of horizontal subsidiarity in respect of sport. Professional sport could no longer, after Bosman, be regarded simply as a matter for voluntary or commercial sector interests. The Bosman case related to two significant elements. The first was freedom of movement of professionals at the end of their period of contract with clubs. But it is the second which concerns us here, in that Bosman successfully appealed against a

UEFA and French Football Association ruling which limited the number of foreign nationals playing in professional teams in domestic or European competition. This element of the Bosman appeal was based on the argument that such quotas for foreign players restricted freedom of movement of professionals within the EU.

The Bosman ruling has important implications for the production of 'local' talent. Among the anticipated economic effects of the removal of European tariff barriers was an expectation that production would develop in a borderless Europe on the basis of regional specialisation. Cars, for example, would be produced in those regions where production could be accomplished most cheaply, or where the greatest level of required skills was available. This logic implies that some nations/regions will not have a car production capacity, but that this will be compensated for by those industries where the region does possess key market advantages. If this economic rationale were applied to professional sport (as implied by the Bosman ruling), then a likely consequence would be a major decline in the local production of sporting talent for some member states. A national or regional economy can, of course, survive without the capacity to produce cars, but can a national culture survive without a capacity to produce sporting stars, when sport is a strong feature of national identity? The impact of the Bosman ruling is visible throughout Europe. In Britain, expensive imports of high-quality players dominate the Premier Leagues of English and Scottish football, while cheaper (often Eastern and Central European) imports are increasingly taking up places in the lower divisions of the domestic leagues, restricting the opportunities of the development of home-grown talent. UEFA requested in 2000 that the EU reconsider the position of sport as a special case, arguing that culture and broadcasting had been treated as exceptions to aspects of competition law, but this request was rejected.

If the rationale that underpins the Bosman case is that sport is an industry like any other, and should therefore be treated in exactly the same manner, a different type of argument has been mobilised in the revision of the *Television without Frontiers* directive (1997). According to the directive, access via television to selected sporting events for the general population can be protected by national governments which may reserve for free-to-air television the broadcasting of a limited number of sporting events of particular national importance. In other words the rationale here is that sport is more than simply a product, and that its broadcasting rights cannot therefore be simply sold to the highest bidder. Sport is, in effect, part of a nation's cultural heritage and may be subject to protectionism. This provision of special treatment for sport stands in stark contrast to the thinking behind the Bosman ruling.

One aspect of the special status of sport is however reflected in the revisions to the transfer system agreed in 2001 between the Commission, FIFA and UEFA. This agreement limited the length of contracts to five years, but incorporated a form of compensation for the costs of education and training for a player, so that the smaller clubs, which produced players who then moved on, would be compensated for their efforts.

2 Sport as a tool of economic regeneration

While the initial development of the European Community took place in the period of postwar growth which continued up until the 1970s, it was clear by the time of the first enlargement of the Community, with the addition of Britain, Ireland and Denmark in 1973, that regional disparities were growing, not simply in the non-industrialised regions, but also in those traditional industrial regions which had gone into decline. The development of the Structural Funds (including the establishment of the European Regional Development Fund, targeted principally at lagging and deindustrialising regions, and the expansion of the European Social Fund, aimed at combating unemployment) has been used in the funding of sport and leisure on a quite significant basis (Bates & Wacker S.C., 1993). Although regional funding should form part of an integrated strategy and have clear economic goals, it is clear that some applicants, while rehearsing economic arguments in order to attract funding, are themselves more concerned to achieve social objectives (Matthews and Henry, 2001). The European Social Fund, which is designed to generate new employment opportunities, also has social goals in the sense of targeting disadvantaged groups. Sport and leisure, as elements in the growing service sector, represent areas in which employment opportunities may be generated (Le Roux et al., 1999). Thus in the 1980s a variety of sport-related schemes were developed at local level with social as well as economic implications, such as the Comsport scheme funded under the ESF in the East Midlands of England, which generated job training for women in community sports development (Seary, 1992).

The competitive position of lagging regions is deemed to be a product of a mix of factors including physical, service, educational and cultural infrastructures, and regional policy. Thus, improvement of cultural infrastructure to make regions more effective in attracting capital is legitimately funded for economic development purposes.

Nevertheless there are significant potential social gains claimed by applicants for much of this funding in respect of reducing inequalities. However, as commentators such as Harvey (1989) and Lash and Urry (1994) point out, much of the sporting or cultural infrastructure developed for economic regeneration purposes targets groups such as service-class professionals, who will need to be retained in lagging or deindustrialising regions; consequently the investment in such cultural provision may reinforce rather than challenge social inequities in leisure. The examples of Sheffield in the UK and Bilbao in Spain illustrate this point.

Sheffield attracted ERDF funding for some of the facilities required for the World Student Games which it staged in 1991. The intention of the local authority was to use the Games as a vehicle for reimaging the city and providing new 'state of the art' facilities. However, the Games provided a huge financial burden for the local authority, and though the facilities inherited have allowed the staging of a programme of international sporting events in Sheffield, prices for ordinary members of the community using these new sports facilities have risen considerably (Henry and Paramio-Salcines, 1999). In the case of swimming, despite the provision of new pools to replace old dilapidated facilities, the number of people swimming in the city declined in the post-Games period against a national background of growth in participation (Taylor, 1998).

Similarly, the Guggenheim project in Bilbao represented an attempt to put Bilbao on the global cultural map. Although redevelopment of the river front benefited from European funding, the scheme attracted criticism that local culture was being sacrificed to pander to the tourist market and that cultural budgets on behalf of local governments were totally absorbed by the prestige project (Henry and Paramio-Salcines, 1998). Thus the use of sport and leisure for economic regeneration purposes is not unproblematic.

3   Sport and social integration

Although the initial phase of development of the EC was dominated by economic concerns to set up an area of free trade, the implications of this process for the social as well as economic exclusion of some of its citizens were well recognised, and were reflected in the inception of the ESF in 1962. However, although social policy has been a continuing and growing concern of the EU, with, for example, the introduction of the 'social chapter' in the Treaty of Maastricht, the focus of concern has been predominantly with economic exclusion, or economically related aspects of social exclusion, such as sex discrimination in pay and conditions, or the use of employment initiatives to integrate ethnic minorities into the workforce.

There has, however, been some use of other European funds directly on sport, and this has in large part been aimed at aspects of social exclusion. A budgetary line in relation to sport was first inserted in the EC budget in the early 1990s in response to the expressed interests of members of the European Parliament.[2] The budget represented a small amount, but was not without controversy. In the budget negotiations of the first half of the decade, the Commission (in which sport's interests were relatively weakly represented in a smaller directorate) eliminated the budget only to have it reinstated at the insistence of the European Parliament.[3] The original sports budget incorporated the European Awareness Budget (to which we return below) and funds directed at young people and socially

excluded groups, particularly disability sport. The budget was consolidated into the Eurathlon Programme in 1996, with broadly the same objectives. However, despite enthusiasm in some quarters, particularly among a small group of MEPs who had formed the Sports Intergroup in the Parliament, there were worries that there was no legal justification for EU expenditure on sport *per se*, since sport had not been incorporated as a competence in the founding treaties, and there was some concern on the part of officials that the justification of expenditure was rather tenuous. Apparently as a result of this, the Eurathlon Programme was abruptly discontinued in 1998, when a number of European Commissioners came under investigation for activities in other policy fields, and subsequently resigned over issues relating to use of European funds for activities without appropriate legal justification.

In the period 1995–97, some of the key actors in the European sports scene had been involved in lobbying member states and European Commissioners to establish a competence in the field of sport in the revisions of the Treaty on European Union at Amsterdam (Arnedt, 1998). The support for such a move was by no means universal. UEFA, for example, and some of the other European bodies representing professional sports were very wary, having been profoundly and (as they saw it) adversely affected by the EU through the Bosman decision. This and issues such as the ban on tobacco sponsorship made a number of people in the sports world nervous about increasing the powers of the EU to intervene in sport, nevertheless the amateur sports group were broadly supportive. In the end the lobby was not entirely successful, a competence was not incorporated in the Amsterdam Treaty, but a Declaration on Sport[4] was adopted which dealt specifically only with amateur sport, but which was seized upon by interested MEPs, who subsequently called for a full review of the EU's role in sport (Pack, 1997). This has been used as the stimulus for discussions (such as the First European Conference on Sport in Olympia in 1999) that have incorporated concerns in particular with broadcasting and interpenetration of sports and media ownership, and has also resulted in a fuller statement on sport being added in an appendix to the Nice Treaty in 2001.

4   Sport as an ideological tool

The role of sport in helping to construct a European identity was recognised by the European Union explicitly in the 1980s (Shore, 1993). By the 1980s it had become widely acknowledged that progress with the European project was likely to be impossible without a strong element of financial and political integration. Political integration itself could not be achieved without winning over the consent and the commitment of European citizens: that is, it could not be achieved without citizens of the member states relating to a European identity.

This concern exercised the minds of the European Council of Ministers when it received the Adonino Report *A People's Europe* in 1985. The report highlighted ways in which a cultural identity for European citizens might be developed, such as the adoption of a European anthem, a European Union flag, and the promotion of EU policy in the cultural sphere.

Among some of the ideas rehearsed in the Adonino Report were the establishing of a pan-European Games, the entering of a European Olympic team, and the provision of support for sporting events that promoted European identity. Some of the more radical ideas have not been acted upon but others

found their way into EU policy. For example, the EU has funded the establishment of sporting events such as a European Clubs Swimming Championship, and supported the European Ryder Cup team (even though that represents more than simply the EU states). It also supported during the 1990s developments such as the European Yacht Race – a race which was routed to join various European ports – and the extension of the Tour de France into other countries (The Netherlands, Belgium, Germany, UK, etc.).

This symbolic use of sport to 'unite' the territory has precursors in the pre-modern and the modern eras, at the levels of the local and the nation state respectively. In the pre-modern era, marching or riding the bounds (e.g. in Scottish border towns) was a means of reasserting annually the extent of the boundaries of the township and expressing civic community. Similarly the Breton *pardon*, the tradition in Catholic parishes in Brittany of procession round the boundaries of the parish, on the feast day of the saint after whom the parish church had been named, reaffirmed the sense of religious and political community of the parish. Phillip Dine has illustrated how in the modern era in the early twentieth century, the Tour de France was inaugurated partly as a means of asserting the unity of the French nation, formed as it had been out of diverse regions, sometimes with aspirations for separate identity (Dine, 1997). In the late modern or high modern period of the late twentieth century, it may be argued that the EU support for the European Yacht Race seeks to perform in symbolic terms much the same function, of publicly asserting a symbolic unity of a political entity. Indeed the funding of this event in the early 1990s came from a European Commission budget line entitled the European Awareness Budget.

Whether one accepts this assertion or not, it is difficult to deny that sport has an ideological function. Culture and sport and identity politics are intrinsically inter-related and that there is a tension in the period of late modernity between its use in promoting national, supranational or local identities (Roche, 1998).

5   Sport as a tool of international relations

The use of sport by nation states as a tool for cementing international relations is well established from the Berlin Olympics of 1936 to the ping-pong diplomacy of Richard Nixon re-establishing relations with China. A number of nation states employ sports devel-opment aid as part of a wider programme of international relations. For example, Britain in 1989 signed a Memorandum of Under-standing with Saudi Arabia incorporating the provision of sporting advice, as part of a wider deal between British Aerospace and the Saudi Arabian government to supply military aircraft. UK Sport (formerly the Sports Council) also has a programme of aid for Southern Africa and Eastern Europe.

Although sport has been used by nation states in such a manner, it is interesting to note that in the mid-1990s when Nelson Mandela visited Europe, members of the Sports Intergroup sought to ensure that the provision of sport aid was included in a pack-age to be discussed by representatives of the EU and President Mandela. Sport as a tool of diplomacy was clearly an issue for develop-ment for certain parties in the EU arena.

THE FUTURE OF THE EUROPEAN UNION AND THE NATION STATE IN SPORT POLICY: SOME CONCLUSIONS

The growing role of the EU in sports policy does not imply a diminishing of interest on the part of the nation state in sports policy.

Indeed, as the nation state finds its role challenged to some degree by the rise of transnational entities, so it may use sport to reassert the existence and importance of national identity.

This characteristic is well illustrated in the British case by the circumstances surround-ing the publication of the governmental statement *Sport: Raising the Game* (Depart-ment of National Heritage, 1995) in the run-up to Britain's general election of 1997. *Sport: Raising the Game* was the first major policy statement on sport in Britain for 22 years. The importance of sport for key actors in the government was underlined by the fact that the Prime Minister himself chose to write a preface to the document outlining the significance of sport. The docu-ment, and, in particular the preface, were fairly unequivocally nationalistic, if not jingoistic. John Major for example wrote:

Sport is a central part of Britain's National Heritage. We invented the majority of the world's great sports and most of those we did not invent, we codified and helped to popu-larise throughout the world. It could be argued that nineteenth-century Britain was the cradle of the leisure revolution every bit as significant as the industrial and agricultural revolutions we launched in the centuries before ... Sport is ... one of the defining char-acteristics of nationhood and of local pride. (Department of National Heritage, 1995: 2)

The document focused policy interest in sport on two areas: youth and national perfor-mance. It also indicated the then govern-ment's intention of investing £100m in the establishment of a National Academy of Sport.

This policy statement came at a time when the Conservative Party had reached a low ebb of public support and when the Party itself was manifesting deep and elec-torally damaging divisions on the issue of Europe and the erosion of national sovereignty by the growing power of the European Union. Sport was one policy area in which the government could demonstrate, at least in symbolic terms, its affiliation to the protection of national identity, in a way that was likely to have a wide appeal. Attempts to rectify the decline of Britain's national performance would almost invariably attract cross-party support from among the electorate. Thus ironically sport is being used both to undermine and to reinforce national identity.

There are other good reasons why the nation state seems likely to remain as a significant actor in the sports policy process, including for example its continuing interest in education, or in the economics of the sports industries. Nevertheless there are also important reasons why the role of transnational bodies such as the EU will grow, for example, in professional sport. The interpenetration of media and sports club ownership (particularly in soccer) and the globalisation of sports talent production (e.g. football clubs having feeder clubs in other European countries' lower divisions), mean that transnational regulation will be required if these transnational phenomena are to be controlled. The European Commission's attempts to promote discussion about a *European Model of Sport* in opposition to a North American model, reflect concerns about phenomena such as the potential breakaway European Football League. With the G14 group of clubs such as Manchester United or Barcelona in a dominant market position, their ability to act as a cartel, effectively excluding other clubs because of the lack of a promotion and relegation system, can perhaps only be effectively regulated by a transnational body. On the other hand, issues such as the production of local talent may require national sporting systems to act in a protectionist manner. Indeed, UEFA has since

the Bosman ruling sought to reopen negotiations with the EU on the matter of re-establishing national quotas of players in professional football, and though its most recent attempt met with rejection in 2000, it seems likely to be a running issue.

Although the EU has traditionally sought to distinguish between professional sport as economic activity (where economic regulation generally applies) and amateur sport (which is more directly subject to the principle of subsidiarity) there are important ways in which legitimate policy concerns have emerged even in relation to amateur sport at the EU level. Although the Declarations on sport incorporated in the Treaties of Amsterdam and Nice fall short of according a competence, they indicate a clear concern on the part of the EU with a whole range of issues associated with the governance of sports organisations, in terms of transparency, democracy and solidarity: the need to protect and foster the economic and social role of volunteers; the need to preserve training policies; to protect young sportsmen and women, particularly in terms of health and from the use of drugs in sport; the need to mutualise revenues from broadcast sales; the need to regulate the transfer market for professional sportsmen and women; the need to protect clubs from concentration of ownership (particularly in the hands of transnational media). The Nice Declaration also explicitly recognises the potential role of sport in combating aspects of social exclusion. The Declaration makes it clear that the basis for recognising the competence of the sports federations is their role in assuring such outcomes:

These social functions entail special responsibilities for federations and provide the basis for the recognition of their competence in organising competitions ... While taking account of developments in the world of sport, federations must continue … providing a guarantee of sporting cohesion and participatory democracy. (Annex IV, Treaty of Nice)

It also acknowledges the EU's concerns to ensure that the principles of good organisational governance for sports organisations are identified and, by implication, monitored. The implication of all this may be that if sports organisations fail to deliver on these social gains, the EU may be forced to rethink its position in relation to sport.

To conclude I would argue that, in effect, the European project and the various national projects are incomplete and on-going. Both are organised around the trinity of politics, economics and culture. Sport, culture and leisure are integral to the processes involved in both types of project, and sport, leisure and cultural policies are of significance in each of the three elements identified here. In economic terms sport, for example, is a major contributor to national economies, but as a transnational phenomenon it has to be subject to transnational regulation. In cultural terms sport, culture and leisure contribute to the notions of cultural identity, which are central to issues of the political legitimacy of both nation state and European Union. In political terms the ceding of policy control by nation states to the European Union or vice versa, or to the commercial and voluntary sectors, is politically non-viable and in policy terms impractical, since both the European Union and member states are mutually reliant.

The relationship between Europe and member states is thus both complementary and competitive. I would argue therefore that reference to the impending demise of the nation state is mistaken. It is rather more appropriate to refer to a relatively fluid process of mutual adjustment between these tiers of government as they negotiate and respond to what has been an increasingly complex global context.

Chapter summary

- The transition from Common Market, through European Community to European Union, has marked a steady widening in the scope of the organisation to include, among other policy areas, an interest in culture and sport.
- As the European Union has expanded into new policy fields, it has challenged traditional views of state sovereignty and consequently stimulated renewed interest in debates on identity and the role of sport in establishing and maintaining identity.
- Growth of European Union interest in sport is based on sport's significance for trade, economic regeneration, social integration, ideology and international relations.
- While the European Union is of increasing significance to sport, the nation state remains important: the relationship between the EU and its members is both complementary and competitive.

Further reading

Seary (1992) and Bates & Wacker S.C. (1993) provide general overviews of the role of European institutions in cultural and sports policy. Matthews and Henry (2001) provide an analysis of the capacity of the EU to influence sport through the use of its funding resources. Mann (1997) examines the arguments regarding the future of the nation state. Shore (1993) provides a challenging analysis of European cultural policy. Henry (2001: ch. 8) provides an overview of the relationship between the role of the EU, the nation state and the city with reference to debates about globalisation.

NOTES

1 The term competence refers to an area of policy making in which the EU has a legal authority or competence to act, as defined by Treaty.

2 Interview with John Tomlinson MEP, Chair of the EP Sports Intergroup, February 1996.

3 This was described to the author and a co-researcher (Nicola Matthews) in an interview with a Commission official as part of a 'game' where the Commission would eliminate from budget proposals items which it was confident would be reinstated by the Parliament.

4 A 'Declaration' is of lesser significance than an article. The latter defines the EU as having legal competence, in a policy field; the former simply declares the EU's intention to act in particular ways.

REFERENCES

Anderson, B. (1983) *Imagined Communities*. London: Verso.

Arnedt, R. (1998) 'European Union law and football nationality restrictions: the economics and politics of the Bosman decision', *Emory International Law Review*, 12 (2).

Bates & Wacker S.C. (1993) *Community Support for Culture*. (A study carried out for the Commission of the EC (DGX) by Bates & Wacker S.C.) Brussels: European Commission.

Department of National Heritage (1995) *Sport: Raising the Game*. London: Department of National Heritage.

Dine, P. (1997) 'Peasants into sportsmen: modern games and the construction of French national identity', in P. Dine and I. Henry (eds), *The Symbolism of Sport in France*. Stirling: University of Stirling.

Harvey, D. (1989) *The Condition of Postmodernity*. Oxford: Basil Blackwell.

Henry, I. (2001) *The Politics of Leisure Policy*. 2nd edn. London: Palgrave.

Henry, I. and Paramio-Salcines, J.L. (1998) 'Leisure, culture and urban regimes in Bilbao', in I. Cooper and M. Collins (eds), *Leisure Management: International Perspectives*. Wallingford: CAB International, pp. 97–112.

Henry, I. and Paramio-Salcines, J. (1999) 'Sport and the analysis of symbolic regimes: an illustrative case study of the City of Sheffield', *Urban Affairs Review*, 34 (5): 641–66.

Hirst, P. and Thompson, G. (1995) 'Globalization and the future of the nation state', *Economy and Society*, 24 (3): 408–42.

Laffan, B., O'Donnell, R. and Smith, M. (2000) *Europe's Experimental Union: Rethinking Integration*. London: Routledge.

Lash, S. and Urry, J. (1994) *Economies of Signs and Space*. London: Sage.

Le Roux, N., Chantelat, P. and Camy, J. (1999) *Sport and Employment in Europe: Final Report*. Brussels: European Commission – DGX.

Mann, M. (1997) 'Has globalization ended the rise and rise of the nation state?', *Review of International Political Economy*, 4 (3): 472–96.

Matthews, N. and Henry, I. (2001) 'The funding of sport and leisure through the European Structural Funds in Britain', in C. Gratton and I. Henry (eds), *Sport in the City*. London: Routledge.

Morris, L. (1997) 'Globalization, migration and the nation state: the path to a post-national Europe?', *British Journal of Sociology*, 48 (2): 192–209.

Pack, D. (1997) *Rapport sur le rôle de l'Union européenne dans le domaine du sport*, Commission de la culture, de la jeunesse, de l'éducation et des médias. Brussels: European Commission.

Roche, M. (1998) *Sport, Popular Culture and Identity*. Aachen: Meyer & Meyer.

Schachter, O. (1997) 'The decline of the nation state and its implications for international law', *Columbia Journal of Transnational Law*, 36 (1–2): 7–23.

Seary, W. (1992) *Brussels in Focus: EC Access for Sport*. London: Sports Council.

Shaw, M. (1997) 'The state of globalization: towards a theory of state transformation', *Review of International Political Economy*, 4 (3): 497–513.

Shore, C. (1993) 'Inventing the Peoples' Europe – critical approaches to European Community cultural policy', *Man*, 28 (4): 779–800.

Smith, A. (1983) *Theories of Nationalism*. 2nd edn. London: Duckworth.

Taylor, P. (1998) 'Sports facility development and the role of forecasting: a retrospective on swimming in Sheffield'. Paper presented at the Sport in the City conference, Sheffield.

Temple-Lang, J. (1996) 'Community constitutional law', in B. Laffan (ed.), *Constitution-building in the European Union*. Dublin: Institute of European Affairs.

Van Deth, J.W. (1995) 'Comparative politics and the decline of the nation-state in Western Europe', *European Journal of Political Research*, 27 (4): 443–62.

19

Sport and Globalisation

BARRIE HOULIHAN

In a humorous guide to revision for chemistry examinations, school students were told 'When in doubt say it's "osmosis".' If osmosis is the default explanation of chemical processes, then it has a lot in common with much of the use of the concept of globalisation. Whether the focus of discussion is the spread of Olympic sports, or changes in eating habits, intergenerational relationships, welfare policy or manufacturing work practices, the default explanation is a reference to the often poorly specified concept of globalisation. Globalisation has established itself across the social sciences to the extent that Featherstone and Lash were moved to suggest that globalisation had become the 'central thematic for social theory' (1995: 1). However, paralleling the growing dominance of globalisation as an explanation within the social sciences was a sceptical reaction against the paradigmatic status

that the concept seemed to be assuming. Unease focused on the utility of the concept, its descriptive accuracy and its explanatory potential. For Bauman it was 'a fad word fast turning into a shibboleth' (1999: 1), while Fitch dismissed much of the theorising of globalisation as 'globaloney' (1996).

The overextension and casual use of the concept will add little to our understanding of global change and its implications for sport. There are three aspects of the concept of globalisation in the study of sport that require consideration before the concept can be used with confidence. The first is the need to distinguish between different dimensions of globalisation such as the political, economic and cultural, and consider their interrelation and relative significance as well as distinguishing between globalisation as a process and globalisation as an outcome. Second, there is a need to specify how that outcome of globalisation would be recognised and specify the criteria that would have to be fulfilled before we could confidently state that we now live in a globalised world. The third aspect concerns exploring the reach of globalising forces and the response of the 'receiving' nation/community.

GLOBALISATION AS A PROCESS: DIMENSIONS AND FLOWS

Political scientists make the important distinction between *democratisation*, which is the process of making progress towards democracy, and *democracy* itself, which is the outcome of the process. There is a need to be aware of a similar distinction between process and outcome when considering globalisation and sport. If we use the term 'globalisation' primarily to refer to the *process* of movement away from a world of discrete nation states and their social systems, cultural patterns, political systems and economies, then there is still the problem of defining the outcome of the process. More will be said about the outcome of globalisation in the next section with the focus in this section remaining on an examination of globalisation as a process.

Scholte (2000) identifies five common uses of the term globalisation, namely as internationalisation, liberalisation, universalisation, Westernisation/Americanisation and deterritorialisation (see Box 19.1). Each usage of the term is based on a different balance between economic, political and cultural processes. Some definitions give priority to one process: liberalisation gives clear priority to economic forces whereas universalisation focuses more on the role of culture in globalisation. Other conceptualisations of globalisation, such as Westernisation/Americanisation, reflect a combined emphasis on economic, political and cultural factors.

Box 19.1   Varieties of globalisation

Globalisation as a process of

Internationalisation, reflecting greater cross-border exchanges, especially trade, but also people and ideas, between countries

Liberalisation, whereby government restrictions on cross-border business are removed and to a large extent reflect the efforts of the World Trade Organisation and at a regional level the European Union and the North American Free Trade Area

Examples from sport

Trade in athletes; an increase in the number of international competition circuits

The impact of the European Union ruling regarding the transfer of players and the number of non-national players that a team may field (Bosman ruling), and also the liberalisation of cross-border TV media ownership and broadcasting

(Continued)

Box 19.1   Continued

Universalisation of culture, a synthesis of existing cultures producing a homogeneous cultural experience	The global coverage of the Olympic Games both in terms of the number of countries participating (more countries than are members of the United Nations) and the number of countries receiving television broadcasts, contributing to an increasingly homogeneous sports diet
Westernisation/Americanisation whereby the social structures of modernity, capitalism, rational-bureaucracy, industrialism and representative democracy, are spread throughout the world	Rational-bureaucratic sports structures (written rules, leagues and records of achievement), a scientific approach to talent identification and development, specialisation both on and off the field of play (physiotherapists, psychologists and dieticians, etc.), and commercialisation
Deterritorialisation whereby the spatial organisation of social relations is altered as a result of a dramatic change in our perception of space, location and distance	The development of large fan groups for English and Scottish football teams not just outside the locality but outside the national state boundaries; the live transmission of international sports events

Source: adapted from Scholte, 2000

Because so much of the discussion of sports globalisation focuses on sport as an element of culture, it is important to consider, if only briefly, the relative importance of the various dimensions of globalisation. For most Marxists the answer is fairly clear: economic factors dominate with cultural practices being broadly a reflection of the underlying mode of production. In relation to sport, Marxists would emphasise the commodification of sport and athletes, the domination of sport by powerful media interests which increasingly determine what sport is

practised, especially at the elite level, and what sport will reach a global television market. Thus media interests, especially television, and the major international federations (football, cricket, Rugby Union/League and athletics) share a common concern to produce a marketable global product. Sport is no different from any other product in the capitalist economy where markets are carefully managed and where labour is exploited as the primary source of profit. The spectacular wages of footballers such as Figo, Beckham and Veron, detract attention from the more modest wages and short careers of most footballers and the ruthless exploitation of footballing talent of many poorer nations, particularly in Africa (Darby, 2001). Support for this argument comes from the work of Klein (1991), who demonstrated how the United States Major League baseball teams undertook a crude form of asset-stripping of talent in the Dominican Republic. Although a number of players from the Republic became major stars in the United States, most of the talented young players who were exported to the US were abandoned when they did not 'make the grade'. However, such was the exodus of talent that the domestic Dominican Republic league was systematically undermined.

For Marxists and others who prioritise economic processes, culture is either a tool for incorporating economies through the manipulation of values and attitudes – cultural imperialism – or it is mere froth and not worthy of serious consideration. Examples of the former include Hamelink, who refers to a process of worldwide 'cultural synchronisation' (1983: 3), and Levitt who refers to the world's preference structure becoming relentlessly homogenised (1983). Scholte summarises the arguments as follows: 'Globalisation introduces a single world culture centred on consumerism, mass media, Americana, and the English language' (2000: 23) and one might add a diet of Olympic sport and Western-defined world championships in sports such as soccer, Formula One, athletics and swimming. Rather more bluntly, Brohm argues that global sport

ideologically reproduces bourgeois social relations ... spreads an organisational ideology specific to the institutions of sport and ... transmits on a huge scale the general themes of the ruling bourgeois ideology like the myth of the superman, individualism, social advancement, success, efficiency etc. (1978: 77).

According to Brohm, the value of sport to capitalism is not just as a source of profit but also as a subtle vehicle for infiltrating capitalist values into a society because awareness of the manipulative capacity of sport is so low. Adopting a slightly different view, David Harvey (1989), also arguing from a Marxist standpoint, retains confidence in a traditional base–superstructure relationship between economic processes and cultural forms and rejects the suggestion that the cultural dimension of globalisation – prominent though it undoubtedly is – requires a new conceptual language for its analysis: modern culture including sport is essentially epiphenomenal. Wallerstein (1991) is equally dismissive, viewing the cultural dimension as a slight ideological impediment to socialism by comparison with the underlying economic relations.

Priority to the economic dimension draws attention to the commodification of sport, the creation and management of global markets for sports products, and the increasing vertical integration between television media companies and the sports they broadcast. Christian Aid (Brookes and Madden, 1995) provided a powerful indictment of the practices of sports goods companies. They found that the manufacture of sports shoes was located in the lowest labour cost countries where employment conditions, especially for children, were very poor and, perhaps most damning of all, that less than 5 per cent of the final retail price was received by the factory workers in South East Asia (see also Maguire, 1999: Ch. 6; Sage, 1996; Katz, 1994). As regards the role of sports media in furthering the vertical integration within the industry, companies such as BSkyB, Canal+ and NTL have all sought to purchase football clubs or at least a shareholding (Brown, 2000), thus enabling them to exercise greater control over their key product.

Events such as the Olympic Games are also examples of the careful development of sports products and more importantly the extent to which even an event as profitable as the Olympics is so heavily dependent on American corporations. Around 60 per cent of all income to the Olympic movement comes from US businesses either in the form of sponsorship (eight of the ten largest sponsors are US based) or in the income generated from the sale of broadcasting rights. It is no wonder that the Games have been awarded to US cities three times in the last 18 years and that a recurring preoccupation for the local organising committee for the Games is how best to schedule events to meet the requirements of US east coast television viewers.

Such is the interconnection between economic power and sport that it should come as no surprise that, with a small number of notable exceptions, the same countries that dominate the world economy also dominate international sport. The G8 countries (USA, UK, France, Germany, Canada, Italy, Russia and Japan) share 65 per cent of world trade with the remaining 200 or so other national economies, accounting for the remaining 35 per cent. As in world trade so in Olympic medals where the same G8 countries dominate, accounting for just under half of all gold medals and 44 per cent of all medals at the Sydney Olympics. The figures would undoubtedly have been closer to the G8 level had it not been for the residual effect of the prominence of sport in the former socialist countries of Central Europe and the continuing high political status of sport in the remaining socialist countries such as China and Cuba. In a study of a range of structural factors that might account for success in Olympic competition, Stamm and Lamprecht (2001) concluded that the structural factors of population size and level of economic

development were the primary indicators of Olympic success and were becoming more pronounced.

In the study of the globalisation of sport, economic processes are clearly of central importance. However, this does not mean that culture should be written off as a mere cipher for more significant economic processes. There are a number of students of globalisation who are willing to grant the cultural sphere a substantial degree of autonomy. Hall (1983), for example, arguing from a broadly Marxist position, suggests that despite the clear power of business interests, there is still scope for a reconstruction of everyday practices and a rearticulation of cultural practices, such as in the area of sport. For Hall, capitalist power determines culture in the first, rather than the last, instance. Hannerz (1990) provides a useful attempt to disaggregate dimensions of globalisation and to investigate their interrelationship. He identifies three cultural 'flows', namely: (a) that of cultural commodities which circulate within the marketplace to include sports fashionwear and individual sports or competitions; (b) that which concerns the actions of the state, to include decisions about funding for sport; and (c) that which concerns the 'form of life', which refers to deeply embedded patterns of behaviour, attitudes and values. What is especially significant about this conceptualisation is, first, that it does not suggest that cultural phenomena are only to be found at the superficial or superstructural level and, second, that in order to ask significant questions about global sport, we need to be able to disaggregate culture and distinguish between levels or depths of embeddedness.

For example, within the realm of social relations, we could ask whether sport globalisation is evident 'merely' at the commodity level or has penetrated to the level of deep structural values and practices. A number of the major European football clubs have extensive worldwide networks of supporters' clubs with their own local fan magazines and club products. While such a phenomenon is evidence of some form of globalisation, we might be tempted to dismiss it as functioning only at the surface of society as a fashion. Like all fashions, it will exhaust itself and be supplanted by a new passion for a different team, sport or other cultural product and remembered in later years with a degree of fond embarrassment. However, if the support for European clubs were to be extended through the emulation of some of the less attractive patterns of fan behaviour such as hooliganism and racism, it might prompt the government to regulate fan behaviour. The intervention of the state would indicate that the degree of cultural change was of a more significant kind. If the growing popularity of football led to the establishment not only of national men's leagues, but also of leagues for women and, more significantly, to a decline in local or regional sports, then we might have evidence of cultural change of a far more profound kind.

Similarly, if we were to focus on the political dimension of culture, we would be rightly sceptical of bestowing too much significance on the attendance of politicians, even from countries with a strong football tradition, at major football matches, as this is likely to be an aspect of the froth of electioneering and cheap populist politics rather than an indication of deeply rooted state commitment. However, if the popularity of football were to prompt the government to reorder its funding priorities for sport with the intention of establishing a national professional league or strengthening the chances of the national team qualifying for the World Cup, we would be right to see this as a change of deeper

significance. Furthermore, if the state began to undermine the traditional autonomy of sports clubs in order to pursue its policies, then the degree of cultural change would be far more significant. As should now be clear, there is a danger of reading too much significance into the fact that such a high proportion of the world's population watch some part of the Olympic Games or the soccer World Cup. What is more significant is when the state intervenes to manipulate, support or impose emergent cultural trends. More significant still is when there is evidence of changes to long-established sporting traditions or to deeply embedded societal attitudes and values in relation to patterns of social deference, gender roles or intergenerational relations, such as a move closer to the rational-bureaucratic model of sports organisation or an acceptance of women's participation in the same elite competitive sports as men.

There are two conclusions that emerge from the discussion of globalisation as a process. The first is an acknowledgement that the significance of cultural change must be conceptualised in terms of depth of social embeddedness and that we must be wary of granting too much importance to shifts in the popularity of particular teams, sports or events. The second conclusion is that while the political and cultural dimensions have a degree of autonomy from economic processes, it is economic interests that have become much more prominent in sport in the last 25 years as major sports and sports events have become increasingly a focus for private profit rather than state subsidy.

GLOBALISATION AS AN OUTCOME

In the opening section of this chapter an analogy was drawn between democratisation and democracy on the one hand and globalisation as process and globalisation as outcome on the other. What was not made clear at the time is that while there is a reasonable degree of agreement about what might constitute evidence of democratisation, there is far less agreement about the grounds for declaring that a country qualifies as a democracy. There is disagreement about the criteria for democracy and the relative weight each criterion should be given. It should come as no surprise that there is an equal degree of uncertainty regarding the threshold for a globalised world and the form that that world would take.

The contemporary complex mix of globalising pressures and their ebb and flow over time make it extremely difficult to predict the precise trajectory of the process of globalisation. From the point of view of sport globalisation, there are at least three fairly clearly observable trajectories of globalisation visible in contemporary sport (see Table 19.1). The first is a globalised sporting world where nation and nationality mean little in terms of defining identity, the provision of funding or the regulatory framework within which sport takes place. Sports teams, leagues and events are deterritorialised and no longer defined primarily by national affiliation, but structured according to some other principle such as commercial opportunity, religion, sexuality or ideology. Professional road cycling, where multinational teams compete in a global competition circuit, is probably the best example of organisation around a commercial principle, although it is interesting to note the extent to which regional and national communities adopt teams as their own, even though the link with the territory is often tenuous.

The second trajectory of globalisation leads to an outcome which is characterised by a pattern of intense inter*national* sporting competition. In other words the inter*nationalised* sporting world is defined by the volume of competition between athletes, squads and teams drawn from clearly defined nation states and where these international competitions are considered, by regional and national communities, to be more important than domestic competitions. Whether Liverpool FC beat Everton FC and whether Liverpool FC win the Premier League would be clearly of less interest to their fans than whether Liverpool FC won the European Champions League. A third possible outcome is best described as multinationalised sport, where the nation is still an important reference point for identity and the state a key source of resources for sports development, but the pattern of sports participation and fan identification reflects the increasingly common multiple or nested identities that a growing proportion of the world's population experience, especially in the industrialised countries. In the UK, for example, there has long been a capacity among Rugby Union supporters to support the England team in the Six Nations championships and also the British and Irish Lions (a team drawn from the four home countries plus Ireland, a foreign country) who compete against Australia and New Zealand. England supporters seem quite able to cheer on the Irishman Keith Wood when he is playing for the Lions a few weeks after he was playing for Ireland against England at Twickenham. Furthermore English football supporters of Irish descent seen quite capable of supporting both England and Ireland in international matches and coping with the split loyalty when the two teams have to play each other.

Split, hybrid, multiple or nested loyalty in sport is not the only dimension of an increasingly fragmented identity. Previous generations in the early and mid-twentieth century inhabited societies, in Western Europe in particular, in which identity was subject to powerful homogenising forces of class,

Table 19.1   *Sport and the outcomes of globalisation*

Characteristic	Globalised sport	Internationalised sport	Multinationalised sport
Nation as the defining unit of international sport and nationality as the defining characteristic of sportsmen and sportswomen	Multinational/ nationally ambiguous teams the norm, as in Formula One motor-racing and professional road cycling	Teams defined by their country of origin, e.g. as in the Olympic Games, and international soccer club competitions	The nation is an important, and perhaps primary, reference point for team/ athlete definition. However, athletes/teams will represent their nations, but also other politically defined units whether sub-national (Quebec's participation in the Francophone Games or the participation of Scotland in the World Cup) or supranational (a European team in the World Athletics Championships or the Irish rugby or hockey teams which comprise players from Northern Ireland and the Irish Republic)
Extent of global diversity in sport	Diminishing diversity and/or the overlaying of regionally/ nationally dis-tinctive sporting traditions with an increasingly uniform pattern of Olympic and major international team/individual sports	Maintenance of a vigorous national/regional sporting culture which exists alongside or takes precedence over Olympic and major international team/ individual sports	Increasing diversity in terms of opportunities for competitions, although there may be a decline in diversity among sports themselves with those without an international stage being especially vulnerable to marginalisation through the adoption by governments of selective funding policies
Extent of state patronage of elite sport	Minimal, sports are either financially self-sufficient or attract commercial patronage	Substantial, most Olympic and major international sports depend on state subsidy	Substantial, although some wariness regarding the allocation of national funds to support supranational teams

(Continued)

Table 19.1   *Continued*

Characteristic	Globalised sport	Internationalised sport	Multinationalised sport
Extent to which sports businesses and organisations operate within a national framework of regulation	Self-regulation by the industry or no regulation	National framework of regulation, e.g. licensing of clubs, coaches, sports venues and television broadcasting or supranational framework of regulation, for example, by the European Union	National regulatory frameworks important but both businesses and sports organisations operate within multiple regulatory frameworks, especially within the European Union
Extent to which international sports federations and the IOC are subject to domestic control	Immune from domestic regulatory and legal systems or in countries where the legal system is 'protective' of corporate/ organisational interests	Subject to legal challenge and regulatory oversight at state level, but also at supranational level	Subject to legal challenge and regulation at both national and supranational levels

Source: Adapted from Hirst and Thompson, 1999

religion and nationality. Since then identity has become more multifaceted with an increasing range of dimensions which now include gender, sexuality, ethnic origin and education, and a fragmentation and decline in significance of traditional homogenising forces. The rapid decline of the industrial working class, the rise of new Christian churches and the import of eastern religions through immigration, and the effect of European Union membership on national identity have all contributed to a much more complex and heterogeneous social fabric which is reflected in sport. When the Conservative Party MP Norman Tebbit questioned the 'Britishness' of Asian immigrants who supported touring Indian or Pakistani cricket teams, he not only failed to appreciate the extent to which the concept of 'Britishness' had changed, but also failed to appreciate the long- established capacity of Britons to manage multiple/nested identities. Norman Tebbit did not apply his 'test' to Scots or Welsh who cheered for their countries when playing football and who, it appears, can cope quite adequately with being both British and Scottish or Welsh without running the risk of becoming the 'lost souls' described by Scholte (2000: 161).

Taking each criterion identified in Table 19.1 in turn, the first is the role and significance of the nation as the defining factor or reference point in international sport. The extent to which a nation was ever a clear and unambiguous concept is often exaggerated, but it is undoubtedly the case that the reality underpinning the 'imagined community' of the nation is often both frail and pragmatic. On the one hand governments have frequently been enthusiastic in allowing applications for naturalisation from elite athletes and have, on occasion, actively 'bought' elite athletes from other countries. For example, the South African, Zola Budd, was awarded British citizenship remarkably rapidly so that she could compete for her new country. Fiona May, the British-born long-jumper, was granted Italian nationality and subsequently went on to win a world title in 1995. When May lost her title four years later, she lost it to an athlete, Niurka Montalvo, whose nationality was equally complex. Montalvo originally competed for Cuba but when she took May's title she was a Spaniard. There are also examples of Ethiopian-born athletes competing as naturalised Turks and Sudanese-born athletes competing as naturalised Qataris. Finally, Mohammed Mourhit, previously of Morocco, won bronze in the world 5000 m cross-country event in 2000 in Seville for Belgium and then posed wrapped in a Moroccan flag with his former team-mate Salah Hissou.

On the other hand, there are many examples of athletes who have sought to maximise their opportunity to compete at the highest level by changing sporting nationality. Athletes can thus retain legal nationality with one country while adopting the sporting nationality of another by virtue of ancestry or even residence. For example, the Canadian tennis player Greg Rusedski adopted British sporting nationality; many British-born footballers have opted to represent the Republic of Ireland; and at one time there were more non-English-born members of the England cricket team as players from Wales, Zimbabwe, Australia and South Africa joined the squad.

Merged, blurred and ambiguous national identities would be expected in truly globalised sport. By contrast, under conditions of internationalised sport, the nation would be protected as the defining unit of international sport. The status of the nation as an organising concept for sport is intimately linked to the significance of the state with which it has, in the vast majority of cases, a mutually dependent if not symbiotic relationship (see Houlihan, 1997). Under conditions of multinational sport, the state would retain a central role as a reference point for the organisation of international sport and for the identity of athletes, but it would lose a degree of exclusivity. Increasingly, other geo-political reference points would emerge either based on supranational organisations (such as the European Union) or on geography, with the increasing construction of 'continental' teams (e.g. the European team that competes against the USA in golf's Ryder Cup; the presence of a European team, alongside other national and continental teams, in the IAAF Athletics World Championships).

The second characteristic is the extent of sports diversity throughout the world. Maguire (1999) refers to 'diminishing contrasts and increasing varieties' with regard to sport, while Hannerz (1990: 237) identifies a major impact of globalisation as producing the 'organisation of diversity'. An illustration of Maguire's conclusion would be the increase in the variety of running events (new distances, new contexts, or new combination of running with other sports, e.g. triathlon) but the decline or exclusion of events and sports that are more sharply differentiated from the dominant Olympic programme, such as dog-fighting, bear- baiting and bare-knuckle fighting.

Though Maguire's conclusion is a compelling one, the measurement of diversity is problematic; indeed, determining when a variation becomes a contrast is far from easy. Nevertheless, the conclusions of both Maguire and Hannerz suggest that under conditions of globalised sport, one might expect to find that local/regional sporting forms were retreating in the face of a largely European diet of Olympic sports and major commercial sports and the rational-bureaucratic form of organisation with which they are underpinned. At the very least, one would expect to find evidence of a 'third culture' (Featherstone, 1991) which overlays more localised sports cultures. In essence it would be the anational holders of power, such as the international federations and transnational sports businesses, that would provide the direction and momentum for change at the domestic level. By contrast, under conditions of internationalised sport, the dynamics of change in sporting culture would be substantially national. Moreover, while engagement with, and adoption of, non-traditional sports might be common, it would be the result of choice rather than imposition or coercion. Multinationalist sport would result in an increasing diversity of competition opportunities with, for example, the European Union providing a context for new competitions, but not necessarily any increase in the diversity of sports available at the elite level.

Third, under conditions of globalised sport, one would expect the role of the state as a patron of, and organisational focus for, elite sport to be slight, by comparison with commercial patrons for example. The influence of the state in determining the pattern of engagement with global sport would be minimal. Internationalised sport would be characterised by a key role for the state, which would play a central role in funding and organising elite sport, reflecting a situation where engagement with global sport is determined significantly by nationally set priorities. Under conditions of multinational sport, state patronage would remain important, although supranational state organisations would provide both an additional source of patronage and a further set of constraints on the decision-making freedom of sports governing bodies.

The fourth characteristic refers to the degree to which commercial sports organisations, including professional soccer clubs, broadcasting companies, and event organising bodies, operate within national frameworks of regulation. Globalised sport would be typified by minimal regulation or a pattern of self-regulation while under conditions of internationalised sport national or regional (e.g. European Union) systems of licensing, certification and training would create a mosaic of distinctive regulatory systems and consequently of sports practices. The conditions of multinationalised sport would be similar to those of internationalised sport, except that there would be clear evidence of dual regulation from the domestic and the supranational levels.

The final characteristic is the degree to which international sports organisations, such as the Commonwealth Games Federation, the IOC and the international federations, are subject to control by the domestic political/administrative/legal system. Under conditions of globalised sport, one would expect these engines of globalisation to be substantially immune from domestic systems of regulation or to be located in countries traditionally protective of corporate interests, such as Switzerland and Monaco. Within an internationalised system, international federations and the IOC would be open to legal challenge and interest group lobbying and enjoy no privileges arising solely from their status as global sports organisations. Multinationalised sport would be characterised, in Europe at least, by dual-level oversight and regulation.

A cursory reflection on the pattern of engagement between sport in the UK and international sport would quickly indicate that it corresponds neatly to none of the three ideal types, but rather exhibits a hybrid profile. The nation clearly remains the primary reference point for sports identity, but paradoxes and ambiguities abound. Chelsea FC still attracts passionate support from over 35,000 fans for each home game as well as from the many thousands who are not able to attend matches. Yet Chelsea regularly field eight or nine non-English players and on one occasion fielded a team that had no English players. Moreover its current and two previous managers have been foreigners. The lack of any depth of association between the team members and England, let alone West London, has done nothing to undermine the intensity of support. In marked contrast to this apparent embrace of cosmopolitanism and globalisation, the proposals to merge Oxford FC with a neighbouring club or to move Wimbledon FC out of London to Milton Keynes was met with passionate parochial opposition. In tennis and boxing there is the strong impression that the British public is more at ease supporting Tim Henman and Frank Bruno than Greg Rusedski and Lennox Lewis. Similarly, in Formula One motor racing the fact that many of the top teams are based in Britain is given little weight if the driver is not British. Thus it appears that for some sports (e.g. football), place is important in affecting the public's sense of identity, while for others (Formula One) it is not; for some sports the nationality of the players does not prevent strong identification while for other sports (e.g. tennis and boxing), nationality, or at least accent, remains important.

In considering the extent of sports diversity in the UK, the role of the state becomes sharply apparent. The Conservative government of John Major reshaped the National Curriculum for physical education to ensure that traditional British sports were embedded in the education system and it initiated the reorientation of elite funding policy to prioritise the major traditional team sports and Olympic sports. Given the relative poverty of most sports governing bodies, the power of state patronage is of considerable if not defining importance. The importance of the state and supranational state organisations in shaping the UK's engagement with globalisation is further emphasised by an examination of the regulatory framework within which sport operates. While at the national level state regulation is still modest, it is undoubtedly growing in areas such as the vetting of coaches who work with children, the licensing of major sports grounds, and the integration of coach training into the national system of vocational qualifications. At the European Union level, where a regulatory culture is more deeply entrenched, the impact on sport has been substantial particularly in relation to the movement of players and the control of sports broadcasting.

If the evidence so far seems to be indicating that the current trajectory of globalisation is toward internationalised or multinationalised sport, the relative immunity of international federations and the IOC from domestic state or supranational state regulation and oversight provides contrary evidence. However, the capacity of the United States to call the IOC to account over the Salt Lake City bribery allegations and the role of countries such as Canada, Australia and the UK along with the European Union in forcing the IOC to agree to an independent anti-doping agency (the World Anti-Doping Agency) both demonstrate the capacity of states to challenge the transnational status of international federations and the Olympic movement.

From the foregoing discussion of the three-fold ideal typology, it should be clear that, as in the discussion of the process of globalisation, the state commands a central position in any discussion of the outcome of globalising processes. Whichever examples of globalisation are selected, anti- doping efforts, the development of sports broadcasting, the movement of sportsmen and women between clubs and countries, or the response to soccer hooliganism, the state is of central significance in determining the pattern of engagement between national and global sport and is far from the residual institution that is sometimes suggested (see Houlihan, 2003). This is not to argue that the state is a natural adversary of globalisation. Indeed some states, especially those with an ideological commitment to liberal economics, may well be the primary source of momentum for the intensification of flows between the national and the international. Moreover, it is argued that the capacity of the state to adapt to a changing global environment should not be under-estimated. Any cursory review of the nature of globalisation in sport will provide ample examples of the close relationship between globalisation and regulation by the state or by international governmental bodies. As Vogel (1996: 2) argues, 'the rhetoric of globalisation ... serves only to obscure what is really going on ... [L]iberalism requires reregulation.'

In summary, it can be argued that sport globalisation as a process has no pre-determined outcome. Indeed there are a variety of possible outcomes which would conform to the conventional definitions of globalisation, which stress the more extensive and intensive connections between people and places due to the increasing transnational flow of people, ideas, information, commodities and capital. However, a significant determinant of the trajectory of globalisation in general and of sport globalisation in particular is the behaviour of states.

REACH AND RESPONSE

In the wake of the US-led invasion of Afghanistan and the defeat of the Taliban following the 11 September attack on the World Trade Center and the Pentagon, the Western press was keen to produce stories and pictures of the return to 'normal' life within the country. Two stories that received wide coverage were, first, the contact between the Afghan sports authorities and the IOC concerning the future involvement of the country in the Olympic Games and, second, the revival of a local sport (involving a headless goat and teams of horsemen) previously banned by the Taliban. The celebration of local sporting culture and the conscious embrace of global sport is by no means unusual. Many, perhaps most, countries can provide examples of dual sporting cultures sitting comfortably alongside one another. The Irish have various Gaelic sports yet participate enthusiastically in the soccer World Cup and the Olympic Games; Australia has its parochial sport of Australian Rules Football, but is also active across a wide range of Western team and individual sports; and the USA seems unconcerned that few other countries play American football or baseball.

Just at the time when we are coming to terms with the impact of globalisation, there appears to be a contradictory phenomenon emerging, namely that of localisation. If globalisation reflects the power of universalistic socio-cultural flows, then localisation emphasises spatial definition and socio-cultural specificity. This phenomenon is evident in politics, especially in Europe, where the enlargement of the European Union has been paralleled by the creation of 16 new states since 1989. For Rosenau (1994) the relationship between the two processes is described as 'fragmegration' aiming to capture, if not very elegantly, the dual processes of fragmentation and integration. Robertson (1995) identified a similar phenomenon which he referred to as 'glocalisation'. For Robertson global culture is contested terrain where 'what is taken to be a worthy direction of societal aspiration – is something which is constructed in the global arena in relation to the constraints upon (most) societies to maintain their own identities and senses of community' (1987: 38). Globalisation involves the reconciliation of a paradox which is the 'particularization of universalism (the rendering of the world as a single place) and the universalization of particularism (the globalised expectation that societies ... should have distinct identities)' (Robertson, 1989: 9).

The capacity of globalisation to reach into every community is not denied, but what is less clear is the impact of that 'reach'. As mentioned above, for a number of writers, the impact of globalisation on culture is to lead to synchronisation, Americanisation or homogenisation and, as Scholte observes, 'Depending on one's perspective, this homogenisation entails either progressive cosmopolitanism or oppressive imperialism' (2000: 23). However, there is little evidence of a consensus on the impact of globalisation on culture generally or on sports culture in particular. In contrast to those who see only cultural homogeneity and the 'end of the national project' (Brown, 1995), there is an equally strong view that globalisation is not only compatible with continuing cultural heterogeneity but may even stimulate greater heterogeneity.

Underlying much of the discussion of the impact of globalisation is an appreciation that the basis on which national identity is defined has subtly shifted. It has long been accepted that defining national/regional identity is a mutually constitutive process in so far as identity is defined in relation to

contrasts with 'foreigners'. More recently, it can be argued that there is a set of globally recognised reference points which are now also important in establishing identity and against which each nation or community has to position itself. These reference points range from the relatively mundane, such as distinctive postage stamps, military uniforms, national flags and anthems, to the more significant such as membership of the World Trade Organisation and the United Nations, participation in UN peacekeeping/ making activities, and attitudes towards global 'principles' of human rights, state sovereignty and internal democracy. One of these reference points is clearly participation in international sport and the Olympic Games in particular. Sport is thus an example of the common paradox of utilising a uniform vehicle for the demonstration of difference.

On one level therefore the reach of globalisation should not be equated with homogeneity, as its 'arrival' may be a welcome opportunity to demonstrate community/ national distinctiveness. At another level, the capacity of communities to modify and adapt global culture should not be underestimated. Jensen, in a study of the local response to television news programmes in a range of countries, noted how 'respondents consistently redefined and reinterpreted the agenda offered by journalists and political actors appearing on the news' and emphasised the extent to which 'the varied local cultures manifest themselves in the interpretation of foreign as well as domestic news. Culture shines through' (Jensen, 1998: 194, 195). Hannerz reinforces Jensen's conclusion and observes that peripheral cultures have a clear capacity to absorb 'the influx of meanings and symbolic forms from the centre [and] transform them to make them in some considerable degree their own' (1990: 127). For Hannerz engagement with global culture is an active process according to which communities/groups appropriate selectively global cultural commodities and use them to refine and reform their own distinctive cultural identity.

Hannerz's marketplace model of globalisation overemphasises the element of choice and discretion in peripheral communities but it does have a resonance in developed countries, where engagement with global culture is on more equal terms. Warde (2000) demonstrates the capacity of communities to adapt global culture in his study of eating habits in the UK. He illustrates a number of responses to non-traditional food, including the domestication of the exotic whereby previously exotic ingredients are incorporated into traditional British dishes and where foreign recipes are modified to suit British taste. These closely related processes can be seen in many British sports in recent years, where sports such as tennis, football, cricket, swimming and hockey have imported foreign elite coaches who have each brought with them 'foreign' training methods and playing strategies. Similarly, the influx of foreign players into the Premier League has required an adaptation on their part to aspects of the traditional English game, such as the pace and aggression.

There are a number of parallel examples to the British experience. In his study of baseball and the relationship between the Dominican Republic and the United States, Klein (1991) argues strongly that the game of baseball has been metamorphosed and that far from simply reflecting American cultural hegemony, it has become a vehicle for demonstrating Dominican excellence. Baseball has been reshaped to infuse it with distinctive Dominican characteristics and qualities, suggesting a clear capacity for a community to import, redefine and re-export a sports cultural product. Similar conclusions were reached by a number of writers in relation to the impact of cricket in the West Indies. James (1963) argued that cricket was significant in establishing a West Indian identity, while St Pierre suggests that cricket 'has been reshaped in sympathy with the cultural ethos of the West Indies [and] has been used as a tool to foster and further nationalist sentiment and racial pride' (1990: 23). For Burton the form of cricket might remain English but it has been 'injected with a new, specifically West Indian content and meaning' (1991: 8). The use of four fast bowlers and the panache and flamboyance of play are considered to be in marked contrast to the English playing norms of seriousness, respectability and moderation.

Just as it was difficult to pin down the particularities of the process of globalisation, so it is equally difficult to be precise regarding the process by which outcomes are determined. Table 19.2 suggests a model for investigating the mediation of global culture at the community level (see Houlihan, 1994).

Passivity generally implies an inability to challenge the external culture and would come close to descriptions of cultural imperialism with the relationship between the United States and the Dominican Republic being a good example. By contrast, the development of sport in much of Western Europe and in English settler states such as Canada and Australia suggests not only a deep penetration by external culture, but more significantly, a strongly participative relationship in shaping and mediating external culture through control over media businesses or through influence within international sports bodies such as the IOC. Further examples of participative relationships between the domestic and the external culture include Japan and many of the countries of South East Asia, where the depth

Table 19.2   *Global reach and local response in sport*

Reach of global culture	Response of the local community		
	Passive	Participative	Conflictual
Commodities	Unmediated reception of satellite television sports broadcasts	Gradual widening of participation in major international sports events such as the soccer World Cup and the Olympic Games through the formation/action of non-governmental sports bodies	The manufacturing of high retail value football kit and equipment in low-wage countries
Actions of the state	Ignoring the issue of doping by national athletes	Shifts in public funding to protect/promote particular sports	Olympic boycotts
Deep structure of societal processes	The gradual marginalisation of local sports or their repackaging for global consumption	The arranging of specific sports events for women, e.g. in Iran	Banning of female athletes in Olympic squads in many Islamic countries

of penetration might be lower and where cultural adaptation and reinterpretation are greater. A conflictual response to external sports culture was seen briefly in both Russia and China in the immediate post-revolutionary period and more recently in the 1960s, when a group of mainly Asian states organised GANEFO (Games of the New Emerging Forces) as a challenge to the perceived dominance by Western capitalist and pro-Israeli states of the Olympic movement and the major federations.

CONCLUSION

There can be no doubting the importance of current debates concerning globalisation

in aiding our understanding of a number of key issues in sport, including: the significance of sport in the cultural fabric of a community; the interpenetration of sport with business in general and the international media in particular; and the significance of sport to governments and supranational governmental organisations. Yet, as this chapter has demonstrated, the analysis of globalisation and the consequent refinement of the concept is still in its infancy. As a result there is a need for caution both in the use of the concept and in the conclusions drawn about the nature and consequences of globalising trends.

This chapter has touched on three key debates over the nature of globalisation: globalisation as process; globalisation as outcome; and the reach of globalisation and the response of local communities. In all three of these areas there is a notable lack of consensus which reflects not only the shortage of empirical study, but also the complexity and multifaceted character of the processes under consideration. As regards the process of globalisation, the significance of economic power in sport must be acknowledged, but simply to treat global sport as a cipher for, or a tool of, economic interests is an overextension of the limited evidence available. Moreover, claims that sport is capable of penetrating and altering deeply rooted local cultural practices must also await more substantial evidence. This scepticism is not to deny the possibility that sport may be a leading factor in, for example, bringing about greater equality for women, but rather to suggest that while sport may indeed be in the vanguard of cultural change, it may also be simply a highly visible reflection of change which has originated elsewhere – in the workplace for example.

The discussion of globalisation as an outcome highlighted the importance of treating globalisation as an open-ended set of processes which do not necessarily lead to a fixed destination. Globalisation is a complex and contingent set of processes within which the state plays a key role in shaping their pace, character and trajectory. The state is still the primary reference point for international sport and a central actor in determining the pattern of engagement between domestic sport and international sport. The final discussion concerned the need to appreciate the resilience, dynamism and interpretive capacity of local cultures. The language of sport may be universal but the meaning it carries is as much determined locally as it is in the boardrooms of multinational sports corporations.

Chapter summary

- The concept of globalisation refers to both a process and an outcome.
- Globalisation in sport has been described in relation to some or all of the following: internationalisation, liberalisation of government control, universalisation of culture, Westernisation/Americanisation and deterritorialisation.
- There is a tension between those theorists of globalisation who emphasise the economic basis of globalisation and those who emphasise the cultural basis.
- As an outcome, there is a need to specify the criteria by which a globalised sports world would be recognised.
- It is valuable to distinguish between the outcomes of globalisation, internationalisation and multinationalisation in sport.
- Just as it is important to determine the 'reach' of globalising culture, it is also important to examine the response of recipient cultures which may be passive, participative or conflictual.

Further reading

Scholte (2000) provides a good overview of the debates on the nature of globalisation while Maguire (1999) provides a wide-ranging analysis of globalisation in sport. More detailed studies of aspects of globalisation include Brookes and Madden's (1995) review of the economics of sports shoe production, Darby's (2001) examination of Africa's relationship with global football, and Klein's (1991) exploration of the relationship between the Dominican Republic and the USA in baseball.

REFERENCES

Bauman, Z. (1999) *Globalization: the Human Consequences*. Cambridge: Polity Press.

Brohm, J.-M. (1978) *Sport! A Prison of Measured Time*. London: Pluto Press.

Brookes, B. and Madden, P. (1995) *The Globetrotting Sports Shoe*. London: Christian Aid.

Brown, A. (2000) 'Sneaking in through the back door? Media company interests and dual ownership of clubs', in S. Hamil et al. (eds), *Football in the Digital Age: Whose Game Is It Anyway?* London: Mainstream Publishing.

Brown, R. (1995) 'Globalisation and the end of the national project', in J. MacMillan and A. Linklater (eds), *Boundaries in Question: New Directions in International Relations*. London: Pinter, pp. 54–68.

Burton, R.D.E. (1991) 'Cricket, Carnival and street culture in the Caribbean', in G. Jarvie (ed.), *Sport, Racism and Ethnicity*. London: Falmer Press.

Darby, P. (2001) *Africa and Football's Global Order*. London: Frank Cass.

Featherstone, M. (1991) 'Global culture: an introduction', in M. Featherstone (ed.), *Global Culture: Nationalism, Globalisation and Modernity*. London: Sage.

Featherstone, M. and Lash, S. (1995) 'Globalisation, modernity and the spatialisation of social theory: an introduction', in M. Featherstone, S. Lash and R. Robertson (eds), *Global Modernities. 10th Anniversary Conference*. London: Sage.

Fitch, R. (1996) *The Assassination of New York*. London: Verso.

Hall, S. (1983) 'The problem of ideology – Marxism without guarantees', in B. Matthews (ed.), *Marx: a Hundred Years On*. London: Lawrence & Wishart.

Hamelink, C.J. (1983) *Cultural Autonomy in Global Communications: Planning National Information Policy*. London: Longman.

Hannerz, U. (1990) 'Cosmopolitans and locals in world culture', *Theory, Culture & Society*, 7: 237–51.

Harvey, D. (1989) *The Condition of Postmodernity*. Oxford: Blackwell.

Hirst, P. and Thompson, G. (1999) *Globalisation in Question*. 2nd edn. Cambridge: Polity Press.

Houlihan, B. (1997) 'Sport, national identity and public policy', *Nations and Nationalism*, 3 (1): 113–37.

Houlihan, B. (2003) 'Sport globalisation, the state and the problems of governance', in T. Slack (ed.), *The Commercialisation of Sport*. London: Frank Cass.

James, C.L.R. (1963) *Beyond a Boundary*. London: Stanley Paul.

James, C.L.R. (1977) *The Future in the Past*. New York: Lawrence Hill.

Jensen, C.B. (1998) 'Conclusion', in C.B. Jensen (ed.), *News of the World*. London: Routledge.

Katz, D. (1994) *Just Do It: the Nike Spirit in the Corporate World*. New York: Random House.

Klein, A. (1991) *Sugarball: the American Game, the Dominican Dream*. New Haven, CT: Yale University Press.

Maguire, J. (1999) *Global Sport: Identities, Societies, Civilizations*. Cambridge: Polity Press.

Robertson, R. (1987) 'Globalization and societal modernization: a note on Japan and Japanese religion', *Sociological Analysis*, 47 (Summer): 35–43.

Robertson, R. (1989) 'Globalization, politics and religion', in J.A. Beckford and T. Luckman (eds), *The Changing Face of Religion*. London: Sage, pp. 10–23.

Robertson, R. (1995) 'Glocalization: time–space and homogeneity–heterogeneity', in M. Featherstone, S. Lash and R. Robertson (eds), *Global Modernities. 10th Anniversary Conference*. London: Sage.

Rosenau, J.N. (1994) 'New dimensions of security: the interaction of globalizing and localizing dynamics', *Security Dialogue*, 25 (3): 255–81.

Sage, G. (1996) 'Patriotic images and capitalist profit: contradictions of professional team sports licensed merchandise', *Sociology of Sport Journal*, 13: 1–11.

Scholte, J.A. (2000) *Globalisation: a Critical Introduction*. Basingstoke: Palgrave.

St Pierre, M. (1990) 'West Indian cricket: a cultural contradiction?', *Arena Review*, 14 (1): 13–24.

Stamm, H.-P. and Lemprecht, M. (2001) 'Sydney 2000 – the best Games ever? World sport and

relationships of structural dependency'. Paper presented at the First World Congress of Sociology of Sport, Seoul, July.

Vogel, S.K. (1996) *Freer Markets, More Rules: Regulatory Reform in Advanced Industrial Countries*. Ithaca, NY: Cornell University Press.

Wallerstein, I. (1991) 'Culture as the ideological battleground', in M. Featherstone (ed.), *Global Culture: Nationalism, Globalisation and Modernity*. London: Sage.

Warde, A. (2000) 'Eating globally: cultural flows and the spread of ethnic restaurants', in D. Kalb et al. (eds), *The Ends of Globalisation: Bringing Society Back In*. Lanham, MD: Rowman & Littlefield Publishers.

Index